# NEW YORK NOISE

# Ethnomusicology Multimedia

ETHNOMUSICOLOGY MULTIMEDIA (EM) is a collaborative publishing program, developed with funding from the Andrew W. Mellon Foundation, to identify and publish first books in ethnomusicology, accompanied by supplemental audiovisual materials online at www.ethnomultimedia.org.

A collaboration of the presses at Indiana and Temple universities, EM is an innovative, entrepreneurial, and cooperative effort to expand publishing opportunities for emerging scholars in ethnomusicology and to increase audience reach by using common resources available to the presses through support from the Andrew W. Mellon Foundation. Each press acquires and develops EM books according to its own profile and editorial criteria.

EM's most innovative features are its web-based components, which include a password-protected Annotation Management System (AMS) where authors can upload peer-reviewed audio, video, and static image content for editing and annotation and key the selections to corresponding references in their texts; a public site for viewing the web content, www.ethnomultimedia.org, with links to publishers' websites for information about the accompanying books; and the Avalon Media System, which hosts video and audio content for the website. The AMS and website were designed and built by the Institute for Digital Arts and Humanities at Indiana University. Avalon was designed and built by the libraries at Indiana University and Northwestern University with support from the Institute of Museum and Library Services. The Indiana University Libraries host the website and the Indiana University Archives of Traditional Music (ATM) provides archiving and preservation services for the EM online content.

## PROFILES IN POPULAR MUSIC

### Jeffrey Magee and Felicia Miyakawa, editors

Unlocking the Groove: Rhythm, Meter, and Musical Design in Electronic Dance Music
*Mark J. Butler*

Neil Young and the Poetics of Energy
*William Echard*

Johnny Cash and the Paradox of American Identity
*Leigh H. Edwards*

Jazzwomen: Conversations with Twenty-One Musicians
*Wayne Enstice and Janis Stockhouse*

Choro: A Social History of a Brazilian Popular Music
*Tamara Elena Livingston-Isenhour and Thomas George Caracas Garcia*

Radiohead and the Resistant Concept Album
*Marianne Tatom Letts*

Rush, Rock Music, and the Middle Class
*Chris McDonald*

Five Percenter Rap: God Hop's Music, Message, and Black Muslim Mission
*Felicia M. Miyakawa*

The Songs of Jimmie Rodgers: A Legacy in Country Music
*Jocelyn R. Neal*

Jethro Tull's *Thick as a Brick* and *A Passion Play*: Inside Two Long Songs
*Tim Smolko*

The Megamusical
*Jessica Sternfeld*

# NEW YORK NOISE

RADICAL JEWISH MUSIC AND THE DOWNTOWN SCENE

**TAMAR BARZEL**

INDIANA UNIVERSITY PRESS     *Bloomington & Indianapolis*

*This book is a publication of*

INDIANA UNIVERSITY PRESS
Office of Scholarly Publishing
Herman B Wells Library 350
1320 East 10th Street
Bloomington, Indiana 47405 USA

iupress.indiana.edu

*Telephone*   800-842-6796
*Fax*   812-855-7931

© 2015 by Tamar Barzel

*Manufactured in the
United States of America*

*Library of Congress
Cataloging-in-Publication Data*

Barzel, Tamar, author.
  New York noise : radical Jewish music
and the downtown scene / Tamar Barzel.
    pages cm — (Ethnomusicology
multimedia) (Profiles in popular music)
  Includes bibliographical references and
index.
  ISBN 978-0-253-01550-1 (cloth : alk.
paper)
  ISBN 978-0-253-01557-0 (paperback : alk.
paper)
  ISBN 978- 0-253-01564-8 (eb)
  1. Avant-garde (Music)—New York
(State)—New York. 2. Jews—New York
(State)—New York—Music—History
and criticism. 3. Popular music—New
York (State)—New York—1991–2000.
I. Title. II. Series: Ethnomusicology
multimedia. III. Series: Profiles in
popular music.
  ML200.8.N5B37 2015
  780.89′92407471—dc23

                                        2014027035

1  2  3  4  5    20  19  18  17  16  15

# CONTENTS

# ETHNOMUSICOLOGY MULTIMEDIA SERIES PREFACE

Each of the audio, video, or still image media examples listed below is associated with specific passages in this book, and each example has been assigned a unique Persistent Uniform Resource Locator, or PURL. The PURL identifies a specific audio, video, or still image media example on the Ethnomusicology Multimedia website, www.ethnomultimedia.org. Within the text of the book, a PURL number in parentheses functions like a citation and immediately follows the text to which it refers (e.g., PURL 3.1 refers to the first media example found in chapter 3).

To access all media associated with this book, readers must first create a free account by going to www.ethnomultimedia.org and clicking the "Sign up for free" link. Site visitors are also required to read and electronically sign an End Users License Agreement (EULA). Afterward, there are two ways to access audio, video, and still image media examples. In the search field, one may enter the name of the author to access a webpage with information about the book and author as well as a playlist of all media examples associated with the book. Or, to access a specific media example, the six-digit PURL identifier (the six digits located at the end of the full PURL address below) may be entered into the search field. The reader will then be taken to the web page containing that media example as well as a playlist of all the other media examples related to the book. Readers of the electronic edition of this book may simply click on the PURL address for each media example; once they have logged in to the Ethnomusicology Multimedia website, the live link will take them directly to the media example.

LIST OF PURLS

## CHAPTER 1

PURL 1.1. "Verklärte Kristallnacht." Gary Lucas, guitar. Berlin Jazz Festival, November 1988. Audio.
http://purl.dlib.indiana.edu/iudl/em/Barzel/910284

PURL 1.2. *The Golem* (1920, dir. Paul Wegener and Carl Boese), with original solo guitar soundtrack; music by Gary Lucas and Walter Horn (10 min. excerpt). Video.
http://purl.dlib.indiana.edu/iudl/em/Barzel/910279

PURL 1.3. Shelley Hirsch, "I Am a Jew" (1980). Shelley Hirsch, solo vocal and taped overdubs. On *States* (Tellus, 1997). Audio.
http://purl.dlib.indiana.edu/iudl/em/Barzel/910285

## CHAPTER 2

PURL 2.1. Shrek, "Yo! I Killed Your God," early 1990s performance at the Knitting Factory. Marc Ribot (guitar and vocals), with Christine Bard (drums), Jim Pugliese (drums), Sebastian Steinberg (bass), and Chris Wood (guitar). On *Marc Ribot: Descent into Baldness,* directed and produced by Cassis Birgit Staudt and Joerg Soechting. © Cassis Birgit Staudt and Joerg Soechting. http://www-marcribot-descentintobaldness.com. Video.
http://purl.dlib.indiana.edu/iudl/em/Barzel/910280

## CHAPTER 3

PURL 3.1. Alvin Curran, *Crystal Psalms* (New Albion Records, 1994). Excerpt. Audio.
http://purl.dlib.indiana.edu/iudl/em/Barzel/910286

## CHAPTER 4

PURL 4.1. G-d Is My Co-Pilot, "Mi Yimalel" on *Mir Shlufn Nisht* (1994). Sharon Topper, vocals; Craig Flanagin, guitar; Fred Lonberg-Holm, cello; Alex Klein, bass; Michael Evans, drums; Siobhan Duffy, drums. Arranged and produced by Craig Flanagin. Audio.
http://purl.dlib.indiana.edu/iudl/em/Barzel/910287

PURL 4.2. G-d Is My Co-Pilot, "Ha-Tikvah," on *Mir Shlufn Nisht* (Disk Union, 1994). Audio.
http://purl.dlib.indiana.edu/iudl/em/Barzel/910288
PURL 4.3. Zadikov Workers Choir, "Hay Naalayim" (Joel Engel and Avigdor Hameiri), on *Hayo Hayu Zmanim: Israeli Tunes of Yesteryear 1* (Hed-Artzi, 1960). *Collection of the Dartmouth Jewish Sound Archive.* Audio.
http://purl.dlib.indiana.edu/iudl/em/Barzel/910289
PURL 4.4. G-d Is My Co-Pilot, "B'Nai!" on *Mir Shlufn Nisht* (1994).
http://purl.dlib.indiana.edu/iudl/em/Barzel/910290

CHAPTER 5

PURL 5.1. Shelley Hirsch, *States,* on Roulette TV (2001). Shelley Hirsch, solo vocal, with taped overdubs. Excerpt. Produced and directed by Jim Staley. Video.
http://purl.dlib.indiana.edu/iudl/em/Barzel/910281
PURL 5.2. "Hymie and Harry" (0'00" to 0'36"). Radio version of *O Little Town of East New York* (1992), commissioned by New American Radio. Text by Shelley Hirsch; music by Shelley Hirsch and David Weinstein. Shelley Hirsch. *New American Radio and Performing Arts online archive.* Audio.
http://purl.dlib.indiana.edu/iudl/em/Barzel/910291
PURL 5.3. "Confession Booth" (6'39" to 7'28"). Radio version of *O Little Town of East New York* (1992).
http://purl.dlib.indiana.edu/iudl/em/Barzel/910292
PURL 5.4. "544 Hemlock Street" (2'14" to 4'33"). On *O Little Town of East New York* (1991), filmed on location at the Dance Theater Workshop. Text by Shelley Hirsch; music by Shelley Hirsch and David Weinstein; film and slides, Shelley Hirsch and Eric Muzzy; camera, Eric Muzzy; decor, Shelley Hirsch, Gail O'Keefe, Liz Prince; costumes, Liz Prince; lighting, Lori Dawson; audio, Brooks Williams and David Weinstein. Video.
http://purl.dlib.indiana.edu/iudl/em/Barzel/910282
PURL 5.5. "Maria's House/The Troika" (4'47" to 6'35"). Radio version of *O Little Town of East New York* (1992). Audio.
http://purl.dlib.indiana.edu/iudl/em/Barzel/910293

PURL 5.6. "On the Far Reaches" (22'33" to the end). Radio version of
*O Little Town of East New York* (1992). Audio.
http://purl.dlib.indiana.edu/iudl/em/Barzel/910294

PURL 5.7. "The Jewish People" (7'29" to 8'26"). Radio version of
*O Little Town of East New York* (1992). Audio.
http://purl.dlib.indiana.edu/iudl/em/Barzel/910295

PURL 5.8. "The Jewish People" (20'56" to 21'58"). On *O Little Town
of East New York* (1991). Video.
http://purl.dlib.indiana.edu/iudl/em/Barzel/910283

PURL 5.9. Anthony Coleman, "Jevrejski by night." Live performance
at Issue Project Room, Brooklyn (2005). Anthony Coleman,
piano; Michaël Attias, saxophone, Marco Cappelli, guitar; Greg
Cohen, contrabass; Fred Lonberg-Holm, cello; Jim Pugliese,
percussion; Ted Reichman, accordion, Michael Sarin, percussion,
Douglas Wieselman, clarinet, bass clarinet, guitar. Audio.
http://purl.dlib.indiana.edu/iudl/em/Barzel/910296

PURL 5.10. Ben Goldberg Trio, "Speech Communication: Anglais."
Museum of Jewish Art and History, Paris, June 2010 (94 mins.).
Ben Goldberg, clarinet; Greg Cohen, bass; Kenny Wolleson, drums.
akadém Broadcast by Akadem.org. Video.
http://purl.dlib.indiana.edu/iudl/em/Barzel/910276

PURL 5.11. Anthony Coleman, "8 Objectives: The Abysmal Richness
of the Infinite Proximity of the Same." Live performance at
Issue Project Room, Brooklyn (2005). Anthony Coleman, piano;
Michaël Attias, saxophone, Marco Cappelli, guitar; Greg Cohen,
contrabass; Fred Lonberg-Holm, cello; Jim Pugliese, percussion;
Ted Reichman, accordion, Michael Sarin, percussion, Douglas
Wieselman, clarinet, bass clarinet, guitar. Audio.
http://purl.dlib.indiana.edu/iudl/em/Barzel/910297

EPILOGUE

PURL E.1. "La Radical Jewish Culture," Paris Museum of Jewish Art
and History, April 2010 (141 mins.). Tamar Barzel with Anthony
Coleman, Mathias Dreyfuss, and Nico Schneider, translation.
akadém Broadcast by Akadem.org. Video.
http://purl.dlib.indiana.edu/iudl/em/Barzel/910277

PURL E.2. "Ecouter le flâneur flâner," Paris Museum of Jewish Art and History, April 2010 (13 mins.). Anthony Coleman, spoken introduction, piano and pre-recorded electronics, Ashley Paul, saxophone. akadem Broadcast by Akadem.org. Video.
http://purl.dlib.indiana.edu/iudl/em/Barzel/910278

# ACKNOWLEDGMENTS

I moved to New York City to begin the research that eventually led to this book more than a decade ago. As time has accrued so have the colleagues, friends, and family who have contributed in material, personal, and professional ways to the endeavor. In the chapters that follow, some of their contributions are more visible than others, but they are impossible to rank, and I can genuinely say that over and above all the contributions that I'm grateful to be able to acknowledge here, there have been dozens of occasions for less official kinds of support—home-cooked meals, email exchanges, kind words, and phone conversations—that have been just as important.

None of this would have happened without my friend Mike Rahfaldt, who brought me the recording that led to this project. I would not have been able to see it through without financial support from the University of Michigan, whose generosity allowed me the great luxury of settling in my field site to do research and write almost full time. In its early stages, this project was supported by several fellowships, including a Rackham Predoctoral Fellowship, a Margaret Dow Towsley Scholarship from the Center for the Education of Women, and a stipend from the Rackham Interdisciplinary Institute. Good readers are hard to find, and I've never had better ones than Paul Anderson and Travis Jackson. Thanks are also due to Jonathan Freedman and Sarah Blair for inviting me to contribute an article to the *Michigan Quarterly Review*, which was a first attempt to work out the ideas about the klezmer revival, and to Jonathan for his staunch support of my work since then. I owe special gratitude to Judith Becker for opening up new worlds in my thinking about music, for always knowing exactly which book I needed to read, and for her guidance in all things. Another heartfelt thank-you goes to Rich Crawford for all the years of collegiality, close reading, and fast friendship.

At Wellesley College I was supported by a Mellon Postdoctoral Fellowship, administered through the Department of Music, in 2004–2006. I thank the dean's office for research and travel support, which allowed me to present my work at conferences and funded my research trips to New York City, Paris, and Berlin, as well as for supporting my research leave in New York City in 2009–2010. Thanks also to all my colleagues in the department, who have been unstintingly generous and who it has been such a pleasure working with and getting to know over the years, including Gurminder Bhogal, Marion Dry, Isabel Fine, Charles Fisk, Claire Fontijn, Lisa Graham, Jenny Johnson, Cercie Miller, Paula Zeitlin, and many others; an extra helping of thanks goes to Martin Brody for his steadfast encouragement, wise counsel, and good cheer. I've also benefited enormously from the assistance of music librarian Pam Bristah and the college library staff, who have found me copies of many difficult to access articles, scores, and books. Among my other colleagues on campus, I would like to thank in particular Carol Dougherty, whose kind invitation to sit on the Newhouse Advisory Board sparked all kinds of new connections, as well as Alice Friedman, Salem Mekuria, and Larry Rosenwald for their unwavering support; thanks also to Stanley Cheng, David Teng Olsen, and Peggy Levitt, whose invitation to present a paper at the Transnational Studies Initiative spurred me to develop many of the ideas about memory and place that found their way into chapter 5. Fellow ethnomusicologists Kera Washington (at Wellesley) and Sandy Graham (at Babson College) have offered a particular kind of collegiality that only birds of a feather can provide. Finally, big thanks to Magdalen Christian, as well as the student assistants in the Music Office, who have helped out in so many ways and without whom none of this would be possible.

There are a few things in this book that happened only because of someone else's expertise. Kenny Freundlich and Jordan Tynes gave invaluable assistance with audio/video clips and the *Kristallnacht* waveform analysis, Joe Mulholland set the musical examples into Finale, and

Maia Rusco and Emily Nice transcribed interviews. My thanks also go to Peter Stastny, Albert Thimann, and Eric Usner (who also provided translations from the German) for helping me to procure out-of-press recordings; to Yoav Weiss and Ofer Pasternak for help with the Hebrew; to my uncle and aunt Uri and Aviva Barzel for their kind hospitality in New York City and for connecting me with the Histadrut Ivrit; and to my uncle and aunt Raanan and Eva Barzel for hosting me so graciously in Paris and for hunting down a copy of Chantal Ackerman's *Histoires d'Amerique.*

In New York City, I was a fellow for a semester at the Center for Jewish Leadership and Learning (CLAL) in Manhattan; thanks to CLAL and in particular to David Kraemer, now at the Jewish Theological Seminary, for his help in procuring the Gefen Haggadah, and to the archivists and staff at JTS for their help in tracking down bibliographic information for the song "Halutz, Beneh." For helping to make fruitful professional connections of various kinds, I thank Ralph and Liz Alessi of the School for Improvisational Music. I was also in two writing groups in New York; for helping me to "workshop" my chapter drafts I thank my fellow ethno/musicologists Adriana Helbig, Lara Pellegrinelli, and Uli Sailer. I also learned a great deal from colleagues in my interdisciplinary writing group, whose work in music, art history, African American studies, Asian American studies, Jewish studies, gender studies, and literature gave me new perspectives that have all had a hand in shaping this book; thanks to all the *kulturhedz,* including Marion Jacobson, Nikki Stanton, Nick Syrett, Grace Wang, and Margie Weinstein. Thanks in particular to two friends from that group, Alisa Braun, for answering all my late night questions about Yiddish, and Libby Garland, for her great generosity and smart advice in reading drafts of the book through all its growing pains. There's no way either the book or I would be here without her.

During my research leave in New York City, I was lucky to work with Rabbi Ellen Lippmann and Cantor Lisa B. Segal, as well as the rest of the staff at synagogue Kolot Chayeinu in Brooklyn, which hosted the event featured in the book's epilogue, "Practicing: A Concert and Conversation," in 2010; once again I thank Marc Ribot, who made the whole thing happen, as well as all the participating musicians for donating their energies to the discussion and the wonderful concert that followed. Mathias

Dreyfuss, Raphaël Sigal, and Gabriel Siancas curated an excellent exhibit on RJC at the Paris Jewish Museum in 2010, shared the artist interviews they videotaped, and invited me to convene an event at the museum on which I draw in chapter 5 and the epilogue, and to which Anthony Coleman also generously contributed. Thanks in particular to Matthias for putting me in touch with Alexander Kluge and for answering a thousand questions, and to Marie Blanquet for making all the arrangements for the trip. At the Berlin Jewish Museum, where the exhibit traveled the following year, Marie Naumann invited me to contribute an article to the museum journal and went out of her way to share all kinds of useful information. Thanks are also due to Shula Reinharz and everyone at the Hadassah-Brandeis Institute for the Study of Women and Gender, where I was a scholar-in-residence in the spring of 2012, and from which I also received a research award. It was a stroke of luck to find two simpatico fellow scholars in this program, entitled "Jewish Women in the Arts." Dance historian Nina Spiegel and art historian Michelle Gewurtz shared their work with me and offered invaluable comments on mine, contributing insights in particular to the material that wound up in chapters 4 and 5. At the *Journal of the Society for American Music,* editor Leta Miller provided crucial feedback on an article in which I first explored the ideas about musical language that inform this book. In presenting aspects of my work in different forums, including the Society for American Music, the Society for Ethnomusicology, and the Society for Jewish History, I have received invaluable feedback from too many colleagues to name here, but for inviting me to present some of this research in its early stages I would like to thank George Lewis and Robert O'Meally of the Columbia Jazz Studies Group; Judah Cohen, Mark Kligman, Michael Leavitt, and Jim Loeffler of the Jewish Music Forum at the Center for Jewish History (CJH); and the organizers of the conferences Makom III (in Potsdam), ReJewvenation (at the University of Toronto), and Improvising America (at the University of Kansas). For extending invitations more recently I thank Charles Carson and the Center for American Music (at the University of Texas, Austin) and Tony Michels and Hasia Diner of the Working Group for Jews in New York City (at the CJH).

This book's website is supported by the Mellon-funded Ethnomusicology Multimedia project at Indiana University Press. I am grateful to all those who granted permission to include their work online, including Helen Thorington at New American Radio and Performing Arts, for sharing the radio version of *O Little Town of East New York*; Rachel Wetstein at Transcontinental Publishing for sharing the sheet music to "Halutz, Beneh!" and Alex Hartov and the Dartmouth Jewish Sound Archive for sharing the song's archival recording. Thanks to Mickael Bendavid and Sigalit Lavon at Akadem for sharing video footage from the Paris Jewish Museum; to Alvin Curran for sharing the audio from *Crystal Psalms*; to Jim Staley and Roulette Intermedia in New York City for sharing the video of Shelley Hirsch performing *States*; to Tanisha Jones at the New York Public Library, Jerome Robbins Dance Division, for her help procuring the video of *O Little Town of East New York*; to Beatta Wiggen and Alexander Kluge at DCTP television in Germany for sharing a video of *Kristallnacht*; to Gary Lucas for sharing his audio and video footage from *The Golem,* and WNYC for sharing the original audio; to Anthony Coleman for sharing recordings and scores; and to Cassis Staudt and Joerg Soechting in Berlin, as well as all the musicians involved, for sharing the footage from *Descent into Baldness.* The book is also enriched by the work of many photographers, including Laurent Baillet, Yaël Bitton, Michael Dorf, Scott Friedlander, Peter Gannushkin, Kevin Kolben, Ziga Koritnik, Martin Mooijman, Ben Rosengart, Dan Sagarin, and Daniel Sheehan.

It has been a pleasure working with everyone at Indiana University Press, from whom I have learned what a group effort it is to shepherd a book through the production process. Thanks in particular to my wonderful editor Raina Polivka for supporting the book from the outset, as well as to assistant editor Jenna Whittaker, copy editor Eric Schramm, production coordinator Dan Pyle, and project manager Darja Malcolm-Clarke. I am also grateful to the staff at IUP Ethnomusicology Multimedia project, including Mollie Ables and Allan Burdette, for their expertise and assistance. This book is much better than it would have been otherwise because of the careful attention given to the manuscript by Judah Cohen as well as another, anonymous, reader for the press. I am also grateful to all the people who took the time out of their busy schedules in the past year to read my manuscript, including Jonathan Freedman, Leta Miller, John Szwed, Sherrie Tucker, and Chris Washburne, along with a number of colleagues to whom I am particularly indebted for generous professional and material support, including Charles Hiroshi Garret, Mark Katz, Ingrid Monson, Carol Oja, and Kay Kaufman Shelemay.

Of course, this book's existence depends on the artists I've met over the years, who have been unfailingly open to my work, giving me access to their rehearsals and performances, handing me concert programs they had saved and essays they had written, sharing unreleased recordings, and spending the time to talk about all of it, both in formal interviews and in many hours of conversation. Like these exchanges, not all of my interviews made it into the book directly, but they all contributed in crucial ways to my understanding of the downtown scene. On this front, I thank Joey Baron, Jim Black, Don Byron, Uri Caine, Greg Cohen, Matt Darriau, Michael Dorf, Dave Douglas, Mark Dresser, Bruce Gallanter, Vijay Iyer, David Krakauer, Alan Licht, Frank London, Jessica Lurie, Rudresh Mahanthappa, Roy Nathanson, Ted Reichman, Elliott Sharp, Brad Shepik, Matthew Shipp, Daniel Zamir, John Zorn, and an anonymous contributor. Thanks are due in particular to interviewees Anthony Coleman, Marty Ehrlich, Craig Flanagin, Shelley Hirsch, Gary Lucas, and Sharon Topper for so generously sharing their work, time, and ideas with me. I am also indebted to Marc Ribot for giving me his unpublished essays and all the concert programs he saved from the RJC years. All these artists invited me to attend their concerts free of charge, an offer I tried not to take them up on too often. (Zorn was the only one who was not willing to share his work for the book, but as of this writing most of it is readily available online.)

Writing a book, even one that involves talking to musicians and going out to hear them perform, turns out to be a pretty solitary business. I have had long stretches of hibernation when deadlines have taken precedence over almost everything else, but whenever I have reentered the land of the living, my friends and family have been standing by without a word of reproach. I can't thank you all enough—except to say that I couldn't have done any of it without you. And to my parents, who have been there for me in so many ways over the years, all my love.

# NEW YORK NOISE

# Introduction

## *Radical Jewish Music in Manhattan*

THIS BOOK BEGAN WITH A GIFT, CASUALLY BESTOWED BY A
friend who worked at our local record store. In those pre-Internet years,
he had enviable access to all kinds of under-the-radar music, and I hardly
knew what to make of this particular find: a CD entitled *Jewish Alternative Movement: A Guide for the Perplexed* (1998).[1] I was dimly aware of the
*Guide for the Perplexed,* a medieval talmudic treatise with an amusingly
modern name. But I was stumped by the phrase "Jewish Alternative
Movement." The liner notes to the recording told me that "J.A.M." was a
new imprint for recordings held by the Knitting Factory—the scrappy,
subterranean club, familiarly known as "The Knit," that was the nerve
center of Manhattan's cutting-edge downtown music scene. In college
in the 1980s, I had heard about an underground art world on New York's
Lower East Side that was the stomping grounds for my most intimidat-
ingly hip peers, known as PIBs—People in Black. But, as I had gathered
in bits and pieces over the years since then, the downtown scene was far
more than that. In fact, it was one of the most innovative and multifaceted art scenes of the twentieth century.

So many of the artists who had shocked me out of suburban malaise in high school—Talking Heads, Jim Jarmusch, the Ramones—were part of it. I didn't know quite what I was hearing, but when I slid my sister's *Horses* album out of its paper sleeve and onto the turntable, unleashing Patti Smith's punk anthem, "Gloria," straight into our living room, I knew it was important.[2] What I was hearing, a decade after Smith and her cohort of poet-rockers had heralded the birth of punk rock at CBGB, was some New York Noise, a bit of DNA from the downtown music scene on Manhattan's Lower East Side.[3] By the 1980s, that neighborhood had become a kind of open-air lab for creative misfits of all stripes. It drew together experimentally inclined musicians with varied backgrounds, in jazz and free improvisation, garage rock, blues, and classical composition, who were intent on the unlikely prospect of bringing all these idioms into dialogue. A boundary-pushing American original, the multifaceted downtown scene attracted its share of hangers-on, but it also pulsed with ideas and energy, and its influence resonates loudly in contemporary jazz, popular music, and film soundtracks. To borrow a phrase coined by Bob Dylan, it was a place for "musical expeditionaries," restless seekers open to influence from any quarter—or almost any. As far as I knew, Jewish music had no place on New York's downtown scene, and so *Guide for the Perplexed* was a puzzle. The Knit's graffiti-laden walls were no doubt imbued with layers of meaning, but the club struck me as an odd place to invoke the Talmud, an ancient compendium of Jewish law and commentary. In fact, the band names and song titles on *Guide for the Perplexed*—Hasidic New Wave, Hanukkah Bush—made me wonder whether the recording was a joke. But when I listened to the music, it was impressive, daring, and polished. I couldn't yet parse out all its idioms—neo-klezmer, hardcore and acid rock, neo-Yiddish cabaret, free verse, free jazz, and electronic sound canvases—but I could tell it was *something,* and I wanted to know more. I said my goodbyes, packed up a moving truck, and drove to New York City to find some answers.

As I discovered soon after arriving in the summer of 2000, the Knit had recently hosted a spate of themed concerts, public Passover seders, and other events that drew on the unconventional, Jewishly identified music that downtown experimentalists had been producing over the past several years. *Guide for the Perplexed* was a musical sampler from that period. And the phrase "Jewish Alternative Movement" (J.A.M.) made a statement about the new sense of purpose shared by artists who until that point had not seen their Jewish identities as particularly relevant to their creative work. I learned that J.A.M. (which sometimes turned up in an alternate format, "Jewish Avant-Garde Music") had been modeled on another rubric, one that ultimately had a more lasting impact on the downtown music scene and on American music as a whole. That rubric, "Radical Jewish Music," was coined in the 1990s by saxophonist John Zorn, a prominent composer on the downtown scene, who was also central to the outpouring of creativity I explore in this book.

The downtown music world was actually a crisscrossing network of different music scenes. One of those scenes consisted of artists with diverse musical backgrounds who aimed to bridge their stylistic differences. By coming together in varied formations to perform, write, and improvise, they ultimately developed a flexible, multifaceted musical language that, while drawing on a legion of influences, was also strikingly original. Zorn and his circle of frequent collaborators were central participants in this collective project. Many of them were Jewish, and in the 1990s they ventured into new creative territory. How, they wondered, could they write new music that was Jewishly identified and yet also in keeping with their other work—unconventional, experimentalist, and with wide-ranging musical influences? This seemingly straightforward question proved to have surprisingly complicated implications about the nature of Jewish music and identity. Although these artists could look to colleagues who, in other times and places, had sought ways to consider culture and heritage through music, there was no simple way to map that work onto the process of bringing both things Jewish and things downtownish into dialogue. This book chronicles the roughly six-year period during which downtown artists grappled most intensively with the work of writing music that was both experimental and Jewishly relevant, during what I call the Radical Jewish Culture moment.[4]

In September 1992, Zorn had curated what became that moment's signal event, the Festival for Radical New Jewish Culture, a weekend of concerts, films, and readings in Munich. By now this festival may be best known for its premiere of *Kristallnacht,* Zorn's programmatic chamber piece, which commemorated the Nazi-orchestrated anti-Jewish riots of 1938. But for many artists, the festival was also a personal and cultural milestone. It represented a pivotal opportunity for mutual recognition about an aspect of identity whose significance, and indeed existence, had so far gone largely unacknowledged in their creative lives. The festival was followed by a flurry of activity. For the next half-decade, musicians presented their new work at annual RJC festivals, most organized by Zorn, each with several days of themed programming.[5] Zorn, who tried out a few versions of his defining rubric, finally settled on Radical Jewish Culture (hereafter RJC) with the establishment of his record label, Tzadik (Hebrew for righteous man), in 1995. Knitting Factory founder Michael Dorf, who had begun producing annual klezmer festivals at the club in 1990 and releasing neo-klezmer recordings soon thereafter, followed suit in 1997 by inaugurating the J.A.M. imprint on Knitting Factory Records as an umbrella for that label's Jewishly themed releases, which included *Guide for the Perplexed*.[6] Tzadik's RJC series ultimately dwarfed J.A.M. in scope. Intending to spark a body of "Jewish music beyond klezmer," Zorn has expanded that series into a catalog with around 200 Jewish-themed releases to date. Indeed, with RJC only one series in Tzadik's diverse library, the label has established itself as a major presence in the landscape of adventuresome new music.

The festivals, the record label, and the shared energy that sprang up around the rubric Radical Jewish Culture have led some observers to call RJC a "movement." Participating artists have sometimes objected to this description, as it implies that RJC was a widespread effort with shared political aims. Although some artists had political ambitions for RJC, it was ultimately a creative phenomenon with social implications and not a political or social movement. Nevertheless, artists found RJC immensely important for being, in clarinetist Marty Ehrlich's words, "an *open* space, and in many ways a *safe* space in the sense of having the support of one's friends & colleagues, to explore & express these artistic leanings [whether] in a straightforward, or in a deconstructive, way."[7] If RJC was not a movement per se, it was nevertheless a collective endeavor that crackled with social and creative electricity. It gave artists a platform for staging an urgent confrontation between two fundamentally important aspects of their lives, Jewish heritage and creative voice, which had heretofore felt disconnected. That confrontation was at its most intense during its first few years, when it spilled out of the musical realm and into the discursive one, resulting in the rich body of writings and conversation I explore in these pages. Rather than "movement," then, I have settled on "moment" as the best term to describe the phenomenon that is my book's subject.

RJC's impact did not end in 1998; to the contrary, a great deal of interesting music emerged over the next decade and continues to do so. Why, then, identify 1992–1998 as the RJC moment? Above all, I focus on these years because of the potent blend of music, writing, and talk that characterized the artistic production of radical Jewish music during this time. Artists produced provocative new work while engaging discursively with the personal and conceptual issues it raised. And they were acutely thoughtful theorists of their own cultural moment. From their unique vantage point at the fringe of mainstream music but the vanguard of American experimentalism, downtown artists contributed in innovative and profound ways to the language of, and the discourse around, contemporary Jewish music and identity.

In its mode of spirited exchange, the downtown scene was heir to the culture of talk that historian Christine Stansell describes as central to the hurly-burly of Eastern European and Russian Jewish bohemian culture on the early twentieth-century Lower East Side.[8] The scene's talkiness spurred artists to develop their ideas about RJC in tandem with each other, enacting a kind of community-wide call-and-response. Sometimes acrimonious and often exhilarating, this dynamic conversational milieu led artists to hone their thinking about the purpose and meaning of RJC. The work they subsequently developed, in both music and writing, offers a signal contribution to Jewish arts and letters. To be sure, artists involved in the U.S. klezmer revival, which began in the 1970s and grew in scope and momentum through the heyday of RJC, had preceded RJC in addressing similar questions about Jewish identity and contemporary music, and in some ways the RJC moment functioned as an extension of ideas klezmer revivalists had already proposed. Downtown artists who led neo-klezmer bands, including clarinetist David Krakauer and trumpeter Frank London of the Klezmatics, were key participants in the RJC moment as well. But because of their stubborn adherence to the principle of grounding new Jewish music in the experimental language special to their milieu—and not in klezmer—the artists on whom I have chosen to focus took their own music and discussions into new territory. Jewish identity and heritage, for these artists, was as malleable and multifarious as their musical idiom, and experimental music, which had once seemed to exist at a reasonable and natural remove from Jewish heritage, could be pushed to give expression to contemporary Jewish experience in unprecedented ways. Because each artist insisted on articulating a radically personal Jewish musical voice, what emerged from their enterprise was a newly articulated sense of both Jewishness and experimental music, with each helping to constitute the other. Their new music was idiosyncratic, to be sure, but it is this very trait that allows their work to intervene provocatively into the broader relationship, beyond the RJC moment, between contemporary Jewish identity and musical aesthetics.

## Coming of Age in New York City

This book is based on nearly a decade of interactions with musicians in New York City, first when I was completing the main research in 2000–2004, and then, after I moved to Boston, during shorter visits a few times a year until 2009–2010, when I returned to the city for another long stay. Like other ethnomusicologists based in urban centers, in my fieldwork I traversed not only live performances but also pre-concert rehearsals and post-concert hangouts in diners and living rooms, coffee shops and street corners. I listened intensively to commercial recordings and dug up those that were out of press, as well as audio and video recordings that had never been released. Systematic collections of music and materials from the downtown scene are still scarce, and so from artists' contributions I amassed my own archive, a unique collection of documents that includes unpublished essays, concert programs, home recordings, and other ephemera. As an amateur pianist among professional musicians, I deepened my personal involvement in my field site not as a performer but as an interlocutor—as a lucky participant, that is, in the scene's spirited conversational community. Over the years, my conversations and social interactions with artists added depth and texture to the formal interviews I recorded and transcribed. Along with artists' original writing and music, these interviews, in which my interlocutors share thoughts that are heartfelt, witty, and intellectually dazzling, lie at the heart of this book's narrative and analysis.

Doing fieldwork on the downtown scene raises interesting questions about the nature of representation in ethnographic research. One of the aims of ethnomusicology is to privilege what anthropologist Clifford Geertz famously called "local knowledge," attending to the way cultural insiders use, derive meaning from, and theorize local musics.[9] To represent a musical community from an insider's perspective is to go a long way toward representing it fairly, and many classic ethnographic monographs are based around a community whose shared aesthetics and creative principles also serve as a unifying focus for the published ethnography.[10] Since the 1980s, with the onset of postcolonial studies and the expansion of fieldwork into culturally diverse, transnational, and urban settings, ethnomusicologists have interrogated conventions of representation, which had developed originally in response to relatively homogenous communities, by addressing issues of cultural heterogeneity, social hierarchy and power, insider/outsider dynamics, personal taste, and conflicting narratives about musical meaning. The downtown scene presents its own peculiar challenge to the question of how best to represent a musical community. Although it is, on one hand, a tightly integrated creative scene with shared aesthetics, practices, and principles—a shared musical culture—on the other hand, iconoclasm is one of its bedrock principles, pushing against notions of community and mutual intelligibility. What exemplifies the musical culture of the downtown scene, in other words, is an understanding that although there are undoubtedly shared aims and practices, no single musician's voice can or should be taken to represent the whole. Indeed, creative entropy and cohesiveness were in constant play on the downtown scene. It was made up of dissident, sometimes uncompromising personalities who were focused on developing their own work and careers. But composer/improvisers also operate in a medium that depends on communication, one in which ideas are fostered collaboratively, and one that promises artists a unique kind of mutual creative development they could not achieve alone. That tension is at play in this book, which addresses the concerns that shaped the scene as a whole while attending to the stubbornly distinctive, sometimes conflicting perspectives of its individual participants.

As intellectually engaged as artists were during the RJC moment, they were also absorbed in their immediate work, and for the most part they were more intent on articulating their own ideas than in stepping back to assess RJC as a whole. I have taken on that role in this book, framing the RJC moment with a wide lens, contextualizing it both as part of the larger downtown music world and in regard to its historical moment, and tracing the themes that run through the music and the discourse that surrounded it. Thus, before turning to closely engage the work and ideas of four artists who contributed in distinctive ways to the RJC idea—Zorn, vocalist Sharon Topper with her queercore No Wave band G-d Is My Co-Pilot, vocalist Shelley Hirsch, and pianist Anthony Coleman—the book tells the story of the RJC moment: how and why it emerged when it did, and how it was shaped by its unique creative context.

Like the scene itself, the nature of these artists' creative work presented me with an interesting methodological challenge. Improvisation being central to their craft, downtown artists never perform one piece in the same way twice, and much of their music is never recorded or commercially released. Indeed, both in regard to developing a full appreciation for the music and in order to build the relationships with musicians that led them to talk freely with me, it was crucial for my research (not to mention a privilege and pleasure) to hear these musicians perform live, regularly and in varied contexts. However, downtown artists also release recordings. Like written musical scores, recordings of improvised music assume the function of primary texts, and, like photographs, they are not simply objective representations of past events but rather unique sonic objects in their own right. Whether based on in-studio performances or live concert tapes, professionally engineered recordings are carefully crafted works of art, and in choosing to write about music in detail, I have turned to recordings as the objects of analysis rather than relying on my impressions of live performances. Nevertheless, each piece of music has a much wider and more varied scope than any one recording can suggest. My understanding of their recorded work is informed by my years of immersion in the scene, but there is no doubt that to analyze these artists' recordings closely is to address only one facet of their creative output.

Live performances, of course, are also inflected by physical and social context in a way that recordings are not. My experience of attending performances transformed my sense of what the downtown scene
was about, creatively and socially, a sense that has fed back into how I
apprehend recordings of music that came out of the scene. Most important was the way in which built space and social mores acted mutually,
if subtly, to bolster the sense that audience and artists were collectively
involved in the musical performance. Although I attended some formal
shows in concert halls, including Merkin Concert Hall and the Rose
Theater at Lincoln Center, I usually found myself at small downtown
clubs or other intimate venues without much distance between performers and audiences, including the Knit, Tonic, ABC No Rio, Roulette,
Issue Project Room, and CB's Gallery.[11] Many of the shows I attended
were filled to capacity, and in addition to simply being in close proximity to other audience members, my sense of being part of a whole was
heightened by the nature of these spaces, where audience members usually sat or stood on a level floor rather than in raked seating, so that the
audience was either below the stage, in which case we were collectively
looking up, or on the same level as the musicians, an arrangement that
created a kind of implicit social leveling for the duration of the performance. Second, although at clubs like the Knit and Tonic, there would
sometimes be a low-level hum at the bar or some talking near the back
of the room, for the most part once a performance began, audiences
were wholly attentive. There would usually be applause after a musician's
solo, and individuals might voice appreciation through an "All right!"
or a "Yeah!" but otherwise audiences seemed to share in a social compact, rarely broken, to focus quietly on the musical performance. (Most
shows I attended were either unamplified or would not have been loud
enough to cut through crowd noise, with some notable exceptions, including an ear-splitting tenth anniversary reprise of Zorn's *Kristallnacht*
at Tonic in 2002.) Casual interactions between performers and audience
members also suggested that concerts were shared social endeavors.
Particularly at Tonic, a club that by the early 2000s had supplanted the
Knit as the central musical hub of the downtown scene, artists almost
always stayed onstage after the show to speak with a coterie of fans,
sometimes mingled with friends and colleagues in the crowd, and could

often be seen making plans to go around the corner for a late night meal. While the relaxed social mien of these shows made it easy for me to meet and talk with musicians, I also understood that what I was witnessing at the clubs was tied to the scene's special kind of interrelatedness. The music that emerged from the downtown scene was contingent on social intermingling and a sense of shared purpose—between performers and audiences at concerts, but also in the creative community as a whole. A map tracing the varied creative collaborations among downtown artists on a single recording would be a messy one indeed. The recordings I discuss should thus be considered as unique but not isolated musical works, as they were suspended in the same creative webs and contingent upon the same social relationships that constituted the scene as a whole.

It was through the twinned processes of collaboration and after-hours social interaction that downtown artists shaped RJC into an unruly collective concept. The Jewishly identified work that ensued differed dramatically from most of the other Jewish music of their era. Chapter 1 addresses the question of how to conceptualize that work, with attention to ethnomusicologist Philip Bohlman's formulation of the narratives that contemporary audiences and artists have often constructed in order to make sense of their relationship to new Jewish music. One of these narratives, which hinges on the idea of "getting Jewish music right," was also at work in the U.S. klezmer revival, and it serves as a key foil for the most provocative work of the RJC moment. I propose the notion of "getting Jewish music wrong in order to get it right" as a critical lens through which to make sense of RJC, an idea I elaborate through an exploration of Zorn's *Zohar* (1995), an ersatz archival recording of cantorial music, whose creative content is inseparable from its apparent flaws and fakery.[12]

As performers, downtown's composer/improvisers were in the public eye, with jazz and rock as models. Whether in the commercial mainstream or on its fringes, Jewish performers in those idioms had rarely been vocal about their heritage. Chapter 2 brings into view the complicated social and historical dynamics that contributed to a similar quietness around Jewish heritage among downtown musicians, illuminating how the gender and race dynamics prevalent in rock and jazz at mid-century played a key part in determining downtown artists' relegation of Jewish identity to the private sphere. Many had strong personal senses of Jewish identity, but they expressed that identity most freely in a personal and familial context, rather than making it part of their social lives on the scene or their public personae as performers. This quietness prefigured the surprising intensity of the Munich festival and the RJC moment.

Amidst the outpouring of talk, writing, and music of that moment, Zorn was not one of its most active discussants, but he was undoubtedly RJC's main protagonist and most prolific composer, and he has remained its central figure to the present day. Chapter 3 uses close readings of Zorn's seven-movement tone poem, *Kristallnacht,* and three versions of the piece "Idalah-Abal" from the Masada songbook—Zorn's book of several hundred original pieces, which he arranges for his various Masada ensembles—to address his compositional vision for RJC. These pieces suggest the counterintuitive arc of Zorn's project, which now spans two decades, of developing a new oeuvre of Jewish music. *Kristallnacht* took as its impetus a terrible moment in Jewish history, the Nazi-orchestrated anti-Jewish pogroms of November 1938, but in his subsequent Masada project, Zorn developed work that, through sound and iconography, retreated from historical particularity. His Jewishly identified work thus took shape through a hyperreal intensity, but it ultimately attained a mystical remove. Underlying this shift were Zorn's convictions about the artist as outsider and mystic, notions he presented in both *Kristall-nacht* and Masada as closely allied with Jewish identity and history. The musical terms, concepts, and notated examples in this discussion will be more accessible to specialists than to general readers, but I have balanced my musical analysis with close readings of Zorn's images, packaging choices, and iconography, which Zorn himself cites as crucial to his creative concept.

On the multifarious downtown scene, there were as many readings of Jewish identity as there were artists to engage it. Chapter 4 focuses on one of the most provocative contributors to this conversation, the No Wave band G-d Is My Co-Pilot, or GodCo. With an emphasis on anti-virtuosity and rawness, 1980s No Wave repudiated the polished genre dubbed New Wave, which had emerged out of the Lower East Side's underground rock scene of the 1970s. During the RJC moment, this slyly subversive No Wave band changed the spelling of "God" in its name to "G-d," in a nod to the traditional Jewish proscription against fully writing out the name of the deity, lest it be accidentally erased; but as G-dCo the band presented Jewish songs in a decidedly non-traditional mien. In collaboration with Craig Flanagin—the band's co-leader, arranger, and main songwriter—lead singer Sharon Topper enacted a queer and musically radical subject position through her vocal stylings, self-presentation, album art, and, for G-dCo's Jewish-themed concerts, elaborate hand-drawn pamphlets. Postcolonial theorist Homi Bhabha's notion of the "in-between space" has proved fruitful for scholars of gender and sexuality, contemporary popular music and identity, and I draw on it here to illuminate the intriguing ideas about Jewish identity and inauthenticity that lay behind the band's studied artlessness.

The concept of the "lieu de memoire" (memory place) plays an important role in the klezmer literature, but RJC has sometimes been characterized as a rootless music without memory. Unlike the music of the klezmer revival, RJC's critics tended to frame it as culturally unmoored and lacking in historical resonance. As I explore in chapter 5, such characterizations of cultural rootlessness link to negative assessments of "schizophonia"—the term proposed by composer R. Murray Schafer for the separation of a sound from its source—and its role in contemporary Jewish music. In this chapter I address work by two artists, Shelley Hirsch and Anthony Coleman, work that is notable precisely because it engages the emotional ambivalence and frayed historical connections that have led some observers to dismiss RJC as cursorily Jewish and thus insubstantial. Even as these artists turned their attention to the Jewishly powerful meanings that lie in personal memory, their music trafficked in pluralistic references and non-tonal abstraction. Indeed, it was through privileging such sounds and techniques that they were able to shape the RJC moment into a special kind of Jewish memory site.

Through their subjective and quirkily creative forays into the territory of memory, downtown artists added a new dimension to the notion of Jewishly usable music: such music, they contended, could usefully reflect imperfect cultural transmission, cultural and national in-betweenness, or simply personal ambivalence. Although such ideas went against the grain of trends in contemporary Jewish music, these artists were not alone in this enterprise. In fact, they were the contemporaries of a new generation of writers among whom similar ideas were brewing, and who have been bent since then on expanding the purview of Jewish American fiction along similar lines. In a sense, the music of the RJC moment functioned as a rejoinder to the work of Philip Roth and other American novelists who had "probed the condition of postwar American Jewish life, summoning into collective awareness both our disconnection from the 'little secrets' of the shadowed past and the inadequacies . . . discontinuities and incoherencies" that inhere in postwar Jewish American subjectivity.[13] The kind of humorous, self-excoriating, and sophisticated investigation into Jewish American experience that typified Roth's writing, and the explosions in syntax and narrative propriety of twentieth-century American arts and letters at large, offered downtown artists an intriguing glimpse of the path their radical Jewish music might take. Indeed, although the 1990s represent an unusually rich flowering of ideas, as I discuss in an epilogue, long after the RJC's moment's collective intensity had waned, downtown musicians continued mulling over questions about the nature of Jewish identity, the shape of Jewish heritage, and how both might relate to their particular kind of pluralistic musical experimentalism. This book, then, offers a chronicle of the RJC moment, delves critically into the music and ideas that constituted it, and considers RJC's lasting presence in the musical and cultural landscape, both in New York City and elsewhere.

## Jewishly Secular Subversives

The RJC moment gave voice to a twentieth-century Jewish American community that has received little scholarly attention. This is hardly surprising, as that community began to recognize itself as Jewish only in the mid-1990s. Downtown artists involved in the RJC moment had different relationships to religious practice and different levels of Jewish education, strongly felt Jewish identities but loosely personalized relationships to traditional religious worship and observance. Of course, the notion that Jewish practice is subject to highly personal interpretation was in line with their global stance toward American culture, and American music, at large. Most had grown up during the 1960s and were part of a cohort that was ready to subvert any aspect of American life, including American Jewish life, with which they disagreed. Yet, although the art scene in which they found a creative home was surely a secular one, the term "secular," which is useful in describing most of my interlocutors to some extent, falls short in other ways.[14] "Jewishly secular" is perhaps a more appropriate term to describe these artists, many of whom have not only written Jewishly identified music, but also gather on Jewish holidays, read widely in Jewish literature, and have given their children Jewish educations. But no matter what their relationship to Jewish identity and practice, if they were to make Jewishly identified music under the rubric of RJC, it would have to resonate with their creative concerns as downtown experimentalists. During the RJC moment, they consequently became interested in the work of Jewish artists and thinkers who had preceded them in mapping out related terrain.

To place RJC in a wider context of American Jewish history, we need to frame its musicians as heirs to the multitude of artists whose work informed the downtown scene. As part a new cohort of creative renegades on the scene, artists downtown looked to both like-minded contemporaries and predecessors in order to build intellectual biographies that spoke to them as strongly as their putatively inherited ones. That cohort included jazz musicians, and particularly artists in the jazz avant-garde, who inhabited a narrow and professionally precarious cultural margin but insisted on the viability of their radical creative ideas. Iconoclastic classical composers, including high modernists and Cageian experimentalists, were another creative touchstone. Downtown artists also understood their work, and their own peripheral cultural position, as affiliated with that of the social outcasts who had developed underground rock and proto-punk in the 1960s—including Velvet Underground founder Lou Reed, who startled his downtown colleagues by appearing at the Munich festival for Radical New Jewish Culture in 1992—followed by punk rock a decade later. The advent of RJC spurred artists to consider their own creative biographies in a way they had not done before—that is, to recover an intellectual tradition of creative Jewish subversives. In this sense they were taking up an old practice of Jewish "self-fashioning"—one ascribed, for example, to the nineteenth-century philosopher Solomon Maimon, who in his autobiography "crafted [a] narrative to his key Jewish intellectual antecedents."[15] For downtown artists those ante-cedents included figures from the Beat Generation: visual artist Wallace Berman, whose work Zorn has memorialized in his live score to Ber-man's film, *Aleph;* comedian Lenny Bruce, whom Coleman has cited as a model for his own conception of RJC; and poet Allen Ginsberg, whom guitarist Marc Ribot and other downtown musicians accompanied on spoken-word recordings in the 1990s.[16] In musicians' interviews and dis-cussions about RJC, a panoply of other figures emerge as well: Hannah Arendt, Walter Benjamin, Paul Celan, Heinrich Heine, Jacques Derrida. Downtown artists might well have engaged some of these figures with-out the advent of RJC. But with it, the possibility emerged that thinkers and artists who, from one perspective, populate the margins of Jewish culture, might be understood as central to an alternative kind of Jewish tradition—one with which downtown artists qua artists could closely identify and to which they might have something unique to contribute. Through their involvement with RJC, then, artists inserted themselves into a discursive tradition of Jewish thinkers and artists, each of whom had created work that articulated ideas with a critical bearing on modern Jewish subjectivity at a particular cultural and historical juncture. The main work of the RJC moment was to add to this legacy by refracting into music their own idiosyncratic subject positions, as Jews, Americans, and musicians.

Was the music of the RJC moment—particularly at its most abstract and esoteric—"Jewish music"? Given the geographic reach and complex history of Jewish people, that deceptively simple phrase calls for a multi-faceted definition. Indeed, defining any musical genre, particularly one preceded by a national modifier, is a tricky proposition. Definition im-plies succinctness and clear boundaries, whereas phrases such as "Ameri-can music" or "Jewish music" are oversimplified conveniences, gestur-ing toward a messy range of musics that refuse to be easily contained. If "Jewish" can be a religious, ethnic, cultural, or national descriptor, with a great deal of variation within each of those categories, then it is hardly surprising that, as ethnomusicologist Edwin Seroussi remarks, ever since the concept of "Jewish music" emerged in the late nineteenth century, "all attempts to define it have faced many difficulties."[17] But as with other such rubrics, rather than defining "Jewish music" narrowly, ethnomusicologists have conceptualized it as a network of interrelated musical practices and genres that either (a) incorporate Jewishly referential material, including texts in Hebrew, Yiddish, or Ladino, references to those texts, and melodies associated with Jewish liturgy, whatever their original (or earliest known) source; or (b) have a social function in a Jewish community, broadly defined.

If a music's social function is contingent upon its uses and meanings within a community, scholars of Jewish music have recently turned to the notion of usability, which links to the aesthetic preferences of individual artists while also suggesting a self-conscious, quintessentially modern preoccupation of grappling with the nature of Jewish art.[18] Although they did not define it in these terms, downtown artists were concerned with the notion of developing a Jewishly usable aesthetic in music. However, they differed from most artists who had come before them in positing just what constituted usability—in regard to their personal preferences, to the nature of Jewish music, and to the question of the social, emotional, and conceptual work to which their own experimental music was best suited. Artists involved in RJC sought, first, to write music that manifested their many creative fidelities. Jewish identity was one piece in the pluralistic puzzle of their American identities, and if their music were not usable on this front, then it would not be Jewishly usable either. Second, they conceived usability in relation to their own creative processes. That is, if things Jewish—whether memories, texts, or melodies—were usable to them as artists, this would be because engaging those things led to interesting new work that could not have been created otherwise. Artists were less concerned with whether their audiences would draw from the end result exactly what they had drawn from the act of composing and performing the music. It was in this very quality, in the ability of music—particularly experimental music—to function as an open text, that it became usable as art. Indeed, for some artists, Jewishly usable art might very well have an esoteric or conceptual connection to its Jewish sources or inspirations. Whether artists conceived their music's Jewish usability as contingent upon a pluralistic creative purview, as deriving from a highly personal creative process, or as resting on a deliberately unstable ontological foundation, the music of the RJC moment demands our attention—not because it solves the conundrum of how to define Jewish music, but because it changes the nature of the question. In the process of grappling with the issue of how to use experimentalist musical resources to engage with Jewish heritage, downtown artists opened up new avenues for conceptualizing Jewish music itself. It is no accident that this particular intervention into the nature of Jewish music's usability developed among artists involved with New York's downtown music scene. Understanding the RJC moment involves delving into the downtown scene's defining social and creative qualities. Those qualities, which emerged out of the neighborhood's unique history, illuminate why RJC emerged when and where it did.

## The Downtown Scene: A Creative Ecosystem

Manhattan's Lower East Side has long been a magnet for musical iconoclasts, and it has served as a crucible for many signal developments in American expressive culture. So many boldface names in twentieth-century music and art have been based there that even a partial lexicon quickly becomes a long list: Jean-Michel Basquiat, David Byrne, Ornette Coleman, Philip Glass, Jim Jarmusch, Meredith Monk, Nam June Paik, Steve Reich, Patti Smith. Now a gentrifying enclave, like so many New York City neighborhoods the Lower East Side has shifted through multiple identities. Representatives of its many pasts—as a crowded immigrant quarter, a multifaceted Latin music scene, a political hotbed, and an artists' haven—now share the sidewalks with residents of its gleaming luxury apartments.[19] For most of its history it was an embattled neighborhood, and in the 1970s it became a desperate one, as an economic crisis and city budget cuts led to crumbling storefronts, gang warfare, and a rampant drug and sex trade. In some ways, the neighborhood's dire circumstances fueled its creative vitality. Lax city oversight spurred a wave of activism from Latino residents, who developed a public murals project and chartered a new cultural center with an art gallery and auditorium.[20] Abandoned buildings, convenient spots for illicit activity, also meant that rents were low and studio space cheap. Successive waves of artists followed, setting up shop in unheated lofts, which doubled as makeshift galleries and rehearsal spaces. By the late twentieth century, the Lower East Side was home to one of the most dynamic creative communities in the United States.

Alongside its vibrant visual arts, theater, and dance scenes, the area included an ever-diversifying music scene—or rather an overlapping series of sub-scenes that included jazz and free improvisation, punk rock, and contemporary classical composition, and whose practitioners got to know each other and each other's music through concerts, collaborations, and after-hours hangouts at local bars and restaurants, which were havens of warmth and camaraderie during New York's freezing winters. With converted industrial lofts well suited to the needs of improvising musicians, the Lower East Side had been a vital center for jazz since the 1960s. As evidenced by a recent spate of commemorative activities around the club CBGB—including a display of its toilets at the Metropolitan Museum—punk rock and its pop-friendly sister New Wave were both born on the gritty Lower East Side of the 1970s, followed soon thereafter by No Wave, punk's avant-garde incarnation.[21] During the same period, contemporary concert music—New Music—had a strong presence downtown, anchored by composers whose work was an uneasy fit with the high-modernist "uptown" schools cultivated at Columbia and Princeton. The Lower East Side offered something special to jazz musicians, punk rockers, and classical composers alike, but if the neighborhood's plentiful studio space gave musicians the opportunity to work together on a dizzying variety of projects, professional venues and paying gigs were scarce.[22] Just a few commercial venues fueled downtown's main musical sub-scenes. Philosopher Bernard Gendron has chronicled four venues that served the three primary "streams" of the 1970s downtown music world: the Mercer Arts Center and CBGB (punk rock); Studio RivBea (loft jazz); and the Kitchen (experimental concert music).[23] As a new cohort of artists began convening downtown in the 1970s and 1980s, their work developed into a fourth stream, whose primary venue was to be the Knitting Factory. When the RJC idea emerged in the 1990s, it was carried along by that fourth stream, whose composer/improvisers drew fluently on idioms from across the downtown music world.

Amidst all these influences, jazz gave the downtown music scene its central creative model, that of the composer/improviser, and provided its central creative tenet, that of developing a personal voice that was at once compositional and performative. Of course, composer/improvisers of the late twentieth century draw on multiple sources, and when addressing the value they place on originality or individualized language it can be difficult to separate jazz's influence from that of other idioms, particularly the classical avant-garde, where individuality and the search for new language are also essential values. Indeed, the artists I discuss often mention modernist composers when they talk about their strongest influences. But despite sharing common interests with classical composers, downtown artists are beholden to their local scene precisely because it offers them, as composer/improvisers, something different from the classical paradigm.

In the United States, the art of composition/improvisation is tied up closely with the history of jazz, a genre that has expanded to include music that, although it may not sound like straight-ahead jazz, shares many of the genre's performance practices and values. Paramount among these values is an emphasis on personal voice. As bassist Mark Dresser explained, emphasizing jazz's significance among his diverse musical experiences, "I've had a kind of a typical American musical performance experience as a bass player, having played everything from European classical music, professionally, to having grown up playing folk music, to playing rock and roll [and] Latin jazz. And believing the whole time that . . . the challenge and the gift and the lesson of jazz was to be yourself, and find your own voice [and] language. . . . Not trying to be a stylist, [not trying] to do something that's been done. But trying to find one's own music."[24] The multifaceted notion of personal voice in jazz includes an individual performer's sound—distinctive timbres, articulations, inflections, and phrasing. In regard to preparing and performing jazz improvisations, personal voice denotes elements that are conventionally considered compositional, such as melody, harmony, and motivic development. And the notion also encompasses a jazz artist's ideas as an author of original music in the fully traditional sense, as a composer of written music outside the context of a performance. The aim of seeking out one's own original voice, so central to jazz, had important consequences for RJC. As we will see in the chapters that follow, during the RJC moment downtown composer/improvisers were willing to push that concept to its limit, chancing unintelligibility in the service of writing highly personal music.

The notion of personal voice in jazz also had a crucial valence during the RJC moment in that it gave artists a mandate to develop Jewishly identified work that, like jazz, was simultaneously sui generis and historically grounded.[25] Jazz improvisers use practices of signification—musical commentary linked to the African American expressive practice of signifying—to articulate a personal, sometimes contentious, but always historically aware relationship with jazz tradition.[26] It is this dynamic that has led scholars to understand jazz as an intertextual field, one in which musical sound, history, and personal commentary intermingle. Part of "thinking in jazz" is thus to conceive of the music in this multivalent fashion, as signifying on multiple fronts.[27] Similarly, the artists I discuss have been intent on developing original, sometimes esoteric work, and yet, through both music and text, they have consistently used that work to address their place in history and their relationship to artists and thinkers who have preceded them. Just as a jazz-based relationship between personal voice and historical precedent permeated the downtown scene broadly, it also imbued the RJC moment. If we approach their music with this dynamic in mind, we can understand it as signifying on the relationship between an artist's Jewishly personal voice, his or her creative voice, and the relationship of both to Jewish heritage and tradition.

Even as downtown musicians sought to develop unique creative voices, they shared an interest in bridging high-low cultural divides and bringing many different musics into dialogue. Zorn, with his embrace of music from cartoons and so-called "spaghetti westerns," on one hand, and his references to modernist composers such as Arnold Schoenberg and Karlheinz Stockhausen on the other, is the most prominent example of the scene's wide purview. There was no academic program, no artistic residency, no music conservatory, and no commercial context that came close to the Lower East Side in offering these artists a forum for exploring their wide-ranging interests, but the downtown music world seemed tailor-made to suit them. That world might best be understood as a creative ecosystem, one formed by musical subcultures, bands, and individuals who came together because of shared interests, while simultaneously cultivating the very traits that would make them distinct.

Much like any ecosystem, the downtown music world changed with the seasons. The arrival of a new club or new artist could instigate changes that rippled through the wider scene. Composer/improvisers affiliated with the Chicago-based Association for the Advancement of Creative Musicians (AACM), for example, many of whom had moved to New York City by the 1980s, changed the scene indelibly through their work and influence, and Zorn himself helped to foment a major shift in the Lower East Side's musical ecosystem. Soon after he arrived downtown in the late 1970s, a group of musicians began meeting to jam, rehearse, and perform in a small West Village basement space he leased, called Studio Henry; in the years that followed, Zorn's ensembles, compositions, and conducted improvisations drew together a network of simpatico collaborators. This is the group of artists to whom the phrase "downtown scene" often refers, and it is likewise the group on whom I concentrate in this book, but these artists occupied only one of the wider scene's many strata. To be sure, it is a messy, ragged category. Artists downtown constantly circulated through different musical contexts. By "downtown scene," then, I mean not only the musical production that happened amongst Zorn and his most frequent collaborators, but also downtown's other crisscrossing musical networks.

The artists in my purview were new arrivals on the scene in their twenties and thirties, drawn together by a shared interest in developing their voices as experimentalists and composer/improvisers. Some had moved downtown straight out of degree programs in jazz or classical composition and performance, while others were already playing professionally in jazz, blues, rock, or soul bands. Some had delved into experimental rock and No Wave, and a few had experience in avant-garde theater. Most had studied with, and had been profoundly influenced by, artists in the jazz avant-garde. All had cultivated wide-ranging listening habits and were hungry for like-minded collaborators. As Hirsch recounted of her artistic projects of the late 1970s:

> I did a lot of different kinds of music. Like I was singing for a Korean dancer, I was working with a downtown minimalist composer . . . [and] singing with [pianist] Kirk Nurock. . . . I'd hang out with . . . [Jeffrey Lohn's No Wave band] Theoretical Girls. . . . And then I met [pianist] Joel Forrester and started singing bebop songs with him. And then I joined a rock group. So I was always in different worlds! Always.[28]

As a vocalist in a scene made up mostly of instrumentalists, Hirsch is unusual, and she even among her peers also has remarkable creative flexibility, moving fluidly among widely divergent musical contexts. But such accounts are typical of composer/improvisers. On the downtown scene, these omnivorous listeners could perform and collaborate in an exhilarating variety of creative contexts that spoke to their diverse musical interests.

Soon after opening on Houston Street in 1987, the Knit became the central nucleus for artists on a downtown scene that had not yet been named. The club focused on composer/improvisers, both those who were new arrivals and those from established avant-garde jazz circles. Dim and stuffy though it was, the Knit created a collective flash of self-recognition: the downtown music scene, even if it did not yet have a distinct name or identity, was palpably more than the sum of its parts. At the Knit, where artists encountered a shifting series of microcosms of the downtown music world, they could consider the role played by their individual work and ideas in relation to the whole. As clarinetist Don Byron recalled in 2004:

> Everybody lived within walking distance from the old Knit [i.e., the club's original location].... There was a lot of intermingling, and people heard and got to respect [one another].... There's no place like that anymore, where the scene is so alive that I just want to be there *tonight,* to see what's gonna come down.... Being able to hear that kind of a range of music, at one place I frequented—that's so me. I mean, anybody that knows me, knows that's so what I'm like. That's what my *house* is like. So I felt completely comfortable at the Knitting Factory.... Anything could happen on a given night. [That was] the way I thought about music. *I* could be playing anything on a given night. So, I liked going there more than I liked going to Bradley's [a jazz club in the West Village]. Bradley's didn't express all of me. Nor did going to the New York Philharmonic, or going to the Met. Those things only expressed a part of me. The Knitting Factory expressed quite a bit of me.[29]

My interviewees shared Byron's warmth toward the sense of community the Knit engendered. Of course, if the circulation of artists and ideas was one of downtown's great attributes, it was not a perfectly free flow. Downtown's musical sub-scenes—which were supported by venues and delimited by genre and performance practice—were also, and relatedly, mitigated by reified boundaries of race, class, and access. Although the Knitting Factory's programming was remarkably varied, it was hardly a full representation of the Lower East Side's music world. By and large, despite the presence of a large Latino community and vibrant Latin music scene on the Lower East Side, the club did not program Latin music, nor was it a venue for hip hop, despite that genre's burgeoning presence in the neighborhood and its influence on the downtown visual art scene.[30] But the club—a commercial concern that presented music for paying customers, protected its own interests, and fomented its share of disputes with performers over pay and copyright—also served an important social function among the artists who gathered there to play, hang out, and stay in touch with new creative developments.[31] Through both its programming and its humming social dynamic, then, the Knitting Factory did something unprecedented. The downtown scene's multiplicity was normally an inchoate quality, experienced in fragments. In a way appropriate to its name, the Knit brought together those quicksilver flashes, unifying them briefly each night and making that multiplicity tangible to both artists and observers.

## Iconoclasm, Pluralism, and the Search for New Language

Downtown's denizens of the 1980s were such a heterogeneous group, and they followed such idiosyncratic creative paths, that it is fruitless (and misleading) to try to identify one common style or aesthetic. But they did share some key concerns. First, in addition to their wide-ranging interests, they were creative misfits who had come of age in the 1960s during an era of dramatic changes in the American musical landscape. In talking about their formative musical experiences, my interviewees' recollections ranged widely over live shows by Frank Zappa, Charles Mingus, and Duke Ellington, Busby Berkeley films, workshops with artists from the AACM, the premiere of John Cage's *Renga with Apartment House (1776)*, and recordings of all kinds. Those who undertook formal training in the 1970s and 1980s tended to be stymied by the creative constraints they encountered in their studies, while those who performed professionally recall searching for a forum that would allow them to synthesize their interests and experiences. Second, these artists shared an interest in noise, especially as this notion encompasses not only high volumes, dissonance, distortion, and "unmusical" sounds, but also conceptual noise, that is, in a loosely Attalian sense, the breach of convention. This value

**Figure 0.1.** The "Old Knit" on Houston Street, c. 1988. *Photo: Michael Dorf.*

led artists to a third common concern, that of tweaking codified styles or working outside them altogether. In disrupting common practice, their outré musical language amounted to a kind of defamiliarizing syntactical noise—hence the scene's association with the phrase "New York Noise." Artists downtown tended to manifest this interest by juxtaposing idioms that ostensibly did not belong together, thereby disrupting the hierarchies of taste that often underlie judgments of artistic quality. Although they incorporated a panoply of stylistic influences, their music seldom hewed to any one style. When it ostensibly did—for example, in Naked City, Zorn's hardcore rock band—artists invariably used formal innovations to subvert that style's typical constraints.

On one hand, these artists, who drew on such a wide range of idioms, found incoherence to be a risk worth taking in the service of forging open-ended, flexible musical syntax out of many constituent parts. In Coleman's words, "What I'm looking for is to . . . let the references in language flow more freely and anarchically and make sense out of *that*. I'm interested in people who risk incoherence."[32] On the other hand, in an ensemble, incoherence was a stage to be moved through along the way to fruitful interactions. Thus, as saxophonist Roy Nathanson asserted, "The [Jazz] Passengers, and all the other bands I was with, were really about mixing language. People from different cultures, different backgrounds, coming together and finding some kind of common language . . . and invent[ing] something new. And I think that's the richest of the American things you can do."[33] A pluralistic approach to genre and a preference for working outside style led composer/improvisers of varied creative backgrounds to collaborate in ensembles, in which they then worked through (or failed to work through) their musical differences. Indeed, by making a connection between common musical language and American pluralism, Nathanson articulated a position shared by colleagues who linked their social ideals to the search for new creative paradigms. As Ehrlich explained:

> Anthony Braxton put out his solo saxophone record (*For Alto,* 1969)—and inside [in the liner notes] he said, "I listen to James Brown, Karlheinz Stockhausen, Charlie Parker, Mozart, and the [Baka] Pygmies, and Marvin Gaye," or something. . . . That blew my mind, as a young kid! . . . My generation's defined by that. Both a desire, and the fact that everything became available. . . . And I think that's a radical thing. I think we're breaking down the [walls]. And that's been one of my passions.[34]

On both a creative and social level, such pluralistic principles were at play during the RJC moment. To be sure, some artists were wary of participating in a project focused around cultural identity. Insofar as personal experience and identification were wrapped up in the project, RJC would be not only a Jewishly identified scene but also most likely a white one; as creative individuals, musicians might well want to plumb the depths of their own Jewish experiences, but if whole ensembles were formed around this idea, no matter what the intention, RJC would be lending de facto support to white homogeneity on the downtown scene. My interviewees, though committed to following through on the creative promise of the RJC idea, took a jaded view of it in this sense, and this is one reason they were ambivalent about taking the whole as an enterprise, a movement, or anything more than the sum of its parts. At the same time, pluralism was central to downtown artists' conceptions of Jewish identity, and they were intrigued by the idea of developing work that could engage the multitudes they inhabited, and by which they were inhabited, as Jewish American experimentalists.

Historian Jonathan Freedman has proposed a model of Jewish American identity that is particularly useful in regard to making sense of this goal. In Freedman's view, that identity is "mobile, multidimensional, transactional."[35] "Jewish" and "American," he argues, are equal players in "Jewish American identity"—that is, this identity is shaped fundamentally both by a sense of Jewish identification and by an immersion in a pluralistic, culturally diverse society. In an essay about RJC titled "Reflections in J," Coleman has neatly illustrated the applicability of this model to his downtown colleagues. He glosses the Lower East Side as analogous to Spain's medieval "Golden Age," when Spanish Jews lived in relative harmony with Christians and Muslims. "They weren't really in *love* with each other during the Golden Age of Spain," he observes. "They just didn't run around killing each other. But that's already a lot. It kind of reminds me of New York. Everything interpenetrates everything here—up to a point." Artists' investment in this kind of cultural interpenetration also informed the RJC moment. In his Lower East Side neighborhood, he explains:

> The Puerto Ricans are blasting their car radios, Trust Fund Babies experi-
> ence the *frisson* of living in a cutting edge neighborhood for $2000 a month,
> tortured Jewish bohos (myself included) channel the history of Downtown,
> not just the *stetl* of the early part of the century, but the Ginsbergian–Keroua-
> cian–Burroughsian history too. . . . Then there are the Polish and Ukrainian res-
> taurants left over from that period of East Village history . . . our local Mosque.
> . . . homeless people (still!) of all stripes . . . 24-hour Korean delis, Pakistani
> newsdealers, a completely Japanese street. . . . You get the idea. Radical Jewish
> Culture came out of all this—and it recedes back into it.[36]

Coleman is skeptical about the connection between embracing the neighborhood's diversity and affecting wider social change, adding, "Can this change the world, providing a model for how people can live together in all their variety? Probably not." But as he intimates in his depiction of the dynamics of his neighborhood and the workings of his psyche, for him and his cohort, Jewish identity participated in the puzzle of American identity in general, and downtown Manhattan identity in particular. Indeed, with its dense city blocks and multi-layered past, the Lower East Side streetscape brought into sight a particularly diverse American-ness. And like many New Yorkers, downtown artists identified strongly with this aspect of their city and felt that for all its problems, it realized the promise of American pluralism in a way that was unmatched anywhere else in the country, and was often unappreciated. As guitarist Elliott Sharp remarked drily, monologuist Spalding Grey "had a great line. He said, 'New York is a small island off the coast of America.'"[37] If downtown's musicians were "American" in the way that their city and neighborhood were American, their Jewish American identities had a similar character. In Coleman's view, RJC's main promise would be realized through music that reflected upon this reality, in a downtownish mien.

In embarking on this project, artists had the tools they needed close at hand. The downtown scene, after all, derived energy from multiplicity, and the praxis of composition/improvisation was one of the main avenues through which artists engaged the music they found most vital— whatever the era or idiom. Artists were already immersed in developing musical language that spoke to them with unique contemporary and personal relevance. They were thus already involved in bringing their individual voices into a community-wide conversation. And yet, Jewish artists had engaged this project largely without considering whether things Jewish—experiences, languages, melodies, texts, memories— had any bearing on the process. On a scene where personal voice was paramount, this absence was notable. Although one could readily point to ensembles downtown that commented on aspects of identity, including gender, sexuality, race, and African American heritage, Jewish identity was not part of this discourse.

This absence was all the more puzzling in that many downtown artists recalled Jewish musical traditions as having been interwoven into the musical landscape of their youths, particularly cantorial music and Yiddish songs. For example, Ribot grew up with regular Friday night dinners with his family that revolved around the music of the Yiddish theater. Similarly, Nathanson explained, "I grew up in a Jewish neighborhood, in Midwood [Brooklyn]. . . . I did have some passing acquaintance with . . . klezmer music. . . . But more than that, Yiddish music, because my uncle . . . was the translator for Joseph Singer [brother to Yiddish writer Isaac Bashevis Singer]. . . . And during our family [Passover] seders in Brooklyn, we sang Yiddish songs."[38] (With the exception of Nathanson, downtown artists, like most of their peers in the klezmer renaissance, did not recall having heard much if any klezmer music in their youths.) Ehrlich, Hirsch, and drummer Joey Baron all recount having been strongly affected by cantorial singing—in Baron's case, on recordings his parents listened to at home, for Ehrlich during his family's regular synagogue attendance, and for Hirsch when she snuck into services at the local Orthodox *shul*.[39]

The RJC idea, then, developed into a new dialogic challenge. With the scene's multitude of influences, its emphasis on personal voice, and its sizable cohort of Jewish composer/improvisers, why had Jewish heritage been virtually absent from its artists' music and creative self-concept? Did that heritage, in fact, have any bearing on the work artists had developed up to this point, even if they had not been fully aware of the connection? And could their music, and the creative processes of downtownish composition/improvisation, be used to signify compellingly and in new ways on Jewish heritage, identity, or experience? These questions led to a rush of music and conversation, shaped by differences of opinion that both animated the RJC moment and, at times, threatened to derail it.

## Contesting the Meaning of Radical Jewish Culture

The idea for what came to be called Radical Jewish Culture emerged out of conversations that had sprung up among a group of musicians who began to meet regularly in the late 1980s to discuss the relevance of Jewish heritage, or the visible lack thereof, to the downtown scene. The Knit, which hosted the first RJC festivals, was a key locus for these conversations, but it was not the only one. As Coleman recalled, RJC "created

... for a little while, a forum. ... We were meeting here [in Mogador, a Moroccan restaurant and East Village hangout] *all* the time. ... A real community was happening, and there was a lot of meeting going on."[40] As the RJC moment gathered momentum, artists' conversations delved into its aesthetic possibilities, conceptual challenges, and sociopolitical implications. Such discussions about Jewish heritage had bubbled up here and there over the years, but they reached a new intensity just as identity politics were becoming a major force in popular music. In the late 1980s, hip hop, which had been a presence downtown since its early years, had broken out onto the national stage, as the band Public Enemy made the genre a forum for black solidarity and social critique. By the early 1990s, performers were taking on issues of gender and sexuality in underground rock bands such as the "riot grrrl" band Bikini Kill and queercore (queer hardcore) band Pansy Division.[41] And when RJC offered artists downtown a similar public forum, it was also recapitulating earlier identity-driven movements in improvised music, including Asian Americans in the 1980s Asian improv scene, and of course African Americans throughout the history of jazz, and conspicuously during the 1960s.[42]

Even as the politics of identity were emerging as a powerful musical force in marginalized communities, conflicts inevitably followed. As musicologist Benjamin Piekut has illustrated in a discussion of New York's Jazz Composers Guild in the 1960s, identity-driven musical projects have long been prone to conflicts over ideological lines, and the conversations preceding the Munich festival had likewise been roiled with differences of opinion about the purposes and meanings of RJC—both the concept and the rubric. Whether the moniker was Radical Jewish Music or Radical Jewish Culture, "radical" was the main sticking point. Whether or not Zorn deployed the word with the intention to provoke, it tied in with a number of interlinked issues about which artists in his circle heartily disagreed. Ribot, for example, asserted that in seeking a name for the Munich festival, "my suggestion was 'Loud and Pushy Music'. . . [which] at least had descriptive value. But almost every word in [Radical Jewish Culture] is problematic to me."[43] Ribot and Sharp articulated the most forthright objections to the phrase, but "Radical Jewish Culture," which worked as a commercial hook, also struck other artists as overly brash and not descriptively useful. Some felt that RJC, an essentially creative phenomenon, could not claim to be radical in the political sense the term implied. Several downtown artists had a history of engaging around political causes historically associated with the Jewish left—including labor organizing, tenants' rights, civil rights, union building, and antiwar activism—and just as hip hop and queer-core artists had used their music to advocate for social change, a few artists thought the idea of Radical Jewish Culture might engage their Jewish colleagues downtown with grassroots community organizing around political issues.

By and large, artists were frustrated in their ambitions to pair art with political action. Under the guise of RJC, artists did collaborate on some politically oriented projects, including two "Artists Against the Occupation" benefit concerts in 2002 and 2003, which contributed funds to Israeli and Palestinian organizations, but RJC's ultimate failure to materialize into a more concerted form of political action should not have been surprising. As Ehrlich asserted, "I think anyone who's ever done political work knows that actually the work of changing material conditions is a much different process [than the work of making art]. That's its own sort of work. That doesn't take away from the importance of art—I think it's as crucial as anything. We all make our different peace with these sort of things. Or we make different choices. . . . I think the question of what is radical and what is Jewish, and how they intersect, is . . . interesting for us Jews to ponder, [but it is not at the crux of] the burning question of how we continue to make a creative, pluralistic American culture."[44] Not all of Ehrlich's colleagues were as even-handed in their assessment of the phrase Radical Jewish Culture, as some took a hard line against what they saw as a specious claim to radicalism that deflected attention from what they saw as the burning issues of race, class, and difference in American social discourse and the political sphere. They were driven by a question articulated by historian and religious scholar Daniel Boyarin: "How can I ethically construct a particular identity which is extremely precious to me without falling into ethnocentrism or racism of one kind or another?"[45] More than an interest in building Jewish solidarity, they voiced concerns about holding the line against reactionary forces in the United States, and about the slippage that can occur between celebrations of cultural pride and the "ethnocentrism or racism" to which Boya-rin alludes. Indeed, Sharp maintained that RJC was radical in neither its musical language nor its political presentation: "Radical Jewish music [i.e., the real thing] is radical because it is [musically] radical. Unfortu-nately, what happened was 'Radical Jewish Music' came to be defined as klezmer, or [music] that . . . [is] reduced to Jewish signifiers. And it's not radical music, for one thing, and the politics in which it's presented are not radical. [They don't] challenge authority." Sharp also objected to the word "radical" because he associated it with the hardcore nation-alism of Israel's right-wing parties, ultra-Orthodox communities, and American groups such as Meir Kahane's Jewish Defense League. As he explained, "I understood the definition of quote unquote 'Radical Jew-ish Culture' in the same context of, you know, radical white culture, as a reactionary notion, not as a progressive notion. That it was . . . nation-alistic—'we are cool, we are right,' that kind of thing, reveling in group identity."[46] With their personal and artistic identity bound up with their position at a cultural and creative margin, downtown artists are generally skeptical of what Sharp calls "reveling in group identity." As Nathanson explained in regard to RJC's potential to activate community pride, "I think that nationalism and identity politics in some kind of way, given the vicissitudes of racism, and all this kind of stuff, is such loaded shit. . . . And I think it's best probably left alone." But Nathanson tempered this ambivalence with an appreciation for what RJC had meant to the Jewish musicians involved: "But—be that as it may—[RJC] was very honest at that time. Very honest at that time. We really did think so."[47] As Nathan-son's comment indicates, downtown artists who were wary of identity politics were not rejecting Jewish communitas. Indeed, many saw the conversations and spirit of the RJC moment as having represented an important alternative space for Jewish community building. But they were determined to keep in full view the value they placed on American racial diversity and cultural pluralism, a value that played a defining role in their lives and music.

The issue of defining the meaning of "radical" touches on a compli-cated tension that arose between the artists on whom I focus and their downtown colleagues involved in neo-klezmer. Neo-klezmer is a loosely defined genre that describes some of the music on Tzadik's RJC series, and in its most abstracted guise it has some points of overlap with the music on which I focus. Although both groups of musicians were seeking to engage American Jewishness through innovative musical means, they disagreed sharply about the best way to do so, with artists in the RJC camp insisting that klezmer music, which seemed celebratory, was problematic in that what it was celebrating was the connection to an imagined past, a rhetorical move of which they were politically suspicious and creatively leery. Neo-klezmer artists disagreed. London, for example, contended that getting involved in klezmer music had strengthened his commitment to social and political causes. As he wrote in 1993, "Learning from the Women's, African-American's, and Native American [movements], and all movements of oppressed groups, group pride and identification are primary steps in our empowerment. The universalist in me often cries out against such strong and perhaps divisive group identification. However, the personal strength I have gained as an outgrowth of positive [Jewish] self-knowledge and identity enables me to work to create a better world. In Jewish terms, this [kind of work] is our taste of 'Tikkun.'"[48] As London indicates by mentioning the Jewish ethical precept of *tikkun olam*, or "repair of the world," he and his cohort of neo-klezmer artists proved to be passionate about the genre's role in championing minority identities—Jewish, queer, and experimentalist. Indeed, with its role in the Queer Yiddishkeit movement, neo-klezmer (in particular London's band, the Klezmatics) gave the klezmer revival the very sociopolitical focus that some of London's downtown colleagues found lacking on the RJC scene. There was thus both irony and frustrated idealism underlying their ambivalence toward RJC as a cultural enterprise.

Scholarly debates about the notion of diaspora help illuminate artists' conflicts on this front. In fact, the differences of opinion provoked by the word "radical" played out along the lines of tension between competing scholarly assessments of the politics of diasporic consciousness. Neo-klezmer artists tended to position the klezmer revival as a positive act of diasporic community in the sense denoted by postcolonial theorists, for whom, as anthropologist Pnina Werbner wrote in 2000, articulating a diasporic subject position was one way "to transgress . . . hegemonic constructions of national homogeneity." In the sense championed by these artists, then, their work played a part in allowing those with repressed histories and marginalized identities to recoup a sense of dignity and pride, and thence political agency. This view had obvious traction in the way some neo-klezmer artists made diasporic Jewish consciousness-raising a platform for queer activism. However, scholars have also turned a more critical eye to claims of cultural solidarity among marginalized groups, pointing out "the continued imbrication of diasporas in nationalist rhetoric."[49] In contrast to their colleagues in neo-klezmer, RJC's core artists were warier of such imbrications, and they were skeptical about the whole enterprise of writing music that celebrated a culture they purportedly shared, but which they had never experienced firsthand. Indeed, some downtown artists were determined not only to steer clear of klezmer in their own work—but also to make work that was resistant to the notion of cultural or ethnic pride altogether.[50] What would be radical about their music, then, would be its resistance to easy identification with any Jewish music of the past, and its traversal of creative and emotional terrain left unaddressed by any other Jewish music they had so far encountered. Over the course of the 1990s and beyond, artists would continue grappling with the relationship among Jewish identification, community affiliation, and creative voice. In so doing they would not settle their differences, but they would develop truly radical means for configuring contemporary Jewish music and identity.

## ONE

# Jewish Music

*The Art of Getting It Wrong*

IN HIS EPILOGUE TO THE BOOK *JEWISH MUSIC AND MODERNITY*, ethnomusicologist Philip Bohlman describes several narratives by which musicians and observers frame the character of Jewish music in Central and Eastern Europe today. Each of Bohlman's narratives functions as a conceptual lens one looks through to bring "Jewish music" into focus in a unique way. That is, each lens constructs a particular notion of Jewish music, and each of these notions is based on a selective interpretation of contemporary music-making. Bohlman's subject is dramatically different from that of RJC, and the site of Europe as the near annihilation of Jewish musicians and musical culture creates, in one sense, a chasm between the two contexts that cannot be bridged. But in a less contextually determined sense his insights are extremely useful in conceptualizing the Radical Jewish Culture moment.

Among the mostly non-Jewish performers and audiences Bohlman addresses, one narrative lens renders contemporary Jewish music exotic. A quality of exoticism inheres not only because the music is Jewish per se, but also because Jewish culture carries a "patina of pastness," denoting both something ancient and something gone. Like other exotic artifacts, this lens makes Jewish music, and by association Jewish culture and history, easy to consume.[1] As ethnomusicologist Mark Slobin has observed, in the 1990s klezmer filled a complicated niche in Europe on the level of the exotic, offering Europeans "a vision of [Jewish] Americans as representing a romantic, faraway musical tradition" that has had little to do with the concerns of present-day Jews in the European body politic.[2] Indeed, a perception of Jewish music (and Jews) as "exotic" has played an important role in the creative lives of downtown musicians when performing in Europe, just as it has with their colleagues in the klezmer revival. As artists have attested interviews and in writing, their perceptions of this attitude have influenced the way they have presented themselves and their Jewishly identified work. But audiences, both Jewish and not, bring many different stories to their encounters with Jewish music, and the presence of one narrative lens does not preclude that of another, seemingly contradictory one. Thus, alongside the lens that construes Jewish music as exotic, another construes it as something not to be assessed as "other" but to be adopted as one's own—an object of neglect that should be embraced and reanimated with as much fidelity as possible to the original. This view, which is typical of musical revivals in general, has resonances with the outlook of the early klezmer revivalists in the United States (with the obvious difference most revivalists were Jewish, whereas most of Bohlman's subjects were not)—just as it does with the mostly middle-class urbanites who instigated the U.S. folk revival of the 1960s, adopting rural idioms and championing the values they associated with rural communities, in a process one historian has memorably called "romancing the folk."[3] There is yet another lens that corresponds closely not to the viewpoint of strict revivalists but to that of their colleagues in the neo-klezmer scene. This lens focuses contemporary Jewish music into that which is not revived but rather revitalized. Artists who frame Jewish music in this fashion are driven by a "desire to discover the vitality of a tradition that can live in the present rather than an urge to salvage one that had already died in its own day." It is just such a view that led klezmer historian and musician Henry Sapoznik to argue for the term "renaissance" rather than "revival" to describe the surge of interest in klezmer music in the United States in the late twentieth century.[4]

Bohlman's insights into the role played by revitalization have a unique resonance for Radical Jewish Culture, offering a basis for understanding RJC's signal contributions to Jewish music and musical discourse. However, this is not so because downtown artists adopted revitalization as central to their cause. To the contrary, the musicians on whom I focus developed their work and ideas in part as a reaction against the idea that revitalization—updating old genres, klezmer in particular—should be the main engine for creating new Jewish music. To make sense of their critique, it helps to turn back to Bohlman's discussion of his third conceptual lens, which speaks saliently to downtown artists' views on revitalization. He notes that the artists participating in the project of revitalizing tradition "want to put glitter and guilt behind them, instead *going about the serious business of getting a contemporary Jewish music right*. Doing that means learning languages, especially Yiddish and Hebrew, and it also means scholarly study, whenever and wherever that is possible."[5] The phrase "glitter and guilt" is striking, but I would like to pause here to take note of the latter part of this passage, for it is through the notion of "getting a contemporary Jewish music right" that this lens brings the most crucial and compelling quality of RJC into sharp focus. To bring that quality into full view, one must (to stretch the metaphor slightly) look through the wrong end of the telescope.[6]

Rather than seeking to get the new Jewish music right, then, the artists on whom I focus were motivated by the creative and cultural potential that lay in getting it wrong. It was precisely by sidestepping received notions about the proper way to go about making new Jewish music that they were able to channel their Jewish subjectivities and creative concerns into the project of the RJC moment: to make work whose language and praxis resonated with the particularities of their own Jewish experiences as well as with their creative concerns as experimentalists. These artists, like those Bohlman describes, "come from a new generation, and they are interested in telling their own stories" to make music that draws on the sounds of the past while resonating with a contemporary soundscape.[7] Their Jewish "stories" were both highly personal and downtownishly musical. That is, the stories were peculiarly their own and no one else's, both in that they reflected individual, subjective experience and because, as both composer and performer, each artist told his or her "story" in an idiosyncratic musical voice. The challenge was to create art that represented a compelling symbiosis among all these qualities.

Artists envisioned this music as offering listeners a paradigm for engaging aspects of Jewish American identity and subjectivity that could not be addressed in a more familiar musical way. Certainly, focused historical and language studies could form one basis for developing new Jewish music, but downtown artists sought another. If the Jewish qualities of their stories were highly personal, and thus hard to hear in the music, so be it. In developing music to reflect on the particular qualities of their Jewish experiences, they were, in Geertz's classic formulation, seeking to use art to "materialize a way of experiencing; bring a particular cast of mind out into the world of objects, where men can look at it."[8] These aims saw their first major public manifestation in September 1992, at the Festival for Radical New Jewish Culture in Munich. In the years that followed, artists vigorously debated the panoply of issues that arose in conjunction with their creative project. These discussions emerged with such force in part because they contained the seeds of ideas that had been germinating on the scene, in the guise of occasional Jewishly identified pieces that artists had developed in the years that preceded the festival.

## Before RJC, Jewish Music on the Downtown Scene

Downtown's Jewishly identified pieces were isolated efforts, and their very sparseness, amidst the scene's otherwise prolific character, points up the absence of a Jewishly creative milieu downtown that could match the contemporaneous klezmer renaissance. The early pieces can also be difficult to document. The evanescent quality of musical performance and the centrality of improvisation to the downtown scene means that much of its music has not been written down, and the informal nature and tight budgets of most downtown venues meant that live performances often went unrecorded. But when several of these early efforts are taken together, it is clear that RJC gave a community-wide platform to concerns that artists had begun to address well before the Munich festival.

Some of the pre-Munich music was released in commercial press-
ings that are no longer easily available. One such early project was *Geduldig und Thimann: A Haymish Groove,* a compilation compact disc produced during the 1980s by two semi-professional musicians whom Zorn
later invited to the Munich festival. The recording includes several New
York–based artists, including guitarist Elliott Sharp and clarinetist Don
Byron, who contribute arrangements of traditional Jewish tunes using
musical language characteristic of the downtown music world, with formal structures that include free improvisation, or an evocation of it, as
both an expressive and a structural element. Byron's composition, for
example, mimics a group of musicians warming up backstage before a
performance, but they are subtly responding to each other and to the
clarinet as it extemporizes on a traditional melody.[9] In other cases, artists
remembered making Jewishly identified work, but it was not recorded, or
the recordings never resurfaced. Many musicians made personal recordings of their performances, but as saxophonist Roy Nathanson noted
wryly when I asked about finding one recording in particular, "You'd
have to go through hundreds of hundreds of [cassette] tapes to find it.
Buckets of tapes." "Are they labeled?" "No. That's the problem." As he
explained:

> RN: My friend Ray Dobbins is a playwright, and [in the early 1980s] we did
> a bunch of things for the theater, I would write music for him.... We did a
> piece about these two gay men who ran an antique store, and they died and the
> antiques came alive, and danced. And that had a kind of klezmer [sense]. There
> were a bunch of things I did for theater, [where] I was still playing around with
> [klezmer].
>
> TB: And is there anywhere I could find it?
>
> RN: No. Well, like I was saying, there are so many things that are just gone.

In Nathanson's recollection, somewhere in his "bucket of tapes" is a recording of his performance of "a trumpet and sax fanfare version" of a
song he used to sing on Passover with his family.[10] He performed this
piece at the Knitting Factory in 1990, as part of a set he presented with
Anthony Coleman. Their performance, in preparation for which Coleman explained that "we were just grabbing signifiers from everywhere,"
was a precursor of the RJC scene to come: it included an arrangement
of the Yiddish song "At the Rabbi's Table" and an early version of two

pieces each artist would develop further, Coleman into *Jevrejski by night* (Jewish by night) and Nathanson's into a solo piece, *Kaddish,* which he wrote in memory of his brother.[11] As Coleman's phrase indicates, their early work contained the seeds of ideas they would develop more fully during and after the RJC moment.

In other cases, artists' personal tapes have resurfaced. For example, upon arriving in Berlin for a gig at the Berlin Jazz Festival in November in 1988, guitarist Gary Lucas recalled, "I noticed that it was the fiftieth anniversary of Kristallnacht. And . . . I resolved to make a comment on it through music. . . . I put a piece together called 'Verklärte Kristallnacht,' which was a pun on [composer Arnold] Schoenberg's *Verklärte Nacht.* And I announced it after I played the piece. It closed my show."[12] Lucas interpolated into his improvisation phrases from "Ha-Tikvah"—the Zionist hymn that became Israel's national anthem—as well as the national anthem of what was then West Germany. He cites this impromptu improvisation as a precursor to his soundtrack to the silent film *The Golem* (1920), in which he likewise indexes Jewishness through melodic motifs from "Ha-Tikvah," and which he and Horn debuted in 1989 at the Brooklyn Academy of Music's Next Wave Festival (PURL 1.1 and PURL 1.2).

Some of the Jewishly identified work that artists presented in Munich had been developed over a period of several years before the festival, but it was not recorded in full until later. A notable example is vocalist Shelley Hirsch's *O Little Town of East New York,* but, about a decade before she began to develop that piece, Hirsch wrote what is, to my knowledge, both the most forthright example of Jewishly identified music by a downtown composer/improviser and the earliest. In 1980, Hirsch recorded a brief, poignant piece called "I Am a Jew." Her arrangement prefigures her work in the long-form *O Little Town,* both in the way she integrates Jewish references into a downtownish syntax and in the way she treats those references musically—particularly as she layers different versions of her own voice, each representing a different character, an effect she expanded upon to dramatic rhetorical effect in the later piece. *O Little Town* is closely autobiographical, but although Hirsch titled "I Am a Jew" in the first person, she slips into character by taking on a distinctive vocal persona. That piece was not yet concerned with exploring the personal "little secrets" that were to emerge as one of the central concerns of the RJC moment (PURL 1.3).

In *O Little Town,* Hirsch denotes the interpenetration of past and present both through performing different versions of her own voice, as an adult and a girl, and by deploying techniques of layering, juxtaposition, and electronic sonic manipulation. In "I Am a Jew," she likewise uses these techniques, but in this case they imply a dialogue between one character, who is declaiming the title phrase, and another, perhaps an alter ego, whom that character is channeling.

To open the piece, an agitated alto voice performs a rhythmically ragged quasi-ululation over a crisp, melodically clapped ostinato; an ethereal female duet—one soprano voice, one alto—wordlessly glides through the melody of "Ha-Tikvah" in two different keys; and a woman's voice rhythmically declaims the phrase "I am a Jew" three times. As another character emerges at a near-subconscious level from within this mix of sounds and voices, an elderly woman's tremulous, Yiddish-accented voice laments:

> There's so much suffering in the world. Why—why—we did not learn the lesson! More killing! More killing! The nice boys and the girls.... Haven't we learned? ... The people that have learned all the time.... Haven't you learned how people—suffer maybe, but learn, too? Kill? Nice!

Just as Lucas did in his guitar improvisation a few years later, Hirsch also interpolates a tonally decentered "Ha-Tikvah" melody into her musical fabric. A slight acceleration in tempo and the insistent, competing presence of the other musical layers—claps, ululation, off-kilter "Ha-Tikvah"—make the old woman's declamation of her last phrase particularly intense. Hirsch also gives each word in the last phrase an upward lilt, pausing between them and drawing them out, so that when she says "kill?" in her quavering voice, the previous word is recast: Not "too?" but "to." Rather than "suffer maybe, but learn, too?" we hear "suffer, maybe, but learn—to—kill?"[13] (The phrase "learn too/to kill" is doubly suggestive here because learning is a concept of central importance in Jewish tradition, not only in the general sense but also because "learn" is a translation of the Hebrew term for studying Torah.) In performing this lament Hirsch takes on the persona of a woman, whom we may infer is a Holocaust witness or survivor, who despairs that despite Jews' experiences of persecution and genocide, Jewish ethical tradition, and the Jewish emphasis on peaceable study, Jews, too, have learned to kill. This piece, which was written during a period of escalating tensions between Israel and Lebanon and which, in Hirsch's recollection, "was made in response to the violence taking place in the Middle East at the time," suggested but did not name the Israeli army as its focus.[14] At under four minutes in length, the piece might seem insignificant, and, as Hirsch pointed out, it was also an anomaly in her body of work: "It wasn't that I was doing Jewish *material,* it's just that I was conscious of what was going on in Israel and felt strongly enough about it to make a little piece about it."[15] Nevertheless, the insistently repeated statement, "I am a Jew," marks this piece as a bold act of self-exposure in a Jewish community that had not yet come to grips with itself.

Other pre-RJC pieces are also interesting for the way they barely, almost inaudibly, nod toward klezmer music, thus intimating the main concerns of the RJC moment—without fully realizing them. For example, Elliott Sharp's "Obvious" (1980), an avant-funk tune originally titled "Obvious Nose," made references to Jewish music with a touch so light it was all but indiscernible. As Sharp explained, the piece "used a C-harmonic minor scale . . . but it was a funk tune. I didn't try to overstate the [Jewish] flavor. I wanted there to be just enough flavor that you'd say, 'Oh, maybe that sounds kinda Jewish.' And . . . that was about as far as I wanted to go."[16] Sharp's piece does not use Jewishly identified melodies or texts, and so its "Jewishness," if it exists, is not audibly evident, but his comment reflects colloquially on a notion that scholars have interrogated and historicized, the issue of "Jewish looks," which Sharp tweaks here to address the idea of Jewish sounds.[17] Some listeners might dismiss the piece's Jewish qualities as superficial, and any claim to its being Jewish music as specious. And indeed, from one vantage point, that is surely the case. However, among the harmonic minor scale, the piece's original and modified title, and Sharp's comment about it, what does become apprehensible is a conceptual quality whose implications go beyond this particular piece: the quality of traces—of things barely remembered, of erasures and of ghosts, whose presence in contempo-

rary Jewish culture is powerful precisely because it is faint, an idea that
has been explored by visual artists, memoirists, and novelists.[18] If one
brings to this piece an awareness of such traces, then "Obvious" takes
on a deeper resonance, as much by implication as for its musical content
alone.

Such an apprehension of the piece, of course, is highly subjective.
One of the most intriguing aspects of the RJC moment is the way, in
regard to Jewishness, some of its music partook of a now-you-see-it, now-
you-don't quality. In one sense, such pieces do not hold up to scrutiny as
"Jewish." One cannot extrapolate too much from Sharp's "Obvious," as it
seems ridiculous to argue that any piece with a harmonic minor scale is
Jewishly relevant or interesting. But are such extrapolations necessary?[19]
Given an understanding of its genesis, pieces like "Obvious" emphasize
the way listening involves interior emotional resonances that, to particular listeners at particular personal junctures, imbue a piece of music with
meanings more profound than its formal qualities might suggest. Moreover, even as such hearings feel highly personal, upon discussing them,
listeners may realize that their interior experiences of the music have
been partly determined by larger social and historical forces that are, in
fact, widely shared. In a mirroring of the burst of communal recognition the RJC moment evinced on the downtown scene, such works can
materialize a shared experience among listeners who would otherwise
apprehend the music's Jewish traces, if they understand them as such,
only in isolation. In musical terms, "Obvious" is not a particularly signifi-
cant part of Sharp's oeuvre, and one should not place too much weight
on this particular piece. But, as I take up in more detail in chapters 4 and
5, the existence of pieces like "Obvious" suggests why a Radical Jewish
Culture festival can productively include work whose Jewishly affective
traces, which to some listeners will sound like nothing, can also lead to
a Jewishly resonant listening experience.

"Tikkun," a piece recorded by Nathanson and trombonist Curtis
Fowlkes's Jazz Passengers in 1988, raises related interpretive questions.[20]
*Tikkun olam* is a concept of kabbalistic origin that was adopted more
widely by American Jews in the twentieth century. A conception of Jewish *tikkun* as a mandate to engage in social activism came into wide public circulation in American Jewish life in 1986 with the debut of *Tikkun,* a

magazine of political and cultural commentary aimed toward the Jewish liberal-left. On its release in 1989, then, "Tikkun" had a clear Jewish referent. More directly than "Obvious," through its title the piece implied a connection between, on one hand, Jewish ethics and spiritual practices, and, on the other, the healing spiritual force of jazz and improvisational music.[21] But otherwise, as with "Obvious," the connections to Jewish identity, heritage, and vocal idiom are suggestive, not direct. As a piece of instrumental music that is formally and stylistically congruent with the rest of the Passengers' work, "Tikkun" does not stand out in any obvious way as Jewishly identified.

What, then, to make of Nathanson's citation of three sonic aspects of his childhood synagogue experiences as influences on his saxophone voice: the keening quality of the cantor's voice; the heterophonic texture of group prayers, which are half-sung, half-recited; and the presence of heterophonic and diachronic motivic repetition?[22] Nathanson has suggested that both his saxophone playing and his compositions for the Jazz Passengers were influenced by the rhythms of congregational prayer he heard in synagogue, and that, as a result, "I play in a cantorial, keening, querulous way that, hard as I try, isn't black."[23] In describing his saxophone sound, then, Nathanson both links it to cantorial singing and notes that such singing has a particular timbral character that is reproduced in his playing, much like an accent one cannot erase. He implies that musical timbre, like a Brooklyn accent, inscribes itself onto the voice. Indeed, Nathanson makes the interesting assertion that he plays with a "cantorial" timbre not out of intention, but because he cannot help it: this timbre is literally part of his (saxophone) voice. The saxophone part in "Tikkun" is also full of a particular kind of motivic repetition—a rapid reiteration of brief sixteenth-note motives that obsessively outline an interval that grows larger with each set of iterations—minor third, augmented fourth, minor sixth. This kind of quick repetition is arguably analogous to the reiteration of words and phrases in Jewish cantillation, while the ebb and flow in Nathanson's dynamic contours could be heard as mimicking the ebb and flow of group prayers.[24] But although Nathanson's particular Brooklyn Jewish accent and intonation are easy to hear when he speaks—indeed, he has recorded spoken-word pieces with texts that refer directly to his Jewish background—and although his piercing timbre, dynamic swells, and shaping of the attack and decay of individual pitches illuminate what he means by "querulous"—it is not straightforward to identify his playing as "cantorial."[25] Moreover, this section of "Tikkun" is strongly influenced by jazz in its melodic content, timbre, and rhythmic phrasing, and the piece's second, swung section is clearly grounded in African American jazz and blues.

To make sense of the cultural valences in "Tikkun," it is useful to revisit anthropologist Steven Feld's notion of "interpretive moves," a theory of the construction of musical meaning in which that meaning is inflected by listeners' "prior musical and social experiences," which in turn affect how they perceive "coherences . . . between sound and the social domain." Such coherences "may change with accumulated life experience . . . and may even be altered by the listening process itself."[26] What one reads into (or hears in) music, then, depends in part on the associations it sparks, even as the act of listening itself breeds new associations. "Tikkun" leads us to take this idea even further. That is, the piece pushes us to consider not only how different listeners might differently perceive the same sound, but also how one listener can hear multiple associative registers within a single sound. Interpretive meanings can differ among individuals, but they can also layer and shift for one person during the act of listening. Indeed, such shifting layers of meaning can make music feel intimate and emotionally relevant in an acutely personal way.[27] Like "Obvious," then, "Tikkun" is one of those pieces in which one may or may not apprehend audible Jewish references, based in part on whether or not the piece taps into one's Jewish memories, experiences, or associations.

Aesthetic experience, in other words, is socially constructed. Listeners invest music with a multitude of social meanings, and those meanings in turn inflect how (and what) listeners hear, intervening into the "tacit, unexamined, and seemingly completely 'natural'" mode of culturally learned musical apprehension that ethnomusicologist Judith Becker calls a "habitus of listening."[28] In reflecting upon the impact RJC had on their creative lives, artists have referred to it as creating just such a disruption. Their experiences during the RJC moment led downtown composer/improvisers to apprehend music differently, a powerful effect indeed. Guitarist Marc Ribot spoke forcefully to this point in one of the unpublished essays he wrote about Radical Jewish Culture. At the 1992 Munich festival, he recalled, he began to hear new resonances in music he already knew well:

> Although I had heard most of these performers before, hearing them in this context seemed to add or reveal new layers of influences, meaning, or metaphor. At the [Munich] festival, punk anger and abrasive dissonance were given [Jewish] historical context. . . . Collective improvisation . . . could be heard with its [roots in] New Orleans jazz *and* its possible roots in synagogue chant. East European or North African musical influences could be heard as more than eclecticism. . . . Lou Reed's famous deadpan voice could be heard in its New York Jewish hipster context, rather than simply generic hipster or ahistorically as just Lou Reed. A wide range of experiences were described by that voice. . . . That voice, those experiences, that poetic tradition could be heard as inscribed in a newly understood history of Jewish music, a hearing that in no way prevented it from also being inscribed in the other histories it also addressed.[29]

Interpretive moves are thus both culturally determined and highly subjective. "Tikkun" presents us with an example of the sort of extreme subjectivity that was also at work when Ribot, upon hearing music with which he was already familiar, found himself apprehending that music differently when he heard it in a new context, at a festival of "Radical New Jewish Culture."

Whether or not "Tikkun" is Jewish music, by suggesting through its title that listeners consider it for its Jewish resonances, elusive as they may be, the piece manifests the idea of listening as a creative act, and perhaps—that is, in opening up a conceptual space in which to apprehend suppressed, repressed, or silenced voices—also as an ethical one. During the RJC moment, some artists developed work whose structural connections to Jewish texts and traditions would have been apprehensible only to listeners who were aware of the work's genesis and development. The music contained small clues, however, that suggested particular kinds of interpretive moves. On his piece titled "Hanukkah Bush," for example, Anthony Coleman embeds a twelve-tone row derived from the holiday song "Oh, Hanukkah" into a jazz-inflected piano solo that is itself based on Abraham Goldfadn's well-loved Yiddish song "Raisins and Almonds" (*Rozhinkes mit Mandlen*). "Hanukkah Bush" is a reference to the phrase used by American Jews to describe Christmas trees in Jewish homes, a practice associated in the United States with post–World War II

Jewish suburban culture and typically "seen as an index of assimilation, even self-hatred."[30] Coleman obscures the tone row for the same reason he titled the song the way he did, and for the same reason he eventually developed his mordantly titled Selfhaters ensemble: he was reflecting musically upon an upbringing in which his Jewish parents celebrated Christmas but not Hanukkah, and in which "Raisins and Almonds" was the only Yiddish song he could remember his Yiddish-speaking grandmother having sung to him.[31] To some listeners, the titles "Hanukkah Bush" and "Tikkun," even with their evident Jewish referents, will not lead to any new interpretive insights, but to others, the titles may spark an interrogation of the music's multilayered meanings. Indeed, it could be argued that such acts of interrogation, themselves resonant with Jewish discursive and textual traditions, constitute a Jewishly inflected way of listening.

## Where to Turn? RJC's Musical Precursors

Downtown artists were not alone, of course, in striving to write music that addressed cultural heritage in inventive ways. Among their most direct precursors were composers of Jewishly identified music in the European classical tradition, as well as groups of composer/improvisers who had developed shared, identity-driven creative efforts at other places and times. The RJC moment also developed on the heels of the U.S. klezmer renaissance, and downtown composer/improvisers overlapped, both creatively and conceptually, with the artists who were transforming klezmer music into "neo-klezmer." Indeed, there were a few downtown composer/improvisers who became central innovators in modern klezmer, preceding RJC in opening up new directions for contemporary Jewish music, as well as new conversations about the nature of U.S. Jewish identity and musical expression. Notably, Byron's involvement in the klezmer scene went well beyond the compilation recording mentioned above, and in fact he was one of the first downtown composer/improvisers to bring neo-klezmer to the Knitting Factory; his repertory band, Music of Mickey Katz (MMK), created an important bridge between the klezmer renaissance and the nascent RJC scene.[32] RJC was driven in large part by artists' search for language that would resonate with their own Jewish experiences; Byron, although he did not share those experiences, brought a similar sensibility to MMK. As his comments and writings attest, he drew on his own multiple subjectivities—as downtown composer/improviser, African American, and experimentalist—to delve into MMK's social resonances. In both a musical and social regard, MMK was a harbinger of the RJC moment. The Klezmatics—a play on the Plasmatics, an outrageous downtown punk band fronted by the sexually brazen vocalist Wendy O. Williams—had formed downtown in the late 1980s; the band incorporated influences from rock, jazz, and global musical idioms and played a central part in addressing Jewish culture at the margins through their involvement in the Queer Yiddishkeit movement.[33] The band's queer thematics also resonated with the Lower East Side's role as an enclave for transvestite theater and a relatively open space for LGBT artists. As the RJC moment unfolded, the band Hasidic New Wave—led by downtown musicians Frank London (also co-founder of the Klezmatics) and guitarist Greg Wall—brought neo-klezmer into an acid-rock context that was built on a repertoire of hasidic *nigunim,* or wordless songs. And in Klezmer Madness! clarinetist David Krakauer expanded the idiom's emotional range by developing an extended clarinet syntax and pushing against the formal constraints of traditional klezmer to develop varied, larger-scale structures for his work. His original compositions and arrangements made dramatic use of electronic effects and took advantage of the band members' creative range, with the wide array of influences and effects available to electric bassist, guitarist, and drummer.[34] In regard to musical language, RJC's closest precursor was the West Coast–based clarinetist Ben Goldberg and the New Klezmer Trio (NKT).[35] Indeed, NKT was the model on which John Zorn had based his first Masada ensemble, the Acoustic Masada quartet. NKT took contemporary composition/improvisation (including influences from rock, electronics, and world idioms) as its basic language, and wove klezmer ideas (melodies, rhythms, and fragments or modifications of both) into that canvas.[36] In a way that recalls Nathanson's description in chapter 1 of the Jazz Passengers' search for a common language, NKT functioned as a kind of collective workshop for developing its own idiosyncratic idiom of multiply inflected Jewish music.

But if some downtown artists drew inspiration from the klezmer renaissance, others saw klezmer as a creative foil. Indeed, a core group of downtown artists—Anthony Coleman, Roy Nathanson, Marc Ribot, and Elliott Sharp—took a strong stance against making klezmer the basis for new, Jewishly identified work. (Coleman and Nathanson did develop work that drew on klezmer, but in an abstracted context.) Whatever klezmer's musical properties, to this cohort the very fact that klezmer was a "revived" genre made it problematic. Klezmer's two-decade lapse from the public eye meant that few of the artists who got involved in the klezmer renaissance or RJC had heard the music before the revival. This generation of musicians, including those with strong Jewish educations and community ties, had grown up during an era in which their grandparents' 78 r.p.m. klezmer discs had been relegated to the attic. It was because they experienced their relationship to klezmer as essentially a nostalgic one, and not one based on direct cultural experience or transmission, that many downtown artists found the genre unsatisfying as the basis for contemporary developments in Jewish expressive culture.[37] Ultimately, then, while downtown artists were divided over klezmer's usability, all the artists on whom I focus in this book sought to write new music that was outside klezmer's purview. Indeed, artists' incisive critiques of the revival were among the most confounding and productive discontents of the RJC moment. Such critiques were confounding because the revival was culturally important and richly creative. But the critiques were also productive because, by insisting on working outside of klezmer, downtown artists developed a distinctive oeuvre of contemporary Jewish music.

As indicated by Lucas's reference to Arnold Schoenberg in naming his commemorative guitar solo "Verklärte Kristallnacht," the tradition of Jewish-themed concert music formed another potential model for artists involved with RJC. Foremost among their close contemporaries, and a colleague in downtown's New Music circles, was Steve Reich, who in 1982 had released a recording of *Tehillim* (Hebrew for Psalms) and who later won a Grammy for his Holocaust-themed piece, *Different Trains* (1988).[38] Composers Alvin Curran and Richard Teitelbaum, both well-known figures on the downtown scene, had also recorded Jewish-themed pieces—including two pieces released the same year as

*Different Trains,* Curran's *Crystal Psalms,* and Teitelbaum's *Golem I*—and Zorn invited both to bring new work to the 1992 Munich festival.[39] But even though there existed a tradition in classical music of thematically Jewish work, the creative model most closely aligned in concept with RJC came from outside a Jewish context. Instead, downtown artists had the most in common with other composer/improvisers who had come together to develop identity- and heritage-driven work.

Notably, the Association for the Advancement of Creative Musicians (AACM), whose participating artists had such a strong creative influence on the scene, was also an organization whose mission was informed by a focus on African American identity and community. By convening around principles of artistic exploration and resisting reified genre categories, while both drawing upon and expanding notions of African American music, the AACM served as the bellwether for related efforts among other groups of artists, including Asian American composer/improvisers who, about a decade before the advent of RJC, had come together to explore the relationship among heritage, identity, and creative affiliation in concerts, discussions, and writing. But whereas the AACM loomed large for artists involved in the latter effort, downtown artists were less likely to position RJC as parallel to the AACM or other organizations formed by African American artists. Indeed, doing so would have amounted to a willful blindness to the social mechanics of race. Artists in the AACM and other groups in the black avant-garde had framed the politics of race as a centrally important point of reference, as had artists on the Asian improv scene. Jewish artists on the downtown scene who were interested in delving into the particularities of Jewish difference were well aware of the destruction and discrimination that had been visited upon Jews in the specious name of racial purity. But although Jewish artists were attentive to the way their own histories and self-concepts did not always line up neatly with whiteness as a U.S. racial category, they also understood that, according to the contemporary American racial calculus, they were white. Because of the privileges that designation accrued, the artists I interviewed were wary of drawing neat parallels between their own issues and those of their African American and Asian American colleagues.[40] Indeed, in some cases they confronted this idea head-on; Ribot, for example, wrote the song

"Clever White Youths with Attitude" for his band Shrek (Yiddish for anger), which he had convened during the RJC moment. In regard to hip hop, another genre that confronted issues of race (and, relatedly, class) in the United States, Ribot noted, "That was *deeply* nationalist music.... So, you know, that started me thinking . . . , 'Well, okay, I'm not saying the Jewish situation is the same, but *where is,* you know, where is, where is *Jewish* anger in all this?' You know? Is it simply because things are so fabulous, that it isn't expressing itself, or is it—repressed?"[41] Thus, although downtown's Jewish composer/improvisers knew they were in some ways following in the footsteps of other artists, they also understood their own efforts as shaped by different cultural and historical forces. If they could not look directly to the AACM and related efforts for models, neither could RJC take shape without attention to the aspects of Jewish difference, and the cultural and historical particularity of the American Jewish experience, that had shaped its artists' outlooks. It was the very process of coming to terms with these issues that gave the RJC moment such force, as artists found themselves delving into the host of personal and social matters that arose as a result of their initial creative turn.

### Getting Jewish Music Wrong, Redux

What, then, was involved in getting Jewish music wrong? Downtown artists generally insisted that, by whatever name, the "radical" Jewish music of their moment should share in the formal and stylistic concerns of their scene as a whole. For the most part, then, the music that fell under this rubric might include boundary-pushing syntax, extremes of tempo and timbre, musical language that fell outside stylistic norms, pluralistic references, a grounding in jazz or rock, or alternatives to formal plans underlain by functional tonal harmony. But as getting Jewish music wrong is a conceptual aim as well as a sonic one, a catalog of stylistic traits cannot fully encompass it. In the context of a performance at a 1995 RJC festival, Ribot faithfully rendered songs from Jewish weddings in pursuit of what I am calling "getting Jewish music wrong." By playing these songs, he asked audiences to consider the Jewish and downtown-ish relevance of the blandly "American" music that served an important social function in the suburban Jewish community in which he had been raised. Knowing that this music would not seem particularly Jewish to his audience, Ribot played it in order to draw attention to the limits of that perception, which in his estimation did not encompass something crucially important about the American Jewish experience as he knew it—that Jewish life-cycle events were often accompanied by un-Jewish music. *Zohar* (1995), which Zorn composed with vocalist Yamantaka Eye, serves as a useful example of a different approach to getting Jewish music wrong. On its surface, unlike Ribot's wedding music, *Zohar* seems to aspire to Jewish and historical authenticity. However, when one attends closely to the recording, it becomes clear that Zorn's aim is to tweak this very notion, in order to illuminate what he presents as a more salient kind of truth.

In its mixture of trenchant wit and grimly uncapturable pastness, its deployment of archival sounds, and its cryptic sonic sensuality, *Zohar* showcased Zorn's flair for absurdist commentary. *Zohar* is a self-deprecatingly fake historical artifact whose avant-garde musical language is buried in, and partially obscured by, its sonic ambience—that is, the way the recording sounds, which is linked to the real or implied physical space in which the recording's sounds exist. Whether recording engineers capture the ambience of an actual physical space or simulate one in the recording studio, ambience is a deliberately constructed aspect of a musical recording, a "mediating force that gives form and character to the sound world of the recording . . . providing the illusion that the recording exists in some unique place, the true world of the disembodied voice."[42] On *Zohar*, ambience seems to have been deployed in order to index the "patina of pastness" that Bohlman describes as being intertwined with contemporary conceptions of Jewish music. But *Zohar* is tricky: close listening reveals that its scratchy ambient noise is, in fact, a tweak on the nostalgic notion of pastness. It functions, instead, as a Wittgensteinian "gesture of pastness." As such it has a rhetorical function, indicating to listeners that what they are about to hear is not simply a representation or a recollection of the past, but a fable about it, with a lesson to impart.[43] The phrases "Long, long ago" or "Once upon a time" fulfill this function in the storytelling realm. *Zohar*'s ambience fulfills it in the musical one.

That ambience is filled with the crackle and hiss of surface noise from an old 78-r.p.m. disc. This noise recalls the old klezmer recordings that revivalists discovered in the 1970s, stacked in dusty attics and forgotten archives, and which were then remastered and released on compact disc. But *Zohar* aims to comment upon this ambience, and not simply to duplicate it. Thus, muffled by the rough throb of a rotating "disc," we hear a minimalistic, minor-mode reed-organ line, which accompanies Eye's unpredictable yowls, groans, and ersatz cantorial moans. Eye's "cantorial" singing is melded here with his extended vocal syntax, and the joke is on anyone who faults it for its inauthenticity. Indeed, Zorn deflects the potential for such criticism by taking on a clownish guise; both he and Eye use assumed names, Rav Tzitzit and Rav Yechida, and he released the recording under the moniker of the Mystic Fugu Orchestra.[44] As one often finds in Zorn's work, the self-deprecating humor on this recording is simultaneously lighthearted, self-serious, and loaded with provocation. On *Zohar*, even as the scratchy ambience is paired with Eye's paralinguistic vocalizations, that ambience takes on a rhetorical function as an intentional but ultimately ironic indicator of pastness. Indeed, if mimicking an old recording were the main point, Zorn would not have ended each track recording cleanly and abruptly, an aural cue that this work is also "about" the mediating quality of the recording process. Sound recording does not simply represent its subjects, but rather allows (or requires) recording engineers to construct sonic artifacts, which they can render more or less naturalistic at their own discretion. The sudden silences between tracks on *Zohar* thus draw attention to the quasi-authenticity of its ambience, and to the intervening role of the recording process in creating it, in a way that gradual volume fades would not.

On the liner notes to the disc, Zorn includes a quotation that clarifies his purposes in creating this recording, whose evident "content" (the evocations of cantorial music and klezmer, shrouded in a fog of historical noise) one has to strain to recover. This passage is ostensibly about the elusiveness of kabbalistic truth, and, appropriately enough, Zorn obscures whatever "truth" the quotation contains, as it appears only in the original German. Because the *Zohar* is the main text of the Kabbalah, Zorn seems to be suggesting a link between the music and the liner notes, but in a deliberately occluded way. Those notes suggest that *Zohar*'s surface noise is in fact an essential part of the piece, and not a distraction from the recording's "real" content. In the quoted passage, Kabbalah scholar Gershom Scholem discusses the process of seeking out the "truth" of that mystical tradition. In Scholem's estimation, scholars of Kabbalah are misguided in "claim[ing] that there is a tradition of truth that can be transmitted." In point of fact, Scholem asserts:

> The truth that is at stake here cannot be transmitted at all. It can be seen, but not transmitted; and exactly what can be transmitted of it, does not comprise it any more. Real tradition remains hidden; only decayed tradition becomes an object and it is only in its dilapidation that its greatness becomes visible.[45]

In the context of *Zohar,* this quotation implies that it is futile to expect historical accuracy ("real tradition") in musical performance to yield artistic truth. A musician who is concerned primarily with historical accuracy—a klezmer revivalist, perhaps—will miss the real meaning of artistic expression. In *Zohar,* Zorn offers instead a piece of "decayed tradition" whose artistic truth lies not in its audible historical quality but in its creative deviation from tradition. In doing so he is not simply taking a swipe at artists who are sticklers for historical accuracy. He is also proclaiming his adherence to another kind of faith—a faith in the creative process, which is inseparable from his own "real tradition," that of the musical avant-garde. Thus, in *Zohar,* Zorn couches musical elements that call attention to themselves as being disruptive of convention and tradition—attenuated syntax, timbral extremes, glossolalia, noise—in a sonic environment that would seem, upon first hearing, to invoke ethnographic or historical authenticity. To locate *Zohar*'s central truth, then, one must look not to its faithful reproduction of old music, but to its creative rendering of artifacts into art.

If *Zohar* is a quintessential example of the creative potential that lies in getting Jewish wrong, it also illuminates the varied tools downtown artists had at their disposal in taking up this project. Although they were invested in the notion that their Jewishly inflected music should reflect both their pluralistic creative outlook and the nature of contemporary Jewish American identity, this aim did not imply a straightforward stylistic mapping of the former onto the latter. It is true that artists were curious about the parallels between the notion of "complex identities" and the mimetic representation of those identities through their music, and in the position statement they wrote for the 1992 Munich festival, Ribot and Zorn did suggest general correspondences between the nature of Jewish diaspora writ large and the "patchwork" nature of downtown music. However, even as artists took an interest in the connections they might draw between patchwork identities and multi-referential music, they also used music to theorize those connections in highly specific ways, drawing on individualized musical syntax and refracting personal memories to write works that they intended to sound like nothing else. Just as *Zohar* engaged the RJC idea without resorting to mimetic representation, the most compelling music of the RJC moment avoided the trap of "glibly [ascribing the fragmentation of language] to a literalization/textualization of diaspora: a scattering, a diffusion, great spaces between units of 'meaning,' partial and discontinuous utterance, difficult linearity or nonlinearity . . . [an] aesthetic in which the formal properties of the work enact a diasporic mapping."[46] Certainly, as artists sought to develop their creative Jewish voices per se, those voices were inflected both by the shared complexities of the modern Jewish condition and by the particular complexities of their generation and cohort. The scene's modus operandi, however, was to make sui generis work. The resulting music married downtown aesthetics to "Jewish music" in ways that were as idiosyncratic as the individuals who were involved in making it.

Few of these artists wanted to claim that they were, in fact, making something called *Jewish music*. The complexities folded into that claim led them to steer clear of it. But that awareness did not prevent them from striving to make music that signified, in personally compelling ways, on the particularities of their Jewish experiences. They hoped their work would resonate with audiences, but they were also motivated to find where this process could lead them creatively. If the new music felt Jewishly usable to them, it might for audiences as well, and it would thence perform a Jewishly important function that other music could not. But artists did not want their music to fit seamlessly into Jewish musical tradition as they understood it; they wanted instead to suggest new perspectives on the notion of Jewish music itself, and they were will-ing, in Coleman's words, to risk incoherence in order to do so. Indeed, on the downtown music scene, the goal was to get *all* music "wrong"—each artist in his or her own way.[47] And although, over the years, individual artists had made occasional forays into applying this principle to Jewish music, it was not until the RJC moment that they took up this project as a community involved in a shared endeavor.

# Breaking a Thick Silence

*A Community Emerges*

IN AUGUST–SEPTEMBER 1992, THE MUNICH ART PROJEKT CAME to the Gasteig, Munich's grand arts center. The Projekt was two weeks of music with a rotating roster of curators; that year, they included John Cale, Ornette Coleman, Philip Glass, Paul Hillier, Gidon Kremer, Arto Lindsay, and John Zorn.[1] True to form, Zorn chose a provocative name for his two evenings at the Art Projekt: the Festival for Radical New Jewish Culture. This two-day festival stands as a watershed moment on the downtown scene. Rather than being simply one more gig in a busy touring schedule, the festival turned out to be transformative for many artists. It made them suddenly aware that they shared a heritage with many more of their peers than they had realized; it made startlingly evident the personal impact of social and historical currents that had caused that heritage to remain hidden in plain view; and it held out the exciting prospect that flowing beneath all this might be an untapped source of great creative potential.

The packed program included many of Zorn's close colleagues from the downtown scene, gathering together representatives from the worlds of composition/improvisation, classical composition, punk rock, and neo-klezmer. Some (including punk rocker Lou Reed, electric harpist Zeena Parkins, and saxophonists Tim Berne and John Lurie) performed music without an evident Jewish identification, but Zorn had invited most artists to participate based on topically Jewish work they had recently composed. West Coast–based clarinetist Ben Goldberg played post-bop, deconstructed klezmer with his New Klezmer Trio. With keyboardist Walter Horn, guitarist Gary Lucas performed an original score to accompany a restored print of the 1920 silent film *The Golem (How He Came into the World)*, a dramatization of the Jewish legend. Guitarist Marc Ribot brought a trio to perform pieces he had developed for his band Rootless Cosmopolitans, including his sarcastic original "Yo! I Killed Your God," whose message was hard to miss, as well as a cover version of a piece he "felt in the context referred to the same thing," Howlin' Wolf's "Commit a Crime" (PURL 2.1).[2]

Drawing on Yiddish theater traditions, pianist Anthony Coleman and saxophonist Roy Nathanson presented a music and comedy duo act they had been honing since 1990. Guitarist Elliott Sharp made a geopolitical allusion through the title of his new thirty-minute piece for string quartet, fretless electric guitar, and clarinet, *Intifada*, which he described as "a series of snapshots, moods, and reflections" on the recent Palestinian uprising.[3] Vocalist Shelley Hirsch and keyboardist David Weinstein performed excerpts from Hirsch's radio play, *O Little Town of East New York*, and composers Richard Teitelbaum and Alvin Curran played in ensembles that performed new topical pieces: Teitelbaum's ". . . 1492 . . . 1942 . . . 1992," written for the occasion, and Curran's "Why Is This Night Different from All Other Nights?" which he had recently developed.[4] There were also non-musical events, including a panel discussion, entitled "Radical Jewish Music Today" and moderated by writer Lynne Tillman. Reflecting Zorn's interest in avant-garde cinema, the festival presented films by Jewish artists, including experimentalist Ken Jacobs and cult-film directors David Cronenberg and Alejandro Jodorowsky.[5]

Although artists could perform hundreds of gigs in a year, a decade later many of the festival participants singled it out as important and remembered it with vividness and emotion. As Hirsch recalled, "That was an amazing event, because it brought together all these people—I never knew [bassist] Mark Dresser was Jewish, I never knew Lou Reed was [Jewish]. . . . And then you said, 'That's incredible! I never thought of that person as being Jewish.'"[6] Today, Hirsch's assertion startles. With revivalist klezmer bands now established in many of the nation's cities, with Jewish references now a familiar part of the landscape of popular media, and with the publication over the past decade of a spate of books focused on the role of Jews in rock, jazz, and popular culture, it comes as no shock to learn that some downtown musician or another is Jewish, or that Velvet Underground founder Lou Reed (the grandson of Russian Jewish immigrants), along with other seminal figures in punk rock— including Joey Ramone (b. Jeffry Hyman), Tommy Ramone (b. Tome Erdelyi), and guitarist Lenny Kaye—were born and raised in Jewish families.[7] But in the early 1990s, Hirsch's sense of surprise about Reed was typical of her downtown colleagues. It reflected the accrued experience of decades in which American entertainers in the public eye had determined that the path to professional success involved deflecting attention away from their Jewish backgrounds. With the notable exception of comedians, most Jewish performers left Jewish matters out of the public sphere.

To be sure, historian Jonathan Sarna has called the 1940s and 1950s a "new era" in Jewish American visibility. Jewish American writers, notably Eastern European immigrants, had begun addressing Jewish themes in novels and essays soon after arriving in the country; by the 1960s, their descendants were engaging squarely with contemporary Jewish life in the United States, creating a body of literature that became central to the heretofore jealously guarded world of Anglo American letters.[8] When Hirsch and her peers were adolescents and young adults, similar cultural changes were brewing in the sphere of popular song—the soundtracks from *Fiddler on the Roof* (1964 and 1971) and *Funny Girl* (1964 and 1968) being two of the more visible examples.[9] But the nostalgic gloss of *Fiddler* and *Funny Girl,* and the populist polish of the musical theater productions from which those films were derived, were exactly what downtown-based artists were fleeing when they left home, literally and figuratively, to immerse themselves in the fray of new American music—jazz, garage rock, soul, funk—and to explore the realms of contemporary concert music and avant-garde theater.[10] By the 1960s, if the dynamic of Jewish quietness—by which I mean not referring to one's Jewishness in contexts that, while not overtly hostile, are nevertheless perceived as unwelcoming—was less prevalent in some contexts than others, it continued to hold true for Jewish jazz and rock musicians. Although novels, musical theater, and films all offered recent examples of media in which Jewish heritage was addressed in a forthright way, jazz and American popular music, particularly the branches downtown musicians were most invested in, lagged far behind. Jewish performers in rock and jazz tended not to address their Jewish backgrounds in interviews or mention Jewish things onstage, nor did they make overtly Jewish musical references. And although the klezmer revival of the 1970s had drawn part of its impetus from young musicians' dawning awareness of this very issue, it is striking that, even in that atmosphere of celebration and pride, the tradition of not being too obtrusively Jewish prevailed: the word "Jew" did not appear on the cover of a revivalist recording until the Klezmatics released *Rhythm and Jews* in 1990, when the revival had been underway for about two decades.[11] On this front, then, jazz and rock had an impact on the downtown scene that was as sociological as it was musical.[12]

The strength of that impact becomes clearer when one considers that this dynamic of quietness prevailed even though the downtown scene took shape in the iconic seat of early twentieth-century Jewish American culture, and in a city whose character and history were strongly influenced by the large Jewish immigration of the early twentieth century—a city in which, according to the subversive logic of comedian Lenny Bruce, even Catholics were Jewish.[13] Certainly, in the 1980s–1990s one could observe old Jewish businesses such as Streit's Matzoh (est. 1925) and Katz's Deli (est. 1888), as well as old synagogues, some closed, one or two still active. Although most of the neighborhood's more recent arrivals paid scant attention to its Jewish immigrant past, some were more attentive to such traces than others. As Sharp recalled, "I felt great to be back on the Lower East Side when I moved here, because seeing the old synagogues, seeing faded writing on the wall—I knew that my father's mother had lived on the Lower East Side when she came from . . . Ukraine . . . in 1905, [but] all that personal history is gone."[14] For Sharp, being surrounded by reminders of the Lower East

Side's once vibrant Jewish community resonated with his family's history. But although that resonance was personal, cultural, and historical, it was not musical, at least not in any overt way. All my interviewees knew the downtown scene had emerged on the historically Jewish Lower East Side, and some recalled having mused on this coincidence over the years, but in the main they did not use this knowledge as fodder for creative exploration. In short, Sharp and his colleagues had moved downtown not because of their attraction to the neighborhood's Jewish history, but because of its experimental music culture, with no evident connection between the two.

Indeed, no matter how important Jewish identity was to artists personally, by their own recollections, their Jewish backgrounds had not seemed particularly relevant to their creative work—at least, not in a way that was transparent or readily communicated. They also assumed that things Jewish, though of personal interest to some musicians, would not have much purchase in downtown's wider social sphere, and would not be of much concern to fans of New York Noise. On this front, it made good sense to attend to such topics in a personal or familial sphere, but not in downtown's wider social one. As a result, Jewish artists were often not visible as such even to each other. Thus, in my interviews, many artists echoed Hirsch's sense of surprise at finding out that one colleague or another, including some of many years' standing, was Jewish. Once the RJC idea seized artists' imaginations in the 1990s, one of the first questions that arose was what connection there might be between the downtown scene and the historically Jewish Lower East Side—and an idea some had been mulling over in private now came into public view.

In regard to the relationship between the neighborhood's Jewish immigrant past and its creative present, one of the more striking documents was the program for an RJC festival held in 1993 at the Knitting Factory. The quaintly rendered pen-and-ink sketch drawing shows a classic turn-of-the-century Lower East Side street scene filled with iconic images: a street packed with vendors; men and women in old-fashioned garb; tenement buildings cluttered with awnings and signs in Hebrew lettering.[15] In contrast to the busy background, in the immediate foreground is an old man sketched in more detail. Glancing outside the

**Figure 2.1.** "The Tradition Continues on the Lower East Side: Radical
New Jewish Culture Festival," program from the Knitting Factory,
New York City (7–11 April 1993). *Image: Burt Levy (1905).*

drawing's frame, he sports a full white beard and soft white sidelocks, small round spectacles, a dark coat, and a wide-brimmed hat: all visual signifiers that the man held to Old World ways rather than capitulating to the secular hurly-burly of the American marketplace that surrounded him. In keeping with this idea is the phrase "The Tradition Continues on the Lower East Side," superimposed on the street scene. But then, directly beneath this man's gaze, is an incongruous second phrase: "Radical Jewish Culture at the Knitting Factory."[16]

At first glance, the cover image and festival title present an odd juxtaposition. It would be easy to see this juxtaposition as glib, and, indeed, such objections were later raised by some of the participating musicians. For one thing, when the drawing was originally published at the turn of the twentieth century, the Lower East Side was impoverished and desperately crowded. Such images were part of a trend to romanticize that neighborhood, from which residents with the money to spare were avidly making their escape, as a haven of *haymish* (Yiddish for homey) lifeways and Old World values. Such a historical gloss was hardly in keeping with the critical acuity many musicians hoped RJC would embody. The cover illustration was also problematic in another way, in that it leapfrogged over the diversity of their current neighborhood to imply that what was most salient to RJC was its link to an idealized Jewish past—a rhetorical move that was precisely what many musicians downtown wanted to avoid. In fact, although in one sense the program cover did a bit of important cultural work in allying RJC with the old Jewish Lower East Side, it was also anomalous in its evident bid for nostalgia. RJC was notable in that through it, artists were beginning to claim a Jewish-identified downtown subculture that counteracted the contemporaneous trend toward "heritage restoration" on the Lower East Side, represented by the Lower East Side Tenement Museum (chartered in 1988) and the project to restore the Eldridge Street Synagogue (incorporated in 1986).[17] Rather than focusing on restoring lost heritage, an idea that aligned more closely with the klezmer revival, the main idea of the RJC moment was to explore the Jewish relevance of their own experimental idiom.[18]

But artists could not embark on this project without grappling with the question of what had caused their long-held quietness around Jewishness in the first place. Why, after all, in downtown's pluralistic milieu, would Jewish artists face any constraints on being as open and expressive about Jewish identity as they wished? Jewish downtown artists had different class and educational backgrounds (in both the Jewish and general sense), and different relationships to Jewish identity in all its senses—religious, national, cultural, secular, and personal. But one thing it would seem they shared in common was the opportunity to attend to each of these dimensions in just the way each would have wished. Indeed, it was just this kind of artistic freedom, coupled with an embrace of individual expression, that had drawn them downtown in the first place, and quietness around Jewish identity, insofar as it was noticed, was generally assumed simply to be one individual choice among many. But as it turned out, this particular choice was more than a result of individual agency; instead, it was partly determined by historical and social forces that came together with unusual strength on the downtown scene. Because that scene ostensibly supported the free expression of difference, those forces could be difficult to discern; artists' views were blocked, in effect, by a false sense of total openness. But as their reflections make clear, their creative milieu, despite its pluralistic values, had some surprising limits in regard to self-expression.

Most of the artists involved in RJC were the grandchildren of European immigrants, third-generation American Jews who had come of age in the 1950s and 1960s, and their stories follow a familiar arc in American Jewish history. Although each artist's family had a different story and a different attitude toward religious practice and education, it is not painting with too broad a brush to say that most of these families had traded wider social acceptance and a greater freedom to self-define for a certain amount of cultural forgetting.[19] Whether it was intentional or not, this process ultimately had an impact on young musicians, who developed the sense that their Jewish backgrounds were irrelevant to their creative interests. In pianist Anthony Coleman's view, this determination stemmed in part simply from a lack of contact with certain aspects of Jewish culture—that is, with what Coleman calls Jewish music's "rootsy side." "Rootsy" is a subjective term, of course, but in this sense it has less to do with the notion of cultural "roots," which Coleman and his cohort stringently critiqued, than it does with the particularities of Yiddish expressive culture that his parents' generation had muffled in order to conform to mainstream (white Protestant) social norms. As he recalled:

> A lot of us, who grew up Jewish in America, we were not in touch with anything rootsy in our culture, because that had been sort of wiped away by the movement after World War II for Jews to become more and more assimilated into the general American culture, and [by] the [number] of Jews that moved out of the cities and into the suburbs. . . . Jews who were interested in becoming musicians [often] became interested in black musics like jazz and blues. The rootsy side of Jewish music became subterranean, became unknown. Became buried. . . . When I was growing up I had glimpses of it, from . . . certain comedians, or certain songs you would hear that were part of the Second Avenue Theater repertoire. . . . [So] it wasn't invisible, but it was buried.[20]

Like Coleman, most downtown artists had little contact with an Old World creative legacy they might have put to use in their music, had they been more familiar with it. A few of them took the very notion of "glimpses" as an important topic to be reckoned with during the RJC moment. As we will see in the chapters that follow, rather than trying to fully recapture what had been glimpsed—or to regain an expressive world that had been lost—Coleman, Hirsch, and Sharon Topper of the band G-d Is My Co-Pilot delved into the question of how to make art whose main substance was those very cultural gaps and historical discontinuities.

Of course, assimilation was not the only cause for the receding presence of Old World expressive culture.[21] Yiddish theater and music, which by the 1920s had already become unfashionable in the European Jewish cosmopole, had been nearly decimated along with Europe's Jewish communities in the disastrous decades that followed. And yet, for downtown artists, knowing about the destruction the Holocaust had wrought was not the same thing as coming to a clear understanding of how it might have affected their creative choices. It was during the RJC moment that many downtown artists fully confronted the legacy of the Holocaust as cause for a quietness around things Jewish in their creative lives— not only because of its destructiveness, but also because of the many kinds of silence that followed in the wake of that trauma. In a statement printed in the concert program to a 1993 RJC festival, French-born vocalist Catherine Jauniaux spoke eloquently to this point:

> When John Zorn asked me to play this festival of 'radical new Jewish music,'
> I was very touched because for the first time I was being recognized for being
> Jewish! Even at home we never talked about our Jewishness because my mother
> had to wear the 'yellow star' and all that it means.... So everything around that
> was strongly and deeply felt...! but not a word was ever said. I think that's why I
> always needed to sing... to break this thick silence.[22]

As her reference to the yellow star implies, Jauniaux was the child of a
Holocaust survivor who had met that disaster with "thick silence." And,
as historians and psychologists have documented, although individuals
have a multitude of different ways of dealing with traumatic memories,
for a sizable cohort of European Jews, silence became the primary means
of coping with the war's trauma, even to the extent of suppressing their
children's awareness of their Jewish heritage.[23] For downtown artists,
part of the work of the RJC moment involved coming to terms with how
this process had affected their own lives, and thus their music, whether
or not it had touched their families directly.

Other downtown artists in Jauniaux's generation, including Americans without family in Europe, attested to having learned, either through
imitation or instruction, to avoid bringing up memories too painful for
their parents to revisit. Even when not directly discussed, past trials and
horrors, or even an awareness of them, could manifest themselves as silence and fear. As these effects were passed down from one generation to
the next, they could be reinforced by new kinds of discrimination. This
process surfaces in a poignant statement by Joey Baron, the percussionist
in Zorn's Acoustic Masada ensemble. In the small Virginia town where
he grew up in the 1950s, he recalled:

> [My parents] were just overrun with antisemitism, and they passed that on to
> me.... I mean, if you're Jewish, you either don't relate to it [i.e., to being Jew-
> ish]—and that's an effect of antisemitism, or you are totally terrified, all the
> time, on a certain level, because you don't know—[laughing, wryly]—you don't
> know when they're comin'!... You don't have to have lived in the Holocaust
> era to have experienced that. Because our parents never had a chance to heal
> from that kind of hurt, and what happens is they try... [to] inflict that same
> fear [of being openly Jewish] in us.... They [did] it for a good reason—it was
> survival. But after the fact.... [it] actually works against you.... I've worked a
> lot, and very hard, to reclaim those [Jewish] memories and experiences.[24]

As Baron's statement indicates, although both he and his parents were
American born, they did not feel safe being seen as Jews, in his parents'

case because of discrimination and cultural isolation, and in his own case because of childhood experiences, as well as lessons he absorbed from his mother and father. As an adult living in New York City, Baron was not subject to the same kind of pressures as his parents had been in their small Virginia town, but coming to terms with this legacy—unlearning the paradoxical lesson that Jewish silence meant Jewish survival—was neither quick nor simple.

In regard to the indirect effect the European genocide had on American Jewish musicians who were nominally insulated from the violence, it is also interesting to note the response by vocalist Sharon Topper to a question I asked her, not about her family history, but about the relationship between her Jewish identity and her music. Topper, who grew up in a large Jewish community on Long Island, answered my question in a roundabout way:

> My family was not at all affected by the Holocaust. And yet, there was a *very* strong [message], "Hide the fact that you're Jewish, so that, if there's another Holocaust, you won't be found." That was really strong in my upbringing! For some reason, it was just like that kind of *Maus* fear . . . [that] was always imparted. I remember being awakened in the middle of the night . . . when I was young. . . . You have to watch, be wakened up in the middle of the night, and taken downstairs in your pajamas, and watch this horrible, horrible footage [about the concentration camps]. . . . That's *all* I was ever told . . . [*mumbling*] *wawawa* being Jewish, and [*speaking up loudly*] how important it is to hide. So this identity stuff was hugely exciting to me. It really was. It was like, "Oh my god, we can be *proud* of being Jewish! We can get on stage, and go, this is who we are!" We were at the forefront of the indie rock scene of the world, and it felt like everybody was watching us. So I guess I answered your question about how it affected my music.[25]

Topper's statement is a testimony to the long reach of genocide. Living in perhaps the safest Jewish community in world history, her parents nevertheless found it imperative to teach their children to be careful about disclosing their Jewish heritage, and Topper recalled the fear of discovery, though irrational, as ever-present. Her experience is one step removed from what scholars describe as "post-memories" of the Holocaust—that is, the memories of the Holocaust that survivors pass down to their children—which "are [part of] the cultural memory and individual consciousness [that] we sometimes refer to as American Jewish identity."[26] Like Baron, Topper's Jewish identity was shaped not by this kind of Holocaust post-memory but by a kind of post-post-memory—the cultural memory of antisemitic violence that her parents, who were not Holocaust survivors themselves, instilled in her for her own safety. Like Baron, she experienced an overwhelming sense of relief at breaking through this silence during the RJC moment.

Although some musicians had parents who imparted the lesson to keep a low profile as Jews, most could not point to a clear reason for their own personal quietness around things Jewish on the downtown scene. But the historical circumstances in which Jauniaux, Baron, and Topper's statements are embedded attest to the notion that to stay quiet about Jewishness did not simply amount to an individual's decision to keep his or her private life out of the public eye. It was instead a choice implicated by a deeper history and a more complicated set of issues. These musicians' statements speak to a complex inheritance of Jewish quietness that generations of American Jews have grappled with in their own fashion, and that downtown's artists set about untangling on their own terms during the RJC moment.

Because of the nature of the downtown scene, some issues loomed large. For example, just as rock music was an important influence on the scene, so were rock's social dynamics. In its early years rock had served as a venue for performers at the social and commercial margins, but rock hardly welcomed all comers. In addition to having offered white musicians a platform that historically was not afforded to their African American colleagues for performing African American music and derivations thereof, rock often trafficked in a machismo that was unfriendly to women, heterosexist, and virtually off-limits to Jews. Scholarship on Jewish masculinity has historicized and explicated the gendered stereotypes of diaspora Jews; such stereotypes, which were common in U.S. popular media in the mid-twentieth century, would have made it difficult for Jewish qua Jewish men to embody any aspect of rock masculinity, be it toughness, hipness, self-destructive excess, or even androgyny. This dynamic was not simple or straightforward to articulate, but those artists who discerned it saw it as a crucial factor in the general quality of Jewish quietness on the downtown scene.[27] For these musicians, it became crucial to think about the relationship between their own Jewishness—as well as public conceptions or stereotypes of Jewishness—and rock's gender norms. As I discuss in chapter 4, Topper took on this issue through writings, song lyrics, and self-presentation in the band G-d Is My Co-Pilot. Ribot grappled with related questions in his unpublished essays, drawing on his own perception of having tried to make a career as a musician in the 1960s and 1970s, and addressing the regulating impact exerted by masculinity dictums, as well as perceptions of hipness, on Jewish rock musicians of his generation.

Whence the quietness around Jewishness on the downtown scene? Ribot located it partly in the social norms surrounding the popular music he and his peers had grown up with. He emphasized that for all of downtown's experimentalism, many composer/improvisers had grown up with ambitions for more mainstream success, or at least steady work, in popular music. And as adolescents who grew up on rock music, they would have been keenly attuned to the politics of style in rock, a politics that admitted virtually no tinge of Jewishness, and no trace of the Yiddish expressive culture that still, albeit in diminished form, permeated many Jewish American communities:

> You learn certain names (Dylan, Shaw, Snow, Ian, King, Mann, Ryder) signify sexy and others (Zimmerman, Arshawsky, Laub, Fink, Klein, Mann, Horowitz) don't. You learn certain noses, accents, and gestures are "sexy," others are "funny," and still others are "exotic." Every casting agent, promoter, and A & R person and every musician or performer who would be employed by them feels this palpably: there is a theological slant to secular American culture . . . and to whatever extent you aspire to enter pop markets, you had better get with the program.

In addition to arguing for its practical implications in musicians' careers, Ribot contended that the exclusion of Jews qua Jews from the sphere of rock music and U.S. popular culture had a profound and far-reaching psychological impact on musicians and audiences. Such exclusion, he contended, "recreates its boundaries within the psyche, limiting imagination, dividing the self, segregating 'Jewish' parts from 'hip' parts [and separating] funny from sexy. . . . For a culture to reproduce, it must have 'sexy.'" Like Baron and Topper, then, Ribot pointed to Jewish quietness as an emotional process that had come to feel natural because it was internalized, and one that would thus take some hard work to excavate and rethink. Ribot also took issue with those who argued that attempts to limit Jews' involvement in American social and civic life were part of a bygone era. There was no doubt that Jews had made great strides since the era of widespread social and legal discrimination, but in his view, narratives that focused largely on such gains were not fully relevant to rock musicians of his generation. Such narratives, which addressed social acceptance and legal gains, were tone-deaf to the internalized effects on adolescents of the Jewish "defeat on the pop culture battleground":

> The apprehension behind the name changes, self-censored behavior, and silence [among Jewish performers] . . . gives the lie to the triumphalist rhetoric . . . that anti-semitism, while still existent, is no longer a powerful force in American life. . . . In this view, fears about public [assertions of] Jewish identity are an unnecessary vestigial hangover from the days of legal discrimination. Yet there are things every sixteen-year-old putting together a rock band feels palpably. . . . For all the access to jobs secured by civil rights gains, these apprehensions and insights about what it takes to 'get over' indicate . . . a defeat on the pop culture battleground, where America determines the content and limits of its core identity by defining through iconic image and sound what is hip, what is sexy, what is normal, what is self and what is other.[28]

In outlining the relationship between "sexy," "hip," and "Jewish" in the pop culture lexicon, Ribot's comments help to explicate the surprise felt by many musicians upon encountering not only their close colleagues but also Lou Reed at the 1992 Munich Radical Jewish Culture festival. Through his work with the Velvet Underground and a solo career that followed, Reed had become an iconic figure, if not *the* iconic figure, of the rock underground of the 1960s and the punk era that followed. Reed's transgressive sexuality and song lyrics put him far outside rock's masculine status quo, and yet, even as he took on a public posture of deviant masculinity, there was little room for including Jewishness in his public image.[29] Given the prevailing depictions of diasporic Jewish masculinity in the popular sphere—and allowing for the exaggerations and simplifications inherent to popular culture's depictions of difference—Jewish qua Jewish men had as little place in punk rock as they did in the rock mainstream.[30] Whether or not Reed, given the choice, would have wanted to emphasize his Jewish background, that choice was not readily available to him. And whether or not this dynamic was endemic to rock or might be amenable to change, as Ribot had pointed out, it was readily observed by young Jewish musicians, and as such, in his estimation, it had affected the music scene they helped to create on the Lower East Side in the 1980s.

Artists also considered the ways in which American racial politics might have played a part in the quietness around Jewish identity that they had witnessed or experienced as young musicians.[31] Because race was a topic of crucial importance in jazz in the 1960s and 1970s, the prevailing discourse around race in jazz had a strong impact on how downtown's future musicians dealt with their Jewish identities as performers. As ethnomusicologist Ingrid Monson has asserted, in those years "everyone in the world of jazz had to cope with the politics of race in one form or another."[32] Moreover, with jazz's popularity on the wane after the 1950s, its creative giants faced with personal and institutional racism, and its artistry undervalued, jazz musicians, Jewish or not, had pressing battles to fight. The urgency of these battles, coupled with the inherited social convention to refrain from too much public Jewishness, seems to have led to a near-monolithic silence around Jewish identity that Baron perceived during his years playing in soul and jazz bands in the 1950s and 1960s:

> Most of us keep it invisible. Jazz musicians in particular. That era, the fifties— [you would] *never* identify as being Jewish! You know, we love the music, and we try to fit in. Used to. Now, times have changed. I think there's a lot more awareness.... Just [the] past twenty or so years, I feel like I can really be myself, and I'm figuring out how to put that out there. But [in the 1950s–60s] I don't think that was much of an [option] for jazz musicians who were Jewish.[33]

In fact, Baron is overstating here—it is not the case that jazz musicians (or critics) in the 1950s never publicly identified themselves as Jewish. But the emotional truth of his statement allies with the general truth that jazz musicians, like other performers, rarely commented on their Jewish backgrounds, or on issues of wider Jewish cultural relevance, in interviews, and seldom sought ways to bring the Jewish music they knew into jazz's creative purview.[34] Thus, in the 1960s, while African American musicians began incorporating more influences from North and West Africa and the Middle East into their work, few Jewish musicians made similar forays into Ashkenazic, Sephardic, or Middle Eastern traditions. In a parallel to the way gender norms affected Jews in rock, this difference can be partly attributed to the place of Jews in the American racial calculus.

Even as the struggles around race and racism in the United States intensified in the 1960s, those struggles, and the terrain on which they were engaged, also affected the American musical landscape. As musicologist Benjamin Piekut has argued, that terrain, though complicated, can be framed as having been divided between two opposing camps: "The heated debates over race and culture in the jazz world of the early and mid-1960s were in essence a struggle between the discourse of *color blindness* held by most white musicians . . . and the paradigm of *race cognizance* increasingly deployed by African American musicians."[35] If color blindness ostensibly embraced an egalitarian outlook by ignoring race altogether, race cognizance challenged the basis for and validity of that stance, attending instead to the structural and institutional basis for social inequity and locating it in a legacy of racial discrimination. Moreover, as Monson argues, "From the early 1950s to the mid-1960s a general shift took place from a colorblind ideology on race within the jazz community to the assertion of a black-identified consciousness on the part of many African American musicians and their supporters."[36] This attention to race, which was crucial for jazz musicians' struggles for cultural recognition, involved for the most part a black-white binary concept, in which the majority of Jews in the United States were understood as white—as, indeed, most Jews in the United States were by that time. Race cognizance was important to the writers who reshaped American music historiography and criticism by insisting on the central importance to jazz not only of African American musicians, but also of African American heritage and expressive culture, and by critiquing white America's misunderstanding and misappropriation of black music.[37] Such issues were also of central concern to many artists involved in 1960s avant-garde jazz, or the "New Thing," and an attention to race cognizance played an important part in the era's key creative collectives, including the St. Louis–based Black Arts Group (BAG), the New York–based Jazz Composers Guild, and the Association for the Advancement of Creative Musicians (AACM).[38] African American musicians, of course, had many differences of opinion in regard to racial politics, but in much of the discourse that prevailed on the jazz scene, as in the United States at large, racial terms were drawn in black and white, and religious or cultural differences among white musicians were beside the point.

In the 1960s, American Jews, who did face blatant discrimination in some contexts, nevertheless did not have the same legal and social battles to fight in the United States as did African Americans. This was why, downtown musicians explained, whatever their personal experiences with antisemitism, they felt those problems to be less pressing than the endemic racism and institutionalized discrimination their black colleagues were contending with. Thus, as clarinetist Marty Ehrlich recalled, even though Jewish identity was centrally important to him, and even though he was well aware of the historical and geopolitical factors that complicated simple depictions of Jews as "white," he tended not to confront antisemitism when he encountered it as a player, nor to speak up as a Jew in general, viewing such concerns as complicating factors in the fight for rights and recognition faced by his African American colleagues:

> I came from a strong Jewish background. And came from some strong family expectations, about . . . the importance of keeping the tribe going. And that was complicated for me, especially as I entered more and more into the jazz world, and in particular began performing in some pretty politicized jazz situations— politicized by race. . . . There was a question of not just how do I fit in there as a white player [but] . . . the whole question of Jewish identity. And at times, there were some definite moments of dealing with antisemitism.[39]

Ehrlich's mention of antisemitism recalls Baron's stark recollection of the discrimination faced by his family in rural West Virginia. Although many of my interviewees recalled enduring antisemitic taunting or bullying as children, most did not discuss experiences that were as intense as Baron's. Along these lines, Ehrlich continued,

> I mean, there's all kinds of levels [of antisemitism]. My parents have their stories of various WASP exchanges [laughs] here and there. Neighbors who didn't like them. . . . A couple times, these Catholic kids would try to beat us up, walking home from school. . . . [But] in America, I did not experience anything approaching a sort of general experience of racism that almost every black friend I have, has had. And it's my sense that very few Jews of my generation have.[40]

Similarly for the other musicians I spoke with, although their childhood encounters with antisemitism might have been frightening, and although they lived with an understanding that they were not far removed from a time and place in which Jews' "whiteness" had not saved them from mass murder, they did not ultimately see their personal encounters with discrimination as comparable to the racism encountered by black musicians.

Just as many downtown musicians got interested in jazz's New Thing, then, the act of music making became racially politicized—in ways they supported, for the most part. But because race had historically played a complicated role in regard to Jewish self-definition, jazz's racial politics intersected in confusing ways with Jewish identity.[41] There were thus some internal struggles involved in the decision to defer discussions of Jewishness vis-à-vis whiteness to another time and place. By the 1960s Jews in the United States were no longer identified as non-white, but in that era "whiteness" tended to signify an American mainstream that was either non-Jewish by default or in which Jewish difference was politely overlooked; as Nathanson recalled, "Judaism in America, you know, it's white people. . . . And when I was growing up that wasn't clear."[42] Working as a jazz musician thus presented Jewish players with an updated version of the old social compact among performers to stay quiet about Jewish identity. For this reason, Ehrlich explained, given his strong Jewish upbringing, "for me, it wasn't easy to get involved in a music I was very drawn to, where a philosophy of cultural nationalism was very strong." But whatever his own self-concept, he understood that his whiteness, and thus his perceived alliance with (and benefit from) a racist social system that devalued jazz as an art form, would usually be taken as an essential defining quality that trumped any differences "white ethnics" perceived amongst themselves. Under these circumstances, he asserted, how could he expect his black colleagues to fully accept him, to say, "Look, 'not only is it no problem [you] being white and playing this music'. . . [and these musicians] are *highly* conscious that their music is meant to be in contrast to mainstream white American culture"—while also expecting them to be "concerned about how I felt about it as being Jewish, as well?" At the time, he accepted that this was not a reasonable expectation: "I didn't *ever* raise that as much of an issue. Until much more recently. But as a teenager, and into my twenties, I didn't. . . . It was the sixties. 'Either you're part of the solution, or you're part of the problem.' And I was trying very hard to be part of the solution. So . . . there were times when it was pretty hard."[43]

Jewish composer/improvisers were thus confronted on multiple fronts with the idea that Jewishness, or a perception thereof, was either irrelevant, antithetical, or disruptive to the social ecology of rock and jazz. It was just such a perception that led Baron to an epiphany regarding Acoustic Masada:

> I realized, "Wait a second! . . . We're being *seen*, as Jews! This is pretty fantastic!" And [that ensemble] is probably the most full-out picture someone could get of me, playing that instrument. I can bring what I love about music—black music, country music, you know—*music*. From all cultures. I can bring everything I've ever assimilated into this situation. . . . So, yeah, it was really quite an awakening for me, to actually have a context to play my ass off, and have it be, like, "Yeah! I'm Jewish!" You know, "I'm human!" It's not better than not being Jewish, it's just, you know, it's part of the picture.[44]

## The RJC Manifesto

If quietness around Jewish identity was so normative it was difficult to discern on the downtown scene, the Festival for Radical New Jewish Culture at the Munich Art Projekt had a dramatically defamiliarizing effect in this regard—as indeed it was intended to do. In a departure from other events he had curated, at the festival Zorn distributed a long statement of purpose, which was printed (in German translation) in the program, and which he also included in the program of the first RJC festival in New York City a few weeks later. As another well-known and outspoken figure on the scene and one who had been emphatic in arguing for the role he wanted RJC to play, Ribot was an obvious choice as a collaborator; Zorn had asked him to draft the original statement, which went through a few rounds of editing between the two authors before being published. This document is now often referred to as the RJC manifesto.[45] If some of its claims are more pugnacious than persuasive, it is worth recalling that the statement was first circulated at a well-appointed, government-funded arts center in Munich, the birthplace of the Nazi Party. The authors took a dark amusement in pointing up their awareness of those circumstances to their liberal-minded German audiences. As Ribot wrote about Zorn's *Kristallnacht*:

> This piece, one of the less conceptual reversals of history at the festival, definitely pushed the envelope on confrontational art. The view from the band

> as Zorn conducted the piece with his back to the audience was unforgettable: Zorn, an avowed sado-masochist, slowly pushing the lever on the [wave form] oscillator past the bearable point, his gleeful expression concealed from the serious gazes of traumatized captive German intellectuals. The Fuhrer warned something like this might happen.

As this passage suggests, although the manifesto took on substantial issues in a serious way, academic detachment was hardly the coin of the realm on the downtown scene, which was fueled by creative intensity, and some of whose artists, including Ribot and Zorn, thrived on the theater of provocation. At the same time, as Ribot recalled, he had been struck in the lead-up to the festival with the "absurdity of the idea that . . . Jewish musicians in New York [living] in the oldest continuous urban Jewish culture [the Lower East Side] could not see the work that they do as relating to Judaism," adding that he had "wanted to break that [perception, and] the way of breaking it was to simply frame the work that we were doing—to present it in a Jewish frame."[46] In framing the festival's statement as such he aimed to disrupt what he felt was an intangible but frustratingly real conceptual barrier, one that prevented artists from thinking about their music as Jewishly relevant. Ultimately, then, although the authors sketched out the downtown scene's historical and cultural context and took pains not to misrepresent their own views as shared by all the participating musicians, Ribot and Zorn's statement served a polemical purpose.

The word "manifesto" applies particularly well to the statement's opening segment, in which the authors contend that in the United States, Jewish musicians, unlike producers and managers, had been rendered "invisible." This was not a specious claim, and at the time, before the publication of what is now a large literature on Jews and popular culture, it had the ring of an allegation that was strongly felt, if not yet fully thought through. After staking out this position, the authors ambitiously outlined the festival's aims, by means of presenting a series of questions about the role of Jewish heritage on the downtown music scene. They used the manifesto to expand on what they called "Jewish paradigms," which included collective memory, Jewish law, exegetical traditions, and group prayer. In suggesting how these paradigms might have influenced the scene in ways artists had not considered before, Ribot and Zorn were

on untested, often shaky ground. Indeed, one of the manifesto's problematic assumptions was that Jewish artists, even those who were quite
disaffiliated, would have had enough contact with Jewish culture, practices, and texts to have deeply internalized their effects. Thus, although
the authors claimed they were not implying something as hazy or treach-
erous as racial memory, there was nevertheless a fair share of mystical
thinking at work in their speculations about the role of Jewish historical
memory and cultural transmission.

The authors, then, made their main contention clear from the start,
opening with an assertion about Jewish invisibility in the realm of "American New Music." This music, they contended,

> has always been noted for its diversity [i.e., the cultural diversity of its partici-
> pants]. It is not the property or creation of any single cultural group. But it is
> safe to say that the participation of American Jews has been particularly strong.
> . . . It is also safe to say that while this music has been labeled and analyzed by
> geography (downtown, east coast, west coast); genre (jazz, no-wave, hardcore,
> avant-garde); politics, race, class and gender; and while Jewish participation
> in music related business roles has been well noted (and often caricatured and
> exaggerated by anti-semites), the phenomenon of intense involvement of Jewish
> musicians has remained strangely invisible.

The phrase "American New Music" can be a bit misleading here, as it
seems to suggest contemporary classical music, which was then called
New Music. However, Ribot and Zorn used this phrase to denote the
downtown scene and its affiliated jazz/rock/noise avant-gardes. The
distinction is an important one. Among their peers in classical music
were composers who had, in fact, written Jewishly identified work in
the years preceding RJC, some to substantial acclaim, and who could
hardly be called invisible. At the same time, although their claim about
invisibility seems exaggerated, Ribot and Zorn were extrapolating from
their own circles in the downtown scene, in which this claim had more
credence. The authors were pointing out the (in)visibility of Jewish qua
Jewish composer/improvisers as performers per se who operated in a
more public milieu than did their peers in the world of classical music
composition. Even though some contemporary classical composers led
and performed in their own ensembles, they worked primarily as composers and not as gigging composer/improvisers enmeshed—socially,

discursively, and creatively—with jazz, rock, and the performance conventions of those genres.

Emphasizing that working as composer/improvisers meant performing in the public eye, then, Ribot and Zorn contended that "the
perception of most Jews working in performing arts [is] that publicly
identifying as Jews will leave them vulnerable to eviction from the American cultural mainstream or highly restricted in the roles they can play."
Their comment about "roles" points up their emphasis on being performing musicians. The implication was that Jewish musicians, like actors,
take on performative personae, which historically have been restricted
in parallel to those of actors but in less obvious ways. In addition to
claiming that perceptions and professional expectations made it difficult
for Jewish composer/improvisers to identify openly as such, Ribot and
Zorn suggested that Jewishness was pointedly ignored (presumably by
critics and audiences) even as other aspects of the music were closely
scrutinized. As implied by the phrase "strangely invisible," despite the
presence of plenty of Jewish artists in their music circles, there was, they
asserted, an elusive but confounding quietness around things Jewish—a
quietness it was time to confront. As we have seen, this determination
was shared by many of their peers.

Having opened their statement with a claim that the downtown
scene was in part a Jewish scene, and should recognize itself as such,
Ribot and Zorn continued by asking if there was a cultural or historical
explanation for why Jews would be drawn to musical avant-gardes and
undergrounds. Might there be, the authors wondered, "shared Jewish
musical or cultural values which the musicians hold in common?" If such
values did draw Jews to the music, these values might also have a bearing
on their own creative work. But how? "Have these artists (many of whom
remain entirely secular or removed from direct contact with Judaism)
somehow reproduced Jewish paradigms in their work?" Music that was
not overtly Jewishly identified might have been shaped, for example, by
an exposure to sounds, practices, or approaches to language that were
culturally Jewish. Ultimately, the authors hoped the festival would "provide a long missing context in which the work of these artists can be
fully heard."

One question they asked was whether Jewish collective memory was linked to the creative choices for which the downtown scene was known, and in particular the qualities of montage, stylistic diversity, and quick stylistic shifts. They were implying an internalized sense among present-day Jews of the Jewish history of enforced movement, as political decrees and upheavals over the course of many centuries had led Jews in Europe and elsewhere to move from one place to the next, with nowhere to fully call their own. Ribot and Zorn wondered whether this history—or, in their view, this collective memory—had manifested itself in the frenetic jump cuts among styles that typified the musical textures (and performance practices) of the 1980s downtown scene. Thus, they took a conceptual leap and asked, "Is the [Jewish] historical memory of statelessness related to the patchwork music that came out of New York in the 1980s?" This question, with its psychoanalytic underpinnings, is probably unanswerable. But again, although Ribot and Zorn's questions might seem musicological, there was little basis on which they could be closely examined. The questions were instead fodder for rumination, for provocation, and for the creative process. In a similar vein, they asked if there was a link between rule-based compositional methods and rule-based Jewish legal and philosophical systems, even among artists who had not spent much time studying Jewish texts: "Do the 'rules' in game pieces like [John Zorn's] *Cobra* (or for that matter, in [composer Arnold] Schoenberg's 12-tone system) reflect a Talmudic desire to codify?"[47] And, asking a revealing question that pointed up a lack of Jewish historical consciousness among many Jewish artists on the downtown scene, they suggested that Jewish colleagues who were drawn to Eastern European or Middle Eastern music might have been unwittingly influenced by the Jewish historical resonance of those places. The basis for this particular query is striking. Unlike other times and places in which Jewish artists have deliberately turned to such idioms in order to explore Jewish themes, on the downtown scene, the authors implied, artists were operating out of instinct, not intention. Thus, although artists might believe they were simply taking an interest in, say, Balkan or Moroccan music, they might actually have been drawn to the music because of its Jewish resonances, which they had never stopped to consider.

Ribot and Zorn suggested that, in general, a Jewish artist's ostensible interest in Eastern European music might actually stem from a less conscious desire to reconnect with a missing piece of Jewish history. Anthony Coleman had begun thinking more intensively about his relationship to Europe as a Jew after he began touring in Eastern Europe in the early 1980s, subsequently settling in what was then Yugoslavia; the authors asked, "Is . . . Coleman's longtime fascination with the music of Eastern Europe part of a search for continuity with a destroyed past?" They also addressed the possible influence on the downtown scene work of Jewish communal prayer and cantorial singing. They knew Nathanson had long been convinced that his saxophone playing had been influenced by the congregational prayers and cantorial singing he had heard as a child in the synagogue, and so they asked, "Does the loose, motivic group improvising in . . . Nathanson's work derive in part from Orthodox prayer traditions (in which members of the group may read the same text at different speeds)?"

In one of their more convoluted rhetorical moves, the authors conjectured that a familiarity with archetypal Jewish stories from the Hebrew Bible and related texts might have led Jewish artists to express their dissatisfaction with mainstream music and mores through punk and hardcore rock. In a series of logical leaps, they suggested, first, that such stories might have given contemporary Jews a precedent for developing a structural view of present-day events. (The underlying logic seems to have been roughly analogous to a Marxist model of base and superstructure, in which the course of human events can be understood only if one recognizes the underlying forces that determine it.) Next, this point of view, combined with the Jewish tradition of interrogating texts for new meanings, might give artists the means to challenge social structures that others might not discern. In other words, Jewish tradition involved delving into familiar stories—Abraham's binding of Isaac, for example—in order to consider how and why they were structured in a particular way; the authors implied that a familiarity with this way of thinking might lead Jews to discern, and then challenge, the deeper structures and processes that undergirded ordinary life. They also suggested that these processes could have played into the attitude of artists who took on rock's rebellious attitude toward establishment values. Thus, they asked, "Has the Jewish genius for the construction of archetypal stories been useful in the angry deconstructing [by] punk, hardcore and their rock predecessors?" Building on the theme that punk rockers' anger toward political passivity and social complacency might be a manifestation of inherited Jewish anger, they concluded, "For those whose work contains the signifiers or influences of punk and hardcore [rock], does their rage at yuppie complacency connect with prophetic Jewish rage at a history of exile and aggression?" This was strong stuff, and it was meant to be. Although the authors' interest in exploring these issues was sincere—as is evident from Ribot's writings in the years after the festival—they also wanted their statement to spur an impassioned response. The manifesto was a polemical position paper in which a scrupulous attention to logic was not the main point. The questions it raised might be unanswerable, but the authors were content with letting them remain that way. The manifesto was intended not as a call for systematic research, but as a prod to action.

## Why Munich?

Munich was a potent locus for the first Festival for Radical New Jewish Culture, and the festival's location was one reason Ribot and Zorn imbued their statement with such urgency. In addition to its historic role as a seat of power in Nazi Germany, Munich, and Germany in general, were also home to some of the downtown scene's most loyal audiences, and the irony of the situation was not lost on the festival's protagonists. In post–World War II Western Europe, government support of the arts had proved invaluable to American experimentalists, and it remained so for avant-garde jazz musicians in the 1960s–1970s, after the onset of the rock era severely curtailed professional opportunities in jazz. In the 1980s, European audiences, who had robustly supported jazz in the postwar era, also embraced the innovative music emerging from the Lower East Side. Interest in New York Noise was particularly strong in Germany, where both residents and visiting performers benefited from state-sponsored subsidies of the arts. Avant-garde jazz and improvisational music had far less institutional support and a smaller following in the United States, and the resultant difference in creative and professional opportunity led composer/improvisers to perform and tour regularly in Europe, as they continue to do today.⁴⁸ As Sharp explained:

> There was a lot of money for culture in Germany. And New York was always in favor in Europe.... During the seventies, the loft scene, the black free jazz scene, and what evolved from it, was very very celebrated in Europe.... [Downtown musicians] were operating in relative obscurity in New York, but we would then go and play for huge audiences in Europe. And especially when the Communist menace was there. Germany, to show that there was an alternative, pumped a huge amount of money into their alternative culture scene.... And we were the beneficiaries of it. This was our audience.⁴⁹

But if European audiences were a mainstay for downtown musicians, although that support was welcome, it inevitably raised the specter of the decimation that had preceded it. Tours to Europe brought musicians into regular contact with the traces—and the absence of traces—of the devastation of European Jewry, Roma, and other Nazi victims. Just as klezmer musicians touring Europe were forced to grapple with what ethnomusicologist Mark Slobin has termed the "cultural hieroglyph of klezmer," with the advent of RJC artists were led head-on into a maze of issues that were simultaneously unavoidable and, for the scale of their horror, impossible to assimilate.⁵⁰

Germany's destructive past, its contemporaneous support for experimental music and musicians, and the quietness of Jews qua Jews on the downtown scene provided a complicated backdrop for the Munich festival and manifesto. On one hand, many of the Jewish musicians I spoke with told stories about making non-Jewish German friends and enjoying the German arts scene. On the other hand, they encountered frequent reminders of Nazism and the Holocaust. Coleman, for example, recounts as surreal the experience of traveling to Europe for the first time. Ethnomusicologist Hankus Netsky, then a fellow performance student at the New England Conservatory (and founder of NEC's Klezmer Conservatory Band), "made me a tape that one side was old klezmer and the other side was new klezmer? . . . I took it with me . . . the first time I went to Eastern Europe by myself, the '81 trip. . . . And so there I was [*gently self-mocking sing-song*]: *A Jew, riding the trains, listening to klezmer.*" Continuing in this vein of morbid humor, he added, "I mean, you know, the first time you go to Europe as a Jew and ride the trains, you gotta

riff out. . . . 'This one goes to Auschwitz! Next stop!' You know?"[51] Like
Coleman, other downtown artists testified to having felt a confounding
mix of good fortune, anguished awareness, and psychic displacement as
they built careers touring in European cities. A few were only a generation removed from genocide, and being forthright about Jewish identity
while in Europe was a way to mitigate their ambivalence about being
there at all. For example, Lucas recalled, "When I first started playing in
Germany years ago, I had severe doubts about my endeavor. I remember
my Grandpa describing how he refused to set foot on German soil after
the war, refusing to leave his cruise ship when it docked in Hamburg on
the Grand Tour. 'They didn't bomb enough here . . . they didn't bomb
enough.' I reject this attitude." Lucas's close relatives had perished in the
Holocaust, some during the massacre of Jewish villagers in 1941 by their
neighbors in Jedwabne, Poland. His parents had made only veiled allusions to this event, but after it became the subject of a widely discussed
monograph, the family history came to light. Lucas wrote about attending a memorial ceremony sponsored by the Polish government on the
sixtieth anniversary of the massacre:

> We place stones on the memorial, and blue *yahrzeit* [memorial] candles. . . .
> Cantor Joseph Malovany from the Fifth Avenue Synagogue sings a prayer to
> conclude the ceremony as the wind whistles in our ears. His voice reaches to
> the heavens and echoes in the surrounding fields. It actually cracks as he sobs
> with grief. Now we move into the graveyard. I wait for the prayer service to
> conclude. And then I take up my guitar and play . . . at first tentatively . . . "Ha-
> Tikvah.". . . The church bell rings, it's three o'clock. The time sixty years ago
> when the burning of the Jews of Jedwabne began. No bells were heard ringing
> in the local church that day.[52]

Even for musicians farther removed than Lucas from the genocide, an
awareness of the Holocaust could not fail to affect their perceptions
of Europe during their tours and travels. As Hirsch recalled of her
childhood:

> Nobody ever talked about the Holocaust. No one ever talked about their roots!
> To this day, I asked my family where they're from, and they had no answers:
> "We're American." But these people in the [neighborhood] grocery store were
> from Germany, and I remember how they handed me [a loaf of] bread one time,
> and I saw the numbers [concentration camp tattoos] on their arm. And it wasn't
> 'til I went to Germany that I really started to feel the weight of this Jewishness,
> and I [understood] it in a very different way.[53]

Touring in Europe had a strong impact on Hirsch in regard to her creative work, and one result was a new attention to Jewish heritage, which she addressed in 1980 with her brief piece "I Am a Jew," in *O Little Town of East New York,* and more recently in other work, including "Hitchhiking/Heinz" and *Tohu Wa Bohu.*[54]

Finally, in addition to its personal and creative effects, some artists saw the festival as a statement in defiance of the neo-fascist and neo-Nazi groups in Europe that had reemerged during the late 1980s and early 1990s. As Ribot and Zorn wrote, some artists chose to participate in the Munich festival "out of a positive desire to identify, others as an act of political will during a period of renewed anti-semitism in the U.S. and Europe." The targets of neo-Nazi violence and ill will included people of color, foreigners, and Jews, and musicians sometimes encountered such jingoism firsthand when they were on tour. In describing the genesis of the festival in an essay he wrote in 1996, Ribot foregrounded this political context:

> We didn't only read about the re-emergence of fascist groups in the news. Starting in the mid/late '80s, you could see the skinheads hanging out at train stations [in Europe]. I usually toured during this period with bands that were at least partly Black (the Lounge Lizards, Jazz Passengers, Rootless Cosmopolitans), and . . . we could feel ourselves being checked out, especially in Bavaria or Austria, where you could buy the collected works of the Führer at station newsstands for relaxation on those long Alpine train rides. Sometimes the graffiti was intense. . . . In any event, after the re-emergence of openly fascist groups in Europe and the U.S. (with their supporters in the skinhead neo-nazi hardcore [music] movement), silence about Jewish identity began to feel like collaboration, especially for those of us . . . who used elements of hardcore in our own music.[55]

Before the festival, Ribot had argued vehemently that rather than simply claiming downtown music as radically Jewish, RJC should create an impetus for discussion and principled action. As his comments above attest, he was spurred in part by the rise of neo-Nazism in Europe, which was also linked to a disturbing trend throughout hardcore rock, both in Europe and the United States.[56] Because hardcore rock had a high profile on the downtown scene, the festival was an opportunity to rebut that trend. In a similar vein, a few years before the festival, in the cooperative heavy-metal trio Slan—"the first all-Jewish heavy metal band"—Zorn, Sharp, and drummer Ted Epstein had addressed hardcore's proclivity to jingoism through performing a piece ironically titled "z.o.g." (Zionist-Occupied Government).[57] The troubling relationship between hardcore rock and racist movements, and the importance of hardcore to the downtown scene, added more ballast to Zorn's idea of producing a Radical Jewish Culture concert in Europe. In this sense, the festival represented a modest but meaningful statement of solidarity with Europe's targeted minorities, and a refusal by Jewish downtown musicians to retreat into the nondenominational, unmarked mode of "white American" in the eyes of their German audiences. Thus, it was in the context of a close but complicated relationship with Europe that, in mid-1991, Zorn chose a Jewish theme for his portion of the Munich Art Projekt. It was a prescient choice. More than any other moment before or since, those days in Munich had a profound effect, generating a wave of creative exploration and making plain a simple but startling truth: there was a Jewish community on the downtown scene.

Once that community had recognized itself, downtown's Jewish artists sought out ways to build upon that recognition. The RJC festivals, Zorn's founding of Tzadik records, and the spate of music that followed—not the least Zorn's own work—all helped create the conditions under which owner Michael Dorf made the Knitting Factory the improbable site for a series of public Passover seders, a development that would have been virtually unthinkable in previous years. The seders had a major musical component, but with their holiday theme they also materialized downtown's Jewish community in a more ambitious way than the music festivals had. The festivals, after all, were based on a familiar model. As affirmations of communal identity, the seders were bolder in marrying Jewish religious and cultural tradition to the experimental Jewish music percolating on the downtown scene.

Seders that added performative elements to the Passover ritual have a history going back to the turn of the century, and they cropped up in New York in the mid-1990s, as part of the Queer Yiddishkeit movement.[58] Dorf began staging seders at the Knit in 1995, and he continued doing so annually through 1998; after a lapse of a few years, in 2004 he began convening his "Downtown Seders" in new locations. The seders were hybrids—part public ritual, part family observance, and part theater.[59] They included pauses in the Haggadah reading for video clips, and the reading was also seamlessly integrated with instrumental performances by the attendees. Dorf emphasized both the seder's collective aspect and its theatrical one by conceiving of the events as "Cyber Seders" to be simulcast over the Internet. Fittingly for a seder held at the Knitting Factory, the downtownish musical aspect was evident from the first moment. As New York–based music journalist Howard Mandel observed:

> Here was [vocalist] Shelley Hirsch offering the age-old blessing over the ritual dinner's first cup of wine, with splatter/squeak/wail obbligato from clarinetist David Krakauer.... Behind banquet tables jammed to overflowing on the Knit's balcony, trombonist Art Baron... played tuba in a standup trio with soprano saxophonist Steve Elson... and accordionist Ann DeMarinis to accompany the tradition dipping of vegetables in salt water.... [Saxophonist] Roy Nathanson ... sniggled the *Pink Panther* theme on his alto ... trumpeter Frank London spun out rampant klezmer licks while a video of Brooklyn Hassids baking the holiday's unleavened bread was screened.... Nora York sang "Go Down Moses," and the hall stilled for a grainy videotape of Dr. Martin Luther King Jr. delivering his "I have a dream" speech. Bassist Mark Dresser and his daughter introduced the Four Questions... followed by [vocalist] Laurie Anderson.... Then Steven Bernstein with a pocket trumpet and his toddler came on.... Finally John Zorn, drummer Joey Baron smiling broadly behind him, unleashed an ear-piercing alto sax howl as the Rude or Rebellious Child, who demands pointedly, "What does this service mean to *you?*"[60]

Some artists had reservations about this mélange of Jewish observance, family tradition, performance and spectacle. As Marty Ehrlich recalled in 2002, "When they had the seders at the Knitting Factory, all I had to do was just call and say, 'Hey, I want to do this,' and everyone would be glad for me to come. But for me, Passover's about my family. And teaching my kids. And I didn't see it as something for public performance."[61] But whatever artists' personal responses to the Knitting Factory seders, these events were remarkable for two simple but powerful reasons: their unprecedented visibility, and their affirmation of Jewish community on the downtown scene. Before the first RJC festivals, it would have been hard to imagine such a freewheeling acknowledgment of Jewish identity, much less a public celebration of Jewish communal ties, among the scene's creative iconoclasts.

# THREE

## From the Inexorable to the Ineffable

*John Zorn's* Kristallnacht *and
the Masada Project*

THROUGH HIS PROLIX CREATIVITY, HIS LEADERSHIP AND management skills, and a seemingly tireless dedication to his cause, saxophonist John Zorn played as decisive a role in shaping the RJC moment as he has on the downtown scene as a whole. In addition to commissioning a great deal of new work on the Tzadik label, Zorn, with his particular gift for composing music that challenged notions of tradition and genre, pushed RJC into compelling creative territory. From his work in *Kristallnacht* (1992), which engaged viscerally with themes of destruction and survival in Jewish history, through the Masada project (1993–present), which has framed Jewish music as a site for spiritual healing, Zorn created new landscapes for imagining and engaging Jewish heritage through music. His vision for RJC looms large, a result of his high profile on the downtown scene, his role as a producer at Tzadik, his own prolific musical output, and his attention to iconography and packaging. Although he was less involved than some of his colleagues in the writing and talk that developed around the RJC idea,

Zorn's interpretation of "radical Jewish culture" is as particular as that of any of his peers.

In the early 1990s Zorn embarked on a new project of writing and commissioning Jewish music, drawing on the creative interests and compositional methods he had developed after moving to the Lower East Side in the 1970s. For example, *Kristallnacht*, his first substantial foray in this direction, reflected his interest in both hardcore rock aesthetics and modernist compositional techniques, also drawing on formal devices from the innovative "game" and "file card" pieces he had developed during his early years on the downtown scene. Like much of his earlier work, *Kristallnacht* aimed to overwhelm audiences with an experience of extreme psychological intensity, a quality that was supported by programmatic scaffolding, including images, liner notes, and titles. *Kristallnacht* is unique in Zorn's oeuvre, however, both in its programmatic scope and for the scale and immediacy of the events to which it alluded.

In addition to drawing upon his established interests, writing Jewishly identified music ultimately led Zorn into new stylistic and formal territory. Notably, beginning in 1993 with the advent of his post-bop quartet, Acoustic Masada, he launched his first sustained compositional foray into jazz, conventional (head-solo-head) song form, and melodic lyricism, writing several hundred short compositional sketches (charts with melodies, harmonies, and some other notated material) that are collected into three "Masada songbooks": *Book I* (1993–1997), *Book II: Book of Angels* (2004), and *Book III: The Book Beriah* (2014).[1] In retrospect, the project of writing Jewishly identified music, which has shaped his career for the past two decades, takes on an interesting arc. *Kristallnacht* addressed an indelible, historically immediate wound, but Zorn followed up in the Masada project with music that, through both sound and dramatic framing, celebrated Jewish fortitude while retreating from historical particularity.[2] This shift, from concrete particularity to free-floating signification, played out sonically, particularly in regard to his use of melody and his choice of formal plans, and it was mirrored in the text and iconography with which he surrounded his recordings.

## Zorn's Early Career: Structured Improvisation, Maximalism, and Trash

Both *Kristallnacht* and the Masada project were informed by Zorn's strategies for directing group improvisations. In the 1980s, he had developed a series of game pieces, each based on a set of formal limits for improvising musicians. Zorn (or another leader) conducted the ensembles using a vocabulary of hand signals and other prompts, but the players retained control over all the content and most of the structural decisions—including when to play, whom to play with, and when to switch to a new idea. The game pieces led to file card pieces, which involved more pre-composition. Rather than providing performers with rules and strategies they could manipulate at will during a performance, in a file card composition Zorn sketched out a score and then worked with performers in rehearsals to realize it fully. To generate the sketch, he made cards, each representing a discrete moment of music. Some cards used musical notation—for instance, a set of chords—and others consisted of phrases or images that served as conceptual prompts: "rain and thunder," "car crash."[3]

Both the game pieces and file card pieces reflected Zorn's engagement with "block forms"—that is, formal plans that juxtapose discrete musical blocks rather than developing along more conventional lines—whose genesis he ascribes to exposure to work by Igor Stravinsky and Charles Ives and to music on television.[4] The cards' content and the logic of their ordering depended on a thematic focus, the best-known example being Zorn's tribute albums to composer Ennio Morricone and writer Mickey Spillane. Arnold Schoenberg was another influence—one that was also to inform *Kristallnacht*. In his early twelve-tone pieces, in the absence of a conventional harmonic underpinning, Schoenberg used texts and dramatic themes to create cohesion. Likewise, Zorn recalled, in file card pieces such as *Spillane,* he "needed something to tie all the different genres together, so I used dramatic subjects. . . . Each moment of music related to the dramatic subject in some way." After arranging the cards into a cohesive sequence and sketching out a score, Zorn brought the sketch to the recording studio, where he and the performers developed the piece into its final form: "When I could see the whole arc of the piece, I would go to a bunch of improvisers and say . . . 'Let's go in [to the

**Figure 3.1.** John Zorn, *Hip Hop Cobra* at Tonic, New York City. 2000.
*Photo: Peter Gannushkin.*

recording studio] and create a piece.'"[5] Ultimately, then, the "score" of a
file card piece resides not in the written notation, but in the recording
itself: "Without my explanation or the tape itself, the paper scores aren't
going to mean much to anybody."[6] The same principle holds true for

most of Zorn's work, although he has also published a substantial catalog of fully notated scores.

The file card pieces had long creative gestations, and Zorn attenuated his approach in his hardcore bands of the 1980s, notably Naked City, which he convened in 1983 and whose sonic influence is evident in Zorn's Electric Masada ensemble.[7] For Naked City, Zorn wrote arrangements that made rapid jump cuts through a panoply of musical idioms and ideas, at punishingly high volumes and breakneck tempi, with many of the musical "blocks" lasting only one or two seconds. Zorn conducted these jump cuts in performance, leading the band from his saxophone and using musical cues and hand-signals. The exhilarating flow of crisply articulated musical moments created a sonic spectacle that, as observers often noted, mimicked the act of flipping through radio stations, but at an exaggerated pace and intensity.[8]

Looking to set his work apart from the so-called minimalism that dominated classical composition in the 1970s, Zorn aimed for "maximalism," cultivating techniques for "packing as much information as I possibly can into a piece." As we will see, this principle, which held true in *Kristallnacht,* stands in marked contrast to his work in Masada. But during his period of involvement with Naked City, maximalism was a central aim, with densely packed "information" that included (a) extremes of tempo, volume, and timbre; (b) clashing stylistic juxtapositions and a high rhythmic density of musical blocks; (c) many short pieces, some under one minute long, performed during a single evening performance or included on one recording; and (d) multiple levels of allusion to other pieces, artists, or artworks, some of which are legible only to Zorn himself. Maximalism functioned in another important way in this band, as Yamantaka Eye's virtuosically calibrated stream of guttural sounds, screams, and gibberish served as a paralinguistic foil to the band's hyper-real idiomatic fluency. Thus, the band not only offered audiences syntactical overload, but also gave them information that was designed to be unassimilable into any syntactical system.

Throughout Zorn's oeuvre, a compositional interest in the unassimilable has taken on social implications, as he has linked an interest in socially unacceptable sounds to the experience of working, as an artist, in a social margin. Musicologist John Brackett has drawn our attention to the way Zorn's fascination with seemingly illogical juxtapositions in music can be traced to his interest in philosopher Georges Bataille, particularly Bataille's formulation of a sphere of "heterogeneity," a conceptual space outside the sphere of a rational social order. To this sphere are relegated human waste, religious faith, madness, and sexual deviancy—in Zorn's words, "that which was thrown away."[9] Zorn's avowed interest in this sphere informs his sonic choices and his formal strategies. He incorporates sounds that would otherwise register as noise or "trash," obvious examples being Eye's blurts and vomiting sounds and Zorn's syntax of duck calls (derived from hunters' bird and game calls), which he performed on saxophone mouthpiece alone. Zorn also uses formal means to create a zone ruled by a principle of unassimilability, in which the musical information he presents cannot be taken in, as "the musically irrational or impossible intrudes on and disrupts our musical expectations: [including] the extreme tempos and stop-on-a-dime shifts of Naked City or the harmonic 'swervings'. . . that often occur between successive musical moments."[10] Indeed, Zorn has described his investment in art as stemming not only from its ability to transmute sonic trash into music, but also from the way art can transform social detritus into an object of power and value: "You could say 'turning lead into gold,' [or] you could say, 'making art out of garbage,' which is what [filmmaker] Jack Smith basically taught me, that great art is made from the detritus of society. And the secret of alchemy is transforming that which was thrown away into something that's treasured. And that's what making art is, kind of, for me."[11]

Zorn shared this interest in trash with many of downtown's visual artists and filmmakers. Like those colleagues, as well as precursors in underground rock (notably Frank Zappa), Zorn embraced lowbrow culture —cartoons, popular music, and B-grade films—and what was elsewhere decried as musical garbage—popular music—moves that flew in the face of the European classical tradition he had encountered in his private and academic studies in classical composition. If John Cage and his cohort had defied modernist principles by embracing sounds and structures that stood outside the realm of high art, Zorn took that stance to a new extreme, championing genres that had little purchase in modern concert music of any kind.

Ultimately, Zorn places himself in a creative lineage of artists who make their work out of material their predecessors have dismissed as antithetical to art's purposes.[12] But despite his challenges to the Western classical tradition—or because of them—in the scholarly literature, Zorn is typically framed as a composer in that tradition, without much attention to the scene of composer/improvisers in which he works. And yet it is the unique creative context of the downtown scene that has made it possible for Zorn to develop his particular formal innovations and his methods of real-time composition. As he has been the first to acknowledge, he could have developed his body of work only among a cohort of composer/improvisers. For example, in regard to *Cobra,* probably his best-known game piece, he asserted, "Content is left up to the performer. . . . I don't tell people *what* to play but create a structure that tells them *when* to play."[13] Likewise, it was no accident that Zorn chose virtuosic composer/improvisers as his side musicians in Naked City. Their unique training and versatility made it possible for him to accomplish an impressive feat: bringing formal innovations—including abrupt and unpredictable entrances, exits, and leaps among contrasting musical styles and ideas—to hardcore rock without sacrificing that idiom's core aesthetic.

This is not to say that Zorn cedes his artistic vision to his side musicians. To the contrary, his creative control is close and exacting. For example, in Electric Masada, Zorn makes compositional decisions on every level, including, for guitarist Marc Ribot, "choosing . . . my guitars and specifying distortion levels and reverbs, stylistic/genre nuances, and degrees of dissonance."[14] Ribot asserts that in this ensemble "it is impossible to overstate the extent to which Zorn 'composed' my sound [and] the sound of my 'improvisations.'" Trumpeter Dave Douglas has concurred, noting that in the Acoustic Masada quartet, an audience might well perceive a musician as freely improvising when he or she is actually following notated parameters. One of the hardest things to let go of in Masada, he recalled, was "the mind-set of the improviser . . . [one in which] no one should interrupt [and] improvisation is mystical. . . . The first time you play with John, that goes out the window. . . . I was surprised to be told from one moment to the next what to do in an improvisation." Ordinarily, as a jazz musician, he would have conceived of a solo as "my improvisation," he continued, but playing with Zorn he learned that "my improvisation is part of the composition."[15] Although as a bandleader Zorn showcases each side-musician's individual voice, he does so in a closely directed way, and in this sense he fulfills a traditional role as composer. But in the sense that Zorn's music is fully realized only through a collaborative process and depends on the individual voices and ideas of his side-musicians, it aligns more closely with jazz—with the developing tradition of composition/improvisation—than it does with fully notated concert music. Zorn thus provides a useful example of why received notions of "composition" are too limited to serve the needs of twentieth- and twenty-first-century music. And just as Zorn and his cohort challenged established ideas about the nature of musical composition, during the RJC moment they also argued for a new relationship between creativity and identity, thereby proposing a new template for "composing" notions of Jewish identity and tradition.

## Approaching *Kristallnacht* through Imagery, Text, and Sound

As Zorn's first major Jewishly identified piece, *Kristallnacht* broke new compositional ground, but it also shares analytical challenges with the work that had preceded it. Among these challenges is the way Zorn often surrounds his work with visual and literary cross-references. In conjunction with his sonic maximalism, such cross-references create a saturated semiotic field that deflects monolithic readings. He also uses references to achieve just the opposite aim: not oversaturation but clarity. In his longer pieces (such as *Spillane* and other file card pieces), he has deployed text and image to create extra-musical themes that guide listeners' interpretations, thereby lending conceptual frames to works with otherwise disparate elements.[16] If Zorn deploys references and iconography to multiple ends—sometimes to deliberately overcrowd the semiotic field and sometimes to simplify it—he maintains that presentation is integral to the work as a whole: "I think that the visual nature of a presentation in a package is very important, and I love working on it. . . . And I am addicted to the connection of visual with sound. . . . To me, they are intrinsically connected."[17] Both the composer's claims and his wider artistic engagements, with film in particular, suggest that in approaching Zorn's recorded work it is important to assess the relationship among sound, image, text, and other elements that make up the "webs of significance" in which his recordings lie suspended.[18]

To be sure, Zorn's use of visual signifiers has sometimes proved controversial. Although he has taken an interest in making art that triggers multiplex reactions and sees image and sound as dual participants in this process, he has often seemed to be unaware that the images he uses might trigger antagonism—directed toward the images and Zorn himself—in his audience. The cover and inset to *Torture Garden* (1985) and *Leng Tch'e* (1992) elicited a particularly negative response.[19] By using photographs of East Asian women in S/M rope bondage, grotesques from Japanese erotic *manga,* and documentary photographs from an early twentieth-century torture session in Beijing, Zorn opened himself up to charges that he was fetishizing the Asian body and glamorizing its violation. But in a way that would later resonate with his creative choices for Masada, rather than engaging such critiques on their own terms, that is, with attention to the racial and gendered aspects of the images, Zorn explicated his work as addressing something less specific: his own (and by extension our) fascination with depictions of intense subjective experiences (of both pain and pleasure). In discussing such depictions without attention to nuances of race, class, or gender, Zorn seemed out of touch with prevailing critical discourse, but his statements also illuminate his particular creative concern with deceptive depictions of violence and serenity. The visual representation of apparent serenity might belie a violence that is less easy to discern, and vice versa, or two antagonistic physiological states might appear to exist simultaneously. For example, as Zorn explains in the liner notes to the 2011 reissue of *Leng Tch'e,* the album's disturbing photograph shows a man who appears to be in an ecstatic trance, even as he is dissected alive.[20] The appearance of quietude belies a deeper violation, as the violence recently visited upon the man's body is both evident and eerily absent from the scene.[21]

Zorn followed up his most visually controversial work with *Kristallnacht,* whose packaging was if anything more provocative.[22] That packaging also extended Zorn's interest in using visual signs whose subtext conflicts with their surface. The album's liner notes were bookended with images of two human bodies, both photographed in an attitude of crucifixion. Rather than presenting the images without any explication as he had often done in the past, however, Zorn made his purposes a bit plainer by including a caption with each. One, subtitled "The Nazi Ideal: Josef Thorak 'Hingebung,'" is a photograph of a female nude sculpture by Thorak, the Nazi artist, and the other, subtitled "The Nazi Reality: Bergen Belsen," is the well-known, horrific photograph of a man's grimacing, skeletal corpse.[23] These captions provide an important glimpse into why Zorn used these images: in a link to his previous work, they illuminate his interest in exposing the gap between that which appears to be disgusting and that which is truly depraved. By including a photograph of the Thorak sculpture and alluding to its relationship to the Nazis' cult of physical perfection, Zorn foregrounds the degradation that is (mis)represented by the statue's classical beauty. Likewise, the image of the frighteningly sub-human corpse elicits horror, but the true horror lies in the genocidal ideology that produced it. Even in the presence of such difficult images, in turning to a Jewish subject Zorn, as a person of Jewish heritage, might well have expected to avoid the critiques he had sustained earlier in regard to his representation of Asians as exotic others. But *Kristallnacht*, rife with interpretive complexities and grim historical allusions, was as controversial as any work Zorn had yet produced. In this long-form tone poem, Zorn set out to do nothing less than to "tell the story of the Jewish experience, [including] survival through the Holocaust, the building of a Jewish state, diaspora Jewry and its attraction and resistance to assimilation, the rise of Jewish nationalism and the ultimate problems of fanatical religious fundamentalism."[24] The theatrical, sonic, and programmatic choices he made in the service of this project all proved to be complicated ones. The piece also brought to the fore his interest, often misconstrued and sometimes clumsily deployed, in using art to champion marginalized individuals and social groups.

*Kristallnacht* is a chamber octet in seven movements, combining pre-recorded material with associative and abstract musical language to illustrate a cinematic program that represents Ashkenazic Jewish history, with the German state-orchestrated anti-Jewish pogroms of November 1938 as the dramatic focus.[25] Many other composers had attempted to address the Holocaust through music, one notable contemporaneous example being Alvin Curran's *Crystal Psalms,* which had been broadcast on European radio in 1988.[26] But at the Munich festival, the combined German and downtownish context made *Kristallnacht*'s Jewish and Holocaust themes all the more striking.[27] With no legacy of thematically Jewish work to build upon in the two genres that had the strongest presence on the downtown scene—rock and jazz—*Kristallnacht* made an emphatic statement about the importance of Jewish history to the scene's (purportedly) culturally unmarked, boundary-breaking experimentalism. Zorn's prominence as downtown's preeminent public figure magnified the impact of this statement.

Zorn ratcheted up the piece's drama by crowding his audience into the concert complex's smallest venue (the Black Box theater), warning them they would not be allowed to leave during the performance, and "providing strong-armed bouncers to carry out those instructions"— provoking more than one attendee to assume Zorn was alluding to the Nazi practice of crowding Jews into train cars and sending them to their deaths.[28] At *Kristallnacht*'s U.S. premiere, he made this idea more explicit by preceding the performance with a long recording of train sounds, leading *New York Times* music critic Jon Pareles to comment: "Before the performance there were recordings of bouncy 1930's cabaret songs and then, for about 15 minutes, the sounds of a train journey; standing in the dark, packed Knitting Factory on Wednesday night, it was easy to recognize an allusion to the sealed trains that carried people to concentration camps."[29] Given the horrifying accounts that emerged from those who survived the Nazi transports, it is difficult to sustain an analogy between those death trains and New Yorkers standing in a stuffy, overcrowded theater. However, Zorn was not the first artist to have pushed audiences to make such a connection. Both *Kristallnacht*'s specific Holocaust allusion and the general quality of crowding and discomfort drew on the legacy of 1960s Happenings, which had routinely treated audiences with some hostility. As Susan Sontag had asserted in 1966, a Happening "seems designed to tease and abuse the audience. . . . Someone may be making near-deafening noises on an oil drum, or waving an acetylene torch in the direction of the spectators. . . . The audience may be made to stand uncomfortably in a crowded room, or to fight for space to stand on boards laid in a few inches of water." Indeed, in describing an event she attended in the late 1960s, Sontag might just as well have been discussing *Kristallnacht*'s pre-concert atmosphere:

> In Allan Kaprow's *A Spring Happening*... the spectators were confined inside a long box-like structure resembling a cattle-car; peep-holes had been bored into the wooden walls of this enclosure through which spectators could strain to see the events taking place outside; when the Happening was over, the walls collapsed, and the spectators were driven out by someone operating a power lawnmower.[30]

Like Kaprow, Zorn used an intrusive sound to heighten the oppressive "cattle car" atmosphere at the premiere, asking his side-musicians (who were wearing earplugs) to perform the piece at a punishingly high volume.[31] In describing this aspect of the Munich premiere, in comparison to a very loud performance of *Kristallnacht* I had attended in 2002, bassist Mark Dresser said roundly, "That was nothin'!":

TB: Really?

MD: That was *nothin'* [emphatically]!

TB: You mean volume-wise?

MD: Volume-wise, that was not—I mean,
[in Munich the volume] was much more intense.[32]

Volume was not the only combative sonic element in the piece. *Kristallnacht*'s sixth movement, "Barzel" (Iron Fist), fused high volumes with menacing timbres and machine-like rhythms, extremes of register, and syntactic overload, pummeling the audience with an onslaught of guttural, distorted, electronically created low-frequency noise, shot through with the sound of sirens and accompanied by William Winant's machine-like playing on the drum set.

Audience members who were familiar with Zorn's hardcore bands, which he had developed into what can fairly be termed a theater of excess, would have been prepared for a similarly overwhelming experience at *Kristallnacht*'s premiere.[33] However, in *Kristallnacht*'s twelve-minute second movement, "Never Again," Zorn pushed both sonic intensity and avant-garde theatricality to a more disturbing place than he had taken his work before, or has done since. Bringing to mind musicologist Suzanne Cusick's discussion of sound in relation to CIA definitions of "no touch torture," "Never Again" was expressly designed to inflict on his audience a particular kind of pain and physical damage.[34]

In this movement, Zorn used a waveform oscillator to generate and sustain several piercingly high sine tones, which at high volumes amounted to a physical assault on the audience. Rather than writing music that was harsh, confrontational, or uncomfortable—as one might characterize Penderecki's *Threnody to the Victims of Hiroshima* (1960), or, in Curran's *Crystal Psalms,* an unpleasant, high-frequency sound reminiscent of screeching car brakes—Zorn constructed a piece of music that was literally debilitating (PURL 3.1).

As Zorn wrote in his oft-quoted liner notes to the recording, the movement "contains high frequency extremes at the limits of human hearing and beyond, which may cause nausea, headaches, and ringing in the ears. Prolonged or repeated listening is not advisable as it may result in temporary or permanent ear damage."[35] This was not an exaggerated claim. High volumes at any frequency can cause hearing damage, but "Never Again" includes inaudible high-spectrum frequencies, some of which are "louder" (of greater amplitude) than the audible ones. As a spectrum analysis reveals, throughout most of the movement there is a constant presence of low amplitude noise between 12,5000 and 22,000 Hz, at frequencies ranging from very high to well above the range of human hearing (which for children is around 20,000 Hz and for middle-age adults around 14,000 Hz). There are also (inaudible) "louder" high-frequency peaks throughout the movement—most occurring at frequencies around 15–16,000 Hz, and a few at around 18–19,000 Hz. Because of their inaudibility, some of these pitches have an insidiously damaging effect, because their amplitudes are greater than the rest of the music in which they are embedded. And yet, for all this sonic aggression, if Zorn used "Never Again" to push his customary provocations to new extremes, the movement also resonates with his early career interest in art whose visceral surface, implying violence, belies an underlying serenity, or vice versa. "Never Again" also brings to mind Zorn's interest in realizing "how music could be done without sound."[36] Not only do some of the sounds in "Never Again" exist outside the range of human hearing, but also, because the sine tones make it impossible to listen to the movement in detail, it can never be fully heard.

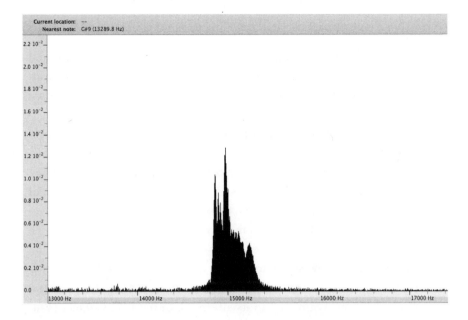

**Figure 3.2.a.** "Never Again" frequency spectrum. High frequency peak at G♯9 (~15,000 Hz). The vertical axis is amplitude; the horizontal axis is frequency.

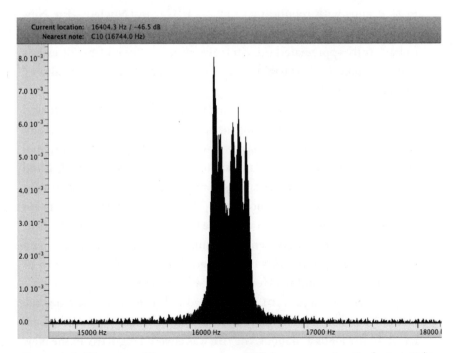

**Figure 3.2.b.** "Never Again" frequency spectrum. High frequency peak at C10 (~16,000 Hz).

Thus, by partaking of a blend of humor, seriousness, and hubris—and as a counter-intuitive counterpart to *Zohar,* Zorn's much gentler historical parable (discussed in chapter 1)—"Never Again" embodies its own directive.

Taking a wider view of the piece, one can see that *Kristallnacht* was distinct in Zorn's oeuvre for both its length and ambition.[37] Its historical program, however, included confusing elements, some deriving from slippage between the piece's Hebrew and English titles, both of which are included on the compact disc insert. The piece's seven movements are titled in Hebrew, transliterated Hebrew, and English, with the English titles in parentheses. It begins in the Eastern European *shtetl* and urban Jewish ghetto, in the movement entitled שטטל[*sic*]-I-Shtetl (Ghetto Life). It alludes to the Holocaust in the next movement, לא עוד-II-Never Again, and to its aftermath in גחלת-III-Gahelet (Embers). In the fourth and fifth movements, תיקון-IV-Tikkun (Rectification) and צופיה-V-Tzfia (Looking Ahead), it moves through the steps of healing and hope. After a shift to militancy in ברזל-VI-Barzel (Iron Fist), it ends with rebuilding in גרעין-VII-Gariin (Nucleus–The New Settlement).[38] As with his images on *Torture Garden,* Zorn seems not to have fully appreciated the controversy at least one of his titles was likely to elicit. It is probably for this reason that he eventually altered the piece's program.

Although the Tzadik website today describes the piece's historical sweep as addressing assimilation, nationalism, and religious fundamentalism, none of these issues has an obvious counterpart in the original program. Zorn seems to have added the latter elements, nationalism and fanatical religious fundamentalism, in response to a backlash against the title of *Kristallnacht's* sixth movement, "Barzel" (Iron Fist). The concept of "Jewish iron," which might well have been the inspiration for the title, dates from early twentieth-century Zionist ideologies of self-defense and self-determination, but this title caused Zorn some trouble due to its contemporaneous political resonances with the violent, ultra-right-wing Jewish Defense League (JDL), which used an iron fist logo and allied the idea of "Jewish iron" with their call for the violent eviction of Arabs from Israel. In the 1980s and 1990s, the JDL was covered regularly in the New

York press for "escalating its tactics from rhetoric to terror" by fomenting violence against both Jews and non-Jews in the United States and Israel.[39] But the association some of his colleagues made between the title "Iron Fist" and Meir Kahane's group seemed to have caught Zorn (who freely admits that he rarely reads the paper or follows current events) unaware, leading him to reorient the program toward an issue all would agree on—fighting religious fanaticism.

"Iron Fist" was not the only title in the piece with a muddled programmatic intent. Although Zorn's titles suggest an informed engagement with Jewish history, languages, and texts—the key elements of "getting Jewish music right"—there is some slippage between the English and Hebrew. Thus, the translation of "Barzel" as "Iron Fist" is also a loose one; "barzel" is simply the Hebrew word for "iron," and the title "Never Again"—a phrase with an important role in U.S. Holocaust discourse (and which was also taken up by Kahane and the JDL)—has no such resonance in the Hebrew version (לא עוד), which translates simply as "no more." Moreover, whereas the English title "Looking Ahead" (צופיה, incorrectly transliterated as "Tzfia") is a vague, historically indeterminate phrase, in Hebrew, the striking word *tzofia* has a unique connotation. Because *tzofia* is a peculiar word, it is readily associated with the most prominent (if not the only) text in which it appears: "Ha-Tikvah," the Zionist national song and Israeli national anthem, in the line, "My eye is looking toward (צופיה) Zion." The title "Tzofia" thus programmatically frames *Kristallnacht*'s fifth movement as alluding not to a general renewal of hope after the trauma of the Holocaust, but to the "hope" of classical Zionism to free Jews from their vulnerable position of statelessness, and the realization of that hope in the establishment of the State of Israel in 1948. Insofar as *Kristallnacht* rests ontologically on literal sonic references to the written program, the English-Hebrew slippage muddles the context in which the music's sonic signifiers are doing their ontological work.[40] In sum, *Kristallnacht*'s "packaging"—the images and liner notes, the texted program, the venue, and the yellow stars—all served to frame a musical rendering of Jewish history that centered around an indelibly concrete event, but that sometimes rested on shifting ontological ground.

## *Kristallnacht:* The Music

After bringing the piece to Munich, Zorn conducted *Kristallnacht*'s U.S. premiere at the Knitting Factory, then brought the ensemble to the studio to record the piece on 9 and 10 November, the anniversary of the Night of Broken Glass. In performance and on the recording, the ensemble included Mark Feldman (violin), David Krakauer (clarinet and bass clarinet), Frank London (trumpet), Marc Ribot (electric guitar), Anthony Coleman (harmonium, and Ensoniq ASR-10 sampling keyboard), Mark Dresser (contrabass), William Winant (percussion), and Zorn on waveform oscillator. In a counterpart to the question of how to approach its theatrical and iconographic presentation, *Kristallnacht* presents us with the question of how to sonically analyze a stylistically disparate piece that is shot through with multiple musical and cultural references. Structurally, *Kristallnacht* reflects Zorn's longstanding interest in creating a formal frame, built upon pre-composed material, that allows for some improvisation. But as he noted in 1993, the piece also used "varied styles and compositional techniques, the most eclectic I've yet used in a single work."[41] For example, he used twelve-tone methods as the basis for one movement, and he modeled another on his unpredictable, strategy-based game pieces. At times in the piece he used electronic sampling and layering techniques reminiscent of such earlier recordings as *Locus Solus* (1983) or built textural "walls of sound" as he had in his hardcore bands, but at other moments he invoked the textural clarity of his classical compositions. Indeed, the piece serves as the culmination of Zorn's compositional identity to that point.[42] It drew together elements from the improvisations and game pieces, hardcore rock and avant-garde classical idioms, modernist compositional methods, short and long-form compositions, and the layering and juxtaposition of electronic samples and found sounds.

In this stylistically diverse piece, Zorn also deployed thematic organizational techniques just as he had in his earlier work, creating, in addition to his programmatic narrative, sonic guideposts for listeners, some easily apprehended and others embedded at the structural level. In conjunction with the piece's historical program, which begins and ends at a place of apparent calm, harmony plays an important organizing role. The piece is not grounded in functional harmony, but its large-scale harmonic framework rests on establishing, departing from, and returning to a D-minor tonal center, with the first movement establishing the key of D-minor as a tonal focal point and the last movement unfolding over a D-minor ostinato. Relatedly, F-naturals also feature prominently throughout the piece, and Zorn also repeats and develops various melodies, rhythms, and motives to lend the piece formal coherence. But perhaps his most obvious structural device was also a programmatic one, as he used klezmer melodies and archival cantorial recordings indexically—to allude to prewar Jewish communities in Eastern Europe—as well as metonymically, as a sonic character standing in for those communities throughout his narrative of Jewish history.[43] In this respect, *Kristallnacht* represented a significant shift from Zorn's earlier work. Even though, outside of the reference to the Night of Broken Glass, most of its program was more general than specific, the decision to use klezmer themes and cantorial samples to allude to Jewish people kept the piece more grounded in reality than did the cinematic or fantastical themes of his earlier work. In an ironic contrast, although Zorn built his Masada oeuvre on a similar principle, using klezmer scales, loosely interpreted, to represent Jewishness, in the Masada project he enacted a musical return to a place that was less historically determined than it was mystically conceived.

Zorn has made two claims about *Kristallnacht* that are particularly interesting to consider in light of his interest in finding ways to structure his entropic pieces and limit his potentially limitless compositional material. Although he is known for his no-holds-barred maximalism and his voracious appetite for stylistic variety, like many composers he is interested in limits, explaining that "I try to go [to] new [compositional] places by setting myself parameters and trying to solve the problems they present. How can I create a piece that has only three sounds in it? Or a piece where every bar is a different genre of music?" In regard to *Kristallnacht*, Zorn has mentioned Schoenberg's opera, *Moses und Aron*, as well as the mystical numerological system of gematria, as two of the central devices he used both to generate and to limit musical material.[44] (In gematria, each letter of the Hebrew alphabet is ascribed a number, and words and phrases with the same numeric value are thought to have a mystical relationship to one another.)[45] Zorn evidently drew on ge-matria because of its Jewish significance, but he also deployed it toward the same kinds of compositional constraints he had always sought when writing a new piece of music—for example, to create initial limits on his pitch material, which he then challenged himself to use effectively in writing the piece.[46] Though intriguing from an analytical perspective, insofar as numerological relationships and pitch matrices lend *Kristall-nacht* formal cohesion, Zorn is not forthcoming in much detail about their roles in the piece; and, given as well gematria's various methods of calculation, it is difficult to assess systematically gematria's role in *Kristallnacht*. But one can nevertheless make some general inferences— for example, *Kristallnacht* is in seven movements, and seven is a signifi-cant number in both classical Judaism and Kabbalah—and it is also possible to identify correlations between certain Hebrew words, their gematria values, and rhythmic values in *Kristallnacht*.

The connection to *Moses und Aron,* though also difficult to trace with precision, is more amenable to analysis. Zorn developed several of *Kristallnacht*'s main motives using pitch material he derived from *Mo-ses und Aron,* using a technique carried over from earlier in his career. In the process of using pitch content from a classical work to create a loose correspondence to a new piece, he has explained, "I might pick another composition, like a piece by Morton Feldman, from which I will derive pitch ideas and pitch sets so that the piece will have an integrity in the sense that it's related to another piece."[47] But one aspect of Zorn's creative process means it will remain tricky to discern links between *Kristallnacht* and *Moses:* his practice of altering the pitches from an original tone row, or otherwise choosing and manipulating them to suit his purposes. Thus, for example, in describing his use of thirty pitches from Stockhausen's *Kontra-Punkte* (Counter-Points, 1952–53) in a new piece, Zorn explained, "I'll skip pitches, play around. If there's some-thing I want, like a B-flat major chord, I can find it somewhere in my row. I'll say, 'Okay, if I skip three pitches and then skip four pitches, I'll get my B-flat major chord.'. . . I do what I want with this information. I do this to amuse myself, and if it amuses someone else, that's an added pleasure. . . . Maybe nobody will be amused; maybe nobody will know! . . . But it makes me feel stronger about the piece."[48] This description has something in common with Zorn's attitude toward imagery. Just as he has tended to use images as inspirations or creative instigators, and (outside of *Kristallnacht*) has seemed less interested in addressing their particular cultural or historical dimensions, Zorn's derivation of a B-flat major chord from a serialist work makes it clear that when he turns to a piece of music he admires for creative inspiration, he draws upon it freely and mines it for useful compositional constraints. The new piece's connection to the work that generated its raw material becomes a point of private satisfaction for Zorn, but that connection does not imply a substantial programmatic reference or a rigorously derived formal correspondence. And, just as in his description of *Kontra-Punkte,* the tonal context in which *Kristallnacht*'s first prominent *Moses*-derived material is embedded makes plain the dramatic gulf between the two pieces.

*Moses und Aron*'s dodecaphonic basis nevertheless makes it possible to discern some correspondences between the two works. The most prominent link to the opera comes in the form of a "Moses motif," which Zorn introduces into the opening, klezmer-like theme of "Shtetl," which is set in the *Mi Shebberakh* mode.[49] (I use "motif" instead of "motive" to distinguish this material from other motives in the piece.) The Moses motif is derived from the opera through borrowing, altering, and reordering pitches from various versions of that piece's tone row. This motif, which is shared among trumpet, clarinet, and violin, also stands out for its dissonance and rhythmic angularity in a movement built primarily upon modal melodies played over tonal pedal points.

The trumpet and clarinet both insert part of the Moses motif into the middle of their opening solos. The clarinet's motif (example 3.1), which is constructed from four pitches (C♯-D-D♯-E), corresponds to the first two and last two pitches (in italics) of the *Moses und Aron* tone row in transposition:

1'41"

**Example 3.1.** "Shtetl." Moses motif. Clarinet (over G-minor pedal point) (1'41"). Transcription by the author.

· *Moses und Aron* tone row, transposed to C♯ (P1):
    C♯-D-A♭-F♯-G-F-B-A-B♭-C-D♯-E.[50]

The clarinet follows its Moses motif with a section of discordant laugh-
ing/choking free playing (using a klezmer-derived timbral effect called
a *tshok*). This section sounds like free improvisation, but in its rapidly
articulated staccato line, the clarinet touches on the row P1's remaining
pitches (F♯-G-F-B-A-B♭) concurrently, and then lands on nine iterations
of a dissonant F, a figure that will reappear in subsequent movements
(1'49"). Amidst a freer passage, the clarinet lands again on two iterations
of a drawn-out, guttural F (2'00" and following), then on a long A (2'09"),
and finally resolves on a D (2'15"), suggesting a predetermined D-minor
framework for the improvised passage.

Like the clarinet, the violin also has a Moses motif (example 3.2),
which also corresponds to another version of the *Moses und Aron* tone
row. The main content of the violin's Moses motif, *C-D-B-F♯-F-C♯*, is
identical to the first six pitches of the *Moses und Aron* row, transposed
and in retrograde:

· *Moses und Aron* row in retrograde, transposed to F♯ (R6):
    F♯-F-D-C-B-C♯-G-A-G♯-B♭-E-D♯.[51]

4'51"

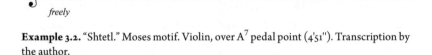

*freely*

**Example 3.2.** "Shtetl." Moses motif. Violin, over A[7] pedal point (4'51"). Transcription by
the author.

The violin's Moses motif, like that of the trumpet and clarinet, returns
at later points in the piece. For example, in the piece's fifth movement,
"Looking Ahead," the violin reiterates its original motif (2'39", now over
B-minor pedal point) as does the trumpet over a D-minor pedal point

(6'19") (example 3.3). A few minutes later in "Looking Ahead" (7'59"), the muted, wah-wah trumpet articulates a twelve-tone row (still over D-minor) that is derived from two segments of the same row (in italics and bold font) from which the violin's motif is drawn, i.e., R6:

- *Kristallnacht,* "Looking Ahead." Pitch content of trumpet row (over Dmi⁷) (7'59"–8'15"): *F-C-F♯-D*-**D♯-G♯-B♭-E-G-A-C-C♯-B**
  *Moses und Aron* row (R6): Segment 1: *F♯-F-D-C;* Segment 2: **B♭-C♯-G-A-G♯-B♭-E-D♯**

0'25"

**Example 3.3.** "Shtetl." Moses motif. Trumpet (over D-minor pedal point) (0'25"). (Parentheses indicate indeterminate pitch.) Transcription by the author.

These correspondences offer a bit of concrete evidence of the way Zorn makes musical references on a structural level, not only a stylistic one. He is well known for the hyper-referentiality of Naked City, which struck some observers as emblematic of a postmodern sensibility, but he built in structural references as well, between Naked City's "block forms" and the block-like forms of other composers, including Charles Ives and Carl Stalling. *Kristallnacht* likewise contains both stylistic allusions and formal ones. Within a piece that often sounds improvised, then, and that sometimes jumps from genre to genre, Zorn uses both tonal references and pitch sets to create an underlying formal unity. However, the most immediately evident unifying sonic device in *Kristallnacht* resides in its literal programmatic elements. As a close reading reveals, this piece reflects Zorn's interest in juxtaposing contrasting styles and sonic characters, both side-by-side and by layering, and also his concern with developing a wide variety of ways to limit and unify this disparate material.

**Table 3.1. Kristallnacht Map**

| MOVEMENT | I | II | III | IV | V | VI | VII |
|---|---|---|---|---|---|---|---|
| Hebrew title and other relevant Hebrew words[1] | שׁ שׁ ל [sic] | לא עוד | נ ח ל ה | ת'קון | צ'יון | ברזל | גרעין [גאולה] |
| Literal translation | Shtetl | No More | Embers | Repair, healing | Looking toward (Zion) | Iron | Kernel, nucleus [redemption] |
| English title | Shtetl | Never Again | Embers | Rectification | Looking Ahead | Iron Fist | New Settlement |
| Length | 5'51" | 11'41" | 3'25" | 3'02" | 8'46" | 2'01" | 7'58" |
| Meter | Free/duple | N/A | Free | N/A | N/A | 18-pulse ostinato | 9-pulse ostinato |
| Tonal center, scale, or unifying pitch content | G *Mi Shebberakh*; D-minor | N/A | 12-tone row, F-pedal point, modal scalar fragments | N/A | Free, with D-minor and other pedal points and pitch set material | N/A | D-minor |
| Formal plan or basis | ABC | ABA' | 12-tone | Block form | Block form | ABAB | ABA' |
| Programmatic/thematic elements | C, K, M, N, O, P, R, Z | C, G, H, I, K, N, P, R, T, Z | B, C, E, M, P | K, M, O, R | C, K, L, M, N, R, W | C, H, L, N, W | L, N, R |

**Key: B**=burning paper; **C**=cantorial singing; **E**=emptiness/spaciousness; **F**=footsteps; **G**=breaking glass; **H**=car horns/sirens; **I**=sine tone; **K**=klezmer melody/modal fragment; **L**=thrash metal/chromatic bass line played on electric guitar; **M**=Moses motif or related pitch material; **N**=Noise; **O**=duple dance or oom-pah rhythm; **P**=pizzicato tremolo; **R**=rhythmic patterning (often corresponding to gematria value of title or related words); **T**=triangle or other bell/chime; **W**=waltz fragment; **Z**=Nazi voices

*Note:* 1. Hebrew spelling as in the liner notes.

## A Programmatic Work, Sonically Realized

Just as he used a historical program to unify *Kristallnacht* conceptually, Zorn also deployed many sonic devices to create unity within this stylistically varied piece. Some of these devices are quite literal, while others are evident only through an analysis of details that are not obviously thematic. But close listening reveals that this piece is woven through with dozens of motivic elements that draw sonic connections between movements and that are as formally important if not more so than the piece's texted ones. Among all the movements, I-"Shtetl" and II-"Never Again" follow the most literal narrative and are the easiest to read for dramatic content. "Shtetl" (5'51") introduces many of the indexical references that recur throughout the piece. These include: modal klezmer melodies (K); archival Nazi speeches and crowd noises (Z); the Moses motifs discussed above (M); a slow, duple klezmer dance (*sher*) with oom-pah accompaniment (O); an *agitato* pizzicato tremolo figure (P); and rhythmic patterning (R, as in the nine prominent F-naturals noted above).

"Shtetl" is also the most tonal movement and the only one that incorporates a regular meter (in its final section). The movement is built over a simple chord progression. It begins with melody instruments in D-*Mi Shebberakh* over a D-A pedal point, moves through G-minor and C-minor, and then (in the metered dance section) transitions to a faster chord progression in D-minor. It can be mapped in a three-part form, ABC: A (unmetered; introduces klezmer melodies and Moses motif); B (unmetered; Nazi speeches over D-A pedal point); C (duple meter, with chord progression in D-minor). The movement ends, without resolving, on a half-cadence in D-minor, followed by a moment of solo clarinet playing a *pianissimo* low F.

"Shtetl" sets up the fundamental dramatic underpinning of the piece, indexing Jewish life at the onset of its violent disruption by the Nazis. In the opening section, each melody instrument iterates a modal klezmer melody. Krakauer (on clarinet) and London (on trumpet)—both members of the neo-klezmer band the Klezmatics at the time—also employ klezmer's distinctive syntax (examples 3.4.a and 3.4.b). "Shtetl" incorporates both juxtaposition and layering. The movement's second section (2'19"), which opens with fragments from a Nazi speech (Z) (over

0'00" (Trp.)

**Example 3.4.a.** "Shtetl." Klezmer theme. Trumpet (0'00")

1'13" (Cl.)

**Example 3.4.b.** "Shtetl." Klezmer theme. Clarinet (1'13"). Transcription by the author.

contrabass, harmonium, and violin pedal point, and with chaotic trumpet vocalizations), includes more such contrasts than the first. The Nazi fragments are soon juxtaposed with the violin's lyrical klezmer violin solo (K) (2'36"). After a new, F♯-minor chord (3'04"), we hear samples of crowds barking out "Sieg Heil!" and in this case the samples are electronically manipulated—jerkily looped and layered—to create a grating cacophony. At a resolution to B-minor (3'08") these samples are joined by clarinet, then trumpet, playing Moses motif fragments. At 3'30", the violin reenters in a series of *agitato* pizzicato figures (P)—a gesture that will reappear in other movements, on both violin and guitar—and, out of the ensuing crescendo, a new clarinet klezmer line emerges (3'53").

In the final A' section of "Shtetl" (4'16"), which is ushered in by an E°⁷ harmony resolving back to D-minor, the guitar, bass, and drums establish a *sher*-like rhythm—a slow, duple klezmer rhythm—as the harmonium takes the lead with a new melody. This oom-pah rhythm (O) is paired variously with the crying clarinet, taped Nazi voices, the violin's agitated vocalizations, and klezmer lines in the trumpet and clarinet (K) (5'10"). As the meter breaks down, the instruments settle on a half cadence, and "Shtetl" ends on an incongruous note, with an archival snippet (in German) of cabaret singer Lale Anderson warbling the popular World War II–era German song "Lili Marleen" (5'29"). The clarinet closes the movement with a pianissimo, low F.[52]

If Old World melodies and archival samples lend "Shtetl" a quality of historical remove, II-"Never Again" (11'41"), *Kristallnacht*'s longest movement and dramatic centerpiece, unleashes an ear-splitting onslaught that pins audiences into an eternal present.[53] "Never Again" includes some tonal elements, but its main unifying device is its program. Two breaking-glass sine-tone sections (G, N) (0'00" and 9'44") bookend a sonic chronicle of the Night of Broken Glass (2'53"), which includes fleeting footsteps and the reappearance of cantorial, klezmer, and Nazi motifs from the first movement. The movement can be mapped in ternary form ABA': A (breaking glass section, with piercing sine tones); B (sonic chronicle, with intermittent sine tones); A'.

"Never Again" juxtaposes and layers different sounds, most of them ominous, which fit together into a meticulously crafted collage. (In performance, the layers were played live, with no pre-recorded overdubs.) The layers include the stylized breaking glass (G), which is a chorused and electronically manipulated sample triggered by Coleman that flows almost continuously through the piece in waves of rapid tinkling attacks. The breaking-glass sound is sometimes accompanied by another unnerving sonic character: a light, rapid, uneven, minimally resonant electric guitar tremolo (P), plucked with both hands at once on the upper strings and placed high on the neck. This tremolo recalls the violin's pizzicato figures from the first movement (and reappears, both in later movements and elsewhere in Zorn's work). Another layer, which includes a low, *agitato* bass solo as well as a threatening bass sound (N), rumbles beneath much of this movement. Intermittently, we also hear soft cymbal shimmers, rapid hand-drum flourishes, and, most prominently, a high, repeated chime on a glockenspiel or triangle (T), which stands out as singular and isolated among the other sounds and, most prominently, echoes the clarinet solo from "Shtetl" by repeating a high F nine times (R) (7'55")—reiterating a number that is to have formal and numerological significance throughout the piece.

Like "Shtetl," "Never Again" metonymically implies the presence of Jews and Nazis through sampled footsteps (F) and shouts (some drawn from the same Nazi speeches as those used in "Shtetl") (Z). After the violence of the opening broken-glass section, there is a sudden halt, and we then hear several sets of frantic footsteps, eerily echoing in an empty sonic environment (E), layered on top of one another and moving erratically through the stereo space. There are, again, samples of male voices and ugly, chanting crowds from Nazi speeches and rallies, made more aggressive by being looped to different lengths, layered, and rapidly reiterated. After another abrupt stop about midway through the piece we hear a new sound: an archival recording of cantorial singing (C), also looped and layered. The cantors' layered voices are answered by the only other lyrical voice in the movement, an *arco* violin, which otherwise chokes out guttural double-stops and rapid, pizzicato bursts (K, N). Throughout, the most central sonic character in this movement remains the sine tone, which, even when it is not present, disrupts the movement's chronological and compositional order. It is loudest in the movement's introduction and conclusion but resurfaces intermittently throughout. Because the piercing intensity of the sine tone is a constant, unpredictable threat, this randomness creates a kind of symbolic terrorist action. Once it presents itself, then disappears, one never knows when it might resurface.

With its gentle, floating quality, sparse texture, and slow tempo *rubato*, the next movement offers a respite to the violence that has preceded it. III-"Embers" (3'25") is played *pianissimo* and is almost inaudible after the assault of "Never Again." A harmonium's modal scalar fragments, which unfold over an F pedal point, undergird this loosely twelve-tone movement. The violin picks up a few of these fragments, as well as some with a more definite melodic contour and thus a stronger klezmer character (2'27") (K). "Embers" also offers a more conceptual kind of program than the previous movements, presenting us with a sonic space whose qualities suggest a post-apocalyptic desolation (E). In keeping with this notion, the recording is mixed to create a sense of breadth, depth, and motion within the stereo space. One of the most obvious examples of this dimensionality is the panning of an eerie electric guitar glissando from right to left channel (an effect achieved with a guitar slide, which Ribot faded in using the volume pedal to mimic the entrance of a bowed violin) (1'12"), and the placement of the sound of burning paper (B) (real paper, crackled during the performance) in the middle of the stereo space and "behind" the other sounds. After "Never Again," this movement's timbres also act as a kind of sonic balm. Winant's gong attacks, in particular, create an unstable sonic environment that envelops the rest of the ensemble. Indeed, all of the instruments use soft attacks, and each has a sound envelope that involves shimmering, wavering, sliding, or tremolo: harmonium, gongs, clarinet, and violin. Ribot plays the electric guitar using several different techniques that evoke a similarly dreamlike state: a light, rapidly plucked tremolo (with little reverb) (2'49" and following) (P), a slide, an Ebow (a magnet encased in plastic that creates sustained pitches), a reverb and echo unit, and volume pedals, all of which create a surreal pulsation on certain pitches.[54] The cantorial voices (C) from "Shtetl" also resurface in this movement (2'40"), and, in addition to this obvious motivic connection, "Embers" also offers a harmonic one. As noted above, "Embers" is a loosely twelve-tone composition with a modal scalar underpinning, internally unified through the slowly unfolding presentation of its pitch content. The movement's harmonically suspended quality reinforces the character of its soundscape, with the dreamily pulsating harmonium, guitar, and violin overlapping in scalar fragments to present the twelve chromatic pitches (example 3.5). The sense of emptiness and unhurried pace of "Embers" are left behind as the next movement opens, not with a ferocious onslaught like that

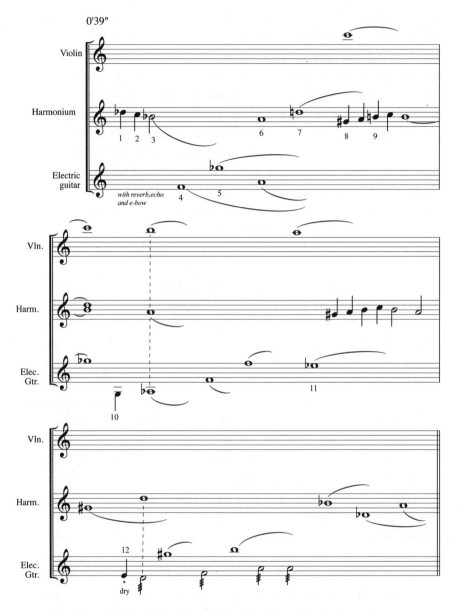

**Example 3.5.** "Embers." Iteration of twelve chromatic pitches by harmonium, violin, and guitar, over F-pedal point (0'39''). (Arced lines indicate sustained pitches, with decay.) Transcription by the author.

of "Never Again," but with a plethora of ideas that skitter unpredictably after one another.

IV: "Rectification" (3'02"), which is quick, lighthearted, and disjointed, is organized around the quick shifts in mood and style that typify Zorn's file card pieces. The violin, the main melodic voice (foregrounded in the mix), and guitar (with no reverb or other effects) open in unison, playing a harmonized, non-tonal eighth-note line (a partial twelve-tone set, with no G or A). They shift quickly into a dissonant, unpredictable call-response dialogue with varied phrase lengths, playing techniques, and motivic material that does not repeat. Rhythmic interjections, played by wood block, triangle or chime, and other small percussion, add to a sense of dislocation. Close listening reveals reiterated patterns, one of which, 3–1–6–30–5, figures prominently in the last movement, "The New Settlement." By one gematria method, this pattern is the numeric equivalent of the Hebrew word *geulah,* or redemption, while applying a second method reduces it to a value of nine. Here and there, we also hear stylistic gestures, for example, an oom-pah guitar pattern (0'53") (O) and a pentatonic, erhu-like melody played by the violin using harmonics (2'35", a timbre that returns in the next movement, "Looking Ahead"). This movement also reintroduces a klezmer presence (K) through a rapid, repeated scalar figure (A-B♭-C-B♭-A-G-F♯-D♯-F♯-G), which will return in the clarinet part in "Looking Ahead." In sum, although it includes elements that will recur in the work, on its own "Rectification" gives little sense of program beyond a general sense of antic dialogue among instruments, with rapid mood shifts and no sense of resolution or unity.

Like "Rectification," V: "Looking Ahead" (8'46") is disjointed.[55] However, it is both harsher and more extreme in its mood shifts, switching from idea to idea every ten seconds or so, with two centerpiece passages, both of which reiterate and develop material introduced in "Shtetl." With shifts among pedal points in different sections, the movement is anchored by a D-minor harmony, although in the first centerpiece passage, a long (in this context) violin solo unfolds, grounded by a pitch, a low B, reiterated in a car-horn-like blast from the synthesizer (H) (2'39"–3'33"). In the second, longer passage, a trumpet solo unfolds over a D-minor pedal point in an active texture to which contrabass, percussion, violin, and harmonium contribute agitated lines (6'42"–8'20"). As noted above, the trumpet's solo in this passage includes klezmer fragments that recall its solo in "Shtetl" (K), and part of its solo is drawn from the same row as the violin's Moses motif (M). This movement also includes blocks of dissonant and unpitched noise (N). Some blocks are grounded tonally by repeated pitches (R), but these pitches are usually undermined by minor seconds (and their octave equivalents). For example, at 2'01", the synthesizer (sounding like a piano) plays a series of repeated pitches on a low E♭, followed by an E♮ and B♭, but each pitch is sounded simultaneously with its chromatic neighbor played four octaves higher on keyboard and wave-form oscillator.

"Looking Ahead" also introduces new material that will signify prominently in the final two movements. It opens with a loud, frightening, and harsh block of noise (N) (created by waveform oscillator, drum set, sampler, and distorted electric guitar).[56] A similar sound will return as the dominant motif of the next movement, "Iron Fist." Just as the intensity of "Never Again" is followed by the quietude of "Embers," in "Looking Ahead" the harsh noise block is followed immediately by a contrast, an *agitato* block of cantorial snippets (C), plucked, reverb-treated guitar tremolos (P), and keening high pitches on trumpet and arco violin. Both blocks return later, incorporating material heard earlier in the piece. Thus, the burning/crackling paper motif from "Embers" (B) joins the cantorial block, and Nazi voices (Z) join the noise block, which also incorporates a new style snippet, a chromatic, thrash-metal bass line (L) played on distorted electric guitar, variants of which will return in "Iron Fist" and "The New Settlement." Between 1'08" and 1'29", Zorn plays frenetically with the idea of contrast, as the noise block trades off seven times with an eerie block created by house keys scratching on the strings of the electric guitar. Quick and unpredictable shifts follow, as the movement cycles through contrapuntal snippets and disjointed melodic lines, reiterated pitches (sometimes as their own block, and sometimes as accompaniment), gong strokes and vibraphone chimes (as well as wood block and glockenspiel), glassy violin harmonics (recalling the harmonics from "Rectification"), and a tutti C-minor waltz

(W, recalling the oom-pah dance of "Shtetl"). Zorn also uses silence thematically in this movement, so that a moment of silence, usually lasting a second or two, becomes one of the blocks (E). ("Looking Ahead" also includes crisply reiterated patterns, articulated by trumpet and clarinet in an overlapping call-response, but the patterns do not have any readily apparent numerological connotation.) Following a section with violin and wah-wah trumpet improvising agitated lines over a D-minor drone, and echoing the opening theme of "Rectification," "Looking Ahead" ends with a harmonized, non-tonal line shared between muted trumpet and violin. After a moment of silence (8'26"), we hear a humorous coda (8'30"): a few more quick jumps in mood, each only a few seconds long, followed by another false ending (8'38") and another quick series of stylistic snippets, made distinct by a cartoonish whooshing sound that appears nowhere else in the piece (8'40").

VI-"Iron Fist" (2'01"), *Kristallnacht*'s shortest movement, is based on a similar compositional principle to that of its longest one, "Never Again": each is thematically unified by an overwhelming sound. "Iron Fist" is built around a block of noise, made up of a threatening mid-range sound, pulsing at about 120 bps and repeating every eighteen pulses, over a bass-noise ostinato (N) moving between E-F♯. This blast of noise is interwoven with several versions of a (European) siren-like ostinato (H), the most prominent one using the pitches A-C-A-B in octaves with pitches above, against intermittent, prominent A♭ (for example, at 0'34"). While the mid-level noise continues, the bass stops playing its ostinato (0'46"–0'57" and 1'24"–1'34"), a change that helps foreground archival cantorial snippets (C) over a B♭-C ostinato, with pitches A-B♭ prominently sounded simultaneously in the first cantorial block, and pitches A-C-A-B sounded prominently in the second. This movement's large-scale form can thus be mapped as ABABA, with A the full noise blocks and B the cantorial sections. The siren sounds, distorted blast of noise, and the underlying, jackhammer-like pulse all embody the combative quality suggested by the title, which, as discussed above, seems to index the nineteenth-century Zionist ideology of Jewish resistance to oppression and state-sponsored violence. But despite this evident connection, the programmatic connotation of the noise blocks in juxtaposition with the cantorial scraps is unclear.

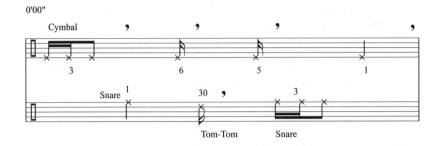

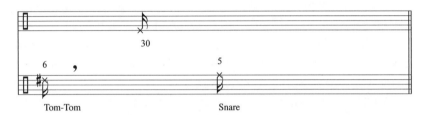

**Example 3.6.** "The New Settlement." Opening drum solo excerpt, with rhythmic groupings corresponding to gematria values in גאולה (Hebrew for "redemption") (3+1+6+30+5=45=4+5=9). Transcription by the author.

Finally, in keeping with the notion of change suggested by its title, VII-"The New Settlement" (7'58") is unified by a new method: here, the drum set (alternating among cymbals, snare, tom-tom, and bass drum) reiterates the kind of rhythmic patterning (R) that was present but less prominent in "Rectification." As noted above, these numbers, 3–1–6–30–5, correspond numerologically to the Hebrew word for redemption and reduce to the number nine (example 3.6).

The "redemption" rhythm both begins and ends the movement, which returns us to the D-minor tonal center established by "Shtetl." "The New Settlement" also includes intervallic leaps that recall the Moses motif and its extensions (M), and it presents variations on the distorted, chromatic electric guitar lines from "Looking Ahead" and "Iron Fist" (L). Overall, however, it is the drum set's uneven but insistent rhythmic iterations (R), along with Cohen's ostinato bass line, that lend the movement its unifying structure. Both parts underpin the movement's centerpiece, the electric guitar solo. Like Winant's shimmering gongs in "Embers," here the drum's dry rat-a-tat-tats shape the sonic environment for the solo, which alternates among dissonant intervals, ascending D-minor and chromatic scalar fragments, moments of free improvisation, and intervallic leaps. The guitar also plays iterations of pitches and intervals in the same numbered groupings as the drum set, for example, repeated F-F♯ minor ninths in a 1+1+1+6 rhythmic pattern (R), another grouping of nine (1'55"). After the guitar solo ends, a brief free bass solo follows, and the drum set closes the piece with a reiteration of its opening rhythmic figures, now divided differently among the cymbals, snare drum, and tom-toms.

This movement, "The New Settlement," whose title at first seems to bring the program to an uncomplicated dramatic close, in fact returns us to the question of how to assess the multiple meanings into which Zorn's work can refract. As we know, he weaves conflicting references into the sonic fabric, and he embeds other references structurally in a way discernible to a smaller number of listeners or only to himself. The movement also suggests interpretations that might well run counter to his original intentions. Zorn has described *Kristallnacht*'s program variably, as culminating either in the establishment of the State of Israel or in the flourishing of a postwar Jewish community in New York City.[57] As he wrote on the occasion of the piece's New York City premiere at the Knitting Factory in 1993, "This piece deals with the Jewish experience before, during and after the Holocaust, taking us right up to today; here in NYC. (We ARE Garin—the new settlement.)"[58] In the sense he described in 1993, then, the phrase "new settlement" refers to the contemporary Jewish community in Manhattan and perhaps to downtown's Jewish cohort (the "we" of "We ARE Garin"). In 2010, however, he wrote that "The New Settlement" refers to the founding of the state of Israel.[59] Unlike the other movements, however, "The New Settlement" has no samples or other musical material that immediately suggest a programmatic depiction of either Israel or New York City.[60] It does, however, seem to gesture to a seemingly unrelated work: Ornette Coleman and Don Cherry's famous recording of "Lonely Woman" on *The Shape of Jazz to Come* (1959), a piece that Zorn, who included a cover of "Lonely Woman" on *Spy vs. Spy: The Music of Ornette Coleman* (1988), would undoubtedly have known by heart.[61]

Whether it is intentional or not, a correspondence between the two pieces is immediately evident, as "The New Settlement" opens with three taps on the cymbal, indexing the instantly recognizable opening to "Lonely Woman." (In "The New Settlement," unlike "Lonely Woman," the opening taps lead into a solo drum part, and not directly to the bass entrance.) In the section that follows in "The New Settlement," Cohen's nine-note descending pizzicato bass line shares a family resemblance with Charlie Haden's nine-note bass line in "Lonely Woman," for its D-minor tonality, its held C♯ (the longest note in each bass line), and its placement before the entrance of the melody instrument(s) and after the cymbal taps.[62] In articulating a descending tritone, Cohen's bass line also has some melodic kinship with the (loosely twelve-tone) melody of "Lonely Woman." Moreover, although Ribot's guitar solo with its ascending scalar fragments using the raised 4th degree might be heard as alluding to a D-*Mi Shebberakh* scale (or to the chromatic and modal scales common in heavy metal music), it also features stepwise patterns (D-D♯-E-F♯ and D-D♯-E-F-F♯-G-A) that recall the motives Cherry plays to accompany Coleman's solos after the statement of the theme. (It is worth recalling here that these note choices are almost certainly Zorn's, who exerts meticulous control over nearly every parameter of the solos his side-musicians play.) Finally, like the soloing melody instruments (alto saxophone and trumpet) in "Lonely Woman," the electric guitar of "New Settlement" drops out, and the movement ends in a coda with bass and drums. In the coda of "Lonely Woman," the bass reiterates a single pitch (D, the tonic) several times, and the drums use the same cymbal attacks that opened the movement, but with the three distinctive opening taps now sped up and set into a skittering ride pattern. The coda of "New Settlement" has a longer bass solo, followed by a drum solo that reiterates exactly the drum's opening numerological patterns rather than varying them. Again, the correspondence between the two pieces, though suggestive, is not exact.

Given the iconic nature of Coleman's recording, it is difficult to imagine that Zorn did not have it in mind when he wrote "New Settlement." If the correspondences are intentional, then the movement can be read as Zorn's programmatic allusion to downtown New York City and the Five Spot, the legendary downtown jazz club where Coleman

premiered the pioneering music that led to *The Shape of Jazz to Come,*
pointing to New York City and the downtown scene as the site of "The
New Settlement." If not, then the correlation simply stands as one of the
work's many prismatic refractions of meaning, and an example of the
principle of multiplex interpretation Zorn sees as central to his work.
The first conclusion would suggest that in addition to Zorn's written program, this piece rests on other programmatic allusions he has chosen not
to reveal, and that, once known, would reconstitute or even undermine
the hermeneutic frame he has proposed. The second conclusion suggests
that despite Zorn's attempts to guide listener's understandings of the
piece, in our sonically saturated cultural moment it is virtually impossible to sustain such a guide, as the jostling panoply of musical material
now available to any listener has rendered moot the notion of "interpretation." Alternatively, I would suggest that such contradictions reveal
something important about the milieu and the medium in which Zorn
and his colleagues work, and thus the nature of the music they developed
during the RJC moment. It is true that their idiom, and experimentalist
music in general, is difficult to "interpret"—and indeed it is sometimes
constructed to resist interpretation. On the other hand, it was the very
act of framing this kind of ontologically malleable work that allowed
downtown artists to develop contemporary Jewish music that spoke,
in its distinctive way, to the condition of contemporary Jews. And yet,
perhaps because it proved so tricky in *Kristallnacht* to marry concrete allusion with conceptual freedom, Zorn surrounded his next engagement
with Jewish music with a more elusive set of references.

## Masada, Melody, Melos

*Kristallnacht* augured Zorn's new compositional direction into writing
Jewishly inflected music, which he would pursue for the next two decades. But it differed from the work it preceded, particularly his mas-
sive Masada project. This difference inhered in *Kristallnacht*'s scope, its
variability in mood and sonic material, and its thematic organization,
and also, strikingly, in the retreat the Masada project represented from
*Kristallnacht*'s historical specificity. With Masada, Zorn also shifted gears
musically, composing tonally grounded melodies that, in most cases, un-

folded in a familiar and logical formal plan. He did not leave intensity behind, but he launched a sustained exploration into writing music that conveyed a sense of wholeness and integration rather than an unresolved confrontation among oppositional ideas. In *Kristallnacht* Zorn had created an immersive tone poem that mirrored an epic sweep of Jewish history, incorporating Jewish musical "characters" into musical settings shaped by both harsh precision and flights of interpretive fancy. Even as he transmuted those characters—klezmer melodies and archival cantorial singing—into an original book of modal melodies and interpolated them into his compositions for Masada, he did so in the context of a new narrative, one that was ostensibly still Jewishly inflected, but now historically ambiguous. In Masada Zorn scaffolded all this music with iconography that included Hebrew letters and ancient scrolls, Jewish symbols and images of ritual objects, desert landscapes, and quotations from Jewish thinkers. Ultimately, by building a particular lexicon of allusions—both musical and not—into the Masada world, Zorn proffered a vision of Judaism that aligned with his convictions about art as a project of unheralded heroism whose aim was to "heal the world."

Zorn leads several ensembles that go by variations on the name Masada, and he both leads and plays alto saxophone regularly in two of them. But the name refers first and foremost to a body of work and not a band. The Masada ensembles perform the Masada songbook, three sets of pieces (more than 600 in total) that debuted about a decade apart, based on the pitch content of two Ashkenazic synagogue modes. These are not fully composed works but sketches of a few lines, and they operate like jazz charts, supplying a melody and chords, often a bass line, and directives as to tempo, mood, and scale. In the first decade of the project, Zorn arranged the pieces for his own ensembles, writing both through-composed scores and arrangements that allowed for improvisation. With the advent of *Book II,* he began inviting other artists to write, perform, and record their own interpretations, which now make up about half of the forty-odd recordings on Tzadik devoted to the Masada songbook. In recent years Zorn has also staged several Masada "marathons," concerts with several hours of music devoted to the Masada songbook, in San Francisco (2009), Milan and Montreal (2010), and Manhattan (annually since 2010).[63]

**Figure 3.3.** Acoustic Masada quartet. In the foreground, Dave Douglas (left) and John Zorn; background, Joey Baron (left) and Greg Cohen. *Photo: Maarten Mooijman.*

In 1993, Zorn had convened an ensemble with alto saxophone (Zorn), trumpet (Dave Douglas), contrabass (Greg Cohen), and drums (Joey Baron) to record his sound track to the film *Thieves' Quartet*. Originally named after the film, the quartet, which blended post-bop lyricism with "out" playing and modal improvisations, became the vehicle for Zorn's first Masada book. (The ensemble is now usually referred to as Acoustic Masada. For a model, Zorn could look to a West Coast–based ensemble, the New Klezmer Trio, led by clarinetist Ben Goldberg, whom Zorn had invited to the 1992 Munich festival.) Acoustic Masada also became an occasion for Zorn to reconnect with jazz, an idiom that had so far not played a direct role in his work, although its relevance to his work was evident in such projects as *Spy vs. Spy*, his Ornette Coleman tribute hardcore band of the 1980s.

Acoustic Masada recorded ten studio albums and several live ones, numbered and titled using the Hebrew alphabet (1=Alef=א, 2=Bet=ב and so on), with varying styles, most with head-solo-head arrangements and occasional "events" pieces that, like Naked City, consist of conducted streams of disjunct musical moments and components of free improvisation.[64] Electric Masada (a jazz-rock fusion band) is another core ensemble, which has some sonic affinity with Naked City and Zorn's other hardcore bands, and which like Acoustic Masada incorporates occasional elements from Zorn's game pieces, along with extended jams and occasions for free—or semi-free—soloing. Zorn has also convened a shifting group of chamber-oriented ensembles to record his most accessible arrangements of pieces from the Masada songbook, developing a genre he has characterized as "instrumental easy listening."[65] His medium tempo arrangements for these ensembles—including the Masada String Trio, the Bar Kokhba Ensemble, and the Masada Sextet—involve occasional opportunities for the kinds of "out" soloing he incorporates into Acoustic and Electric Masada, but for the most part these are straightforward settings, and they gently mix in influences from straight-ahead jazz, classical music, Latin music, and surf guitar. But although Zorn's Masada ensembles have spanned a wide stylistic range, that range can be deceptive. As a group they all manifest a new intention to produce broadly appealing work. Thus, he explained, in the Masada book, "the harmonies are very simple, and it's a sound that I really love, it's very soulful and it's very accessible to a wide range of people."[66]

In addition to simple harmonies, the Masada project's "soulful" quality hinged on another musical parameter with far-reaching consequences: melody. Before 1993, when he formed Acoustic Masada, recalled Zorn, "the traditional concept of melody was not a large part of my creative language."[67] Given his early investment in the punishing aesthetic extremes of hardcore rock, this assertion might be read as sarcastic. Zorn, however, was in good company among his contemporaries in avoiding the "traditional concept of melody," not only aesthetically but also formally. In Zorn's overlapping creative circles—modernist and

**Figure 3.4.** John Zorn and the Masada String Trio. Left to right: Mark Feldman, Greg Cohen, Erik Friedlander, John Zorn. *Photo: Peter Gannushkin.*

experimental concert music, free improvisation, hardcore rock, and to some extent the jazz avant-garde—melody and lyricism were rare.

Melody (as conceived in the European classical music tradition, which has influenced jazz and popular music in this regard) does not imply lyricism alone. Instead, melody is one aspect of the system of tonal harmony, and melodic themes play a key part in the unfolding of "organic" formal plans based on that harmony. Thus, allied with Zorn's disinterest in melody was his interest in block forms, whose internal logic did not depend on harmonic development. His block-form compositions might include melodic snippets, but such snippets functioned as foils to melodic lyricism. That is, rather than beckoning listeners into a flight of lyrical expression, as a melody would do, the melodic snippets served

**Example 3.7.a.** *Mi Shebberakh* scale. Described in Idelsohn, *Jewish Music: Its Historical Development*, 184–85.

**Example 3.7.b.** *Ahavah Rabbah* scale. Described in Idelsohn, *Jewish Music*, 84–89.

to emphasize the non-tonal, montage-based quality of the compositions in which they appeared. In their attenuation, and in their presence within a quicksilver stream of stylistically disjunct moments, melodic snippets in Zorn's work telegraphed the absence of traditional melody (and thus the absence of a tonally based formal plan). In contrast, Zorn's first Masada ensemble, which in style and instrumentation recalls Ornette Coleman's 1960s quartet with Don Cherry, also reflected Zorn's admiration for Coleman as a melodist and his interest in writing a book of original melodies just as Coleman had.

As noted above, Zorn wrote the pieces in his Masada books using scales derived from two synagogue modes, *Mi Shebberakh* and *Ahavah Rabbah* (examples 3.7.a and 3.7.b).[68] Zorn's use of lyrical melodies in the Masada project points up the historical importance of melody, both to Jewish musical expression and to notions about the musical expression of Jewishness. Melody, of course, plays a key part in the Jewish liturgy, and melodies define a body of Jewish folk and holiday songs—forming the basis for the "table songs" that are traditionally part of holiday celebrations at home. Historically, writers have also gone so far as to describe melody as the expression of a Jewish soul, probably most famously by Sholem Aleichem in his novel *Stempenyu*, whose hero's violin "would moan, and wail, and weep over its sad fortune, as if it were a Jew. . . . It was as if every note found its way upwards from out of the deepest depths of the soul."[69] And, as this passage indicates, it is not only melody, but also the way the melody is inflected—through moans, wails, and weeping—that gives voice to a Jewish soul per se. In Masada, Zorn used scales derived from klezmer music (which were in turn based on synagogue modes) to develop lyrical melodies, but he did not include either klezmer's distinctive syntax or its dance rhythms.[70] Instead, he developed jazz, rock, free and Latin rhythmic contexts for his Masada ensembles and treated the modal scales just as ordinary scales would be treated in a modal jazz context, addressing them simply for their pitch material and melodic contour without adding any timbral inflections that would have connected them to liturgical singing or klezmer music. Zorn's decision to use the scales in this way stemmed from his original view of RJC as a platform for developing new Jewish music outside the klezmer idiom.[71] He did not share with some of his colleagues a deep skepticism about all aspects of the klezmer revival, but he did state that klezmer should not define new Jewish music: "Klezmer is not synonymous with Jewish music. Jewish music is really a lot broader than just klezmer." He explained that in Masada, he tried to "look toward the future [of Jewish music]" rather than looking to the past, which, in his view, klezmer represented.[72] Together with the new focus on melody and relatively straightforward harmonic language, in most of his arrangements of tunes from the Masada book Zorn moved away from the block forms that had dominated his earlier work and that played an important part in *Kristallnacht*. Three different arrangements of "Idalah-Abal," from *Masada Book I*, offer a useful opportunity to explore Zorn's method of fleshing out a chart's basic outline using a familiar formal plan drawn from jazz or popular music, tailoring the arrangement to suit each ensemble and exploiting the talents of each performer:

(1) *Masada 1 (א, Alef)* (Avant, 1993)
Acoustic Masada quartet: alto saxophone (Zorn), trumpet (Dave Douglas), contrabass (Greg Cohen), drums (Joey Baron).

(2) *The Circle Maker: Zevulun* (Tzadik, 1998)
Masada Sextet: violin (Mark Feldman), cello (Erik Friedlander), electric guitar (Marc Ribot), drums (Baron), percussion (Cyro Baptista), contrabass (Cohen).[73]

(3) *Electric Masada: At the Mountains of Madness* (Tzadik,
2005) <u>Electric Masada</u>: alto saxophone (Zorn), keyboards
(Jamie Saft), laptop and electronics (Ikue Mori), electric
guitar (Ribot), electric bass (Trevor Dunn), drums (Baron),
drums (Kenny Wolleson), percussion (Baptista).

**Example 3.8.** "Idalah-Abal" theme.

**Example 3.9.** "Idalah-Abal" theme in $\frac{4}{4}$ setting, with one measure each of $\frac{5}{4}$ and $\frac{6}{4}$ (eleven measures total). Transcription by the author.

"Idalah-Abal" has a forty-seven-beat A-minor theme, whose uneven note lengths and shifting downbeat emphasis create rhythmic interest and a sense of mutable meter.[74] (The melody, using an A harmonic minor scale, shares the pitch content of a D-*Mi Shebberakh* scale, but the tonal center is on A.) When played in a $\frac{4}{4}$ metric context, as it is in all three recorded versions, the theme falls into nine bars of $\frac{4}{4}$, one bar of $\frac{5}{4}$, and one bar of $\frac{6}{4}$, or eleven measures total (examples 3.8 and 3.9). The three arrangements follow a similar but not identical formal plan. All hew to the same basic harmonic framework and include solos that venture "out" harmonically, with the Sextet being the most diatonic and Electric Masada the most dissonant. Each arrangement has introductory material with an unmetered solo of variable length (I), followed by a statement of the theme, which is repeated with minor variations ($AA^1$), a series of solo choruses ($A^2$, $A^3$), a return to the theme (except in the case of Acoustic Masada) ($AA^1$), and a coda (C) sometimes followed by more closing material (D). The general template is thus: I ($AA^1$) $A^2A^3A^4$ ... ($AA^1$) C (D):

| | |
|---|---|
| Acoustic Masada (6:15): | I ($AA^1A^2$) $A^3$ $A^4$ $A^5$ C D |
| Masada Sextet (7:41): | I I2 ($AA^1$) $A^2A^3$ ($AA^1$) C |
| Electric Masada (6:33): | I ($AA^1$) $A^2A^3$ ......... ($AA^1$) C D |

Both Acoustic Masada and the Sextet are sparsely orchestrated, with a transparent texture and moderate dynamics. Aside from Zorn's occasional forays into avant-garde timbral territory in Acoustic Masada, both arrangements favor timbres that are smooth, warm, and round. In the Sextet, Ribot's characteristic ringing surf-guitar sound, often described as "reverb-drenched," adds another rich timbral presence. (The quiet, ghostly presence of high, rapid, and dissonant violin arpeggios recalls a similar sound from *Kristallnacht:* Ribot's quick plucking of the high-register guitar strings in "Never Again" and a bowed pitch in "Idalah-Abal" recall the swooping glissandi of "Embers.") In both versions, Cohen's Latin-inflected, walking, and two-beat bass patterns create a gently syncopated groove. The percussion instruments—primarily tom-toms, splash cymbal, and gongs—are played with mallets and mainly add color and punctuation, not forward propulsion or rhythmic density. In Acoustic Masada, Zorn and Douglas take several solo choruses, in which Douglas sometimes plays the theme or a ground bass under Zorn's solo. In other choruses they solo simultaneously, doing the kind of modal exploration to which Zorn refers above, at times incorporating, as he suggests, a blues influence.[75]

In contrast to the Acoustic Masada and Sextet tracks, the Electric Masada version of "Idalah-Abal" is a wall of sound, with the whole band playing at high volume throughout.[76] With four electric instruments—electric guitar, bass, keyboards and laptop/electronics—plus two drum

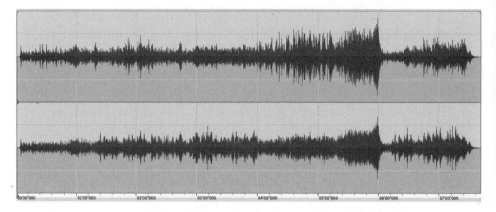

**Figure 3.5.a.** "Idalah-Abal" waveform, Masada Sextet, on *The Circle Maker: Zevulun* (Tzadik, 1998). The vertical axis is amplitude; the horizontal axis is time.

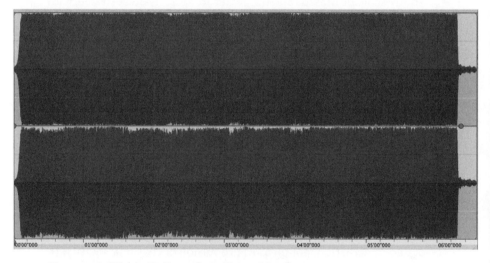

**Figure 3.5.b.** "Idalah-Abal" waveform, Electric Masada, on *At the Mountains of Madness* (Tzadik, 2005).

sets, percussion instruments, and an alto saxophone, Electric Masada offers a great deal of potential range in timbre, texture, and amplitude—but unlike the other two versions of the piece, this one does not exploit subtle timbral shadings or expressive dynamic shifts. As the waveform images illustrate (figures 3.5.a and 3.5.b), in the Electric Masada version noise is a constant presence, a result of the level of instrumental activity, the electric instruments, and an unremitting level of feedback and distortion. This quality, which is of course immediately evident when listening but difficult to represent in transcription, comes across in a comparison of the waveforms of Electric Masada versus that of the Sextet.[77]

In the Electric Masada version, timbres are often guttural, and the high, squealing saxophone improvises not a lyrical line but an a-melodic sheet of sound. In contrast to the Sextet version, here Ribot's guitar sound is distorted, heavy, and rough. There is also a great deal of rhythmic activity in the electric bass and drum set, instruments that together create a busy groove whose rhythmic feel varies between hard rock (mixed quarter, eighth, and sixteenth notes) and thrash (mostly sixteenth notes). Finally, the melodic theme is iterated by the guitar in its low register, giving it a darker, heavier character than it had when articulated in the previous examples. Developing over several choruses during Electric Masada's extended jam, the instrumental solos are often dissonant and dense enough to have a non-tonal quality. Indeed, because of the dense texture, distortion, and number of instruments, and the ubiquitous presence of unpitched sound and instruments playing in extreme registers (high squealing saxophone, drum set with plentiful cymbal attacks, gongs, shaken percussion, low electric bass, keyboard and electronics effects, ghosted pitches in guitar, distortion), it is difficult to discern all the separate instrumental parts in the fabric of the Electric Masada track. However, although the ubiquitous presence of noise and distortion destabilizes the tonal landscape, the theme serves as a stable point of reference, and the rhythm section instruments also contribute to the sense of stability by playing ostinati over an A-minor pedal point throughout, with unison arrivals on the tonic pitch. As these three sketches of "Idalah Abal" indicate, despite stylistic variations among his Masada ensembles, by embracing a relatively conventional musical idiom—and by basing his Masada oeuvre on singable melodies—Zorn set aside most of the overwhelming qualities of his previous work, and he balanced an interest in catharsis with an exploration of relaxation and simplicity. Even amidst the sonic overload of Electric Masada, he offers listeners a clearly defined melody and a series of simple harmonies, and thus a way to relate. In a striking departure from his work up to and including *Kristallnacht,* Zorn clothed his Masada recordings in "pretty" packaging, and he described the project as "beautiful and positive" and thus, perhaps not coincidentally, unlikely to provoke controversy.[78]

### Doubly Alienated, Doubly Chosen: The Artist, the Jew, and the Mystic

In his retrospective notes to *Masada: Sanhedrin* (2005), Zorn discusses the music and the experience of playing with Acoustic Masada in terms of healthiness (using the terms "organic," "natural," and "fresh"), magic (chemistry, telepathy, flow), positive emotions (love, passion, sensitivity), and the indescribable (amazing, inspiring, perfect). These descriptive terms are a good illustration of the difference, which could not be more striking, between *Kristallnacht's* disturbing visual imagery and Masada's misty photographs and gorgeous presentation.

Each of the first ten Masada releases (on Avant, the record label Zorn ran before starting Tzadik) included an image of rocky desert hills (presumably the Judean Desert, where the ruins of the Masada fortress are located) and scraps from the Dead Sea Scrolls, neither of which are identified.[79] Tzadik's RJC series, on which Zorn re-released these recordings, exchanges these images for a similar kind of corporate identity kit—a font, signature color palette, and other design elements that distinguish a product line or brand. Although the Tzadik discs do not include Avant's sepia-toned desert scenes, the inserts have a color signature of gold, black, red, and white, and they include a prominent Star of David as well as other images that allude to Judaism, such as ornamental crowns for Torah scrolls and depictions of the hand sign associated with Cohanim, the Jewish priestly caste. Finally, in the inserts Zorn includes quotations by Jewish thinkers, including Kabbalah scholar Gershom Scholem, Ahad Ha'am—"the father of cultural Zionism"—and, as I discuss below, Rabbi Arthur Hertzberg.[80] In sum, and in stark contrast to *Kristallnacht,* the unifying concept to which all Masada's elements contribute is that of a Jewishly inflected dream world. It is a world shot through with references to strength, integrity, endurance, and ancient things, and although it touches on the ideas of important Jewish thinkers and alludes to ideological positions, it does so without staking a definite claim, instead floating free of too much historical or political detail. Thus, whereas in *Kristallnacht* Zorn grounded his narrative of Jewish history in a violent event of terrible concreteness, here Jewishness functions less as a historical legacy to be reckoned with, and more as the entrée into an all-encompassing state of mind that transcends historical particularities.

Although Masada's concatenation of signs does represent a historically unmoored world, a consistent underlying narrative also unifies these signs. In order to fully understand that narrative, we must look outside the Jewish frame. Because Masada's iconography is Jewishly if not historically specific, it can be difficult to see it for what it is: a narrative about Judaism embedded in a narrative about art. However, a close consideration of Zorn's liner notes and other writings makes it clear that a set of convictions about artists as outsiders and seers has determined Zorn's idiosyncratic depiction of Judaism in the Masada project.

In 2010 Zorn established the Obsessions Collective, an arts advocacy project for which he articulated a personal credo about art and laid out his views about the role of the artist in society. This credo overlaps strikingly with his textual and iconographic engagement with Judaism in Masada. The organization is devoted to unrecognized visual artists, whom Zorn describes in terms that, when considered in tandem with the Masada material, sound remarkably familiar. These artists, whom he calls "special individuals," have been specially chosen to do the work they do. Zorn ascribes to them a primary place in the cosmological order, asserting that "since the beginning of time . . . [these individuals] have been compelled to create objects that seemingly have no function or purpose." Moreover, it is often a spiritual force that drives them to create, whether they are "channeling the spirits, communicating with higher forces, wrestling with demons, defining themselves, appeasing the Gods or working through their own inner thoughts and passions." These artists have also singled themselves out in order to remain faithful to their ideals rather than being motivated by money: "Creation has been their only motivation, the work their only reward." Indeed, they have removed themselves from the capitalist process of turning art into commerce. Thus, they are "honest, passionate, imaginative and technically proficient, [and] they work independent of the established art scene and without support or assistance from patrons, grants or commercial galleries." Zorn counts himself in their number, being devoted to supporting artists on the margins and to creating alternatives to the art market: "Founded and curated by New York composer John Zorn . . . the Obsessions Collective is a non-profit alternative to the commercial Art scene. . . . 100% of the income derived from all sales go directly to the artists." Finally, he reveals that those who buy the artwork will be contributing to a higher cause, because the project is founded upon spiritual principles: "More than anything else, the Obsessions Collective believes that Art can heal the world."[81] The elements that figure so strongly into Zorn's figure of the Artist—the chosen-ness, the unheralded good deeds, the spiritual and ethical motivation, and the marginalization, by choice and by society—also shape his conception of Jews and Judaism as he presents them through the Masada project.

Perhaps most salient in this regard is Zorn's view that the people who catalyze the alchemical process of turning detritus into art belong to a chosen class and are called upon by a greater power to perform this task for the social good. Thus, when asked in 2000, "How do you see your own place in the scheme of things?" he replied:

> I look out at the world and I see chaos. And that's kind of the formula for being an outsider. You don't want to be an outsider, you want to belong and you're burdened with these human frailties. You . . . want to˙be understood even though you're doing something that's a little difficult; you want your work to be appreciated; you want to be loved. We're burdened with this. But . . . [artists are] creating something that is a little bit scary to most people. It challenges their view of the world. Most people think the world is a perfectly ordered place and they love it. The outsider looks at that and goes, 'Man, this is chaos. This makes no sense at all.' And then, they try to tell the truth. And they're compelled to tell the truth. They can't help but tell the truth by some inner sense of responsibility.[82]

Over the years Zorn has been forthcoming about his views about art's social and spiritual purpose: artists are outsiders and truth-tellers, mystics and seers, charged with a spiritual mission to heal the world. His presentation of the Masada recordings and the Radical Jewish Culture series on Tzadik illuminates the way he allies a notion about the chosen-ness of artists with that of Jewish chosen-ness. It would seem that deriving the traits of the Jew from those of the artist has led him to privilege and sometimes romanticize particular aspects of Judaism and

Jewish history, including the historical role of Jews as "abject others" who are aliens in a hostile society and are subject to its whims.[83] With the Masada project, he has also drawn a parallel between his own artistic mission and a Jewish determination to stand down one's oppressors or die trying. And, as indicated by the name he chose for his record label, Tzadik, he has been drawn to a Jewish ideal of righteousness and of living according to a credo based on doing good deeds that are likely to go unrecognized. Finally, Zorn takes a Romantic view about artists as suffering outsiders, and art—underground art in particular—as a pursuit with ethical and spiritual dimensions. In full agreement with the statement of outsider-ness famously articulated by modernist poet Arthur Rimbaud—"Je est un autre" (I is an other)—as an artist Zorn frames himself as belonging to a class apart, by calling, by choice, and because of social bias. His statements about Jews and Jewish history are likewise peppered with references to Jews as outsiders. For example, in the 1993 RJC Festival at the Knitting Factory, Zorn made a striking statement, describing Jews in the United States as being "alien" to their surrounding society and as having uniquely Jewish "native identities." In a discussion of the genesis of the RJC idea, he wrote, "The ability to live peacefully and respectfully in a relatively alien, and sometime hostile culture does not presuppose the loss or denial of one's native identity. In fact it can bring it into sharper focus. What can be more Jewish than the impassioned outcry of the alienated outsider?" Zorn's depiction of American Jews as alienated outsiders who are not "native" to the United States was not only polemical in its own right, but it also formed a dramatic contrast to the way his colleagues describe American pluralism and diversity as central shaping forces for their own identities and Jewish values.[84] Indeed, even if Zorn was exaggerating to make a point, such a notion is an odd fit with his lifelong immersion in and commitment to American popular and vernacular musics. But here, again, his narrative about art was working to shape his statements about Jews.

On this front, one of the most telling quotations Zorn has included in his Masada liner notes is by Conservative rabbi, activist, and civil rights champion Arthur Hertzberg: "Judaism is the faith of those who are dissatisfied with the society around them and have a critical sense of the hollowness of worldly success—and only through such people can

Judaism survive, or have reason for survival."[85] The statement is notable
not only for what it expresses, but for what it does not. Hertzberg was
renowned for his activism in social and political causes, but Zorn did not
quote him in order to frame Judaism as a mandate for undertaking ethical actions that engage with wider social and political causes. Instead,
he chose a quotation that emphasizes Judaism as a faith to which adherents are bound not by deeds, but by a steadfast belief in their innermost
convictions. This quotation thus encapsulates a particular view of Judaism that is similar to Zorn's view about art. Jews, like artists, are (1) at
odds with wider social mores and values ("dissatisfied with the society
around them"), (2) spiritual seekers put off by material rewards ("have
a critical sense of the hollowness of worldly success"), and (3) charged
with a higher responsibility for upholding the special values of their faith
("only through such people can Judaism survive"). This quotation, in
other words, describes Judaism in terms that are nearly identical to the
way Zorn frames the practice of making art. Both figures, the artist and
the Jew, are informed by a notion of chosen-ness, and both are misunder-
stood social outcasts who are, in the words of anthropologist Jonathan
Boyarin, "solitary hero[es] whose intentions are carried out despite the
world's impingement."[86] Zorn, however, inverts the normative framework in which the Jews are God's original chosen people. As he outlines
in his credo for the Obsessions Collective, artists are the chosen ones.
In the Masada project, he frames Jewish history and Judaism as morally
and spiritually compelling insofar as they parallel the chosen-ness of the
artist.

This is not to say Zorn lacks a credo for putting his principles about
art into action. Indeed, it could be argued that Zorn has devoted himself to art not only as a vocation but also as an engaged kind of faith.
After moving downtown in the 1970s he played a crucial role in cultivating an emerging creative community, and he has been unstinting
in advocating for experimental music ever since. In addition to curat-
ing the Avant imprint and running Tzadik, in 2005 Zorn established a
not-for-profit venue, the Stone, which has been steadfast in maintaining
experimental music as a presence in the East Village even as downtown's
creative community has dissipated.[87] He supports both the Stone and
Tzadik financially as well as through his own labor. He has also edited

and published five volumes of essay collections, called *Arcana,* devoted to publishing original writing by fellow artists, and he regularly performs in and organizes benefit concerts for social and political causes.[88] Not surprisingly, Zorn focuses his ambition to "heal the world" through the lens of art. Thus, although his framing of the mutual outsider-ness of artist and Jew has suggestive resonances with similar conceptions by Jewish thinkers—for example, Hannah Arendt's influential formulation of the Jew as "self-conscious pariah"—the correspondence is not complete. Arendt's notion, for its part, was based on activating one's outsider status as a Jew into a wider civic and political engagement that would lead to Jewish (and human) emancipation. Zorn might have similarly ambitious goals for art, and indeed for Jews and the human race. However, he does not use the Masada project to contribute substantially to a critical discourse that engages social or political topics, such as Jewish identity and nationhood, or that link in direct and ideological ways to his images and quoted material.[89] Instead, Zorn's presentation of Masada resonates with his long-held convictions about the artist as an outsider, social outcast, and visionary. These convictions align with his framing of Jews as alienated from the rest of society, as a special class of people who are bound by inner ideals and not moved by worldly rewards, as a righteous group whose contributions go unacknowledged, and as proud defenders of their faith against incursion and oppression. Even as Zorn developed his Jewishly identified Masada project, he was also shaping it in ways that were congruent with his interest in art's more generic spiritual and mystical dimensions. Jewish allusions run through Masada's music and its packaging, but Zorn's creative vision for Masada seems to have been most deeply informed by his interest in art's ecumenical mystical properties.

Zorn's interest in mysticism had been sporadically evident throughout his earlier oeuvre, but it informs Masada in a thoroughgoing way. Mysticism had played a part in his compositional process since at least the 1970s, during performances he staged at his apartment in which he explored the idea of "music without sound." In these performances he used mystical diagrams such as the grid and the square to create ordered sequences of objects, to which he applied permutation processes derived from serialism. When he used gematria to derive some of *Kristallnacht's*

**Figure 3.6.** John Zorn, with "Abracadabra" in Hebrew lettering on T-shirt. 1998. *Photo: Daniel Sheehan.*

rhythmic sequences, then, Zorn was drawing on a longstanding interest in marrying compositional processes with mystical systems. But, more so than in the work that preceded it, this coupling of mysticism with music runs through the Masada project, helping to determine Masada's sonic qualities. Those qualities seem designed, individually and en masse, to gesture toward a contact with the ineffable.

Zorn has described his engagement with mysticism in spiritual terms, as having to do with an unseen power that guides the artist's hand, and this imbues his framing of the Masada project through the notion of "Masada magic." He has recently related, for example, the process of writing a score that "grew to about sixty-one musical moments scattered across the sheets in semi-chronological order, approaching the random. Hearing these fragments in the sequence they appeared on the page was a revelatory experience. . . . Magically the piece had been through-composed and written in sequence from beginning to end on some kind of deep, intuitive level."[90] In conjunction with the idea of Masada as having magical properties, perhaps through its connection with a higher power, one can understand the Masada project as having been shaped by Zorn's intent to write formally unified, thematically legible music to accompany a state that transcended reality. Like the ecstatic or anguished ruptures of his previous work, this state transgressed normative physical boundaries, but in a less confrontational way.[91] Instead, the hundreds of Masada melodies, arrangements, recordings, and marathon performances make up a sonic world that Zorn linked through titles and iconography to an idealized Jewish realm. Ultimately, the music was designed to end up in a place of "magic"—non-denominational, non-political, and ahistorical.

Zorn's inscription on the recording of Acoustic Masada's first recorded live performance speaks to this point:

> a diamond in the rough . . . thieve's [sic] quartet . . . eye of the peacock . . . loose heads [ . . . ] running over charts during the break . . . the center of the tone . . . trouble in paradise . . . masada magic.[92]

One can glean a few concrete references from this cryptic stream of snippets: the *Thieves' Quartet* was the film for which Zorn originally created the ensemble that was renamed Acoustic Masada, and *Trouble in Paradise* (1932) is an Ernst Lubitsch comedy. However, it seems clear that Zorn's aim in writing this passage was not transparency or precision, but rather to gesture poetically toward a flow of experiences culminating in the final snippet, "masada magic." The notion of "Masada magic" also informs a passage in which Zorn ascribes to a mystical power the process of composing the *Masada Book II*:

> In one hour I'd have like ten tunes. And after ten tunes you begin to get exhila-
> rated.... I'm telling you, it's something very unusual. After like six, seven tunes
> you start laughing like man this is getting crazy, let's try another key. And you try
> another one and after about ten tunes, then it's getting scary. Then you realize that
> you are not alone. You can't do something like that alone. That there's something
> else clearly ... tapping into that sensibility that maybe is so ineffable and so inexpli-
> cable that to talk about it would be a big mistake, so let's take another question.[93]

Although these descriptions rest on an indescribable experience, Masada's scaffolding—the photographs of Jewish ritual objects and the ruined fortress, the Star of David motif, and Zorn's references to historical figures—made manifest this quality of magic and transcendence. Taken singly, each of these images might give a sense that the project was historically grounded, but as the sum of its parts the Masada world was instead a historically unmoored, abstracted Jewish space. It is a world that presents audiences with the possibility of escaping the most contentious political and ideological issues in American Jewish life, not engaging them. As a concept, "Masada" has political and historical substance, but Zorn constructs the Masada world as a place where substance slips away, replaced by magic. A critical reading of the Masada world yields an idiosyncratic interpretation of Jewishness, which overlaps with Zorn's philosophy about art and its mystical powers.

If Zorn frames Masada's compositional process as tapping mystically into a higher power, "Masada magic" also has a musical component with an intriguing historical genesis. Zorn's references to magic, and to transcending the physical plane, link to a body of work he has cited as "a primary influence on the Masada songbooks": the piano music of G. I. Gurdjieff (1866–1949). Not only does this music share family resemblances with the Masada oeuvre, but on a large scale, in its design and expressive function, Masada also shares intriguing points of congruence with Gurdjieff's modally inflected music, which he shaped in accordance with the mystical ambitions he held for his art. An exploration of these works' common points suggests that Zorn shaped his Jewishly inflected Masada project in accordance with a similar creative vision. Gurdjieff, the charismatic Armenian-born philosopher, collaborated with Ukrainian-born composer Thomas de Hartmann in writing a large body of chorale-like piano music, which he used in developing his methods of awakening one's higher consciousness through music and movement.[94] Many musicians describe themselves as spiritual seekers, but, having achieved a guru-like stature among his disciples, Gurdjieff is unusual in having developed a multi-faceted system for reaching spiritual enlightenment through a series of proscribed movements set to a body of original music that was tailored for this purpose. This body of work offers a revealing glimpse into Zorn's musical and mystical conception for the Masada project.

As a contemporary of Bartók, Kodály, and other European folk song collectors, but not a trained composer or ethnographer, Gurdjieff had traveled throughout western and central Asia and East Africa, Tibet, and Siberia learning local ritual practices and, accompanied by Hartmann, transcribing melodies. He also drew on the ritual movement of Turkish Sufi dervish orders to develop a series of choreographed "gymnastics" that were meant to lead his coterie of followers to a higher plane of consciousness. Participants performed these movements in conjunction with the piano pieces he and Hartmann wrote, which were based on their collection of folk melodies. The musical pieces were collected in large-scale suites, with, for example, both *Seekers of the Truth* and *Movements* made up of nineteen brief pieces. In keeping with that era's conventional practice among composers when setting folk melodies to a classical idiom, Hartmann drained most of the culturally specific detail from their collected melodies by transcribing them into standard European notation and harmonizing them for piano, a tempered instrument that could not replicate the timbral or microtonal nuances of the originals.[95] (This discrepancy is particularly evident in the suite *Songs and Rhythms from Asia,* whose modal melodies are named for their places of origin.) With their majestic tempi, ample use of the harmonic and natural minor modes, tremolo figures, the occasional pedal point (e.g., *Seekers of the Truth,* Part 2), and a lack of conventional harmonic development in spite of the hymn-like progressions and cadences (e.g., *Seekers of the Truth*, Part 5), the Gurdjieff/Hartmann piano pieces created a grand yet accessible, hypnotic, and culturally deracinated musical environment for disciples' meditations and movements.[96] Hundreds of these pieces would be played successively to accompany disciples' four- to five-hour daily movement sessions and their even longer performances.[97] Gurdjieff had developed these sessions according to the precept that "the function of all art . . . was not the invocation of aesthetic beauty or the imitation of surface reality, but rather the initiation of the recipient into a completely different plane of understanding . . . to awaken him into experiencing a cosmic sense of place and time, to permanently shatter and enlarge his socially delimited sense of personality."[98]

In both conception and scope there are striking similarities between Gurdjieff's oeuvre and the Masada project it inspired. First, as with the non-Western modes and melodies of the Gurdjieff/Hartmann music, in Masada, klezmer scales derived from synagogue modes anchor the music, but Zorn does not attempt to simulate the inflections of the idiom from which they are drawn. There are virtually no klezmer-inspired micromoves, none of the corresponding dance rhythms, and no emulation of the cantorial singing that Zorn deployed to such dramatic effect in *Kristallnacht*. Instead, he presents these modes in stylistic contexts— post-bop, jazz-rock fusion, string trios—more familiar to a general audience of American and European listeners. Second, although the Masada project is far more varied than the Gurdjieff/Hartmann music, both oeuvres couch their mode-based melodies in arrangements that are, for the most part, harmonically straightforward and broadly appealing. Along with Zorn's shift toward melodic lyricism in Masada, after his innovative deployment of block forms that typified his earlier work and that he continued to use in other contexts, this nearly wholesale shift to head-solo-head forms was notable. Third, both oeuvres are made up of a mammoth collection of short pieces, each of which functions as an expression of the larger idea, which is itself articulated through titles and scaffolding. In Gurdjieff's case, his teachings and long lectures, the piece and suite titles, and the context in which they were performed all contributed to the work's unifying concept, that is, shattering individual subjectivity and transcending the ordinary "plane of understanding." Moreover, along with the accompanying physical movements, the music's qualities were designed to make participants reach this aim. For disciples, the culturally unspecific but vaguely Eastern melodic quality of the pieces, their otherwise familiar and accessible style, and their harmonic stasis all contributed to hypnotic effect, even as groups of adherents moved silently and in strictly proscribed ways to the accompaniment of perhaps a hundred such pieces played successively over several hours.

In not only its musical qualities, but also its scale and its unified iconography, Masada has an interesting correspondence to the Gurdjieff/Hartmann music. Indeed, Zorn frames his music in ways that support and articulate the purpose of creating a path to transcendent experience. In both sets of pieces, an integral part of the work's character includes the monumentalism of the oeuvre, especially, for Zorn, at the Masada Marathons. Even by comparison to other parts of Zorn's prodigious compositional output, Masada stands out for its scope. The multi-faceted Masada project includes a book of several hundred pieces, multiple ensembles, more than forty recordings, and many years of touring regularly with Acoustic and Electric Masada—whose performances Zorn numbers in the thousands—as well as recordings by other musicians, the Masada marathons, the iconography of the packaging, and the quoted texts of the liner notes. By virtue both of its sheer size and its thematic unity, Masada functions as a world unto itself, and it differs markedly from Zorn's previous oeuvre both for its musical qualities and in regard to the way he has framed the work. When we take Masada in all its facets, we can discern an interplay between its musical qualities—lyricism, modal inflection, harmonic simplicity, stylistic accessibility—and its extra-musical ones—scale, imagery, and text. All this helps us make sense of a notion of Jewishness that is at once underlain by Zorn's romantic artistic credo and embedded in his vision of art as a means of apprehending the ineffable.

Even though the Masada world was ostensibly a Jewish one, through both iconography and sound, Zorn shaped it in a way that resonated with his ideas about music's ecumenical mystical possibilities. Many of his recent recordings reflect this interest, both in regard to a focus on magic and mysticism, and in light of the approach he takes in framing and titling them. Indeed, the recent Electric Masada release from which this book's example of "Idalah-Abal" is drawn is encased in images from Tibetan scrolls and paintings, with the South Asian Buddhist god Mahakala pictured on the front and a Tibetan mandala hexagram, which looks like a Star of David, on the back. Ultimately, through Masada, the artist and the Jew—who had been shaped by the artist's image—converged into a single, ineffable, and culturally indeterminate figure: the mystic. In retrospect, Masada reveals itself as leading toward a more ineffable, less culturally specific place than the Jewishly particular one that Zorn's titles and iconography would suggest—and Zorn's Jewish oeuvre, which had taken shape through a hyper-real intensity, ultimately attained an otherworldly remove.

# FOUR

## Rethinking Identity

### *G-d Is My Co-Pilot's Queer Dada Judaism*

IN 1994, JOURNALIST ROEE ROSEN PUBLISHED AN ARTICLE IN the Jewish community newspaper the *Forward,* in which he shared his impressions of a musical performance he had heard at the Knitting Factory:

> On the stage of a downtown Manhattan club, G-d Is My Co-Pilot, an aggressive, rough-edged hardcore band, is producing its trademark sound, a spasmodic noise whirlwind supported by two drummers. Soloist Sharon Topper starts off with a series of short, sexually suggestive songs like "Smooch" and "I'm in Love With a Girl." Then she segues into "Ha-Tikvah," Seder favorites like "Khad Gad Yo" and even a few Hebrew musical relics of socialist Zionism.... Ms. Topper descends the stage to offer the crowd Halvah bars and other Lower East Side delights—along with a pamphlet titled "Haggadah of G-d Is My Co-Pilot," a hybrid of Xerox art, personal reflections on gay sexuality and ruminations on things Jewish.[1]

The band God Is My Co-Pilot, or GodCo, was led by a married couple, music director and guitarist Craig Flanagin and vocalist Sharon Topper. Soon after forming in New York City in 1990, GodCo became a regular presence at the Knitting Factory and other downtown venues, and the band also recorded prolifically, releasing more than thirty recordings (including seven-inch vinyl records, compact discs, and cassette tapes) in six years. Melding avant-garde techniques with punk rock's visceral appeal, GodCo was a central player on downtown's No Wave scene, where the band stood out both for its innovative musical arrangements and for the subject matter it addressed in its original songs. Building upon punk rock for its aesthetic stance, its humor, and its mode of social critique, GodCo drew a novel connection between two bodies of music: songs celebrating queer sexuality and international folk songs. When Flanagin and Topper turned their attention to Jewish music during the RJC moment, they blended the band's potent anti-establishment ethos with an interest in translation, confusion, and liminal cultural spaces, thereby—through their music as well as their commentary on it—generating a working theory of RJC that was uniquely their own. GodCo was not at the 1992 Munich festival, but the band played at the RJC festival that was held soon after in New York City, taking its place among RJC's core interlocutors. In contrast to John Zorn, who created sweeping narratives for Jewish music—and, after *Kristallnacht,* situated it in an otherworldly zone—Topper and Flanagin embedded their Jewishly identified work in a decidedly un-idealized, even confessional context. They were particularly interested in dramatizing the imperfect transmission of Jewish songs from one generation to the next, turning their attention to the resultant flaws and lacunae, an interest that comes through in their song arrangements and performance style. To the same end, Topper developed two elaborate hand-drawn booklets that she distributed to her audiences at two RJC festivals, and in which she candidly presented the checkered genealogy by which the band had incorporated a collection of Jewish songs into their repertoire.

As a No Wave band, GodCo was well positioned to present Jewish music in a way that was both stylistically daring and critically acute. As the antithesis to the pop-friendly genre that the recording industry had taken up as rock's "New Wave," No Wave—so named by critics—had both of these qualities embedded in its DNA. Combining a visceral sonic character, raucous energy, and often a pointed social critique, No Wave was shaped by an identification with downtown Manhattan's underground (punk) rock scene of the 1970s, as well as a resistance to

the branch of underground rock that gained the most commercial success. Although early punk bands and artists—including Richard Hell,
the Ramones, Television, and the Patti Smith band—ultimately had a
major impact on American popular music, in the short term only the
bands more amenable to grooming for the pop world—for example,
Blondie and Talking Heads—met with wide exposure. All these artists
had formed New York's underground rock scene together, but stylistic
differences and uneven industry success among bands eventually led
punk's most adamant champions to view New Wave as a denatured version of the original. Looking askance at New Wave, then, in the 1980s No
Wave musicians took up the legacy of the early punk rockers, who were
musicians and poets who had themselves looked back to an earlier era in
rock to reclaim something they thought the genre had lost.[2] These performers took the highly produced and elaborately orchestrated character
of 1970s arena rock as a symptom of the pernicious effects visited upon
that genre, and upon art in general, by American mainstream tastes and
corporate values. Instead, they emulated the raw energy of early rock—
including 1950s rock 'n' roll and 1960s garage rock—and channeled its
transgressive affect. Punk rock, then, had embedded a social critique
in an aesthetic one, and punk's new incarnation, No Wave, served as a
prime venue for the kind of pointed musical commentary that flourished
on the 1980s downtown scene.[3]

Some No Wave bands attempted to render their work wholly unassimilable into pop music's aesthetic economy—a goal made evident by
lead singers whose vocal production was defiantly unschooled, unsupported, and unmelodic. This cohort—including the Theoretical Girls,
Mars, and the Contortions—were also anchored by the anti-heroic electric guitar style known as "skronk." (This method of attack-as-technique,
which was invented by amateur guitarist Arto Lindsay in the band DNA,
privileged the noise element already present in punk rock guitar soloing.)
These bands favored an abundance of angular dissonances, fractured and
attenuated forms, and barely functional harmony. No Wave musicians
also developed punk in new directions by drawing on the idiom of experimentalist composition/improvisation that had sprung up downtown after punk's heyday. Some No Wave bands—GodCo prominent
among them—also reflected the influence of the jazz avant-garde and the

1960s–70s art-rock underground. With its reach into noise experiments, exploded syntax, and free improvisation, No Wave seems to have been crafted as a catalyst for what sociologist Bernice Martin, drawing on Adorno's theories of music and noise, has called "'moments of subjectivity' which are turned atavistic because they cannot be accommodated by capitalism."[4] That is, in courting unintelligibility, foregrounding harsh timbres and herky-jerky song forms, and often adopting a flat emotional affect, No Wave artists upped the ante on their punk predecessors by embracing an outsider perspective that was valued on the downtown scene, but that had little value in popular music's wider marketplace.

GodCo was at the creative forefront of New York's No Wave scene, notable for its unique affect, creative songwriting, and imbrication with experimentalist musical language. With Topper on vocals and Flanagin on guitar, the band also included electric bass (Alex Klein), drum set (Michael Evans and Siobhan Duffy or Christine Bard), and sometimes cello (Fred Lonberg-Holm) or violin (Samara Lubelski). The presence of classical string instruments was unusual for a punk rock band, as was GodCo's interest in subtle timbral color. To increase its range of timbres and textures, the band not only used two drum sets, but also brought in guest artists on a variety of instruments, including sampling keyboard, Australian didgeridoo, North Indian tabla drum, harp, and saxophone. GodCo sometimes used the full-throttle onslaught preferred by other downtown thrash and noise bands, but at other times its instrumentalists improvised skittering exchanges, judiciously employed electronic distortion and timbral extremes, quick shifts of texture, and fleeting dissonances.[5] Many of GodCo's "songs" were instrumentals, and the band crossed over decisively into the world of contemporary improvisation when it staged a concert using Zorn's Cobra system in the early 1990s; GodCo also collaborated, in performances and on recordings, with many of the scene's composer/improvisers, including pianist Anthony Coleman, saxophonist Roy Nathanson, and guitarists Marc Ribot and Elliott Sharp. The band was also jubilant and witty, projecting an affect that was often described as "Dada punk," both for its deconstructive, deceptively unsophisticated, anti-pop aesthetic and for its sly inversion of punk rock's semiotic codes.

**Figure 4.1.** Sharon Topper and Craig Flanagin. 2007. *Photo: Laurent Baillet.*

Just as No Wave artists took punk rock in new stylistic directions, the genre also served as terrain for tweaking notions of punk rock authenticity. Indeed, on a scene where insider status was paramount, signaled by style as well as music, No Wave could critique punk rock from within, just as punk rock had critiqued the rock mainstream, via mutually intelligible syntactic and semiotic systems. Of particular interest to some No Wave musicians was the way punk, despite a transgressive social stance, could also traffic in surprisingly limited codes of race and gender. In regard to race, punk was (and remains) ripe for critique, as it was not only a musical genre but also a complex of style traits that were coded as "white"; punk's semiotics of style were determined both by early (white) punk rockers—torn clothing, leather jackets, and short, spiky hair—and, in a less obvious way, by the absence of black signifiers. And yet, whereas punk style recalled (white) "greaser" icons from the 1950s—Marlon Brando, James Dean—the garage rock that punk emulated had been based on African American music, in particular the rough eloquence of electric blues and proto-rock.[6] As Ribot recalled about downtown guitarist Robert Quine, "In terms of punk-rock guitar soloing, he could definitely be called the inventor. . . . [But] what many people don't know is that . . . [he] was going and buying records in working-class black neighborhoods in the late fifties and the early sixties. . . . Quine recorded [a cassette] for me. . . . [on which Ike Turner] does a guitar solo on the song 'Matchbox'. . . from 1954 or 1955. . . . [He] takes this completely insane solo on it, which is basically as punk as anything Robert ever played. He put this solo on there and then stopped the tape and recorded the solo three times in case I missed it! This kind of insane soloing is as old as rock and roll."[7] As Ribot is indicating here, punk rock guitar not only had a precursor in black music, but was also closely enmeshed in it. In ways that were generally not addressed through band names, song texts, packaging, or self-presentation, then, punk rock participated in the long American tradition of "love and theft"—that is, the admiration with which white musicians emulated African American music, and then became the names and faces audiences associated with the music.[8] No Wave artists were hardly immune to this dynamic, but with a strong current of identity politics running through their contemporary music scene, they sometimes used their songs to signify pointedly on it.

**Figure 4.2.** Sharon Topper with melodicon. 2007. *Photo: Laurent Baillet.*

For example, Ribot performed his original song, "Clever White Youths with Attitude," with his No Wave bands Shrek and Rootless Cosmopolitans, and the all-white No Wave band James White and the Blacks developed a genre of punk-funk music that sonically intervened into the silence around race in punk rock. No Wave vocalists also gestured toward this issue in a more symbolic way, by magnifying a vocal trend that had been prominent in New Wave, using a nasal, timbrally plain monotone delivery that, while anti-virtuosic and anti-pop, also made a point of not emulating African American vocal or verbal styles. More often than confronting the role of race in rock, however, No Wave artists expanded punk's purview around issues of gender and sexuality. GodCo was at the vanguard of this effort.

GodCo's sexual critiques were issued potently and directly. In a song called "We Signify," for example, the band proclaimed, "We're co-opting rock, the language of sexism, to address gender identity on its

**Figure 4.3.** God Is My Co-Pilot, *Gender Is As Gender Does*
(Funky Mushroom, 1992). 7″ EP.

own terms of complexity."[9] Indeed, even as it distinguished itself stylistically through its affiliation with No Wave, GodCo was also part of the
early nineties wave of female (and primarily West Coast) "riot grrrl"
post-punk bands, including Bikini Kill and Sleater Kinney, and along
with bands such as Nervous Gender, Pansy Division, and Team Dresch,
GodCo was also prominent on the 1990s queercore scene.[10] Like punk
rock, riot grrrl and queercore bands had their own pre-history in figures
like Wendy O. Williams of the Plasmatics (the sexually graphic "Queen
of Shock Rock," for whom the Klezmatics had named their band), Lou
Reed, and Patti Smith. In some ways, punk rock had already served
as a forum for rock musicians who transgressed gender norms; in his

songs Reed had addressed New York's transvestite culture, while Smith, well known for her androgynous gender presentation, wrote songs that frankly confronted anti-gay violence and female sexual desire. Building upon this precedent, queercore bands made homosexuality, and the project of challenging pop music's hetero-normative expectations, their central themes.

GodCo addressed issues of gender and sexuality through the images they included in their packaging and in their songs extolling sex, critiquing sexism, touting women's sexual freedom, and defying social taboos. The titles of the band's queercore miniatures, usually about a minute in length, could be innocent, as in "Crush on a Girl," or allusive, as in "Gender is as Gender Does," or blunt, as in "Pornography and Rape" and "You Smell Like Sex." Like other queercore bands, GodCo conceived of their music as a kind of political theater—within limits. As Flanagin asserted, "We're not a direct action group, we're a band, and our music is what we have to offer. . . . There are better ways to say, 'The workers must seize control of the means of production' than over a heavy backbeat. If you need a message, how about: 'So much noise in the world, so much sex. So many amazing things, and nothing happens that doesn't contradict itself in the happening. I think I will dance now.'"[11] But in fact the band's message was fundamentally political, as GodCo proffered to their audiences a performance of queer identity. Topper and Flanagin identified as a bisexual couple, and through her androgynous self-presentation as lead singer, Topper made it plain that the band was forging new ground in rock for an unabashed expression of queer sexuality, and a free interpretation of femininity. Being out as a bisexual woman, she explained, was a simple decision: "Queer invisibility has so many bad consequences, that being open is just a matter of conscience. How could I not be? . . . It's no shameful secret so I see no need to hide."[12]

Alongside their queer-positive message, GodCo distinguished itself through its forays into international folk song. Indeed, with their typical mix of droll humor and seriousness of purpose, even as the band recorded a multitude of deconstructed folk-punk tunes, Flanagin and Topper saw the band as inserting itself, with deliberation, into the processes of constant reappraisal that has long been part of so-called "folk song." Contrary to the idea of immutable tradition that the idea of "folk music" often conjures up, Flanagin and Topper enjoyed observing the unpredictable way songs could turn up in new contexts and acquire new meanings as they circulated transnationally, and they were particularly fascinated by the imperfect transmission of songs from person to person, both within and across cultures. Helped by a basic familiarity with multiple languages, they sought out new material during the band's international tours and travels. The goal was not to reproduce the songs in a way faithful to the sources from which they had learned them—to the contrary. Instead, they turned their Finnish, Japanese, and Hungarian songs into off-kilter punk rock ditties. One result was to quash cultural differences by applying a similar aesthetic to each tune. However, in doing so, the band was also subverting the idea of the folk song as an indelible marker of national patrimony.

Instead of buying into the idea of a homogenous national "culture" that a folk song represents, Topper and Flanagin conceived of their performances of foreign-language songs as commentaries on the cultural encounters and clashes that describe cosmopolitan culture and American pluralism. As they contended, "There is nothing more American than having a total collision of different languages and cultures. (Although some Americans can't seem to remember that!)"[13] They also foregrounded and naturalized the notion of "in-between" languages, creoles and "pidgins." Flanagin connected their interest in non-normative language to GodCo's punk-rock, DIY outlook on musical technique, adding, "I think this attitude has something to do with how we started the band too. I realize there are different ways to learn guitar, but me, I just picked it up and started to play. Two weeks later I was in a band. Sharon too. Siobhan too. And Laura. We had this thing we wanted to do."[14]

Like their colleagues on the downtown scene, Flanagin and Topper had wide intellectual appetites, and it is no coincidence that the way they articulated their interest in pidgin languages and imperfect cultural transmission had much in common with post-colonial theorist Homi Bhabha's formulation of "'in-between' spaces," which he published soon after the band had convened. This concept, which has been taken up in many disciplines, has also proved useful to ethnomusicologists, who have long been interested in the relationship between cultural insiders and outsiders ("emic" versus "etic" relationships), and who have also sought to interrogate that binary in order to reflect music's role in shaping complex identities and cultural formations.[15] The notion of in-between spaces is particularly pertinent to GodCo not only because of is applicability to queer studies, but also for the way Bhabha discusses notions of national belonging ("nationness") and identity ("selfhood") as being dependent upon the "moments or processes that are produced in the articulation of cultural differences." He calls these moments "'in-between' spaces [that] provide the terrain for elaborating strategies of selfhood—singular or communal—that initiate new signs of identity, and innovative sites of collaboration, and contestation, in the act of defining society itself."[16] If GodCo, as a queercore band, served as "terrain for elaborating strategies of selfhood" and sexual identity, then by adapting folk songs into a No Wave context, the band also brought notions of an insistently personal selfhood into dialogue with the idea of national belonging. In other words, the band did not aim solely to function as an "in-between space" where it was possible to articulate unofficially sanctioned forms of gender and sexuality. With a deft and self-deprecatory touch, GodCo also intervened into monolithic conceptions of nation and culture. Flanagin and Topper developed a method for addressing this disjuncture between the construct of shared national identity and the actual nature of lived, individual experience, learning local songs from people they met in their travels and then arranging them in a way that skewered notions of folk authenticity. As individuals, they implied, the "folk" ostensibly given voice by their international folk songs had multilayered identities, whose many facets were as important to each person's self-concept as was the "culture" the band's songs purportedly represented. Through their idiosyncratic methods of collection and interpretation, then, Flanagin and Topper used folk song, which has been historically regarded as emblematic of a monolithic culture, in order to articulate the in-between spaces in which lived culture—that is, human interaction—rather than imagined, national culture, is created. In turning their attention to Jewish culture, which had a personal valence for many of the band members, they also drew upon this notion in performance, making their concerts into crucibles for forging new connections between downtown mores, No Wave aesthetics, and Jewish identity.

## GodCo, the "In-Between Space," and Jewish Inauthenticity

GodCo took on the mode of No Wave critique and aimed it in mul-tiple directions: not only at the conventional sounds of rock music, but also more specifically at gender politics, and, interrelatedly, at notions of American identity and Jewish tradition. In so doing, they were under-mining another punk rock norm. If there are punk bands today of every religious stripe, an identification with organized religion was anathema to punk's original anti-establishment, anti-social-control narrative. And although ideas about spirituality have played an important part in avant-garde jazz and creative improvisation, much of the downtown scene gen-erally construed itself as secular, if not anti-religious.[17] But just as Jew-ish "secularity" usually does, the RJC moment complicated this stance. Ribot, for example, who had addressed issues of race and class through some of his song lyrics and titles, also "cried out cynical poems about God to the strains of spine-tingling dissonant rock and roll" at the 1993 RJC Festival at the Knitting Factory.[18] (Ribot's "cynical poems" include the song "Yo! I Killed your God," which he conceived as one way to con-front the "invisible Christian values of [the] supposedly neutral public space" of the downtown scene.)[19]

In fact, GodCo had engaged religious ideas before getting involved in RJC. Flanagin, who is not Jewish, wrote songs with Christian tropes, including angels, God, and Joan of Arc—which made it clear that its name, though hardly indicating an embrace of conservative Christian values, did not preclude the band from taking an interest in religious things. During the RJC moment GodCo turned their focus not only to Jewish identity, as did most of their peers, but also to Judaism, bringing Jewish learning, law, and worship into the purview of the band's particu-lar in-between space—that is, a musical-cultural space in which they hoped marginal subjectivities could momentarily become normative ones, where social norms could be upended and identities rethought. The band was also concerned with Jewish community-building and saw it as part of their creative mission to develop the means by which they and their audiences could "reject essentialistic notions of identity and culture, [but] nonetheless remain committed to the perpetuation of a distinct community"—albeit a community made up of strong-willed individualists.[20] In a way that comes through clearly in Topper's statements, the downtownish in-between space GodCo meant to make their own was one that was both Jewishly irreverent and transformative.

Topper's turn toward Jewish music had been spurred by a shock. Zorn had invited the band to participate in the first RJC festival in New York City, where, just as many of her peers had been in Munich, Topper was startled to discover that she had been working in a community that was largely Jewish. As she and Flanagin recalled, the force exerted by this realization, and by the potential RJC offered to counter it, was dramatic:

> ST: We were just really minding our own business, doing our ... No Wave punk rock shit ... playing at CBGB's, and playing at ABC No Rio.
>
> CF: We were playing our "No New York" punk rock Finnish folk songs—
>
> ST: We were touring in Scandinavia, we were touring in Finland, we were taking bits and pieces of everything we heard and creating our own hybrid, but we weren't doing anything related to Jewish music at that point ... until we got invited to do the RJC festival, the first one [in 1992 at the Knitting Factory]. ... And that's where all the identity stuff came in. ... It felt to me, like, "Oh my God. This whole scene that we're in—is Jewish!" And we—and I—never realized it before.

Topper described her dawning sense of amazement at this revelation:

> "The music that we're doing is totally fun, and this is a scene, and oh my God!" Because for me it was always that ... you hide it. It's not cool, it's not something that you want to be proud of, or identify, or get up on stage and say, "I'm a Jew! This is what I do!" And it was all of a sudden, like, "Oh!" Everyone in our scene [was Jewish], from John Zorn to Marc Ribot to Anthony Coleman, to me, to Catherine Jauniaux ... all these people.[21]

The impact of this realization is notable given Topper's conviction that it was important to be out as queer; somehow, the idea of being Jewishly "out," which would seem much less threatening, was also far less accessible. But after Zorn's invitation, Topper launched a major effort to recover Jewish songs she had once learned: "The first thing that I did to prepare for that festival was just ransack my memory. ... I had been Bat Mitzvah-ed, and the thing that I [loved] most about Hebrew school were the songs. ... And I couldn't remember any of them! Except, like, little snippets. ... I was asking everybody, 'Do you know this song?'"[22] She

also wanted to discover new ones. In the same ad-hoc way they had collected their Finnish and Hungarian folk songs, she and Flanagin began
asking their colleagues on the scene about Jewish songs they knew: "We
asked each person, like, 'Go out, find what you can.'. . . . Samara [Lubel-
ski, the band's violinist] came back with a cassette of her grandmother
singing these beautiful, beautiful, Yiddish Haggadah songs."[23] This is
the second grandmother we have encountered as a source for passing
on Jewish songs—recall Coleman's memory of his grandmother singing "Raisins and Almonds"—and in her song-collecting project Topper
likewise turned to her own grandmother and to an older female friend.
Creating a traceable chain of human interaction was already central to
the way GodCo thought about folk songs, but with the chain now linked
to immediate family members and close friends, the process took on a
more urgent, personal cast. Each Jewish song an artist collected came
from someone he or she knew, and by choosing to follow the odd path
of each song's genealogy, Topper and Flanagin approached the songs as
if they, like the individuals who bore them, could reveal as much through
their idiosyncrasies as their conformation to type. Indeed, rather than
seeking out archetypes, as folk song collectors once would have done,
they sought out the versions of songs that bore traces of their passage
through space, time, and cultural change. In this way, Topper and Flanagin used songs to give voice to personal stories that, because they
involved hazy memories and misremembered texts, did not have a clear
place in the familiar narratives of Jewish immigration and generational
change. Maintaining this method was so important to them, recalled
Flanagin, that when they began researching Jewish songs:

> We made a very definite [decision]—I mean, we could have done things, like
> gone to YIVO [the sound archives at the YIVO Institute for Jewish Research],
> that we didn't do.
>
> TB: And why didn't you do that?
>
> CF: Because it was all the point-to-point transmission stuff. It was all about
> learning a song from somebody and maybe getting it wrong.

Using the songs they had collected, GodCo developed a performance set for the Knit's Radical Jewish Culture festival in 1992, which
they reprised, with some new material, in 1993. (When performing its

**Figure 4.4.** G-d Is My Co-Pilot, *Mir Shlufn Nisht*
(We Don't Sleep) (Disk Union, 1994).

Jewish material, the band also took on the spelling G-d, reflecting the
Orthodox Jewish practice of using variants to avoid erasing the name
of God from a written document, which Jewish law forbids.) In the summer of 1994, the band also organized and curated its own weekly "Synagogue Series," which they called "an alternative to the alternative," a
series of Jewish-themed concerts by experimental musicians first held at
a small downtown synagogue, then at CB's Gallery in the club CBGB.[24]
GodCo also began including some Jewish songs, and instrumentals with
Yiddish titles, in their other performances, and in 1994 the band released
*Mir Shlufn Nisht* (Yiddish for "We Don't Sleep"), a recording focused on

Jewish material—including traditional songs and a few originals.[25] It also included songs with Russian, Finnish, Swedish, and Gaelic titles, some with lyrics and some performed as instrumentals. The Jewish (or Jewishly identified) material included the following:

> Two Russian songs, "Raketapisztoly" and "Katoshka"
>
> The Passover songs "Had Gadya" and "Dayenu"
>
> The Hanukkah song "Mi Yimalel"
>
> "Ha-Tikvah" and "Halutz, Beneh!" one of the above-mentioned "Hebrew musical relics of socialist Zionism"
>
> The Yiddish song "Piramidn"
>
> "Hora," an instrumental
>
> Seven originals: "Mia Geht Nach Bodega" (GodCo), "Like/Park" (Flanagin), "Dance for Liz Cohen" (Flanagin), "Sissy Dog" (Flanagin-Elliott Sharp), "Palmcore" (GodCo), "We Don't Sleep" (Flanagin), and "Tanstukolena Yid" (traditional Finnish song, arranged by GodCo)

Some of the song titles are spelled out using Hebrew and Russian letters while others are transliterated, and the liner notes include lyrics in various languages. In GodCo's signature fashion, the arrangements loosely melded avant-garde aesthetics with the rhythmic propulsion and primitivist energy of punk rock. And as always, the band projected an ideal of anarchic cultural pluralism. The compact disc cover and insert mirror the band's cheerful embrace of informal language and mistranslation, cross-cultural communication and misapprehension, and they gesture toward the kind of back-and-forth among languages that characterizes many immigrant homes, and certainly twentieth-century Jewish ones.

*Mir Shlufn Nisht* projects an untutored, anarchic spirit of free exchange that upon close listening reveals itself as having been thoughtfully calibrated. Although the band's disjointed arrangements of these songs include interludes of unmetered free improvisation and noise, even in the busier, louder sections of the recording the texture remains for the most part pointillist, contrapuntal, and parsable, rather than overwhelmingly dense or noise-based. The recording is clear and carefully mixed, and the arrangements retain each song's original lyrics and melody, albeit often in attenuated form. Throughout, Topper's vocal delivery is decidedly punk: unsupported, nasal, and always slightly off-key. She sometimes uses a throaty or screaming timbre, but she more often conveys a flat affect worthy of a Weimar-era chanteuse. It may seem fitting to read an implied critique of her texts into Topper's vocal style, but it should not be assumed that audiences would have heard these arrangements as ironic. To the contrary, in a No Wave context, her vocal style is idiomatic and aesthetically fitting, and the band used similar performance practices for all its material, including songs whose texts about bisexuality and sexual freedom were an unequivocal part of the band's core identity. The band's Jewish songs were thus well integrated into GodCo's whole oeuvre, where a high value was placed on ugly beauty, startling aesthetic turns, and unconventional affect. In sum, a sense of respect for the material's integrity is evident on *Mir Shlufn Nisht,* where the band's creative strategies seem designed to call attention to each song's identity rather than obscuring it.

In collaboration with Flanagin, Topper also created elaborate, hand-drawn booklets for two RJC festivals, which she distributed to the audience, to whom she joked, "You can say you were here at the birth of the No Wave klezmer trend."[26] The booklets wove together reminiscences, reflections about Judaism, and song lyrics, with Hebrew and English handwriting that is playfully off-balance, a result both of Topper's DIY outlook and the way she conceived that exposing the limits of her Jewish education should be an important part of her band's Jewish project. Both Flanagin and Topper knew some Yiddish already and brushed up by taking Yiddish lessons at the local Arbeter Ring (Workmen's Circle, a Jewish fraternal organization), but as Topper admitted in her booklet, "Hebrew school was a long time ago for by me. Maybe for you too!"[27] ("By me" is a Yiddishism.) She also reassures her readers that "there are no definitive versions of these songs—the most important thing is that we are singing them."[28] The theme of personal storytelling came through clearly in the title of one of the concert booklets, "G-d Is My Co-Pilot's Haggadah." (The original is written half in Hebrew, half in English: "Haggadah shel G-d Is My Co-Pilot.") This phrase was framed by a Star of David above and a rakish illustration of a World War II–era

**Figure 4.5.** "Haggadah Shel G-d Is My Co-Pilot." (G-d Is My Co-Pilot's Haggadah). Radical Jewish Culture Festival at the Knitting Factory, 8–11 October 1992. Concert program.

**Figure 4.6.** "What Kann You Mach? Es Ist Amerikeh!" (What Can You Do? It's America!). Radical New Jewish Culture Festival at the Knitting Factory, 7–11 April 1993. Concert program.

fighter plane below. But the booklet was not meant as a variant of the ritual text traditionally used during the seder service of the Passover holiday. The Passover Haggadah chronicles the Jewish exodus from Egypt and redemption from bondage, but, as the contents of the booklet indicate, Topper deployed the term "haggadah" (lit., telling) to denote the "telling" of her own Jewish story through performing with G-d Is My Co-Pilot.[29] She thus fills the booklets with personal touches, such as whimsical line drawings, asides, and family photos, including one "taken by my great aunt Hannah in 1932 @ Ave. C and 3rd St.[of] my great-great grandmother and her 2nd husband."[30]

In the booklets, Topper presents her colloquially worded statements about music, memory, and identity in a naïve way, but she also engages complex issues with which American Jews have been grappling for decades. Most important, the amateurish aesthetic served as an analog to an imperfect inheritance of, and indeed access to, the kind of Jewish cultural knowledge that historically was not learned in school but was passed down in the family from one generation of women to the next. For example, as Topper explained in 2004, "My grandmother still does Passover, and she sneaks . . . into the kitchen, when we're all in the living room eating. She's . . . doing her prayers, with the candles. But she doesn't want anybody to see. . . . She never would say [to me], you know, 'Come here, put this [scarf] on your head, do your prayers this way.'"[31] Like other song collectors before her, Topper found that talking with her grandmother about music opened up their conversations in ways that talking about Jewish identity or religious observance would not have done. To illustrate, in one of her booklets she included a striking passage in her grandmother's hand, in which her grandmother attempted to translate the words to the song "What Kann You Mach? Es Ist Amerikeh!" from Yiddish to English.[32] Demonstrating her interest in language and in written texts that retain traces from their bearers' histories, Topper explained, "This is my grandmother's handwriting. . . . And so she starts writing [*pointing to the text*]. This is Yiddish, [transliterated] in the Roman letters. And then [*pointing*] she just devolves into . . . Hebrew handwriting, in Yiddish—and then [*pointing*] she just starts writing her [secretarial] shorthand."[33]

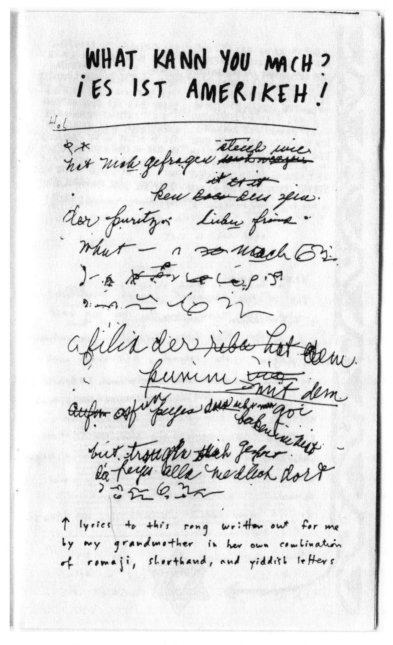

**Figure 4.7.** "What Kann You Mach?" Handwritten lyrics in a combination of languages and alphabets. G-d Is My Co-Pilot concert program, 1993.

As her comments indicate, Topper is intrigued not so much by
what is lost through translation but rather by what one can glean about
a writer whose translation does not succeed in fixing itself into a reified language—a translation that fails because its author cannot com-
partmentalize the different languages in which she writes. This notion,
that personal and historical truths can be revealed only in moments
of mistranslation or unintelligibility, resonates with one of Bhabha's
pronouncements about his "in-between space": "We should remember
that it is the 'inter'—the cutting edge of translation and negotiation, the
in-between space, that carries the burden and the meaning of culture."[34]
That is, Topper's grandmother's translation itself may be impenetrable,
but it is only by being so that it can shed a particular kind of light on her
subject position. With "What Kann You Mach?" rather than a transparent translation from a disembodied source, which would have given us
the lyrics to a Yiddish song in English, we get an impenetrable thicket
of signs. This thicket, however, gives us a glimpse of the "culture" the
song actually inhabits—one that is described by a historically determined and irresolvable in-betweenness.

In this context, handwriting becomes an eloquent marker of lived
experience. In her grandmother's case, the mix of Hebrew and Yiddish
with Latin letters and shorthand speak to a complicated cultural inheritance, one in which it is not clear to which language, if any, her "folk
song"—and by implication she herself—fully belongs. Topper likewise
wrote out brief notes about each song, but her handwritten script and
colloquial style make it clear that her program notes were meant not so
much to edify her audience as to connect with them, by maintaining the
principle of point-to-point contact. In the booklets, her discursions on
female sexuality converge with the feminist truism that women's history
is often written not in official histories, but in the traditionally female
domain of hand work. The booklets also partake of a principle of feminist writing, prominent in American visual and performance art of the
1970s and 1980s, in which the body is understood as being inscribed
upon the word.[35] Like other handmade things, but with an unusually
personal provenance because her booklets are biographical, Topper's
handwriting draws a connection to her physical body, acts as an analog
to her spoken voice, and takes on an embodied presence. Correspond-

ingly, rather than speaking authoritatively in her booklets, she traced how she had learned, forgotten or misremembered, and reconstructed many of the songs.

One striking example is "Mi Yimalel," a Hanukkah song she half-remembered from her childhood. Thus, she wrote: "I learned this from a Catholic girl who lived across the street from me when I was 9—I think it's an Israeli song; no one else I've sung it to seems to know it."[36] By casually adding a jarring element—her Catholic playmate, who learned the song for a choir performance—to the more familiar litany of sources for Jewish cultural transmission, Topper drops us into a lived American reality where a Jewish girl might be less familiar than a Catholic girl with Jewish songs. Rather than sidestepping this discomfiting memory, or studying Jewish songs as a way to leave behind the memory of not knowing, Topper is intent on foregrounding the contingent nature of her own Jewish experience and in leaving seams exposed. Her booklets are in effect performances of cultural inauthenticity. In disclosing the cobbled-together nature of her insider's knowledge, Topper is implying that the discontinuities are as important—in that they have become as much a part of Jewish American experience—as the enduring Jewish symbols and tropes. By turning her gaze on what would normally be construed as inauthentic, Topper creates a discursive frame for exploring the role played in Jewish American life by the "in-between space" (PURL 4.1).

## Dada-Punk Judaism, from Z(ionism) to H(asidism)

In addition to its holiday songs, GodCo recorded "Ha-Tikvah" and an Israeli pioneer song from the early twentieth century, "Halutz, Beneh!" (Build, Pioneer!). These recordings illuminate the band's radical approach to folk song particularly well, as both are national songs that were intended by their composers to give voice to a particular national *melos*—that of the Jewish people and the hoped-for nation of Israel.[37] With their simple, often stirring melodies, such songs were made to be sung together by groups of people; when soloists perform them, whether live or on a recording, a community of listeners is always implied. The songs' identities, in other words, are inseparable from the imagined community they are meant to represent. But GodCo's arrangements seem to turn all this on its head. "Ha-Tikvah," for example, opens with a slow jam that reveals nothing about the song's identity. Instead of preparing listeners for the entrance of the melody, resonant drums (especially a boomy kick drum) and low electric bass guitar, often entering just behind the beat, create a minimalist, relaxed duple groove, above which a violin and alto saxophone engage in an agitated, overlapping, and unmelodic antiphonal dialogue. There is no indication that the "Ha-Tikvah" melody will emerge from this texture, but after about a minute Topper enters with the song's first phrase, singing in her usual nasal, emotionally deadpan style. Even though she is now singing, in Hebrew, "As long as the Jewish spirit is yearning deep in the heart, with eyes . . . looking toward Zion, then our hope—the two-thousand-year-old hope—will not be lost," the song's mood barely shifts. The violin does leave off its quarrel with the saxophone to pick up the melody and, with the bass guitar, accompanies Topper in the verse, but they are in only approximate unison—approximate not only rhythmically, but because the instruments, like Topper, are playing slightly off-key. This No Wave arrangement might seem to belie the song's associations with the Zionist national cause. And indeed, in keeping with GodCo's attitude toward national folk song in general, in this recording there is an element of insistent individualism, and an up-ending of the musical conventions that would normally, in renditions of "Ha-Tikvah," be designed to do the cultural work of indexing the Jewish nation and eliciting feelings of Jewish national belonging. But GodCo's arrangement was meant as an homage to the idea of "Ha-Tikvah," and based on the way it fit neatly into the band's overall aesthetic, their fans would likely have understood it in just this way.

In fact, in seeking to radically update timeworn material and make it part of a contemporary Jewish community-building effort, this avant-punk band was preceded by early twentieth-century modernist composers. In the 1930s, the Jewish National Fund (*Keren Kayemet le-Yisrael*) commissioned several composers—including Aaron Copland, Kurt Weill, and Stefan Wolpe—to write original settings of Israeli folk songs, for voice and piano, to bolster national pride and give contemporary musical expression to the Jewish community of British Mandate Palestine.[38] Although GodCo's work may seem far removed from this context, the band had a similar purpose in performing songs like "Ha-Tikvah" and "Halutz, Beneh!" Indeed, the band located its message of down-townish Jewish solidarity in an earlier era of nation-building in Israel, drawing on old-fashioned exhortations, without much attention to events that had unfolded in the intervening decades, to get downtown's Jew-ish community to build itself up. GodCo's No Wave musical settings of these songs were thus designed with the same purpose in mind as the earlier, modernist ones. Although she paid less nuanced attention to the "national" than the "personal" side of the equation, Topper conceived the RJC festivals as crucibles for generating a new openness about Jew-ish heritage and an affirmation of Jewish community, in a distinctively downtownish way (PURL 4.2).

"Halutz, Beneh!" was part of a different group of songs commis-sioned by the Jewish National Fund. Unlike the modernist settings of traditional melodies, this project focused on pioneer songs, a genre popular in Zionist circles in the early twentieth century.[39] In the pio-neer songs, "images of young farmers tilling the soil of Palestine or . . . [texts] about nature encountered by the pioneers returning to Zion were not only symbols, but calls to explicit action."[40] Accordingly, "Halutz, Beneh!" exhorts audiences to "build Jerusalem/emigrate and build" even when conditions seem unbearable. Taking some poetic li-cense with the original Hebrew, the song's English lyrics read: "Sing of shoes full of holes, sing of shoes without soles, and wherever our feet may turn, there they meet only stone, and they burn. Have no care, Halutz [pioneer]. Jerusalem, go build Her!" The song "Halutz, Build On: Chalutz, Benëh," written in Palestine in the mid-1920s by Russian-born composer Joel Engel and set to a text by Hungarian-born poet Avigdor Hameiri, was published in 1929 in the collection *Mizimrat ha-Aretz* (Tunes of the Land [of Israel]). The songs in this collection were meant to be taught to children and sung at community events, both in Palestine and in Europe, to bolster a sense of Jewish national solidarity, and indeed, the song entered the national imaginary indelibly enough that three decades later, in 1958, it was performed at Israel's tenth jubi-lee concert, during a gala evening of music and dramatic readings. The text on the jacket of the long-playing record issued to commemorate the concert captures the mix of national pride and nostalgia the jubi-lee concert sought to invoke: "These songs were part of the stuff and dreams of Zionism in its beginnings. They came from the hearts of a people who had returned home, at last. And they will sing to you with the same magic."[41]

On this recording, "Halutz, Beneh!" is realized through a lusty performance by the Zadikov Workers Choir of the Tel Aviv Labor Council, in an arrangement that is evidently based on one that had been published in the United States in 1942.[42] Marked *Alla marcia vivo*, this arrangement magnifies the drama of the song's modest text, creating a narrative of struggle and redemption by using extreme dynamic contrasts and theatrical *ritards,* and building to a triumphant climax (marked *fff* in the score).[43] Although both arrangements were intended to stir up an audience's feelings of community and cultural affirmation, it would be hard to imagine a performance farther afield, either musically or culturally, from the one GodCo recorded some thirty-five years later (PURL 4.3).

In the absence of a full-voiced choir, martial instrumental accompaniment, or harmonic underpinning, GodCo flattened this song's narrative of struggle and perseverance. Instead, Topper, who learned the song from an elderly friend, who had learned it as a child at a Zionist summer camp, mimics her homespun rendering of the song.[44] The band arranged "B'Nai!" (as they spelled it) as a duet for voice accompanied by a handsaw chewing through a block of wood. (The sound serves as a kind of index for the "building" of Jerusalem, although that city is built from stone.) The saw, which opens the piece, has a frightening affect: Loud, low, and guttural, it growls and snorts like a wild animal. The saw is also unruly. The only rhythm instrument, it keeps time badly and nearly destroys the duple meter in its projected enthusiasm for independence. When Topper's voice enters, singing the words in oddly accented, sometimes garbled Hebrew in a clear and expressionless monotone, the saw falls into rhythm with her voice, then out again, rushing ahead and adding embellishments and rhythmic figures. If the saw's erratic phrasing suggests an eager but unschooled accompanist, Topper's performance emphasizes this lack of polish. Topper sings in a clear alto that is stridently, fervently off-key. She also pares down the words of the

**Figure 4.8.** Page from Joel Engel and Avigdor Hameiri, "Halutz, Build On: Chalutz, B^enëh / Hay, Hay Naalayim" arr. Avraham Soltes, trans. Babette Deutsch (New York: Transcontinental Music Corp., 1942). Used by permission.

song, which are almost nonsensical to begin with. "Ay, ay, ay, shoes," she intones in Hebrew. "Build, please, shoes. And burns, and burns, and burns, and burns. It's nothing, it's nothing, it's nothing, it's nothing, it's nothing: Build, pioneer! Build, build, build!"[45] She ends out of tune, on the flatted-sixth scale degree instead of the dominant, and the scraper stops abruptly. "Build, Pioneer!" has been rendered as a one-minute Dada-punk song.

How, then, did this odd arrangement fit into Topper's vision for Jewish community-building on the downtown scene? Topper's concert booklet makes the connection plainer than it might appear at first. It includes two images drawn from the lexicon of mid-twentieth-century Zionist visual culture. One photograph is of "pioneers" on the land, young Jewish immigrants cheerfully shouldering hoes and picks while "Marching to Work," probably for the hard labor of clearing fields, breaking up stones, or building roads. (Topper ignores one key aspect of the pioneer movement, the vilification of city life and Diaspora Jews such as herself.)[46] The other image in the booklet, "Arab and Jew Working Together," shows a man, dressed in the traditional Arab garb of a long-sleeve, ankle-length garment and headdress, gripping the wheel of a tractor while another man, evidently an Israeli as he is dressed casually in overalls and cap, leans over him, apparently showing him how to work the machine. Such images, typical of Israel's early nation-building project, were subject to critiques even then, and by 1993 such idealistic captions and images were true chestnuts. Topper and Flanagin knew they were old-fashioned, and Topper included a comment to that effect by journalist Roee Rosen, who had told her that "when he heard us do Ha-Tikvah . . . he thought we were referring to Palestinians." But elsewhere in the booklet Topper presented no inkling of such an interpretation. Indeed, she wrote in response to Rosen's comment that his interpretation had never occurred to her. His statement, she wrote, "didn't lead me to a solution, but it did lead me to think, and to think is a start." This equivocal comment aside, she presents the songs and images in an insouciant way. Thus, superimposed on "Marching to Work" is a text box in which Topper writes: "B'NAI: And for American Jews, there is always Israel—but as each of us is out of Egypt, each of us must build the homeland. B'nai, chalutzim! [Build, pioneers!]"[47] With

**Figure 4.9.** "Sharon Topper and her goyish band present Yiddish masterworks": "Marching to Work," "Arab and Jew Working Together," "Ha-Tikvah," and "B'nai!" G-d Is My Co-Pilot concert program, 1993.

tongue-in-cheek humor but sincerity too, Topper refers to her audience members as "pioneers" and suggests that they get to work "build[ing] the homeland"—not in Israel, but in Lower Manhattan. In this section of the booklet, Topper's purposefully naïve aesthetic seems well matched with her anachronistic points of reference, and here, unlike in the telling of her own story, Topper veers into territory that seems vague, idealized, and kitschy enough—"Arab and Jew Working Together"—to impede a close critique (PURL 4.4).

The booklet's text can be confusing in light of the way GodCo's settings of its Zionist songs reject aesthetic convention, eschewing the Ro-

mantic musical syntax in which national songs are typically rendered—
and that was realized so rousingly by the Tel Aviv Workers' Choir. It
could be argued that GodCo's settings contest the national pride these
songs enact and symbolize. The strange Hebrew, the off-kilter intonation, and the resolutely bizarre character of the two timbral presences
(voice and saw) in "B'nai!" could be interpreted as a subversion of the
song's Zionist text, or perhaps an acknowledgment of Zionism's fractious
history and a comment on the impossibility of fully realizing its ideals
in the State of Israel. But this argument would be based on a reductive
interpretation of the semiotics of punk music. In fact, GodCo did not
mean these songs as critiques. As Topper explained:

> I think I'm coming from such a point of respect for the songs. And yet—just be-
> ing a member of the [downtown] community that I'm a member of, the majority
> of it is very pro-Palestinian, [so] people did ask us [about our intentions]. . . .
>
> CF: It wasn't meant as an ironic commentary. . . . This is mellow for us. We were
> the noisiest band on the block, long before that.
>
> ST: It's hilarious to me that someone would hear [irony or] irreverence. . . .
> Because like I said before, it's just them looking through this perspective that,
> 'Oh, this little punk rock chick from the East Village is getting up there and
> doing this song, so she must just want to be slapping you.'. . . I think that [ir-
> reverence] makes it better. Because it adds an edge to it—otherwise maybe it
> would be completely kitschy.
>
> CF: Yeah. Do we need another straight recording of "Ha-Tikvah?"
>
> ST: It's probably what makes it great, actually. . . . [Humorously] I can't help it if
> I'm punk.[48]

Indeed, Topper included "Halutz, Beneh!" and "Ha-Tikvah" in her
repertoire as forthright expressions of support for the idea of Israel as
a Jewish nation-state: "The theory, the Land, is so important to us as
a people. And it needs to be protected. . . . I think it is important for
Jews to come forward—to question [Israeli political policies], maybe,
but still, we need to protect its land."[49] Her intentions might not have
been clear to all listeners, and the band's transgressions of Jewish tradition and propriety might well have been received with skepticism in the
Jewish communities Topper invoked as her inspirations. But through
the looking-glass of downtown's aesthetic economy, GodCo's treatment
of this timeworn material comprised a tribute, not an ironic dismissal.

What was incongruous instead—and would have been especially so on the No Wave scene—was the song's forthrightly Jewish aspect.

In what would seem an even greater dissonance between the band's social values and its choice of Jewish songs, GodCo also laid claim to hasidic songs as vehicles for the sweaty ecstasy of the rock concert-qua-secular ritual. But, as with her Zionist material, Topper took a pragmatic approach to hasidic Judaism—choosing to celebrate some aspects and ignoring others the rest. Hasidism (lit., pietism) is a mystical branch of ultra-Orthodox Judaism with roots in the teachings of Rabbi Israel ben Eliezer (c. 1700–1760), known as the Ba'al Shem Tov (Master of the Divine Name). Music and dance are central to hasidic worship, giving ordinary people a path to joyful communion with God. Topper proffers an admiring (if self-serving) gloss on hasidic Judaism:

> The Ba'al Shem Tov taught, and Hassidim believe, that creatures of G-d have a duty to enjoy the gifts of G-d: food, sex, dancing. It is a husband's duty to give his wife pleasure! . . . Of course, all man's joy is rooted in living the Law and in study of Torah—this Chassidic song . . . exhorts the dancers to do exactly this. . . . So here we go.[50]

To get her audiences up and dancing, GodCo included the lively Hasidic songs "Sisu V'Simchu" and "Az Der Rebbe Tanzt" in their set. (Topper noted that the latter "sounds like it might have been intended to poke fun"—an accurate impression, as this is a song mocking hasidic ways.) Although the band did not record these songs, one can get a sense of the climate of raucous celebration they hoped the songs would inspire by Topper's graphical representation of the Yiddish drinking song "Tayere Malke" (Dear Queen/The Goblet, words and music by Mark Warshawski), also known as "Bim Bom" for its rousing refrain.

In keeping with the jubilance this image conveys, Topper closes her statement about hasidic songs by enjoining her audience to "co-opt, recontextualize, dance!" Topper is inveighing her audience to appropriate particular hasidic customs in the spirit of rock's joyous anarchy and queercore defiance. That is, she urges listeners to co-opt hasidic songs, recontextualize the songs into a secular/queer-positive milieu, and dance to them. In the context of a virtual showdown between hasidic Judaism and New York–style punk transgression, this little exhortation takes on a dizzying burden of cultural work. On one hand, Topper, like

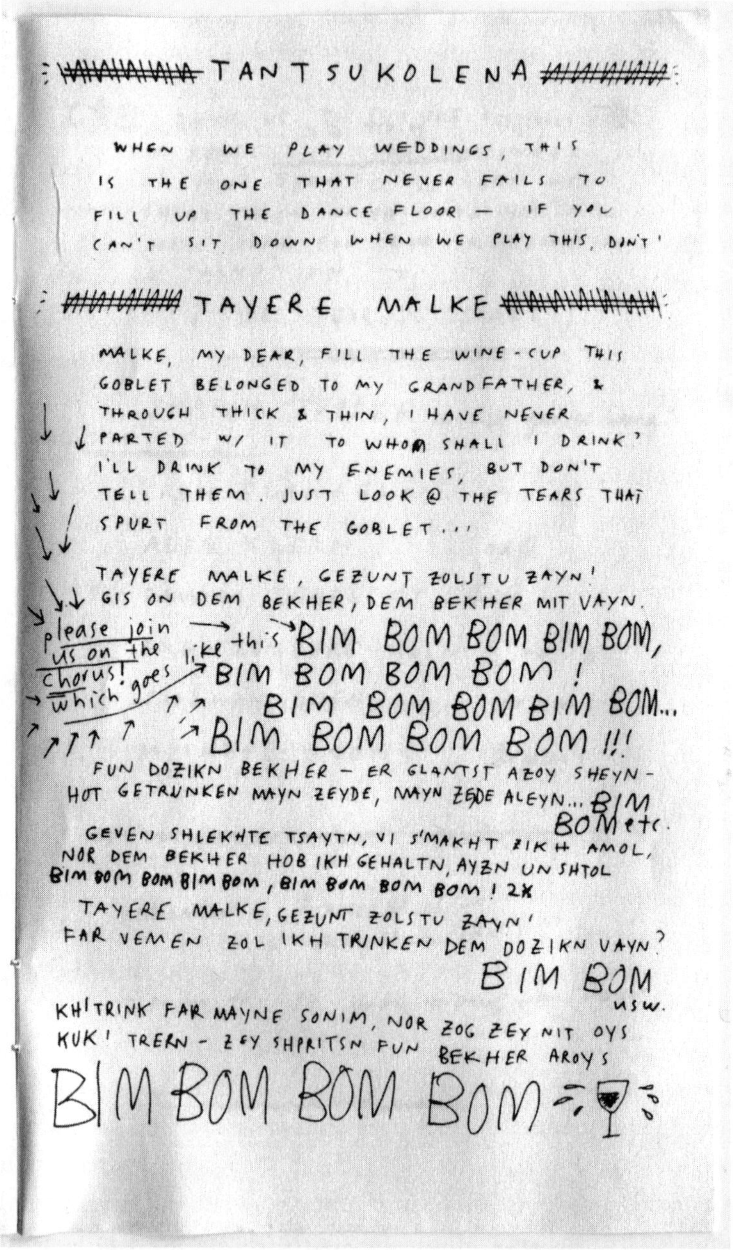
TANTSUKOLENA

WHEN WE PLAY WEDDINGS, THIS IS THE ONE THAT NEVER FAILS TO FILL UP THE DANCE FLOOR — IF YOU CAN'T SIT DOWN WHEN WE PLAY THIS, DON'T!

TAYERE MALKE

MALKE, MY DEAR, FILL THE WINE-CUP THIS GOBLET BELONGED TO MY GRANDFATHER, & THROUGH THICK & THIN, I HAVE NEVER PARTED W/ IT TO WHOM SHALL I DRINK? I'LL DRINK TO MY ENEMIES, BUT DON'T TELL THEM. JUST LOOK @ THE TEARS THAT SPURT FROM THE GOBLET...

TAYERE MALKE, GEZUNT ZOLSTU ZAYN!
GIS ON DEM BEKHER, DEM BEKHER MIT VAYN.
please join us on the chorus! which goes like this
BIM BOM BOM BIM BOM,
BIM BOM BOM BOM!
BIM BOM BOM BIM BOM...
BIM BOM BOM BOM!!!
FUN DOZIKN BEKHER – ER GLANTST AZOY SHEYN –
HOT GETRUNKEN MAYN ZEYDE, MAYN ZEYDE ALEYN... BIM BOM etc.
GEVEN SHLEKHTE TSAYTN, VI S'MAKHT ZIKH AMOL,
NOR DEM BEKHER HOB IKH GEHALTN, AYZN UN SHTOL
BIM BOM BOM BIM BOM, BIM BOM BOM BOM! 2X
TAYERE MALKE, GEZUNT ZOLSTU ZAYN!
FAR VEMEN ZOL IKH TRINKEN DEM DOZIKN VAYN?
BIM BOM usw.
KH'TRINK FAR MAYNE SONIM, NOR ZOG ZEY NIT OYS
KUK! TRERN – ZEY SHPRITSN FUN BEKHER AROYS
BIM BOM BOM BOM

**Figure 4.10.** Sharon Topper's representation of Mark Warshawski, "Tayere Malke" (Dear Queen/The Goblet). G-d Is My Co-Pilot concert program, 1992.

many outsiders to the community, appreciates the importance of song, dance, and celebration in hasidic life. The queer-positive Klezmatics and other freethinking downtown artists also arranged and performed hasidic *nigunim*, and the RJC moment saw the formation of a band called Hasidic New Wave. But as with her colleagues' conditional embrace of hasidic music and ecstatic prayer, Topper's description of ultra-Orthodox Jews as pious scholars with earthy down-home values is selective. Behind her exhortation to "co-opt" hasidic ideas and "recontextualize" them in a secular, gender-progressive context lies an awareness of a far more complicated picture. In an ultra-Orthodox world, secular education is frowned upon, women cover their bodies from head to toe, homosexuality is anathema, and it is generally forbidden for a man to listen to a woman singing unless she is his wife. It is a world, in other words, in which Topper and her audiences do not belong. Like most celebratory rhetoric, Topper's advocacy of hasidic lifeways is both reductive and strategic: reductive in representing a version of Hasidism without the presence of hasidic Jews themselves, who might contradict her or complicate the picture, and strategic in bringing that version into downtown's most iconic performance space. Ultimately, by doing so, Topper undercuts ultra-Orthodox claims to moral authority. She insists that she (and by extension her audience) have as legitimate a relationship to Judaism as do the most strictly observant members of the Jewish community, and she reclaims the "deep Judaism" normally construed as off-limits to (and by) nonobservant Jews.

In her intention to use the music of the RJC moment to address her relationship with Judaism, and not simply her Jewish heritage or identity, Topper was unusual among her downtown colleagues. Although the queer-positive and feminist nature of GodCo's programs was a challenge to religious dogma and social conservatism, this was not a wholesale rebellion. Having inherited such rebellion from her parents, Topper was instead making the typical third- or fourth-generation move of rapprochement. As she explained, "My great grandparents moved to the Lower East Side around the nineteen-teens, and they were kosher, and spoke Yiddish almost exclusively. Then, each generation kind of lost a little bit." By her parents' generation, Jewish observance was not only lost, but derided: "We didn't light candles, we didn't go to temple, we weren't kosher, we ate bacon and we went gambling on Yom Kippur. . . . There was a healthy disdain for the Orthodox. We were all Bar and Bat Mitzvah-ed [but] it just felt like it was [with the attitude of] 'Okay, get your obligation over with, and that's it, you're done.'" But far from rejecting Judaism or foregrounding her ambivalence toward it—as might be expected from her gender activism—Topper considers how it could be wrested from the forces of consolidation and reclaimed for her own purposes.

In carving out a space for a Judaism that made sense to her, Topper did not stop at celebrating aspects of hasidic worship. Although she clearly was not about to become strictly observant, she acknowledged in her booklets that "at the heart of Judaism is the Law," also emphasizing the importance in Judaism of developing a "personal relationship to the Law."[51] Following up with brio on this idea, she drew on the work of feminist theologians and mused on Judaism as a matrilineal religion with an ancestral goddess figure, quoting an excerpt from the revelation discourse called "The Thunder, Perfect Mind," which she named "a Goddess song in Jewish tradition," and from which she and Flanagin were to draw the title for their main recording of Jewish songs, *Mir Shlufn Nisht.* On that recording, she drew a link between the band's feminist and Jewish aspects with a new song, "Liz Cohen Caught Looking," which she described as "a love song for Jewish lesbians everywhere."[52] Along with her interest in feminist theology, Topper, like Zorn, was drawn to the idea of Jewish mysticism as an alternative path to rabbinical authority. Thus, she wrote in one of her booklets, even after Rabbinic Judaism had been established, there remained "movements such as Merkabah mysticism, magical texts, and the later Karaite resistance to rabbinic teaching."[53] She asserted historical precedents for a multiplicity of "Judaisms" rather than a single, unified orthodoxy, writing that "ancient Judaism was a rich tapestry of many different religious tendencies. Recent research . . . [has] taught us to avoid thinking of Judaism as one neat, definable entity called 'orthodox Judaism.'"[54] Of course, there is no such entity. Topper's view of Orthodox Judaism as monolithic betrays her lack of understanding about the interpretive conflicts that divide the Orthodox community. But in a more general sense, in using the RJC moment to posit a feminist and queer-positive relationship to religious Judaism, in a voice that was at once skeptical and sincere, Topper took RJC into different territory than most of her peers.

## Masada Redux: A Gendered Reading

Topper's interest in finding alternatives to orthodoxy led her to allude, like Zorn, to Jewish mysticism and Judaism's "magical texts," but the resemblance ends there. Indeed, GodCo's queer and feminist critique points up the absence of similar concerns in Zorn's presentation of RJC, especially in the Masada project. If Zorn's body of RJC work splinters prismatically into many meanings, one not often discussed is the way it can be taken as a sonic expression of Ashkenazic Jewish masculinity. This is not to say that Zorn excludes female musicians. Indeed, many of the women active on the downtown scene, as well as in experimental music in general, have released recordings on Tzadik, and he has a series on the label, called Oracles, devoted to female artists. (Moreover, his embrace of the free expression of sexuality, which he has expressed through images and liner notes, includes the film score to *Trembling Before G-d*, a film about homosexuality in the Orthodox community.) Nevertheless, Zorn's Masada project begs a gendered critique. On one hand, the acoustic and electric Masada ensembles enact a positive response to the dilemma described earlier: the invisibility of Jewish-qua-Jewish artists in rock and jazz. Electric Masada's gladiatorial quality—in Ribot's words, "the kind of super-muscular chop-soloing that I grew up questioning," which he framed as "kind of like the musical version of the high-school jocks"—brings Jewish men into a musical arena to which they were previously not admitted.[55] On the other hand, both jazz and rock are male-dominated genres that have historically subjected female musicians to gender hazing. Zorn's presentation of RJC and Masada is not sexist, but it does traffic in machismo.

Zorn's visual and written cues also suggest a reading of his Masada oeuvre that puts Jewish masculinity front and center. Nearly every thinker and artist whose work he includes on his covers and insets is male, as are all the artists covered in his Great Jewish Music series. Judaism, moreover, is a religion whose tradition of patriarchal authority feminists have often had to fight. As theologian Melissa Raphael points out, "The male Jew has been the normative Jew: he has been God's allocutor and the tradition's interlocutor and decisor in matters of Jewish law."[56] On the RJC series, Zorn uses images of Jewish ritual objects traditionally associated with male religious privilege, and neither the word *tzadik* nor the images of the ruins of the Masada fortress suggests that he is concerned with countering the normativity of the male Jew. Taken as a whole, Zorn's interpretation of the RJC project comes across as decidedly masculine.

Both as a gendered space and as an idealized one, based on Jewish archetypes abstracted from contemporary world, Zorn's Masada world stands in stark relief to the "in-between space" articulated by G-d Is My Co-Pilot. It is true that Topper indulges in utopian thinking in her booklets. When she discusses Jewish nation-building songs, she skirts any substantial mention of geopolitics in the Middle East, choosing instead to draw on old-fashioned images from an era that, if it ever really existed, is now long gone. On the other hand, Topper was unusual among her peers for using the RJC moment to address Israel at all. (Elliott Sharp's *Intifada* is one of the few instances of a more direct allusion to contemporary Israeli politics.) But GodCo's main contribution to the RJC moment was its radical insistence on incorporating in-betweenness into the notion of Jewish culture. If Jewish weddings, day camps, Hebrew schools, and grandmothers have served generations of Americans as familiar points of transmission for Jewish expressive culture, that transmission has often been less than thorough or complete. Topper's Jewish experience was shaped both by the ruptures of violence, genocide, and loss visited upon previous generations, and by the move away from religious observance that her parents and grandparents had been eager to make. As a fourth-generation American Jew, Topper inherited a historical legacy that left her with a tangle of ties and lacunae vis-à-vis Jewish texts, traditions, and practices. Rather than ignore this tangle, Topper chose to engage it. Rather than hide it, she made art out of it. Insofar as Topper was trying to teach her audiences about Jewish music, this position is open to criticism. However, her goal was not to offer stylistically convincing or historically accurate performances of Yiddish and Hebrew songs. Instead, Topper, Flanagin, and their band took on what I consider to be the central project of the RJC moment, stepping outside the frame of both authenticity and convention in regard to the notion of Jewish music, and particularly songs. The band's ingeniously arranged Jewish songs are not meant as emblems of the Jewish people as a whole, but as testaments to the complex inheritance that has shaped Jewish American identity in the late twentieth century, one person at a time.

 FIVE

# Shelley Hirsch and Anthony Coleman

*Music and Memory from the "Nowhere Place"*

RADICAL JEWISH CULTURE, EMBEDDED IN ITS GEOGRAPHIC
locus and indebted to the people who lived and worked there, was also a
function of a particular moment in history, one shaped by an ever easier
access to music that crossed boundaries of genre, nation, and era. As the
site for a creative scene that trafficked in pluralistic references and non-
tonal abstraction, the Lower East Side's present, more than its turn-of-
the-century Jewish past, informed the music of the RJC moment. Given
this presentist orientation, it might seem implausible that RJC should
have played a productive role as a "memory space"—a conceptual space
for remembering, or for engaging the notion of memory.[1] And yet, downtown artists were able to put some very strange music to work in developing RJC into a peculiarly useful Jewish memory space. They aimed
not to engage historical memory so much as to make sense of their own,
Jewishly complicated landscapes of recent memory. Like GodCo, vocalist Shelley Hirsch and pianist Anthony Coleman used music to mull on
lived experience, on the encounter between memory and history, and on
being Jewish in the world. Through their music, these artists staged an

encounter between individual subjectivity and the larger entities—Jewish history, religion, heritage—that shape it without fully constituting it. If their Jewish experiences had not engendered a thorough familiarity with Jewish texts and traditions, this was a quality they shared with many other Jews of and beyond their own generation and milieu. And that was just the point. Their creative and conceptual forays added a new dimension to the notion of Jewishly usable music: such music, they contended, could reflect imperfect cultural transmission, cultural and national in-between-ness, or simply personal ambivalence. But in their efforts they were not always well understood. Among the misconceptions they encountered, one of the most productive—that is, one that spurs us to consider RJC, and the relationship it posited between music and Jewish identity, in a new way—was that they were coming to Jewish music from a "nowhere place."[2]

The notion of the "nowhere" place had two key components in regard to Radical Jewish Culture. One was downtown artists' evident disinclination to use Jewish musical traditions as the template for their new work, and the other was their quality of "aesthetic detachment"—that is, the detachment of contemporary artists from the cultural sources of the sounds they manipulate into art objects. The first issue was sometimes voiced by participants in the klezmer revival, who suggested that RJC was culturally unmoored and lacking in historical resonance. Without an audible anchor in Jewish musical traditions, these artists contended, new Jewish music would not have much substance or traction. As Coleman recalled, after the initial burst of creativity sparked by the Munich festival, "so quickly it became a cliché, and so quickly it became segmented, that klezmer was one thing, and this other stuff [downtownish music], which *claimed* to be Jewish music, was something else."[3] The second component of the "nowhere place," aesthetic detachment, raises interesting issues about the traits and purposes of Jewishly usable art, particularly in regard to contemporary music; it also has echoes in composer R. Murray Shafer's formulation of "schizophonia"—the separation of a sound from its source, and its entry, via recordings, into a free-floating global "soundscape." In such a soundscape, recorded sound, easily parted from its cultural and temporal origins, offers up music as an object of pure consumption.[4] Thus, the free circulation of recordings creates a "nowhere place" in which contemporary music, and the artists who make it, reside.

The notion of a "nowhere place" may have a hollow ring, but it presents us with a useful spatial metaphor for precisely the emotional territory downtown artists were striving to reclaim as the province of contemporary Jewish music. Artists whose music could appear to betray a lack of interest in reconnecting with a Jewish musical roots—whose work might seem to some listeners to embody either the "depthlessness" of the oversaturated postmodern artifact or the rootlessness of nontonal, abstract experimentalism—were willing to chance being charged with developing work that was nominally Jewish but free of meaningful Jewish content. In fact, accustomed as they were to working on the stylistic and conceptual margins of jazz, rock, and classical music, these artists now aimed to adapt experimentalist soundscapes to suit the so-called "nowhere places" of Jewish identity—and thereby to materialize those spaces, which were otherwise defined by absence, as meaningful creative presences.

To make sense of this idea, it is useful to visit the debates over "schizophonia" and its effects on music's meaningfulness. Since Shafer proposed his notion in 1969, there has arisen a lively dialogue over the implications, pro and con, of the schizophonic state of affairs into which twentieth-century technologies have propelled us. The view of schizophonia as precipitating modern music into a hollow and rootless condition is of course decidedly "con." At its most hollow, that condition is one in which artists ignore (or are ignorant of) cultural losses, favor artifice over knowledge, choose easy pleasure over ethical engagement, and prize consumption above all.[5] Circulating aimlessly through this nowhere place are the sonic artifacts of music without memory. Even as listeners and artists consume such artifacts, in the absence of their awareness of, or personal connection to, the contexts in which the music was created, music loses its ability to evoke any collective memory of its cultural origins. Thus, as performance studies scholar Barbara Kirshenblatt-Gimblett wrote in regard to RJC, "'Nowhere' is a space of abstraction where sounds unmoored from other times and places can be engaged as sound for its own sake. In that place called *nowhere*, musicians can play anything." Moreover, insofar as contemporary music is typified by the "aesthetic practice of detachment," in the context of RJC that detachment is "intensified by the situation of music without memory."[6] The latter notion rests on the idea that music's meaningfulness to a community is determined not only by sounds themselves, but also by the communal uses to which those sounds are put. If music is separated from its thick cultural context, it loses its collective memory-making function. When it is cast out into a world where it is apprehended for its aesthetic content alone, what can it really "mean"?

In the context of Jewish history, the idea of music without memory is a potent one, even more so because collective memory is a central part of Jewish liturgy. That liturgy sustains a community-wide understanding of central events that have shaped Jewish history, and in this process musical sound—including liturgical songs and prayer cantillation—plays a key role.[7] Music has thus become bound up with Jewish historiography—it contributes to the inscribing and reinscribing of Jewish history onto the collective consciousness. In contrast, in the "nowhere" place, downtown musicians seem to appropriate and manipulate sounds whose Jewish cultural content, already frayed in that milieu, is now damaged even further. Empty aesthetic affinities, concatenated into a disorienting range of culturally deracinated references, replace meaningful Jewish connections. Any music that has been separated (by force or forgetting) from its meaning-making cultural context becomes music without memory, but in light of the violent ruptures in modern Jewish history, that loss is particularly acute. The downtown scene, which champions schizophonic aesthetic detachment above historical continuity, community building, or collective memory, becomes a lonely space for Jewish music.

Downtown artists refuted this idea verbally and in writing, arguing that their music, far from exhibiting a lack of attention to Jewish culture, actually gave credence to neglected aspects of that culture. Guitarist Marc Ribot countered the charge in a provocative way. Convinced that the downtown scene was relegated to a "nowhere place" in (and by) modern Jewish historiography, he argued that if the scene were invisible to some observers—and indeed to some downtown musicians—as a Jewish place per se, it was because of the way Jewish history had so far been written and conceptualized. He found particular resonance for his ideas in a thesis that theologian Jacob Neusner had proposed about the over-arching narrative of Jewish historiography. In Neusner's formulation, this narrative describes an arc that begins with exile, moves through destruction, and culminates, with the founding of the State of Israel, in redemption.[8] Part of the narrative's power lies in the way it determines which aspects of the Jewish experience—in its long, variegated history and wide geographical reach—are most relevant to Jewish historiography. Thus, in Ribot's interpretation, "The reason why [the downtown scene] was invisible [as a Jewish community] . . . was because the story . . . of Holocaust and Redemption said, 'Well, there was the Temple, then there was the Diaspora, then there was the Holocaust, and then there was Redemption in Israel.' And so things which exist outside that story don't exist." To partake of the Diaspora-Holocaust-Redemption narrative, then, was to suggest that after the establishment of the State of Israel, diasporic Jewish cultural life had become irrelevant. Whether or not it was articulated outright, Ribot was convinced that Neusner's controversial thesis was implicated in the way artists downtown had once assumed that Jewish heritage had little relevance to their creative work, and vice versa. He and his colleagues, he wrote:

> exist in a mythic nowhere, neither in "the promised land," nor in "exile.". . . [Although] we walk, breathe and write music in the virtual and historic center of the largest, oldest, uninterrupted urban Jewish culture in existence, our creations are visible and audible as everything but the continuation of that culture's history . . . and the music we normally play, while categorized by every other conceivable parameter—geography, gender, style, race, class, politics—cannot be "read" as Jewish.[9]

According to the logic of the narrative on which he drew, the music and creative milieu of the downtown scene were invisible (and inaudible) as Jewish history. Ribot was concerned in particular with the way this narrative cast out the creative innovations of the downtown scene—its distinctive repertoire, performance practices, and approach to musical language. As he continued, "And it doesn't mean that we couldn't live [in the United States]. You could live some place, you could have a house, and a car—but what you couldn't do was create." Indeed, he argued, this view of history had pushed Jewish artists themselves to take a diffident attitude toward the Jewish relevance of their work. This was one reason the RJC moment was so empowering: "And so ... to say, 'No, actually, we have a creative history, here in New York,' [to say], 'There is a "We," and we have a creative history,' is violating [the integrity of that narrative]. Because [being in diaspora] we shouldn't exist. We're just kind of this temporary thing."[10] The RJC moment would disrupt this narrative insofar as artists sought to inscribe their experimentalist, downtownish work into the annals of Jewish history, where they did not by rights belong.

This reasoning suggested that RJC was not only about its own moment, but also about carving out a kind of alternative history. Just as art historians had sought to write work that was not immediately self-evident as "Jewish" into the history of Jewish art, downtown musicians could use their own work to expand upon what was meant by "Jewish music." On one hand, there had been a long tradition of Jewish artists and thinkers whose work was basically secular and not necessarily geared toward Jewish audiences, but who had been influenced by, and remained invested in, Jewish tradition. Indeed, in the RJC moment many downtown artists became curious about whether or how their own work fit into the compass of Jewish creative and intellectual history. On the other hand, with a growing literature that aimed to address it, work that was Jewishly relevant, but not in an obvious way, was hardly as invisible as Ribot asserted.[11] Whether or not Neusner's narrative actually explained the lack of attention of composer/improvisers to that creative lineage, it did some key conceptual work for Ribot, explicating both downtown's pre-RJC quietness and, afterward, what he found to be a frustrating tendency among some of his contemporaries to adopt the paradigm of "getting Jewish music right" by turning to klezmer, instead of looking to the methods and materials of their own scene. He took issue with artists who looked to a diasporic moment and place—early twentieth-century Jewish immigrant life in the United States—that, unlike their own, was an acknowledged part of Jewish historiography. This move, he contended, led artists to turn toward sound sources that lent their new music Jewish historical legitimacy even as they turned away from any Jewish experience that felt, in comparison, blemished and inauthentic. To the contrary, Ribot suggested, downtown music could usefully engage even "a useless inherited Judaism, the past as

hell ... [and] a religious upbringing steeped in hypocrisy and denial."[12]
Rather than writing music that suggested a nostalgic connection to a
Jewish past they had never known, Ribot contended that artists should
use music to engage their own Jewish experiences and memories, just
as they were.

On his own part, those memories encompassed the non-Jewish and
cheerfully un-hip American songs and dances that had played a key social function in his postwar Reform Jewish community, and which, as a
teen in a garage band, he had suffered through at his own bar mitzvah.
Ribot argued that such material should form the basis for the music
of the RJC moment precisely because its evident lack of Jewish content—
and, in the case of traditional Jewish songs styled as American pop, its
decidedly diasporic character—illuminated something important about
twentieth-century American Jewish culture. Ribot was interested, in
other words, in the functional aspect of music within the Jewish community, whether or not that music "sounded Jewish" per se, and regardless
of whether it strengthened artists' sense of communal identification or
spurred them to escape its embrace.

In insisting that Jewish culture resided in his experiences growing
up in a postwar milieu of suburban Reform Judaism—rather than being
something he could acquire through systematic study or to which he
simply had a birthright—Ribot's essays align with a notion developed
by literary theorist Walter Benn Michaels at around the same time. Benn
Michaels had argued controversially that "culture" is no more and no
less than what one does, and that if "identity" is shared, it is only because experiences are shared, and not because of birthright, heritage, or
ethnicity. Thus, he contended, "there can be no 'mark of identity' that
transcends one's actual practices and experiences. . . . [If we perceive
an activity as belonging] to *our culture* [this belief] cannot count as a
motive for doing it since, if it does belong to *our culture,* we already do
it and if we don't do it (if we've stopped or haven't yet started doing it)
it doesn't belong to *our culture*."[13] This argument has been strenuously
contested, but it was just such an extremist formulation of "culture" that
led Ribot to foreground what he identified as the Jewish musical culture
of his childhood at an RJC festival in 1995, when he devoted his evening
on stage to the music of Jewish weddings and bar mitzvahs from the

Reform community in which he had grown up. He identified that music as having exerted a formative influence on his Jewish identity, not as a positive model, but as one of several musical "push" factors that had driven him out of suburban New Jersey and thence to the downtown scene. His own bar mitzvah, he recalled,

> took place in a bright, modern, inconspicuous and unattractive building called Synagogue Oheb Shalom on a leafy street called Scotland Road in suburban South Orange, New Jersey in 1967. The band played the Alley Cat, the Hokey Pokey, [and] Barbra Streisand.... I was profoundly influenced [by this music] —by a wound to my sensibilities over which my subsequent aesthetic formed like a scar. But this is real memory, real influence, and however painful, real familiarity.... Isn't this Jewish culture? What was my Bar Mitzvah then? Isn't my reaction to it, however oppositional, Jewish history? If not, what is it?[14]

By bringing this musical material to the RJC moment, Ribot brought the particularities of his Jewish experience into the light of day, but unlike G-d Is My Co Pilot's treatment of Jewish holiday songs, Ribot presented this material in a straight pop style, without using it as a canvas for his own interpretive treatment. Rather than channeling the songs through his own creative voice as a composer/improviser, as he was otherwise wont to do, he was suggesting that it was useful to present them at an RJC festival just as he had heard them growing up. The bafflement with which his efforts were met resonated with his interpretation of Neusner's narrative. Thus, he mused, "Although I was determined not to treat the material satirically, the overall effect was comic, as anyone who has heard my material can imagine [in contrast to the way he normally played]. But why really? I think part of the laughter was nervous: by tracing, between Babs and myself, the borders of [postwar Jewish] culture ... a space was opened up into which we are conceptually unprepared to look."[15] Those borders, he suggested, also surrounded the downtown music scene, another space artists had little precedent for including in their purview of Jewish history and culture. He saw such borders as posing a formidable conceptual challenge to downtown artists as they sought out materials for their Jewishly identified music. And although his colleagues did not necessarily concur with this interpretation, several did share a similar interest in developing work that reflected, first and foremost, on their own Jewish subject positions. Their music might or might not be construed by observers as falling within the grand arc of Jewish history, but their main concern was to develop music that could engage the Jewish resonances of their own memories and experiences.

## Schizophonia, Redux

Given the ghosts that wander through Jewish history, the possibility of reclaiming memory has become a vital part of the contemporary Jewish musical landscape. Klezmer is a clear example of a music whose communal function, and thus potentially its memory of itself, could be reestablished by artists who cared enough to do so. And yet, the concept of reclaiming lost culture is not sufficient for apprehending contemporary music in general, or RJC in particular. As the large post-Shaffer literature illustrates, contemporary musical creativity, schizophonic though it may be, is not a wholly commodified and ontologically drained cultural free-for-all. On the "pro" side of the schizophonia debates, scholars argue that easy access to music provides opportunities for cultural community-building, makes way for new cultural formations and the articulation of hybrid identities, allows for collaborations across previously intractable borders of class and nation, and provides more equitable access to the materials of modern music. Indeed, the separation of sounds from their sources, which seems to be a product of modernity, also has a long history—probably as long as music history or Jewish history itself. In the sense that contemporary artists will follow their curiosities wherever they lead, nearly all inhabit a "nowhere place." But long before recordings, radio, and even the printing press, songs, those most portable of cultural artifacts, were brought from one place to another and absorbed into their new surroundings as new meanings accrued around them.

Whether they work in the sphere of popular music, jazz, concert music, or contemporary liturgical music, artists inevitably engage with idioms that have been shaken loose from their sources—if indeed they can be traced to a single source—and whose former meanings can never be reconstructed. This dynamic of borrowing and re-adaptation may seem more obvious in Western music, and in particular in music with elements of collage, but ethnomusicologists have documented it as occurring in many different contexts, including non-Western, non-commercial, and ceremonial ones. Indeed, as ethnomusicologists Ellen Koskoff and Kay Kaufman Shelemay have illustrated, "traditional" Jewish communities—among them Lubavitch (hasidic) and Syrian Jews—borrow songs from outside sources and imbue them with contextual meanings quite different from their original ones; such songs then enter into the community's collective musical memory and become part of the local lexicon.[16] In both cases, the process of adapting and adopting the new music is more important to its Jewish communal function than is the source from which it was borrowed. And yet, even if Jewish communities can create Jewishly usable music from non-Jewish sources, the question remains as to what kind of Jewish usability the downtown scene, which had not always conceived of itself as constituting a Jewish community at all, would embrace.

By investigating the very nowhere place in which they purportedly resided, artists involved in the RJC moment offered a novel paradigm for usability in Jewish music. But as part of a scene imbued with jazz's practices and values, they were already working in a creative context that was determined by artists' relationship to their musical past. They thus took their complicated relationship to Jewish memory and history—and their fidelity to a cosmopolitan, experimentalist art scene—as points of serious artistic inquiry. The schizophonic world they inhabited, the strong emotional and often frayed historical connections to Jewish heritage, the common wariness toward religious mandates: all became objects of their artistic attention. In the process, downtown artists ventured into a creative sphere that was Jewishly meaningful by means of its unique musical refraction of American Jewish experience in the twentieth century. Hirsch and Coleman developed two of the most striking, and strikingly different, musical responses to the idea that "people should write from their own memory—their own memory and their own desires, and not from some collective memory. . . . To differentiate between what they actually remember, and what they're being told they remember."[17]

## O Little Town of East New York:
## A Sonic Memory-Space

In her creative engagements with Jewish memory and identity, Shelley Hirsch has exploited her vocal gifts and compositional concerns, using storytelling and vocal mimicry to bring to life multiple characters, and turning fluidly to her own invented kinds of glossolalia to voice what could not be articulated through language. By the 1990s, Hirsch had developed an oeuvre of narrative-driven, often site-specific compositions, many of which incorporated real or fictional characters she admired or identified with, but it was not until the RJC moment that she delved into writing a substantial first-personal narrative. When she did, about ten years after recording "I Am a Jew" and a year before the Munich festival, she drew on her longstanding interest in music as a vehicle for memory to develop a radio play, *O Little Town of East New York*.[18] She used the piece to dramatize and reinhabit her childhood, drawing on the creative process to make sense of its discontinuous Jewish elements in a way she could not have done as a girl. Using the sui generis, fluidly expressive musical language she had developed over her career, she confronted the question of Jewish memory—what it is, what constitutes it, and how to musically apprehend it—and developed an interpretation of RJC that was among the most personal of the artists in her creative cohort.

Developed in collaboration with keyboardist David Weinstein, *O Little Town* stands as one of the key documents of the RJC moment. Using narrative to engage concretely with personal memory, while employing innovative musical means to illuminate the elusive nature of memory, the piece appears to capture memories—but it also uses sound to illustrate the ultimate impossibility of that act. In depicting, through text, a conflicted Jewish girl coming of age amidst a wondrous, menacing, and confounding outside world, *O Little Town* echoed the twentieth-century literary turn toward exploring the discontinuities and discontents of American Jewish life, notably by novelist Philip Roth, and more recently by such writers as Shalom Auslander, Nathan Englander, Jonathan Safran Foer, Allegra Goodman, and Nicole Krauss.[19] Indeed, Hirsch applies experimentalist literary techniques to her text's formal construction in a way that signifies compellingly on the slippery nature of mem-

**Figure 5.1.** Shelley Hirsch. 2011. *Photo: Ziga Koritnik.*

ory, and on the constant interpellation of past experiences into present ones. In leaping between her adult perspective and her child's one, and in moving amongst voices and between past and present tenses, she both makes direct observations about memory and signifies obliquely on the nature of memory. In *O Little Town,* Hirsch has thus created a work in which the music itself does the work of "remembering."

In one of her earlier long-form narrative pieces, *States* (1996–97), one of her characters intones, "The body is the biggest recorder possible," an idea she mined through the process of composing *O Little Town* by improvising with her voice and exploring the memories that arose as a result.[20] Over the course of her career, Hirsch's interest in improvisation and free association had also led her to develop uncon-

ventional narrative strategies to sonically manifest a series of kaleido-
scopic textual shifts. Her narratives leap among sonically embodied
characters, glossolalia, and quotations—real and ersatz—from myriad
musical sources. Like *States,* but set in a fully autobiographical context
(a point on which she has been adamant in interviews), *O Little Town* is a
montage of anecdotes, which are infused with sonic elements and which
sometimes transmute into musical performances. (When she performs
the piece alone, she achieves this effect by vocalizing over a prerecorded
musical track.) *O Little Town* thus incorporates the creative tools Hirsch
had crafted over the course of her career, in pieces that were often site-
specific and that wove together composed and improvised music, text,
movement, and visual elements (PURL 5.1).

O *Little Town* is scored for voice, keyboards, and percussion, and
on the recording Hirsch also uses a vocal harmonizer, multi-tracking,
and digital delays; in live performances, she has included costumes,
lighting effects and projected slides, as well as a sampling keyboard and
dual microphones programmed with contrasting effects. The piece is
peopled with multiple vocal characters from Hirsch's childhood, and in
her musical reconstruction of her neighborhood, as throughout her creative oeuvre, different vocal characters can suddenly emerge, disappear,
and seamlessly transform. Each of *O Little Town's* thirty-five vignettes,
which range from thirty seconds to five minutes in length, enacts and
encapsulates a formative moment, an influential person, or, as in the case
of "Bongos," a sonic character; about half of the vignettes address Jewish
themes or characters—for example, "Hymie and Harry," who were "the
butcher and the fruit man, respectively"—which are embedded into her
larger story about the neighborhood's polyglot mix and its class- and
race-based tensions. She narrates the vignettes over varied melodic and
rhythmic ostinati, which are often woven through with sounds that,
by virtue of both the text they accompany and their own qualities, assume the rhetorical function of memories or ghosts. Hirsch also shifts
between a first- and second-person perspective, at times reminiscing and
addressing her listeners directly, using her own adult voice, in which she
narrates an introduction and "Outro," sections that bracket the work
both formally and as dramatic devices. At other times she retreats into
a dramatically constituted realm to reenact her memories in character

as a young or adolescent girl. In the piece's larger dramatic framework, then, she invites us in, draws us into her multivalent childhood world, and ushers us back out into the present day (PURL 5.2).

O Little Town of East New York is an interesting artifact of the RJC moment in another way: it offers a counter-narrative to the Lower East Side nostalgia that historian Hasia Diner has shown to be central to American Jewish letters.[21] As an artist Hirsch was based on the Lower East Side, and she had lived in its environs since striking out on her own as a teenager, but her sonic memoir is about East New York, the multiethnic, "racially tense" Brooklyn neighborhood in which she grew up, one of the poorest sections in the five boroughs. Within the larger framework of the piece, her encounters with Jewish culture are simply one strand in the fabric of her girlhood world. As she reconstructs this neighborhood musically, evincing a child's fascination without any rose-tinted nostalgia, Hirsch's stories about East New York offer a counter-narrative to the Lower East Side as the quintessential Jewish American memory space.

Like her own sense of Jewish identity, the Jewishness of Hirsch's neighborhood was at once apparent and fugitive. Jewish people lived in this place, so it was a Jewish place, but throughout the piece Hirsch makes evident the fragmentation and fading of its Yiddishkeit, as well as the magnetic force other cultural currents exerted upon her. Hirsch's home life was likewise laced with antipathy toward Judaism, as she recalls: "My mother . . . never spoke a word of Yiddish at home. My father thought it sounded too whiny. . . . I did go to synagogue, almost as a rebellion against my parents. There was no spirituality or any sense of religion [at home]."[22] As she intones in one of O Little Town's more acerbic vignettes, she defied this aspect of her home life in small ways: "I had a little electric menorah / I'd screw the candles in, to light the bulbs up / but my parents always sat in the back room / smoking cigarettes and eating pork chops!" In another vignette, she recalls, "At Christmas time, Dad dressed up as Santa Claus and he'd tell stories to all the kids in the building," but in this case she suffuses the memory with warmth. In O Little Town, then, Hirsch explores her memories of growing up with a strong sense of Jewish identification but a confusion over what that sense constituted. She experienced little by way of Jewish practice or culture (at least, it was not named as such) at home, but as she ventured into her building's hallways and through the neighborhood streets, she was intrigued by encountering Yiddish turns of phrase, intimations of Jewish culture in families quite different from her own, and glimpses of religious practices for which she had little context. In recounting her ad hoc encounters with Jews in the neighborhood, her girlhood self also recognizes historical forces beyond her grasp. But as the piece's adult narrator, Hirsch does not seek to draw out larger themes from her own story. Instead, it is the sensual force of her childhood memories and way of seeing the world that animate the piece. Her main focus is thus not on the role played in her parents' or her neighbors' lives of the larger forces in Jewish history, but on the grain of human experience—its textures, smells, and sounds. The piece hinges on memories that are acutely particular, and it is animated by Hirsch's finely observed details of the differences among the people in her neighborhood—the smell of sardines in one apartment, her friend's mother's false teeth in a glass on the kitchen table, the different accents she learned early on to mimic exactly. By constructing O Little Town as a montage, Hirsch addresses the uneven rhythm in which these things—some Jewish, some not—flickered in and out of her life as it unfolded. In this way, O Little Town fully inhabits, and brings to life, a "nowhere place" in which Jewish knowledge is fragmentary, Jewish history only dimly revealed, religious practice viewed at a distance, and formal Jewish education nonexistent. It is in bringing those very lacunae into view that the piece exerts its power as a substantial Jewish memory space.

As much as the piece meditates on fragmentation and absence, it is also brimming with content. One of Hirsch's main concerns in O Little Town is to represent the multiple musical and cultural influences that shaped her creatively, and to reflect upon the Jewish aspects of her experience as bound up with and mutually constitutive of that whole. Accordingly, on "Songs in My Head," Hirsch sings snippets of about twenty iconic songs from her teens—including Jimi Hendrix's "Foxy Lady," Jefferson Airplane's "White Rabbit," and Aretha Franklin's "Chain of Fools"—in a stream-of-consciousness flow. Throughout the piece, her text gives a narrative context for her leaps amongst musical and cultural idioms, and for the flow she creates as she moves between musical abstraction and topical references. Uniquely among her colleagues during the RJC moment, Hirsch was thus able to incorporate directly into her personal narrative downtown's quality of musical pluralism. And she was thereby able to suggest one biographical genesis for the kind of "mobile and transactional" American Jewish identity discussed in this book's introduction (PURL 5.3).

Hirsch reaches this dramatic end through verismo, not nostalgia. In *O Little Town* she sketches out not only scenes of enchantment, but also those of racial tension, powerlessness, and class rage. In several of her vignettes, including "Killing the Ants," "Confession Booth," and "Vinnie Russo," she slips in reminders of the threats and antisemitic slurs that were part of the world she once moved through. In the first one, she alludes to neighborhood toughs who would kill ants in the street and jeer, "We're gonna kill the caterpillars too. And then we're gonna kill you, we're gonna kill you, we're gonna kill you!" In "Confession Booth," she addresses one of her experiences of antisemitism outright:

> I remember going to St. Fortunado's Church. I'd sit down in a pew wondering if anybody knew I was Jewish. . . . I wanted to go into those little confession booths they had. They looked so romantic with all the dark wood, and red velvet. . . . I wanted to go in, but I had to just sit there, and I had a lot to confess, and there were no psychiatrists or anything at that time. . . . You know, Frank Torretto was really cute, but he hated Jews, and my father was tall and blond and he worked with his arms, and one time I told Frank that my father was Irish. And he believed me, too, for a while.
>
> *Hey Shell! So your old man's Irish, huh? You wanna go to a movie or somethiiiin'?*

If the narrative of *O Little Town* was embedded in Hirsch's childhood experiences, so were its sonic techniques. Hirsch traces her key compositional concerns to her earliest memories, and the piece makes manifest many of those concerns, especially her interest in the body as the repository of cultural *habitus,* and the voice as an embodied medium that could also flow out of its body of origin and enter into the habitus of another, quite different one. She remembers having been drawn since her childhood to music that investigated the speech-song continuum. At seventeen, one of her favorite recordings had been of mezzosoprano Jan DeGaetani's iconic performance of Schoenberg's *Pierrot Lunaire;* even earlier, she recalled, she recognized the potential dramatic connection between, on one hand, speech that flows seamlessly into song and back again, and, on the other, deploying this kind of flexible speech in a theatrical context in order to trigger a surrealistic visual display. As she recalled, "I was totally enamored of Busby Berkeley movies, [film musicals that] influenced the way I think about music turning into language turning into a kind of surrealistic montage."[23] Hirsch's childhood fascination with using music to enact fluid shifts among psychological realms was coupled with an attention to unique sonic spaces, and both interests have informed her work ever since: "Most people go through these [compositional] periods. For me, it's all been there from being a little kid, making a piece site-specific to the staircase in the hallway."[24]

In text and composition, *O Little Town of East New York* addresses the genesis of all her aesthetic concerns, which Hirsch locates vividly in particular moments, places, and memories, each associated with a particular soundscape. Three such soundscapes, which are woven into both the musical and the texted narrative, figure into the recording most dramatically: the sonic ambience of the stairwell outside her childhood apartment, the different voices and accents of the people who lived in her building, and the evenings she spent dancing with her father to jazz records in the living room, which, in her recollection, "was like the enchanted room, dancing with my *very* handsome father, to Frank Sinatra, Nat King Cole, Johnny Mathis." The first soundscape, the echo-filled stairwell, offered her an early experience of the kinds of site-specific musical performance that would continue to occupy her throughout her career, and the diverse denizens of her building provided her with her earliest raw material for the coterie of characters she would later develop, as well as sparking an early fascination with the details of linguistic and cultural particularity. The experience of dancing with her father prefigured her involvement with soundscapes in another fashion, as it led her to inhabit, and be inhabited by, a piece of music. As she recalled, she wanted not simply to dance or sing along, but something more transformative: "I wanted to be part of the music." Her sense of enchantment with those evenings stemmed not only from a girl's adoration of her father, but also from her psychological entrée, achieved through movement and vocalization, into a transporting sonic world. When they were dancing together, Hirsch recalled:

My father might sing the melody, but I was listening to the little instrumental embellishments.... I was listening to all the sounds that connected the melody to the whole orchestration.... I would take [one phrase] into the hallway [and sing it].... In another acoustic space, suddenly there are strands from the music coming out of peoples' apartments, mixing in with it. So it is no longer a tiny part of a phrase, it has become the foreground for this new music.... I was hearing all the other things drift into the hallway with it, and so I never heard just the little musical phrase. I heard it in context [in a particular ambient and social environment].[25]

An interest in fully inhabiting a musical space, and in drawing on that space's sonic qualities to transform her found or original musical material, led Hirsch to construct sonic landscapes during her late teens, when as a member of the San Francisco Actors Workshop and influenced by the ideas of Artaud and Grotowski, she pursued an interest in sound-as-theater through creating site-specific works. She has recalled this experience as the first "totally conscious manifestation for me" of another idea that had long intrigued her. In conjunction with her interest in the continuum between speech and song, she wanted to develop work using music, movement, and theatrical elements to "move out of abstract spaces into narrative spaces."[26] A soundscape, in other words, could inspire new texts and narrative ideas: "We started doing soundscapes, by going to these different environments,"[27] she explained. "We'd go under the Golden Gate Bridge and sing under there, and then take back the sound [the sonic ambience] into the rehearsal space and see how that then moved into language."[28] Like her installations, which were affected sonically by their unique physical terrain, her recorded work also engages this concern with ambience, or the unique character a space effects upon sounds that are produced within it. In *O Little Town,* Hirsch explores the dramatic influence of the sonic ambience of her apartment's hallway, resonant and replete as it was with the "strands" of music and talk from throughout the building. When as a child she began staging theater pieces designed expressly for the hallway and stairwell, that sound-world had a dramatic effect on the way she would henceforth experience her own voice as an intimate partner to its sonic environment.

The musical setting, as well as Hirsch's dramatic performance and vocal presentation, allow *O Little Town* certain expressive possibilities particular to its medium, possibilities Hirsch and Weinstein achieved through layering sounds and juxtaposing recorded and electronically manipulated elements with Hirsch's voice. Electronics also play a part in enacting the flexible subjectivity of the piece's memory space by allowing Hirsch to populate the soundscape with different versions of her own voice, which she likewise juxtaposes, layers, and choruses. Sound, always a potent repository for memory, also makes it possible for Hirsch to represent the process of remembering as a multi-vocal one, with different voices registering in the foreground and background of each reconstituted scene. She uses several compositional devices to create a sonic "memory space" that complements her autobiographical stories. In "544 Hemlock Street," for example, she constructs a sonic environment to mimic the apartment hallway that once entranced her—both as she heard it at the time and as she envisioned it as the site for future musical performances. The layered texture of this section includes a bass-line ostinato, an insistent tapping, and a variety of evocative sounds—swooshes, whistles—to create the illusion (either through the effect of the space in which they recorded the piece, or by using a production effect) that these sounds are echoing in a reverberant space (PURL 5.4):

> Four stories high and our family moved to the top.... There was a window that looked out onto a courtyard, and we shared a clothesline with the people across the way ... and we'd have conversations when we were putting out or pulling in the wash.... And everybody at 544 listened to music.... And all different kinds of music seeped out of everyone's apartment and blended together in the hallways.... George Rifkin used to sit behind his doorway playing his trap set. ... The Dinnersteins, the Donnellys, the Baskins, the Boscos, the Blooms, the Rizzos, the Schneidermans, Mrs. Konnecky and Miss Lynch all mingled in the hallway, with the tiled floors and the marble steps.... And it was like being in some kind of a city cavern, the way it echoed and everything.

The memory space of *O Little Town* also resounds with the rock, soul, and funk that Hirsch heard in her youth, genres she has continued engaging in her work. Like her downtown colleagues, throughout all her involvements with experimental theater, free improvisation, and extended vocal techniques, Hirsch maintained a steady interest in popular music, and the characters that populate her narratives often channel that interest by breaking into a song, which then draws them, and the piece, into a new subjective world. *O Little Town* also includes a few samples from commercial recordings, notably Johnny Mathis's 1957 recording of the romantic ballad "Come to Me," one of the pieces she remembers dancing to with her father. In a way that compounds the idea of the piece as a meditation on the interaction between past and present, in "Singing with Johnny" she inserts her own, chorused vocal harmonies into the song's sweeping string accompaniment—fulfilling her childhood desire to enter musically into its seductive sonic world.[29] Echoing this arrangement are the rippling, unmetered harp arpeggios that usher in the vignette entitled "Maria's House/The Troika," in which Hirsch invokes the romance she associated with a family of Russian Jews, who "served real vegetables, not the olive green kind we used to get in cans," and where she heard her first full-length pieces by Stravinsky and Rachmaninoff— names she draws out to emphasize the way their exotic otherness captured her imagination as a girl. Fascinated by the sound of the Russian language but unable to reproduce it faithfully, in "The Troika" she uses electronic vocal effects to develop her performance of a "Russian" song into a surrealistic fantasia, manifesting her creative interest in moving seamlessly through language and melody into an abstract space, a fantastic and imagined dramatic world of her own devising (PURL 5.5).

Throughout *O Little Town*, Hirsch uses both formal devices and production effects to depict not only different physical spaces, but also the psychological terrain through which her vocalized characters are moving. Thus, the piece both constitutes its own unified "space" and also enacts a sense of shifting spaces. But rather than Hirsch seeming to move through these spaces, as one might experience in a film, they dissolve and reappear in new guises as Hirsch's voice stays in the same part of the stereoscape. The changes in sonic ambience, rather than taking us through a changing physical environment, thus bring us into the subjective field of one person as she is visited by a stream of memories. Hirsch enacts these environmental shifts sonically, not primarily through the use of the ambience effects available to her in the recording studio, but rather through her musical and dramatic architecture. Most of the piece's ostinato-based arrangements are centered around a single tonal center, some are non-tonal or highly chromatic, and a few end on an unresolved harmony. This construction makes each vignette into its own miniature world, whose harmonic logic does not often extend beyond its borders, and it adds to the piece's quality of filmic montage. As the piece's harmonic shifts happen for the most part between ostinati, it is the text and the reappearance of certain thematic elements, rather than the harmonic framework, that give the piece a sense of dramatic cohesion.

Woven throughout O Little Town are distorted or nearly inaudible sounds, which mimic dreams or distant memories in existing just below the surface of consciously apprehension. These sounds include faraway voices that emerge and retreat periodically throughout the composition, and which are often revealed as having been part of the sonic texture only after the other sounds drop away. To signal their rhetorical purpose, Hirsch introduces two wordless female voices, accompanied by a faint, low train whistle, in her opening vignette, "On the Far Reaches"—just at the moment when her spoken narration languidly trails off with a comment about memory: "Thomas Wolfe wrote a book called You Can't Go Home Again. But you can always . . . remember. . . ." The mysterious opening characters (voices and whistle) of O Little Town reemerge about two-thirds of the way through the piece in "Rhapsody," whose sonic space, constructed of layered loops, creates a stylized "jungle" that echoes and develops the theme of an earlier vignette, "Bananas." The final time we encounter these characters is in the "Outro," in which Hirsch describes going back to East New York as an adult. In this final section the dreamy vocal swoops have given way to rapid, layered vocal ululations, and the piece ends with the roar of the elevated train that runs past East New York. It is a testament to the evocative power of sound that even without Hirsch's vocal text, these faraway sounds point us to the piece's nature as a memory space (PURL 5.6).

It is notable that Hirsch foregrounds the notion of glossolalia, as opposed to straight imitation, most strongly in two of the piece's Jewish vignettes. Elsewhere, particularly in "Songs in My Head" and "Dipped," Hirsch acts as a ventriloquist, taking on the exact vocal timbres, phrasing, and inflections of the artists she imitates. But in regard to her Jewish material, instead of imitating outright, Hirsch often deploys gestures of pastness (an idea introduced in chapter 1) to indicate that she is engaging in a commentary on the past and not simply representing it. "Chant" is a striking example. Although she opens this vignette in a masculine cantorial voice, singing a blessing in Hebrew, she soon moves into glossolalia, reconstituting the way she would have heard that unfamiliar language as a child. These distortions of cantorial singing serve a rhetorical function, drawing attention to the key role played by interiority in *O Little Town*. "The Jewish People" includes a similarly stylized version of the cantorial singing she heard in her neighborhood's Orthodox synagogue. Together, these vignettes encapsulate the memory of having followed her elderly Jewish neighbors to synagogue only to be kept at a distance, upstairs in the women's section, from the cantorial singing that fascinated her. (The experience of being kept at arm's length because of her gender was to be repeated early in her career, when she sought to train in Kabuki dancing but was prohibited from doing so because she was a woman.) As she recalls in "The Jewish People," as a child she was struck by the vulnerability of her Jewish neighbors, dwarfed by East New York's housing projects, as they made their way to synagogue services. In a warbling, older woman's Yiddish-accented voice similar to the one she had used on "I Am a Jew," she recounts:

> The Jewish people in the projects looked so tiny there inside of all the big buildings they had. Ah! They used to sneak outta there to go to synagogue on the High Holy Holidays! And it was such an inspirational song the cantor was singing. . . . Ah! And I wanted to go downstairs with the men with the nice silk shawls they had, with the fringes. But we had to sit upstairs. We had to sit upstairs!

Her sense that her Jewish neighbors had only a tenuous and temporary claim on the neighborhood was eventually realized, Hirsch continues, despite the vibrancy of the synagogue services she witnessed: "You know the projects, where it is now, there used to be a big, beautiful synagogue, with marble? I thought stone was forever." With this bittersweet statement, Hirsch once again interleaves present and past, signaling again that *O Little Town* is more than an autobiographical narrative, but rather a space one visits in order to explore the act of remembering.

As in "The Jewish People," in "Chant" Hirsch investigates both her childhood attraction to cantorial singing and her lack of access to the sounds that fascinated her. Here she addresses this tension more conceptually, not only venturing into glossolalia, but also singing antiphonally with harmonized, male versions of her own voice. Just as she inserted her own voice into the texture of Johnny Mathis's romantic ballad "Come to Me," in "Chant" she weaves a masculine version of her voice into the ambient space, using an electronic effect to depict a subjective state. But unlike her memory of dancing with her father, and then using the reverberant hallway to create a rich new musical setting for a short melodic phrase, although she wanted "to be part of the music" in the synagogue, she could not use her own voice to inhabit the sonic space of cantorial singing. Sitting in the women's section, she was farther removed than the men from the cantor and could not, moreover, allow her voice to carry to the men's section. She could, however, imagine herself singing along down below. Inserting masculine versions of her own voice into the texture of "Chant" allows her to depict just such an imaginative act, drawing us into an interior world in which she conjured up a musical experience she could not otherwise achieve (PURL 5.7 and PURL 5.8).

The whole of O Little Town is about memory, but in these two vignettes in particular Hirsch blends narrative, compositional strategies, and vocal techniques in order to call attention to the way her representations of memory function as simulacra. The distorted language, the deliberately unschooled attempts to imitate cantorial phrasing, and the masculine-sounding manipulations of her voice: all these are facets of O Little Town's distinctive encounter with Jewish memory. In this piece, Hirsch is not simply addressing *something that happened*. Rather, she is sharing its residue with us, the memories she holds today of her encounters as a girl with flashes of compelling, mysterious, and inaccessible Jewish heritage. She never resolves the contingent nature of these flashes in the piece. She does not give us a vignette in which she revisits and repairs her fractured encounter with Jewish culture, for example, by fluently singing Hebrew prayers and enacting a return to her roots. In the lovingly reconstructed memory space that is O Little Town, her access to Jewish customs and languages must remain limited, and her understanding of them imperfect and fragmentary.

## Anthony Coleman: The Limits of Memory

Like Hirsch, during the RJC moment pianist Anthony Coleman turned to memory and personal experience to generate musical material. But although he occasionally used storytelling and theatrical frames in his performances, he also pursued, to a more abstract extreme, the idea of mining personal experience in order to develop an original, Jewishly inflected musical idiom. Coleman has composed and recorded a substantial body of Jewishly identified work, including two recordings of straight-ahead piano jazz with his band Sephardic Tinge (material he set in a more experimentalist context elsewhere, for example, on a No Wave arrangement of the traditional Sephardic song "Hija Mija"), two recordings with his Selfhaters ensemble, a recording of traditional Jewish music arranged for the Shabbat services at a Manhattan synagogue, three duo recordings inspired by Yiddish theater traditions with saxophonist Roy Nathanson, and a solo piano recording devoted to the work of composer Mordechai Gebirtig.[30] Like Zorn, Coleman has a diverse oeuvre of Jewishly identified music; to address his engagement with the notion of music without memory, it is illuminating to trace the progress of his unusual engagement with klezmer music, whose arc I trace through discussing an early piece called "Jevrejski by night," and two ensembles he subsequently developed, Sephardic Tinge and the Selfhaters ensemble.

In the early years of RJC, Coleman had particularly appreciated the way that rubric had allowed for interpretive flexibility and even confusion about the interface between downtown aesthetics and Jewish music. He saw RJC's vitality and promise as having two key sources: first, its artists' idiosyncratic voices, and second, its indeterminacy. Describing the RJC moment as a heady one, he recalled its inchoate quality of artistic ferment:

> It was this incredible opening. Because it was this incredible questioning. And that's what was interesting! . . . The questioning was the shit, the questioning was fantastic! I felt so alive, you know? It was like, wow, all these people, and they're all Jews, and they're all making this music, and there is *no* way to say what it is. Sometimes you think you have a glimmer of it—somebody does a little klezmer piece, and you go, "Oh, okay, that's it—" then John [Zorn] does *Kristallnacht*, and there was all this breaking glass, and "Oh, okay, it's a picture, it's an *image* of German-Jewish life, and the Jewish experience," and then Shelley Hirsch does her stories about growing up [in *O Little Town of East New York*], and then you say, "Oh, it's all a biography!" and then me and Roy [Nathanson] did our thing, which had a lot to do with Jewish repartée, and kind of Second Avenue theater [for example, on *The Coming Great Millennium*]— "Oh, it's Jewish *comedy*, right, it's more like that, it's like Jewish life in New York,

it's like going back [in time].". . . . And it was all so real, and it was all so alive. . . .
What was lost was that feeling in the beginning where you would look at it and
say, "What *is* it?" Now we know what Frank [London] does, we know what I do.
We know what John [Zorn] does, we know what Masada sounds like, we know
what [David Krakauer's] Klezmer Madness! sounds like. It is what it is. It's
there, it's a thing. It's reified.[31]

But although Coleman found RJC less interesting for having crystal-
lized, by 2001, into its various creative formations, he had developed a
body of work that resisted such reification—that is, he had composed,
performed, and recorded music that stood outside style and genre and
refused most of the kinds of musical and textual unifying devices Zorn,
GodCo, and Hirsch had deployed to lend coherence even to their more
abstract work. In his Selfhaters ensembles in particular, Coleman enacted a radical revision of the multiplex referentiality that informed
Zorn's and Hirsch's work, devising instead a minimally referential musical landscape that retained just a few tantalizing traces of his source
material. The pluralistic references that informed the music of the
downtown scene found its way into his other work, but in Selfhaters he
was after something different. He had designed this work to instigate
conceptual readings, an aim he elucidated through the notion of an
"open text."

In an intriguing challenge to the notion of the "nowhere place," in
Selfhaters, Coleman created a rigorously abstract musical framework for
articulating a space of failed communications and fragmented cultural
retentions. The work was about hollowness, but he defended it robustly
against a critique that it was itself hollow and thus Jewishly irrelevant.
During the RJC moment, he recalled, he and his colleagues had "felt
like, 'We know what we're doing, and we see how it connects to [Jew-
ish] things.'" And yet they were not well understood in their conviction
that getting Jewish music wrong, primarily through using experimental
language, could be as artistically rewarding as getting it right, through
basing one's work on historical research and reconstruction. Then, he
continued,

you had all these [musicians] who . . . had all the historical knowledge. The ones
who had done the research, the ones who had gone to Eastern Europe, the ones
who had catalogued and written down—you know, the ones who had met with

the last klezmer of Belarus or whatever. And they were saying . . . "[RJC] is just
some people who feel culturally disenfranchised, and they want to feel like they
have something. But . . . what they're doing has nothing to do with anything."
And . . . we had to say, "Well, no! You know what, you're missing the point."[32]

The point in question had several facets, and considering them leads us
to understand the sort of usability Coleman was most concerned with
as he developed his oeuvre of new Jewish music.

Part of the point that was being missed, then, was that downtown
artists, who might seem to be creating works of ironic abstraction, were
also drawing on their customary expressive toolkits, which signified
differently amongst insiders and outsiders, just as GodCo's No Wave
renditions of "Ha-Tikvah" had done. Another aspect of their work, lost
on Coleman's hypothetical interlocutor, was that composer/improvis-
ers were thinking of their Jewishly identified music in tandem with a
lineage of artists and thinkers, including Jewish figures, who were willing to work from the margins of cultural acceptance and intelligibility, a stance with which downtown artists identified. And finally, part
of the point was the value Coleman and his colleagues placed on creating open texts, or abstract musical canvases that are neither devoid
of content nor fully parsable. When apprehending an open musical text,
he explained, "It projects on you, you project on it. . . . There's no point
where you're gonna say, 'Oh, I get it. This is what it is.' You can't get it!
It's never gettable."[33] Indeed, one of the RJC's most intriguing creative
promises, which Coleman pursued most intensively, was that it might
lead artists to develop pieces that were Jewishly compelling in their very
indeterminacy. Some of downtown's earliest Jewishly identified music
had gestured in this direction—recall, for example, Nathanson's quasi-
cantorial keening on "Tikkun," and the now-you-see-it, now-you-don't
matter of its Jewishness—but in retrospect those gestures had not signified in robust enough ways to constitute an idiom. In Selfhaters, on
the other hand, Coleman made indeterminacy a unifying trait. Without
melodies, grooves, thematic development, or clear formal plans, this
Jewishly identified music was, in a fundamental sense, an investigation
into the nature of irresolution and absence.

Coleman was outspoken in his critique of the klezmer revival, but
from his early collaborations with Roy Nathanson in the duo Lobster and

**Figure 5.2.** Anthony Coleman. 2005. *Photo: Ben Rosengart.*

Friend, through his work on the Balkan-themed recording *disco by night* (1992) and through different iterations of his Selfhaters ensemble, Coleman also produced a unique body of work to which klezmer was central. He engaged klezmer's complicated cultural valences and approached the genre not as a source to be embraced for the cultural homecoming it offered, but as an occasion for existential reflection—shot through with a great deal of dry, self-mocking wit. "Poor klezmer!" he had once written. "A music which most of us never heard until the mid- to late '70s has to stand for a completely hybrid and fragmented culture—New York Jewish Culture."[34] Soon after the Munich festival, Coleman recalled, artists downtown were grappling with the question:

> People didn't know what they were getting! They were getting some klezmer, but maybe ten percent, you know? And some obvious Jewish references, but maybe another ten percent, fifteen. That still left seventy-five percent of stuff they had to wade through, and go, "What the hell is it?" Those are the kind of listeners I want. I don't want a bunch of listeners to watch me jump through a fucking hoop!"[35]

Coleman may have been stymied by the problems he saw in the klezmer revival, but even after a moment of crisis in Europe, when he and Nathanson had experienced their own klezmer performances as a macabre kind of minstrel act, Coleman continued engaging the music on his own terms. His compositional approach amounted to both a refusal and an insistence. What he refused was to celebrate a wished-for relationship to Jewish tradition. What he insisted on keeping in sight was a dialectic, that is, the process of making sense of one's relationship, however compromised, to that tradition, or to the idea of it.

### "Jevrejski by night" (Jewish by night)

One of Coleman's earliest ventures into Jewish-identified music drew substantially on klezmer as the basis for a mordant, existential meditation. "Jevrejski by night" is one piece on *disco by night* (1992), an extended musical suite Coleman developed in response to several years he spent in Yugoslavia in the early 1980s before that country and region descended into civil war.[36] The five-minute piece was inspired in part by a visit he had paid to a synagogue in Dubrovnik that was located on "Jevrejske Ulitza," or "Jew Street." As Coleman recalled, "I had read about cities having 'Jew Streets' before. But I had never actually seen a Jew Street. 'Jew Street' had kind of a big impact."[37] And although this piece can be read for its character relationships and narrative content, it also prefigures concerns Coleman would push to a more abstract place in Self-haters, including stasis, depletion, and the limits of communication. "Jevrejski by night" presents us with an existential drama in miniature. Drawing upon a simple, minor-mode dance idiom, it extends its musical materials to the breaking point. Scored for soprano saxophone, accordion, piano, and drum set, the piece has suggestive stylistic connections to klezmer's medium-tempo duple dances, but it is too slow and tired to be a *freilachs,* too depleted and strange to be a *sher,* and far too limited in expressive means to approach a *doina*. Instead, it is weary, limping, and unstable in its sudden shifts of mood. The piece's dramatic quality is determined in part by its slow tempo and irregular metric framework, underlying harmonies, and formal plan. But it is the relationship between the plaintive saxophone and the ragged ensemble, which emerge as the piece's two main characters, that lends "Jevrejski by night" its dramatic heft. In another strategy that resurfaced in Selfhaters, Coleman depicts this relationship with an underlying wit, thereby weaving a strand of self-referential commentary into its narrative fabric (PURL 5.9).

A brief, unmetered opening section sets up these two characters. The saxophone, alone and unsupported, wanders through unstable harmonic terrain; it expresses itself in scalar fragments, first centered in D-minor and then through A♭ and G♭, finally straying to an E♭ on which it settles to let out a series of plaintive cries. Suddenly, an ensemble of accordion, piano, and drum set joins in, propelling the piece back into D-minor and into a more orderly musical universe (0'32"). With the saxophone now incorporated into this motley quartet as a melody instrument, we are presented with four choruses of a twelve-bar, duple-meter dance. This dance, though, is hardly a lively one; if the saxophone, once lost, has now been found, it is given no celebratory welcome. The highest level of rhythmic excitement the ensemble can offer is a cymbal splash here and there. Otherwise, the accordion sleepwalks through what should be a sprightly rhythm, the kick drum plays only once every measure, and even though the saxophone has now settled into its role in the ensemble, playing the minor-mode melody it seems to have been seeking during the opening section, it nevertheless sounds exhausted. All in all, if one infers that these instruments are being played by musicians in character, it is evident that the exhausted players might not have the stamina to make it through an entire performance. Soon enough, the ensemble comes to a halt, having failed even to resolve at a cadence. The saxophone, cast out once again, wanders again in solitude, cries out again, and the ensemble reenters and reenacts the hopeless opening drama (1'47"). The group tries to straggle through one more iteration of the chorus, but this time they are wholly unsuccessful, as ominous dissonances crop up and the form breaks down. Yet again, the ensemble manages to marshal its resources and return to its halting dance (accompanied by clacking drumsticks—a bit of gallows humor after the saxophone has played a Dies Irae fragment [2'25"])—with a bit more energy, and after a repeated series of diminished seventh tutti blasts that resolve to the tonic and then cycle back, again and again, through the same gesture, the instruments come together decisively on a final tonic chord (4'30"). But despite this arrival, the piece's cumulated dramatic effect suggests that any sense of accomplishment is illusory. Although this ensemble has managed to go through the motions of playing a piece of music, it has essentially remained in the same place all along, and in its ragged debility it seems to offer no safe harbor to the lone saxophone that wanders through the piece. Coleman's explanation of the genesis of this piece sheds some light on its discursive field:

> It was when I went to Yugoslavia [in 1981], I started to really feel the absence of Jewish culture, like where it had been. 'Cause in the Balkans you get that much more than you get it in Germany.... In Germany it's all whitewashed and you have the Jewish Museum and the little plaque that says "Germans took the Jews away here" and so on. But the darkness of the Balkans, it still kind of looks like it did in the photos [from soon after World War II]. We went to a synagogue that was like the third-oldest synagogue in Europe, and there was a ninety-year-old guy just screaming about the community and what had happened to it. It was pretty chilling. All these things started happening at the same time and I started thinking, "Wow, it's time to deal with this."[38]

Such impressions give context to the sense of despair and existential pointlessness conveyed in "Jevrejski by night." This piece also reflects Coleman's interest in the narrative strategies—including repetition, atomization, isolation, and stasis—made famous by poet and playwright Samuel Beckett. In the piece's limited musical world, two characters engage in a dialogue of uncertain purpose and irresolution, and in this sense the piece has less in common with klezmer music than it does with Beckett's play of existential frustration, *Waiting for Godot*. A Beckettian mien was even more in evidence in Selfhaters, an ensemble Coleman convened about five years after he recorded *disco by night*. In the interim, he had developed a project that was quite different, but that led him to explore the ideas about cultural ownership that would become the genesis for his Selfhaters project.

In the piano trio Sephardic Tinge, Coleman brought a Spanish and Ladino influence into the realm of the straight-ahead piano jazz he had studied as a teen with Jacki Byard. Although neither Sephardic Jewish culture nor the Ladino language had played a part in his upbringing, he created the trio as a way to reflect on what he felt was by rights "his" culture, if any culture was his to claim. After some soul-searching about his attitude toward klezmer, he had come to understand that he felt skeptical about the genre precisely because of its evident claim as being Jewish "ethnic music":

> I was thinking, what was my problem with klezmer? Where's my unhappiness with klezmer? And I guess it was the feeling [during the revival] that it was *the* ethnic music of Jews, you know? Ethnic music is the music that is around when you are growing up.... Ethnic music for me was ... Latin music, because it was always around, it was really a part of my day-to-day life.... I lived on 160th Street [in Manhattan], there wasn't one sign in the streets that was in English. It was like living in a Spanish city.... Ethnic music is like that: it's the music that you live and breathe. Klezmer is not fuckin' ethnic music to me. I'm sorry. I mean, it's very nice, I like it a lot, but it's not ethnic music to me. It's some kind of ethnic music, but it's not *my* ethnic music.[39]

As in Ribot's formulation of "culture" as that which he had experienced, as opposed to that which was his birthright, Coleman considered Latin music his own—or at least more his own than klezmer music—because he had long been immersed in a predominantly Latino neighborhood, with Latin music coursing out of neighborhood bars and neighborhood businesses advertising their wares in Spanish. Although he did not claim Sephardic music as his own, either, he connected to the idea of it more than he could with klezmer music:

> [The band is] not really Sephardic. I mean, the name comes from the Jelly Roll Morton thing [the notion of jazz's "Latin tinge"].... If you don't get that ... play on words, it's hard to understand what the project is really about. "Tinge" is really crucial, you know? A tinge is only a tinge. [But in the trio] I was trying to look at this kind of combination between [jazz, Jewish heritage and] the Hispanic part of my background, which is not [from] my birth, but from where I [lived], what I loved and what I heard.... Ethnic music is the music you hear that accompanies your rituals. That was the music that accompanied my rituals, so ... that was the sense I was trying to make out of it.... There was no reason for me to say that I had any more right to play klezmer than I had to play salsa music.[40]

After he had recorded three albums with Sephardic Tinge, Coleman began thinking of ways to develop his work in a new direction. Unlike the music that surrounded him in the city, neither the Jewish music nor the Jewish culture with which he was familiar was the stuff to excite his imagination. Rather than drawing on Latin music, Coleman realized he could focus on the confusing lack of inspiring Jewish music he had encountered growing up in what was, after all, a culturally vibrant Jewish city. Citing a common plaint of his generation, he recalled, the suburban

Jewish communities in which his extended family lived seemed to be more focused on comfort and material acquisitions than they were rich sites for creative invention. In contrast, blues, soul, jazz, and funk suggested worlds of meaning far beyond what was close at hand. He and his downtown colleagues wondered where the Jewish music was that could come close to matching these other genres in expressive power:

> Us little white kids . . . either we lived in the suburbs, or our grandparents lived in the suburbs, or our uncles and aunts—*somebody* lived in the suburbs. . . . So there was a certain [materialistic] suburban mentality [close by]. . . . And so things like the blues . . . would make you realize that there's some reality in this world that is not reducible to *things*. And we didn't find this in . . . Jewish music, particularly. . . . Some people knew the cantorial repertoire really well, and they were very touched by that. But those of us who [went] to a Reform synagogue [*sings minor melody laconically, with a bit of stilted vibrato*]. . . . This was nothing that was gonna make someone who liked [blues guitarist/vocalist] Robert Johnson very excited.[41]

Coleman himself had grown up in the city, in a household imbued with the arts, including the modernist composers he would rediscover on his own after a long apprenticeship in jazz and folk music. But although his own upbringing was far from the bourgeois suburban experience shared by some of his contemporaries, it was still, by his own estimation, blandly American and nearly devoid of Jewishly distinctive culture. As he began searching for a new project that could engage his lived Jewish experience, despite what felt like its lack of stimulating creative material, he hit upon the idea that he could approach "his" Jewish culture for its quality of containment. The very paucity of Jewish expressive culture in his home was in fact a substance he could use art to examine, and not simply an absence to be ignored. In retrospect, then, his family's casual and ambivalent relationship with things Jewish loomed just as large as the things themselves:

> My parents were pretty self-hating. I mean . . . way beyond assimilated. My parents . . . would have a turkey on the table for Christmas. . . . A Della Consort record was playing. . . . My parents were Americans, they weren't into [Jewish identity]! Both of them had come out of different kinds of [Jewish] families, but both of them associated their families with mumbo jumbo. . . . They went to synagogue . . . [and] they kept the holidays, but they were . . . [Jewish] the same way that like Middle Americans are Christian. . . . My father's family . . . had some of the madness, you know [*warbling emotionally on a single pitch*] "Oy, I'm gonna

**Figure 5.3.** Selfhaters Ensemble. 1990s. Left to right: Doug Wieselman, Anthony Coleman, Michaël Attias (face obscured), Jim Pugliese, Fred Lonberg-Holm. *Photo: Yaël Bitton.*

> get a heart attack!"... They occasionally would tell a joke, or sing a song—it's like there were little hints, that there was some [other Jewish] world out there.... When you think about the way the Jews were portrayed, in movies ... as talking with their hands, and loud, and seemed like funky people! It didn't necessarily correspond that much to the actual people we were around, who were mostly pretty uptight.... My ex-girlfriend [said] ..."People are always talking about [how] the Jews are the people who ask questions? I've been around these relatives [of yours] and they don't ask me anything! [*cracking up in laughter*]"[42]

That other Jewish world, which he caught glimpses of in his father's family, in Allen Ginsberg's poetry and Lenny Bruce's comedy routines, and which was brought home to him musically by klezmer clarinetist Dave Tarras's 1978 concert in Manhattan, was one he was to spend substantial time and energy investigating.[43] At the moment he convened Selfhaters, however, he recalled drily, "So I thought, *that's* my culture, the culture of the self-hating Jew."[44] His new project grew out of the idea

of using his own Jewish experience as a text that could be read, deconstructed, and mined for creative material.[45] Describing that experience
as "a palimpsest" made up of "little bits of things," he continued,

> There's one dream of what it can all mean. And then there is what is really there.
> And what I have tried to do is to look at what is really there.... The Jewish
> experience is atomized.... Funny, sad, pathetic, weak, broken—so there's a little
> rhythm here, a little phrase there—that's what Selfhaters were all about. That's
> why it's *called* Selfhaters. There was no other possible name for it to have! Like,
> let's own it for what it is, you know? It's not all a big celebration.[46]

## Selfhaters and the Klezmer Cry

If its attenuated allusions to klezmer lend an audibly Jewish stamp to
"Jevrejski by night," the music Coleman created with his Selfhaters ensemble is notable for the rarity of such signifiers—at least in an audible sense. In fact, such signifiers were present, but they were so highly
abstracted that they were hard to recognize, thus becoming their own
meditation on notions of origin. Coleman, who had worked extensively
with sampling keyboards by that point in his career, explained, "I started
to take klezmer phrases like elements of design—like elements of language.... As though you were sampling them, except they were played
by live players." Some of Coleman's pieces are fully scored, but with
Selfhaters, he brought the basic klezmer phrases to the ensemble, and in
rehearsals, through improvising with the material, the musicians developed a dialogic context for Coleman's concept. That context sometimes
mimicked what he describes as the dysfunctional character of communications in his own extended Jewish family. With typical wit, he recalled,
"We rehearsed it a lot, and we knew the rehearsal was successful when we
ended up sitting in chairs looking at the floor, ignoring each other and
not speaking."[47] In addition to finding personal if rueful resonance with
such musical language as it applied to his own Jewish experience, Coleman also related it to the environment on the Lower East Side in which
he and his colleagues were working: "You could see Hebrew letters on
stuff, and [on] the building where the Yiddish-language paper, the *Forward,* had been.... You could still see some of the traces.... [There was]
the Educational Alliance—there were a couple of pickle stores—there

was some stuff. But mostly it was vanished. And so I wanted to do music that would have that same kind of [ambience]. Little traces of this, bits of that, repetitions of that, silences."[48] The bits and traces Coleman derived from klezmer include short, syncopated rhythmic patterns, duple rhythms, and minor melodic motives. With Selfhaters, then, Coleman drew his basic musical materials from klezmer, but he deployed those materials in an atomized musical setting typified by repetition, discontinuity, and attenuation.

In drawing on klezmer for the building blocks of a new, ensemble-specific language, Coleman's Selfhaters present an interesting contrast with another ensemble, Ben Goldberg's New Klezmer Trio (NKT). That ensemble shares with John Zorn's acoustic Masada quartet an immersion in post-bop jazz, and acoustic Masada (which was modeled on NKT) is the band to which NKT is most often compared. However, in regard to NKT's radical intervention into klezmer syntax, the ensemble is more closely aligned with Selfhaters. Like Coleman, Goldberg and his colleagues—composer/improvisers who drew on contemporary jazz, rock, and electronics—had derived a catalog of short phrases, gestures, and rhythms from early twentieth-century klezmer, a genre with which Goldberg was intimately familiar, having spent several years in the mid-1980s in the revival band Klezmorim. Indeed, journalist Howard Mandel suggested that NKT functioned as a kind of postmodernist version of the independently convened *chavura,* or study group, typical of Reconstructionist Judaism. As Mandel observed in 2001, NKT "performs as a de- and reconstructionist study group, breaking down traditional klezmer's gestures and essences, piecing them back together with cracks and gaps showing as if they were pottery shards or bits of memory."[49] Study groups generally focus on written texts, but in this case klezmer was the text under consideration, and when traditional klezmer melodies appear in NKT's musical canvas, they are sometimes fully articulated and sometimes visited in a highly fragmented way. Goldberg has described NKT as an attempt to wrest the control of "klezmer" out of the hands of the most preservation-minded revivalists. As he recalled, "It was important to us to be able to describe (and sometimes defend) what we played as 'klezmer music.'... We felt our task was to look deeply into klezmer, using everything we had, and find out what was there."[50]

**Figure 5.4.** Selfhaters Ensemble. 2002. Left to right: Michaël Attias, Doug Wieselman, Fred Lonberg-Holm, Jim Pugliese, Anthony Coleman. *Photo: Scott Friedlander.*

Before the RJC moment, by using the creative tools of composition/ improvisation, the West Coast–based NKT realized the goal of developing its own, ensemble-specific syntax for new Jewishly inflected music (PURL 5.10).

Like Selfhaters, NKT exploded klezmer syntax in the manner of an exploded-view drawing, so that each of its constituent parts, as well as how they fit together, are visible. The ensemble then obscured and elaborated on those constituent parts; recognizable klezmer references surface at moments, but they are also suspended in, and sometimes re-made by, a new medium of fluid textural shifts. It was in the elaboration and development of such klezmer motives that Selfhaters departed from NKT's creative concept, as Selfhaters used klezmer as the basis for musical language that was wholly abstracted from a jazz idiom. Unlike the ensemble members in NKT, each of whom contributed continuously to a discursive and evolving texture, each instrument in Selfhaters had at its disposal a limited lexicon of musical motives, articulated in near isolation. Instrumental interjections were interspersed with long silences, and only occasionally (and ineffectively) did the ensemble attempt to come together to create a groove. Coleman's ensemble, then, enacted only the most halting and occasional inter-group communication, and this lack of conversational flow became part of the band's core identity—became, in other words, part of what the band was about.

Selfhaters' aesthetic world demonstrated Coleman's affinity for avant-garde poetics. In addition to burying his Jewish references so they could be apprehended only by listeners who were willing to delve into the music's origins and development, Coleman drew on work by modernist minimalists, including Beckett, Morton Feldman, and Giacinto Scelsi, to create nearly static environments that recalled, for example, Beckett's obsessive repetitions and rhythmic irregularities. In this way Coleman used his Selfhaters' concept not only to magnify small dramas, but also to test the limits of memory. Rather than creating a narrative with its own teleological drive—even a non-linear one like Hirsch's—Selfhaters proffered musical landscapes, through which listeners and musicians alike can wander without a definite direction. In a rhetorical context defined by sparse textures, stop-and-start rhythms, and open space, any dramatic events that do occur unfold at a glacial pace. Like "Jevrejski by night," the music in Selfhaters was made up of simple constituent parts—short motives, repeated pitches—but in Selfhaters Coleman deployed those parts in more conceptually challenging ways, to address the question, for example, of how long one could retain the memory of a musical note or phrase, how much repetition would constitute familiarity, and whether silence meant completion.

The first Selfhaters recording (1996), eponymously titled, included both cover versions of well-known pieces, including "You Don't Know What Love Is" (De Paul and Ray) and original music. One original piece, "Hidden Language," incorporates ideas from "Jevrejski by night" but pushes them to a farther extreme; the rhythm section's part simply consists of a repeated pulse, broken up by strained vocal moans, and the ensemble can find a groove only in unison dissonant blasts. Plodding reiteration, it seems, is all they can manage. In both their cover versions and their original work, Selfhaters' landscapes are filled with isolated musical utterances whose ontological richness is conferred not through their transparency of meaning, but through the way they verge on intelligibility and strive for coherence without quite reaching either aim. And although the ensemble is an instrumental one, in a vestige of the character-driven narrative that unfolds in "Jevrejski by night," with Selfhaters Coleman also developed a vocal version of what he termed the klezmer "cry," a warbling call that indexes an idiomatic cantorial moan or a shofar—the ram's horn that is blown ceremonially in the synagogue on the High Holidays—in its approximate intonation and wailing, squeezed timbres; at times the cries are also evocative of the lilts and creaks of spoken Yiddish.[51] The cries were notable, too, in that they were expressed as human vocalizations in an instrumental texture, a contrast Coleman exploited to dramatic effect.

With its limited expressive resources, the klezmer cry was also a manifestation of the limits of the lone human voice that emerged out of Selfhaters' instrumental textures. Far from foregrounding it as a soloist with a story to tell, as composers conventionally do with human voices that are accompanied by musical instruments, Coleman constructed a depleted vocal character with little narrative force and seemingly nothing to say. But despite its restrictions, he was also able to deploy that vocal character for dramatic purposes by using the poetic strategies of the musical avant-garde: "The whole thing in Scelsi where a minor second is *so big*—they spend the whole piece getting up a minor second [*demonstrates, moaning*]. So to me this had something in it, too, that I could connect to the 'cry' of klezmer."[52] By having his side-musicians channel that cry through their instruments, Coleman also deployed it to signify on other music, a function that is particularly evident in Selfhaters' cover version of a piece from the Duke Ellington Orchestra's "jungle" period, "The Mooche."[53] This choice of repertoire was inflected by Coleman's biography, as he had spent many years in his young adulthood immersed in Ellington's music and had a strong early affiliation with this piece in particular. In Selfhaters' rendition, Coleman formally deconstructs and recomposes "The Mooche" while maintaining enough of its thematic integrity, and weaving enough of its familiar referents into the strange new canvas, to allow us to recognize its connection to the original. With Ellington's mid-1920s recordings of "The Mooche" in mind, one can hear Selfhaters' klezmer cry entering into symbolic dialogue with the blues cry that Ellington's side-musicians employed with particular intensity throughout the band's history of playing that piece. Indeed, the blues had formed the basis for Coleman's concept of building new language out of a vocabulary of Jewish cries. As he explained, "There's such a thing as a blues guitar sound, and you don't need to hear more to feel the blues. [We were] trying to distill 'Jewish' music in that sense."[54] Selfhaters' mimetic moans and vocalizations contrast suggestively with the Ellington ensemble's gutbucket blues cries on its many recordings of this piece. Here, then, is a visceral confrontation between the "funky thing" Coleman and his colleagues had admired in African

American music, and the lack thereof in most of the Jewish music they knew. The blues cries are virtuosic, rhythmically authoritative, and vibrant with timbral variation. The Jewish cries are wispy, undirected, uncontrolled, and uncertain, and they exploit a relatively narrow timbral range. Even so, when set into the nearly static textures of Selfhaters, they achieve a dramatic potency.

Outside these cries, it can be difficult to discern klezmer's influence on the ensemble, but "Goodbye and Good Luck," the last piece on the recording, makes the klezmered context clearer. In this piece, which takes its title from a Grace Paley short story, Coleman, whose voice has been heard so far only in weak moans, tells a gently self-mocking Jewish joke, which he intersperses among sections of klezmer music, easily recognizable though disfigured by the ensemble's characteristic syntax. This piece closes, too, with a sample from an archival recording of Mark Warshawski's well-loved Yiddish song "Oyfn Pripetchik" (On the hearth). When these elements are considered in conjunction with the motives that recur on the rest on the recording, it is evident that "Goodbye and Good Luck" functions as a retrospective framing device, obliquely suggesting a "klezmered" reading of the attenuated drum rolls, the minor scalar motives, and the frequent stops, starts, and abstracted cries in the music that has preceded it (PURL 5.11).

By the time of the release of the second Selfhaters' recording (with some changes in personnel and instrumentation), the ensemble's language had become even more radically reduced. *The Abysmal Richness of the Infinite Proximity of the Same (8 Objectives)* (1998) is a suite of eight dreamy, extended moments of minimalist interaction among several instruments and one lone male voice. There are no melodies; there is no harmonic development; there is no clear meter or pulse. Some moments are louder and more intense, with faster rhythmic and melodic motion, but most of the music sounds as if it is happening underwater, with instruments contributing brief, fractured entrances or sustaining pitches at length to create chromatic tension with little forward motion.

Throughout the suite and the two longer pieces that follow it ("His Masquerade," a piece for solo piano, and "Fifty-Seven Something"), each instrument uses its own brief gesture or group of gestures, which it repeats and varies slightly but does not develop.[55] The drum kit, for exam-

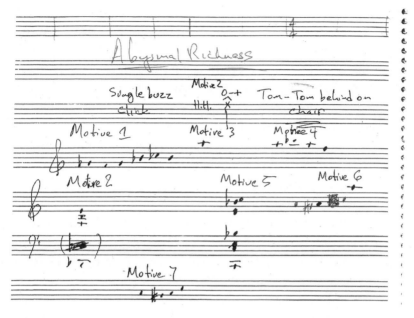

**Figure 5.5.** Coleman's original score with his motivic "bits and traces" from *The Abysmal Richness of the Infinite Proximity of the Same (8 Objectives)* (1998).

ple, uses a sizzle stroke on the high-hat cymbal that is quickly damped, two quick strikes with drumsticks on the edge of the snare drum, and an occasional hit on the bass drum. The baritone saxophone uses a low, rhythmically irregular repeated pitch. The piano intersperses melodic intervals here and there; in the suite's first piece it also articulates a figure, A-Bb-A-F-Eb, which encompasses the recording's main melodic material, as the clarinet, saxophone, cello, trombone, baritone saxophone (the musicians double or triple up on instruments), and piano take turns playing variations on, clipping, holding individual pitches from, and transposing this figure. In this nearly static world, Coleman's lone voice stands out once again, not for what it does, but for what it does not do. A high, wispy wail, the voice takes on no leading role; it is not singing, not talking, and not asserting itself in a robust way as it surfaces only infrequently.

As Coleman noted, this austere context makes the addition of a major instead of a minor second interval, or a new timbre—for example, Coleman's knocking on the piano frame and plucking the piano's strings in "His Masquerade" (2'00" and following)—into a dramatic event. Nevertheless, although all these gestures follow one another in sequence and at times overlap, and although there is some variation among motives over the course of the recording, musical events occur primarily through juxtaposition, layering, and changes in rhythmic density and dynamics, and not through development. In an interesting consequence of working with such limited musical materials, the quality of the relationships among instruments becomes magnified. In other words, the music's "content" becomes not only the minimally eventful musical landscape and limited syntax, but also the circumscribed nature of the instruments' relationship to one another, and the limits to what they can accomplish even when working in concert. Those limits become increasingly clear as the recording unfolds. In the absence of motivic or harmonic development, little can change over the course of the piece, but insofar as anything does, it is only because the instruments come together to create interactive events despite their inability to respond to one another in a broadly expressive way. There are occasional moments of collective action—partial cadences, bits of free improvisation, moments of harmonic concurrence, rhythmic and melodic unisons. Moments of traditional lyricism and even functional harmony also surface in the last piece, "Fifty-Seven Something," which includes rhythmic patterning and unison playing, an *arco,* vibrated cello interjection (4'00"), and a surprisingly robust I-IV-V$^7$-I cadence, in A♭ major (2'13"). But for the most part, the ensemble remains rigorously fixed in an expressive world that, unlike music that develops along more conventional lines, is exactly the sum of its parts. With Selfhaters, Coleman has created a text that is so open that it tests its own boundaries. The music's underlying, klezmered program, though hardly obvious, is more evident in the ensemble's earlier work; by the time of its second recording the concept had evolved into near-total abstraction. But if we take the idiom of the second recording as the culmination of the entire Selfhaters project, then that project as a whole plays out as a meditation on the nature of traces—of culture, of memory—which on some occasions converge into a recognizable form, revealing something to us about their origins or larger spheres of meaning, and which on other occasions do not. Like

GodCo and Hirsch, with Selfhaters Coleman presents us with a commentary on the process of remembering and forgetting.

These artists, and the music of the Radical Jewish Culture moment, were not unique in carving out a compelling Jewish memory space through music. Klezmer, too, has functioned as a complex and contingent kind of "lieu de memoire."[56] But as GodCo, Hirsch, and Coleman show us most acutely, the RJC moment was distinctive for its means of remembering and for the things that were remembered. Having developed out of jazz, one of the scene's guiding principles was that artists craft a personal idiom that engaged musical tradition while also constructing one's own tradition along personal lines. Working from this perspective, then, artists developed an intriguing way of "getting Jewish music wrong" in order to get it right: they used music as a medium for remembering—in the sense of both recalling and reconstituting—Jewish experience, sometimes in ways that seemed unresolved or discomfiting. And indeed, a notion of relationality between present and past was bound up with their idiom. Artists were able to mine this territory by virtue of their fluency in the multileveled musical discourse that flourished on the downtown scene in the 1980s and 1990s. As experimentalists and composer/improvisers, they could draw on an expansive and malleable creative toolkit, and they used all the means at their disposal to address the aspects of Jewish identity and heritage they found most creatively compelling. It is true that some artists turned their gazes toward the lacunae of their own Jewish experiences, toward the doubts, social pressures, and breaks with tradition that had left many without a clear sense of Jewish historical continuity, particularly as that idea applied to their creative interests and milieux. But their work did more than expose a void. To the contrary, these artists expanded the expressive resources of Jewish music by using sound to engage aspects of Jewish subjectivity that had been typically treated with silence.

# Epilogue

IN 2009, I RETURNED TO NEW YORK CITY FOR A YEAR. AS EVER, the city was in flux. Big changes had been building on the Lower East Side for decades, but New York's densely settled neighborhoods reshape themselves on their own peculiar time, with old institutions and new arrivals rubbing shoulders, sometimes for years on end. I did the initial research for this book from a home base in Brooklyn that had yet to see its first artisanal cheese shop, crossing the East River to spend many of my evenings in some of the less well-traveled pockets of downtown Manhattan, which were then on the cusp of a major transformation. Since leaving in 2004 I had been traveling back and forth from Boston to see concerts and exhibits, meet with artists, and continue collecting materials for this study. During my visits I had seen the gleaming towers of the W Hotel rising on Allen Street, one of the Lower East Side's central arteries, but at the same time the punk-activist collective ABC No Rio, which had hosted GodCo and many other No Wave stalwarts, had marshaled its forces and managed to stay planted a few blocks away in the building where it had originally squatted in 1979. But although the

Lower East Side's creative scene had been undergoing a slow shift for decades—over the years I had been away, many musicians who lived there
had decamped to Brooklyn—just as I was settling back in to the city, a
recent economic crash was giving the final push to many of the people
and venues I had been writing about. During the year, my comings and
goings confirmed that the Lower East Side, like my old Brooklyn neighborhood (which now had newly paved sidewalks and more than one
farm-to-table eatery), was well on its way to becoming a hive of upscale
shops and condos.

Experimental music still flourished downtown in places—including
the annual Vision Festival curated by bassist William Parker and dancer
Patricia Parker Nelson, the peripatetic record store and performance
venue Downtown Music Gallery, and Zorn's presentation space, The
Stone (founded 2005)—but both CBGB and the club Tonic, heir to the
Knitting Factory, had closed; experimental music mainstays Roulette
(founded 1978) and Issue Project Room (founded 2003) had moved to
Brooklyn or were about to; and the Knit itself would soon move across
the river to Williamsburg.[1] The scene was now being memorialized in
newspaper articles with titles like "Remembrance of New Music Past,
When Downtown was Magic."[2] Artists' spaces were disappearing, and
downtown's visual art culture was being taken up by museum curators:
in 2005 and 2006, I had come to Manhattan to witness the scene being
historicized in two exhibits, "East Village USA" at the New Museum and
"The Downtown Show: The New York Art Scene 1974–1984" at NYU's
Grey Art Gallery.

The decades-old art world on the Lower East Side had more staying
power than most creative scenes, but its survival was contingent on a
unique set of circumstances that both drew artists to the neighborhood
and allowed them to settle there, in close proximity to a diverse community of peers and to better-paying gigs elsewhere in the city. To be sure,
during my year in the city there were still plenty of creative efforts afoot,
but even as individual composer/improvisers continued to work and
perform where they could, rents were rising ever higher on the Lower
East Side, and it seemed clear that the scene's center would not hold
through the new millennium. Some artists took the changes in stride,
but given New York's uniquely important role for experimental music in

**Figure E.1.** "Radical Jewish Culture: Scène Musicale, New York," Paris Museum of Jewish Art and History, curated by Mathias Dreyfuss, Raphaël Sigal, and Gabriel Siancas. Exhibit poster displayed in the Paris Metro. 2010. *Photo: Tamar Barzel.*

the United States, others were alarmed by the wider implications of the scene's demise—especially given the impact of illegal downloads on the recording industry and those whose livelihoods depend upon it, and the squeeze being put on government subsidies for the arts in Europe, which had long been one of the scene's mainstays. In supporting festivals and concert halls, artists and audiences, European subsidies had been cru- cial to U.S.-based touring composer/improvisers, who had cumulatively helped sustain the entire downtown scene. In 2007, with John Brackett, trombonist Scott Thomson (then co-director of the Association for Im- provising Musicians in Toronto), and Marc Ribot, I convened a panel to discuss whether composer/improvisers, whose craft is so bound up with the process of working out ideas together, could hang on in the absence of major government support at home, in a beleaguered climate where

**Figure E.2.** "Art Projekt" and "Klezmer, NY" sections of the *Radical Jewish Culture* exhibit, Berlin Jewish Museum. 2011. *Photo: Tamar Barzel.*

the arts are now lauded for their civic role as economic incubators. This is a positive view, but not one that is likely to favor, either economically or socially, the formation of creative communities devoted to the risky endeavor of making New York Noise in the twenty-first century.[3]

I was curious about what I would learn about the current state of the downtown scene from another immersion experience, a real reentry into my field site. I had witnessed the scene's changes in bits and pieces, but there is a difference between checking in on a place intermittently and understanding it as a local. I sublet an apartment in Crown Heights, updated my Metro Card, and set about getting fully reacquainted with the city. One of the things I had missed in Boston was the sheer number of performances, and that year I went to hear dozens of concerts by Coleman, Ehrlich, Hirsch, Nathanson, Ribot, Sharp, Zorn, and many of the other artists whose words and work enliven these pages. I also spent

**Figure E.3.** "Radical Jewish Culture," Berlin Jewish Museum. 2011.
Poster kiosk in museum plaza. *Photo: Tamar Barzel.*

hours immersed in conversations with musicians after concerts, over
meals, and on street corners as subway trains rumbled beneath the sidewalks. As I picked up the familiar rhythm of moving between research
and writing, concert-going and pavement pounding, I understood that
if the particular "community of talk" around the RJC moment had ebbed,
artists were still very much engaged with the ideas that had contributed
to its flowering. It was also gratifying to see the way RJC was continuing to
generate interest farther afield. A few years earlier, I had met with the future curators of an exhibit on Radical Jewish Culture in Paris. Fierce in-

tellectuals (Parisians, after all) and music aficionados, they were excited
by the intimations of RJC they had encountered over the years amongst
the downtown artists whose music had long inspired them. As young
Jews who had grown up in France, they were intrigued by the unfamiliar cultural landscape American Jews inhabited, particularly in regard
to the freedom with which Americans interpreted their relationship to
Jewish tradition. The multimedia exhibit they developed, called "Radical
Jewish Culture: Scène Musicale, NY" was mounted in 2010 at the Paris
Museum of Jewish Art and History, which is located in the Marais, the
old Jewish quarter. (The exhibit moved to the Berlin Jewish Museum the
following year.) Like the Lower East Side but with a much darker Jewish
past to contend with, the rapidly gentrifying Marais still retains some
of its old character, and among the ultra-chic boîtes that line the streets,
a few kosher shops and bakeries attest to the larger Jewish community
that had been deported from that quarter some fifty years before. In
conjunction with the exhibit, the museum curators programmed a series
of performances by visiting artists—Zorn presented his live score to
Walter Berman's experimental film, *Aleph*—and in April I convened an
onstage conversation with Anthony Coleman and Mathias Dreyfuss, one
of the exhibit curators. Coleman had developed a piece for the occasion
entitled "Ecouter le flâneur flâner" (Listen to the stroller strolling), for
piano, saxophone, and pre-recorded electronics. In the days leading up
to the performance I followed him through the streets of the Marais as
he recorded volunteers, from among our group as well as Parisian pass-
ersby, reading aloud different sections from *Illuminations* (1968), Hannah
Arendt's edited collection of essays by Wallace Benjamin. In a return to
the sampling techniques he had used in his early career, he incorporated
snippets of this recorded text into the piece.[4] It was an homage to Arendt and to Benjamin, the quintessential theorist of flâneurie, who had
written that "at streetcorners . . . in proximity to particular doorways"
the flâneur (a city stroller, observer, and connoisseur of urban life) "experiences an uncanny thickening and layering of phenomena, an effect
of superimposition, in which remembered events or habitations show
through the present time and place, which have suddenly become transparent."[5] Onstage, as he cast his gaze back to Benjamin and Arendt in a
talk that touched on his interest in palimpsests and contingent identities,

Coleman was also performing.for an audience the process by which, during the RJC moment, he and his downtown colleagues had drawn such figures into a creative lineage of influential Jewish precursors. Benjamin's intense intellectual life and bleak death, his friendship with Arendt, the sounds of the streets of the Marais, the collection of voices reading passages from the book, the way all this relates to Jewish history and identity … when I heard Coleman perform, I could sense these facets of the piece flashing through my experience of it, in ways that felt tangible but, as he had once remarked, never fully "gettable." That event made it clear to me that the energy and ideas generated during the RJC moment would continue to resonate in new work, amongst communities that were in some ways far afield from the work's sources, and in others intimately connected to it (PURL E.1 and PURL E.2).

A few weeks later, I invited a number of artists whom I had gotten to know well in the course of my fieldwork to take part in a similar event, a conversation followed by a concert, at the synagogue Kolot Chayeinu (Voices of our lives), an untrendy venue for liberal Jews in Park Slope, Brooklyn. A far cry from the Marais or the Lower East Side, the south Slope had a stolid character, and its leafy streets, filled with stately brownstones, felt insulated from the creative rumblings that were afoot in other Brooklyn neighborhoods. But the concert was a reminder of the way music and sound can transform a space. In a context far removed in time and distance from the heyday of the downtown scene, the performers, who were mostly longtime collaborators—Ribot, clarinetist Marty Ehrlich, saxophonists Roy Nathanson and Jessica Lurie, and bassist Greg Cohen—channeled downtown's creative energies to perform one of the most remarkable concerts I heard that year. The event was titled "Practicing: A Concert and Conversation"—a pun on the notion of creative and religious practice—and the concert was a testament to the uncanny way a group of composer/improvisers can communicate almost telepathically, distilling ideas seemingly out of thin air—both qualities stemming from a lifetime of "practicing" the art of improvisation. The concert was preceded by an equally intense onstage conversation, in which artists reflected on the relationship between Jewish identity and their creative work. The conversation extended many of the themes I have examined in the preceding pages, and it was interesting to witness these issues

**Figure E.4.** "Practicing: A Concert and Conversation." Synagogue Kolot Chayeinu, Brooklyn. 2010. Left to right: Marc Ribot, Marty Ehrlich, Greg Cohen. *Photo: Kevin Kolben.*

unspooling in the context of a group exchange. In a way that echoed the kinds of talk that had rippled through the RJC moment, artists traded and built upon each other's ideas as they took turns relating the personal—their own memories and experiences—to the themes of memory and language we had agreed upon before the event.

One of the issues that came up right away was the problem of separating Jewish influences from all the others that were part of each composer/improviser's toolkit. Although this question is difficult to rationally parse, the RJC moment had provided artists with an opportunity to reflect upon the push-pull among overlapping influences, as they have continued to do since then. As Nathanson explained at the concert, Jewish tradition was a strong part of his upbringing, but at the same time, "we are defined by this kind of hodgepodge of history in the language that we speak as musicians, and we are [defined in the same way] as sort of modern Jewish people." Ehrlich concurred, noting that he had grown up "in a very Jewish-centered home, with a lot of Jewish singing, very much centered around the synagogue," which was also the site of his earliest formative musical experience. Listening to the cantor in his synagogue had taught him that music "could make you feel both uncomfortable and that you were going to change because of it"—a dynamic that was to become central to his creative life. And yet, he observed, it might be more fruitful to consider Jewish influences other than musical ones: "It's hard to separate out . . . the types of music that influenced us, which might be cantorial or blues or classical or Balkan or whatever, versus what made us make choices in life. And for sure, for me, my Jewish upbringing was the moral ground that I worked from." That moral ground led him to turn toward the jazz's New Thing at a moment closely bound up with black musicians' struggles for recognition, and consequently to set aside his classical clarinet playing and to keep to himself the Jewish concerns that had been central to his upbringing. For her part, in talking about the relationship of Jewish family life to her identity as an artist, Lurie added another female mentor to those mentioned by other musicians in this book, bringing her grandmother into the conversation as a key source for passing on Jewish culture. As she explained, "My father's mother I was very close to, and I have written a lot of songs for her and . . . towards the Jewish memory that she passed on to me in traditions that we shared." But, like her colleagues, Lurie recalled having been too moved by multiple musical influences, and in particular by African American music, to be able to name Jewish music as a strong early influence on her playing. In regard to her involvement as an adult with klezmer music, I was struck that although she is younger than most of RJC's main protagonists and had grown up when the U.S. klezmer revival was in full swing, her feelings about klezmer mirrored their own, recalling Coleman's comment about what "his" folk music really was: "My early memories of the music that I thought was impossibly hip was the Jackson Five . . . and when I think of what [inspired me as] a horn player, [it was] Maceo Parker and Stevie Wonder." Unlike the Motown, funk, and soul music these names conjure up, klezmer hadn't been "her" music as a young player, "because [klezmer] wasn't the music that I grew up with really. Funk is a lot of the music I grew up with." Lurie also addressed the import in her work of the artistic principles of composition/improvisation, more than any single genre per se. Bringing the conversation around to the notion of musical language as a key concern, she noted, "When you think about what really inspires you when you're young . . . [it] is this [musical] language"—jazz—"and then you know klezmer or whatever Jewish music [or other influences] feed into it. . . . Because if you do just look at 'Jewish music' with quotations it would be very limiting. It's like playing Balkan music the way the traditionalists wanna hear it. . . . It's beautiful, but your room for personal expression is constricted." In contrast, she continued, "jazz is a non-static form." In other words, jazz gave her the means for developing her creative voice in a way not shared by other music she knew, including Jewish music. In regard to musical language, Ehrlich followed up by addressing another one of the scene's tenets: the importance of coming together with others in an ensemble, both to engage across social differences and to develop new modes of communicating. Improvising, he explained, is "a collective activity that at a lot of points in my life felt really important, very connected to my politics, to a sense of [jazz as] a field where people were coming together over differences. . . . The excitement was [also] when you're doing a collective improv, or just any improvising, and you find something that doesn't sound like anything you've ever played before. That to me is an incredibly exciting moment." In contrast to the thrill of finding one's voice among a community of like-minded musicians, Lurie, who spent her early career in Seattle before moving to New York City, touched on the social and cultural forces that had curtailed her grandparents' freedom to publicly voice their Jewish identities, the same forces that had eventually contributed to a general quietness around Jewishness on the downtown scene in the 1980s.[6] In her father's family, she explained, there was "this whole big Jewish side in Chicago, and then they moved to Columbus, Indiana where there were like no Jews—two hundred churches to 10,000 people—and you know, Monday morning if you didn't go to church you had to stand up in front of the class and they would pray for you." She continued, "So . . . they were kind of like, 'Wow, it's kinda hard to be Jewish out here.'" With all these experiences and impressions having contributed to a situation in which the Jewish cultural influences on their work, if any, are difficult to trace directly, Ribot addressed his sense that Jewish musicians involved in composition/improvisation might have been drawn to jazz on a subconscious level, in that artists might be "recapitulating these deep structures of

Jewish thought" in their music. Expanding on an idea he had touched on in his essays, Ribot drew a parallel between the way text and interpretation work in jazz and in the process of Jewish textual exegesis:

> The way jazz musicians use memory is a process that's very close to Rabbinic exegesis of sacred texts. The difference is that our sacred text is [saxophonist] Charlie Parker or [pianist] Thelonious Monk. I mean Charlie Parker, for example, took his sacred text as being the pop music of his time, and he took a tune, let's say [the Les Paul/Mary Ford song, now a jazz standard] "How High the Moon." And his solo can be seen as an interpretation of that text.... [It was] written down and became his own song, "Ornithology."... And in "Ornithology," the chord changes of "How High the Moon" constitute a kind of memory of the original song... And then other musicians [continued the process].... Every musician could remember the old tune—the standard that the new [melody] was written on. So in the minds of jazz musicians, it's kind of like a page of Talmud with the original text, the Charlie Parker interpretation, and your interpretation on top of it.

Moreover, he asserted, just as with rabbinic exegesis, jazz improvisation involves developing an original interpretation: "You don't just *read*. If your interpretation doesn't catch fire and doesn't transcend [the original], then your solo stinks. So it's an interpretation of a text, the intent of which is to transcend, and it uses memory and history and also intuition and inspiration." In a way relevant to both the notion of a habitus of listening and a culture of shared practices and values, then, Ribot describes jazz as offering artists a language for inscribing their own interpretations upon a primary text, one that everyone in the (jazz) community is deeply familiar with, and whose multiple layers of interpretation, which musicians also know intimately, inform each new one. As Ehrlich concurred, "And no rehearsal is needed 'cause the side musicians already know the song."

The question of a language's more direct influence on their playing came up as well. Ehrlich contended, " I think it's really clear that language ... has influenced how musicians have played their instruments. ... A lot of [Parker's] rhythmic ideas and his articulation patterns come from black speech patterns, which makes sense, and [*responding humorously to a comment Ribot had made earlier*] no wonder you can't play it." In a way that is nearly as difficult to trace as the "deep structures" Ribot was discussing, language, he surmised, shapes the inflections that help to define a composer/improviser's personal voice. In his hearing, the effect is as much rhythmic as musical: "In Eastern European Jewish music [as a melodist] you never play the downbeat . . . and this [is] connected to Ashkenazy pronunciation. [*Illustrating, moaning*] *Ccchhhuhh, uhhhh, ahh chuchhhh*—it's phlegmatic, you know, and we [he and NEC faculty member Hankus Netsky] joked that . . . the Jews were not going to invent funk"—where the main rhythmic emphasis is on the downbeat. "Eastern European Jews became [proficient] at classical music, and the fact that you always came in [subtly after the downbeat] [*singing*] *nyaaah dah dah dah dah dah,* you ease into it, it's not so much right on." Just as Nathanson had done in regard to his saxophone timbre, Ehrlich speculated that there might be a connection between this rhythmic approach and the Yiddish language or its intonations: "I don't speak Yiddish . . . but I think it's in the air [when you grow up in a Jewish household]. . . . [and] I think that language . . . affects how we play our instruments," particularly in regard to rhythmic phrasing. As Ehrlich's and Ribot's comments make plain, although scholars prefer demonstrable proof, downtown artists are invested in mulling over such connections, and if the connections cannot be conclusively decided they can nevertheless influence artists' creative choices and self-perceptions. Indeed, Ribot made a comment that shed light on the choice he and his colleagues had made during the RJC moment to use music to investigate ideas that might connect conceptually to an ongoing thought process, but in a way that would have been difficult for audiences to fully discern. Thus, he explained, he had wanted to play "How High the Moon" at the evening's concert, particularly because he was performing in a synagogue, because the piece offered a way to posit a relationship between the interpretation of texts in Jewish tradition and in jazz. Audiences might not have gotten the connection, but artists would have, and it would have informed their playing and their experience of the piece. Over the course of the conversation that evening, it was this kind of observation that reminded me again of what an unusual window the RJC moment had opened up onto the creative process, during those intense few years that had led downtown artists to articulate their conceptual concerns as a community, in a way they had not done before and have not done since.

Two issues strike me in particular about the changes that Radical Jewish Culture has wrought and the way the downtown scene has changed. One is that the RJC moment precipitated what I think of as the end of "quietness" around Jewish identity on the downtown scene. Part of the change is cultural and generational, but, given the scene's earlier insularity on this front, had it not been for the disruptions of the RJC moment, that quietness might well have lasted well into the era of *Heeb* magazine (est. 2001), the ensconcing of comedian Adam Sandler's "Hanukkah Song" (1994) into the canon of Jewish popular culture, the Jewish "outing" of Krusty the Klown in an episode of *The Simpsons* (1991), and other products aimed at a pre- and post-millennial generation of Jewish Americans with an untroubled sense of cultural belonging. But RJC did have an impact on the downtown scene, and a dramatic one at that. My return to New York brought home to me how far-reaching that impact had been. Those 200-plus Tzadik recordings on the RJC series now form a major oeuvre of new Jewish music, which Zorn, still an influential figure and a model for younger musicians, has continued to expand. Zorn's Masada project has proliferated into a dizzying variety of ensembles, and since 1998 Zorn himself has generated an enormous and varied body of Jewishly identified music. Indeed, using National Public Radio, the *New York Times*, and the *Forward* as rough cultural barometers, RJC had a wider impact after 1998 than it had before. New cultural formations emerged after the RJC moment, too; in regard to RJC, one I find most notable is the affectionate reclaiming of postwar Jewish culture by such organizations as the Idelsohn Society for Music Preservation, which collects mid-century Jewish LPs, and whose founders published a warm homage to the music of that era entitled *And You Shall Know Us by the Trail of Our Vinyl*, thereby bringing to light some of the "little secrets"—*Barbra Streisand: A Christmas Album* (Columbia, 1987), *Pat Boone Sings Irving Berlin* (Dot, 1957)—that downtown artists had once been so bemused about.[7] There has been a concomitant rise in literature on American identity and popular media in Jewish cultural studies. By the early 2000s, concerts of downtownish music with Jewish themes had become a familiar part of the cultural landscape in New York City and internationally, and they continue to recur regularly. All in all, whereas in 1992 such a thing would have been unprecedented, it is now self-evident that a downtown synagogue, led by a rabbi who as a performing keyboardist once co-founded a downtown band called Hasidic New

**Figure E.5.** Jessica Lurie and Marc Ribot. East Village Radical Jewish Music & Poetry Fest: Jewish Art for the New Millennium. Sixth Street Synagogue, New York City. 2011. *Photo: Dan Sagarin.*

Wave, should convene an "East Village Radical Jewish Music & Poetry Fest," as the Sixth Street Synagogue did in 2011.

It is clear from our continued conversations that artists involved in RJC during its heyday never stopped thinking about the issues it raised. And yet, even though the latter-day RJC-ish events have been meaningful, well attended, thoughtfully produced, and special for their own reasons, they also serve to highlight something that now exists only on the occasions when musicians gather to create it, and not in the same wholesale way it once did. Artists warmly recall social evenings at the Knitting Factory, the neighborhood's vitality and long creative history, the web of interpersonal relationships among colleagues who lived and worked within a few blocks of each other, and the musical experimentation that happened in the neighborhood's lofts, basements, and ad hoc rehearsal spaces. Downtownish music is far from vanished from New York City's soundscape, and new creative efforts, including the Undead Music Festival and Brooklyn Jazz Underground, make it plain that there is no shortage of composer/improvisers with ideas to contribute. But creative scenes, like the neighborhoods that sustain them, rise and fall through a unique combination of circumstances. And while Jewish themes may now be a familiar resource for downtownish music, the creative ecosystem that gave rise to the RJC moment, with its freewheeling exchange of ideas, has waned. Historical retrospectives that address the downtown arts scene have not occupied themselves with considering the scene's dispersal as the loss of a certain kind of Jewish American community. But in addition to all the other things downtown was, and all the musics and cultures it encompassed and inhabited, it also supported a distinctive kind of Jewish community, one constituted by the mandates of originality, pluralism, and shared artistic endeavor, which were among the most important contributions of its creative scene to American music as a whole. Though it was made up by stubborn individualists, the scene also allowed an unusual kind of Jewish community to flourish. New York's downtown scene, then, belongs in the annals of both experimental music and Jewish history. During the rush of creative work, writing, and talk that I call the Radical Jewish Culture moment, it served as an incubator for a conceptually daring body of Jewish music, new ideas about Jewish identity, and far-reaching interventions into notions of Jewish history, memory, and tradition.

# NOTES

### INTRODUCTION

In transliterating from Hebrew and Yiddish, I have followed the guidelines from the *Encyclopaedia Judaica,* in most cases retaining the spelling in common usage in English. Exceptions include instances in which I refer to another source, for example in the discussion of the mode *Mi Shebberakh* in chapter 3, or another transliteration, for example, in the discussion of "Bnai!" in chapter 4. See "General Introduction," in *Encyclopaedia Judaica,* eds. Michael Berenbaum and Fred Skolnik, 2nd ed. (Detroit: Macmillan Reference USA, 2007), 1:23–24.

1. *The Jewish Alternative Movement—A Guide for the Perplexed* (Knitting Factory Records, 1998).

2. "Gloria: In Excelsis Deo/Gloria" (Patti Smith/Van Morrison), on Patti Smith, *Horses* (Arista, 1975).

3. The phrase is drawn from a book and a series of compilation recordings on Soul Jazz Records documenting Manhattan's underground rock scene of the 1970s–80s.

4. "Experimental music" and "avant-garde music" are contested and problematic terms, but it is difficult to discuss the downtown scene without resorting to them. Historically, both terms have been fraught with elitist, racially biased assumptions about the sort of music that can be deemed experimental or avant-garde, and both have been deployed in a way that reifies networks of institutional access and thus cultural recognition, prestige, and professional opportunity. I use the term "experimental" here in accordance with the way downtown musicians tend to use it, which is generally to describe music that follows few stylistic constraints and that transgresses the formal norms of the very genres on which it draws, if any—jazz, rock, Western tonal music—while creating its own poetics out of the process of transgression. For the most part I use "avant-garde" in a more closely bounded way, not to refer exclusively to the high modernist classical avant-garde, but in the context of artists who sought to use experimentalist means to expand the boundaries of a particular idiom or tradition—for example, the jazz avant-garde. For an important discussion of the historical, ethical, and ontological problems embedded in the phrase "experimental music," see Benjamin Piekut, *Experimentalism Otherwise: The New York Avant-Garde and Its Limits* (Berkeley: University of California Press, 2011). Cf. George E. Lewis, "Experimental Music in Black and White: The AACM in New York, 1970–1985," *Current Musicology* (Spring 2001–2002), 100–157.

5. In addition to the Knit, venues included CB's Gallery and Merkin Concert Hall. There were also RJC concerts in Boston, Montreal, Toronto, London, and Jerusalem.

6. Dorf convened an annual klezmer festival at the club until 2003, when the club came under new ownership, and he has continued producing Jewishly themed music events in New York City. His catalog of Jewishly identified recordings on Knitting Factory Records predates the J.A.M. imprint, and includes the compilations *Klezmer 1993, New York City: The Tradition Continues on the Lower East Side* (1993), *Knitting on the Roof* (1998), *Klezmer Festival 1998: Live at the Knitting Factory* (1998), and releases by Frank London, Roy Nathanson, Hasidic New Wave (led by London and Greg Wall), the Paradox Trio (Matt Darriau), and Zohar (Uri Caine and Aaron Bensoussan).

7. Marty Ehrlich, written communication, 29 May 2004.

8. On the notion of a "conversational community," see Christine Stansell, *American Moderns: Bohemian New York and the Creation of a New Century* (Princeton, N.J.: Princeton University Press, 2009 [2000]), 73–119.

9. Clifford Geertz, *Local Knowledge: Further Essays in Interpretive Anthropology* (New York: Basic Books, 1983 [1976]).

10. Many classic formulations in ethnomusicology are based upon this idea; for example, David P. McAllester's discussion of "enemy way music" as a unifying principle among Navajo musicians, Ruth Stone's discussion of "let the inside be sweet" among Kpelle musicians in Liberia, and Steven Feld's discussion of "lift-up-over-sounding" as a "grand metaphor for natural sonic relations . . . as well as social ones" among Kaluli musicians in Papua New Guinea. McAllester, *Enemy Way Music: A Study of Social and Esthetic Values as Seen in Navaho Music* (Cambridge, Mass.: Peabody Museum, 1954); Stone, *Let the Inside Be Sweet: The Interpretation of Music Event among the Kpelle of Liberia* (Bloomington: Indiana University Press, 1982); and Feld, "Aesthetics as Iconicity of Style, or 'Lift-up-over Sounding': Getting into the Kaluli Groove," *Yearbook for Traditional Music* 20 (1988), 74–113.

11. The Knit, then in TriBeCa, is now in Brooklyn; Tonic (closed 2007) and ABC No Rio were on the Lower East Side; Roulette, then in SoHo, is now in Brooklyn; Issue, then in the East Village, is now likewise in Brooklyn, and CB's Gallery was on the lower level of CBGB, the iconic East Village birthplace of punk rock.

12. Philip V. Bohlman, *Jewish Music and Modernity* (New York: Oxford University Press, 2008).

13. Janet Burstein, *Telling the Little Secrets: American Jewish Writing since the 1980s* (Madison: University of Wisconsin Press, 2006), 15. The phrase "little secrets" is drawn from a poem by Paul Celan. Cf. Norman Finkelstein, *Not One of Them in Place: Modern Poetry and Jewish American Identity* (Albany: SUNY Press, 2001). In particular see chapter 2, "Jewish American Modernism and the Problem of Identity," 35–54. As literary scholar Dan Miron reminds us, the enterprise of using literature to plumb the whole of Jewish subjectivity reaches back farther, harking back to at least the turn of the twentieth century, with philosopher Micha Yosef Berdichevsky's contention that Hebrew literature should give "expression to the entire personality, or else it was not expressive at all . . . because the main goal of Hebrew writing should have been to explore the interiority of the Jewish individual, thaw its frozen instinctual and emotional areas . . . map them and make the reader aware of the entire gamut of his subjectivity. . . . The painful experience of paucity and deficit was the source of a possible plenitude, since pain, when authentically experienced, could be as spiritually bountiful as comfort. . . . The sine qua

non condition for the condition of a worthwhile literature was the authenticity of the experience and that of its articulation, not the contents of the experience as such." Dan Miron, *From Continuity to Contiguity: Toward a New Jewish Literary Thinking* (Stanford, Calif.: Stanford University Press, 2010), 93.

14. As historian Jonathan Sarna has observed, in the 1950s, amidst the Cold War and the McCarthy era, "to call oneself secular (as but 1 percent of the national population did in 1952) was to declare oneself subversive, for religion was deemed an essential part of the 'American way of life.'" Jonathan D. Sarna, *American Judaism: A History* (New Haven, Conn.: Yale University Press, 2004), 282. Such was certainly not the case for the downtown musicians born during that era. For a historical overview of Jewish secularisms, see Mitchell Silver, *Respecting the Wicked Child: A Philosophy of Secular Jewish Identity and Education* (Amherst: University of Massachusetts Press, 1998).

15. Adam Sutcliffe and Ross Braun, eds., *Renewing the Past, Reconfiguring Jewish Culture: From Al-Andalus to the Haskalah* (Philadelphia: University of Pennsylvania Press, 2004), 13.

16. A key example is Allen Ginsberg, *The Lion For Real* (Island Records, 1997 [1990]).

17. Edwin Seroussi et al., "Jewish Music," *Grove Music Online. Oxford Music Online,* http://www.oxfordmusiconline.com.luna.wellesley.edu/subscriber/article/grove/music/41322, accessed May 6, 2014.

18. Barbara Kirshenblatt-Gimblett and Jonathan Karp, eds., *The Art of Being Jewish in Modern Times* (Philadelphia: University of Pennsylvania Press, 2007), 8. Cf. David G. Roskies, *The Jewish Search for a Usable Past* (Bloomington: Indiana University Press, 2008). The notion of usability also informs two recent collections focused on literature and visual art: Stephen Paul Miller and Daniel Morris, eds., *Radical Poetics and Secular Jewish Culture* (Tuscaloosa: University of Alabama Press, 2010); cf. Maria Damon, "Alan Sondheim's Internet Diaspora," in *Diasporic Avant-Gardes: Experimental Poetics and Cultural Displacement,* eds. Carrie Noland and Barrett Watten (New York: Palgrave Macmillan, 2009), 51–76.

19. The neighborhood garnered substantial attention in published accounts, memoirs, and novels, each of which cast the neighborhood in a different light. Jacob Riis's scathing 1890 chronicle of "Jewtown" as a den of moral depravity was answered by the measured admiration of journalist Hutchins Hapgood in *The Spirit of the Ghetto* (1902). Polemical memoirs such as Michael Gold's *Jews without Money* (1930) seethed with class rage, whereas Sidney Taylor's mid-1950s children's book series, *All of a Kind Family,* burnished the neighborhood with the nostalgia that would characterize portrayals in the years to come. See Hasia R. Diner, ed., *How the Other Half Lives: Authoritative Text, Contexts, Criticism* (New York: W. W. Norton, 2010). Cf. Tony Michels, *A Fire in Their Hearts: Yiddish Socialists in New York* (Cambridge, Mass.: Harvard University Press, 2009 [2005]). For an important discussion of the role of the Lower East Side in the American Jewish imagination, see Diner, *Lower East Side Memories: A Jewish Place in America* (Princeton, N.J.: Princeton University Press, 2002).

20. See Janet L. Abu-Lughod, *From Urban Village to East Village: The Battle for New York's Lower East Side* (Cambridge, Mass.: Blackwell, 1994), and Christopher Mele, *Selling the Lower East Side: Culture, Real Estate, and Resistance in New York City* (Minneapolis: University of Minnesota Press, 2000).

21. The exhibit was part of a 2013 exhibit titled "Punk: Chaos to Couture."

22. It was due to the dearth of such venues that, having been an important center for free jazz for several decades, the 1970s "Loft Scene" developed downtown; Studio RivBea (1969–1978, run by Sam and Beatrice Rivers) was one of its main focal points. See George Lewis, *A Power Stronger than Itself: The AACM and Experimental Music* (Chicago: University of Chicago Press, 2008).

23. Bernard Gendron, "The Downtown Music Scene," in *The Downtown Book: The New York Art Scene 1974–1984,* ed. Marvin J. Taylor (Princeton, N.J.: Princeton University Press, 2005), 41–65.

24. Mark Dresser interview, 24 January 2004.

25. As I have discussed elsewhere, the music of the downtown scene, which has sometimes been linked to an ahistoricist postmodernism, has, more often than not, a strong historical basis. See Tamar Barzel, "The Praxis of Composition/Improvisation and the Poetics of Creative Kinship," in *Jazz/Not Jazz: The Music and Its Boundaries,* eds. David Ake, Charles Hiroshi Garrett, and Daniel Goldmark (Berkeley: University of California Press, 2012), 171–89.

26. For an exploration of the nature of personal voice and signifying in jazz, see Ingrid Monson, *Saying Something: Jazz Improvisation and Interaction* (Chicago: University of Chicago Press, 1996).

27. Paul Berliner, *Thinking in Jazz: The Infinite Art of Improvisation* (Chicago: University of Chicago Press, 1994).

28. Shelley Hirsch interview, 24 February 2003.

29. Don Byron interview, 12 February 2004. In the late 1980s Byron, a downtown composer/improviser and an alumnus of the Klezmer Conservatory Band at the New England Conservatory, began performing at the Knitting Factory with his neo-klezmer repertory band, Music of Mickey Katz (MMK). This ensemble included several other downtown artists and reimagined the instrumental music recorded in the 1940s–1950s by clarinetist/vocalist/bandleader and Yinglish song parodist Mickey (Meyer Myron) Katz (1909–1985). Despite MMK's Jewish focus, Byron told me in 2004, "I see [MMK] not even as a Jewish music thing, but another one of the acts at the Knit, like [No Wave band] Negativeland, or whatever. It was just another thing that happened at the Knit." By making this comment Byron was not diminishing the band's Jewish cultural stature but indicating that MMK (both the original music, Byron's arrangements, and among the band members themselves) had a downtown sensibility.

30. As the club began programming more rock and hip hop in the late 1990s, the club Tonic, on Rivington Street, supplanted the Knit as the downtown scene's nerve center. The nonprofit organization Roulette (1978–present, founded by Jim Staley and David Weinstein) was another important venue that programmed music from across the downtown music scene.

31. See, for example, Lukas I. Alpert, "Knitting Factory Settles with Musicians," *Associated Press* (1 December 2004), http://www.backstage.com/news/knitting-factory -settles-with-musicians/. Cf. Rebecca Moore, "The Sweet Sound of Success: Knitting Factory Recording Artists Win Historic Settlement," *Allegro* 55/2 (February 2005), http://www.local802afm.org/2005/02/the-sweet-sound-of-success/.

32. Anthony Coleman interview, 13 August 2001.

33. Roy Nathanson interview, 10 September 2003.

34. Marty Ehrlich interview, 1 February 2004.

35. Jonathan Freedman, *Klezmer America: Jewishness, Ethnicity, Modernity* (New York: Columbia University Press, 2008), 194.

36. Anthony Coleman, "Reflections in J" (January 2002). Original manuscript, courtesy of the author. Spelling and capitalization as in the original.

37. Elliott Sharp interview, 18 February 2003.

38. Nathanson interview, 2003.

39. "Shul" is Yiddish for synagogue, typically used to refer to Orthodox congregations. The term "synagogue" is more common among Conservative Jews, and "temple" among Reform Jews.

40. Coleman interview, 13 August 2001.

41. See Theo Cateforis and Elena Humphreys, "Constructing Communities and Identities: Riot Grrrl New York City," in *Musics of Multicultural America: A Study of Twelve Musical Communities,* eds. Kip Lornell and Anne Rasmussen (New York: Schirmer, 1997), 317–42.

42. For a discussion of the Asian improv scene and of Asian American composer/improvisers who have explored cultural themes in their experimentalist work, see Michael Dessen, "Asian Americans and Creative Music Legacies," *Critical Studies in Improvisation / Études critiques en improvisation* 1/3 (May 2006), http://www.criticalimprov.com /article/view/56/89, and in the same issue, Deborah Wong, "Asian American Improvisation in Chicago: Tatsu Aoki and the 'New' Japanese American Taiko," http://www .criticalimprov.com/article/view/50. Cf. Loren Kajikawa, "The Sound of Struggle: Black Revolutionary Nationalism and Asian American Jazz," in *Jazz/Not Jazz: The Music and Its Boundaries,* eds. David Ake, Charles Hiroshi Garret, and Daniel Goldmark (Berkeley: University of California Press, 2012), 190–216.

43. Marc Ribot, in *Shibboleth* (Paris: Museum of Jewish Art and History, 2010) (video). Although it may appear that, by supplanting the phrase Radical Jewish Music with Radical Jewish Culture, Zorn stepped back from denoting Tzadik's series as radical in a musical sense, ultimately both phrases functioned as usefully vague gestures toward encompassing a general aim—to inspire new Jewishly identified music that was not being presented elsewhere.

44. Ehrlich interview, 2004.

45. Daniel Boyarin, *A Radical Jew: Paul and the Politics of Identity* (Berkeley: University of California Press, 1997), 228–29.

46. Sharp interview, 2003.

47. Nathanson interview, 2003. As another artist explained, "I found that the whole idea of ethnically identifying was not embracing. And it's not what I thought [of as] the real power of music. . . . I think for certain people this movement had a real power. It was really liberating, it was really identifying. And I understand . . . how it empowered a lot of people, you know. Gave them spiritual and musical juice. . . . [But] I had [witnessed the role played by Black nationalism in jazz]. . . . I saw how it gave power to the people involved and shut out other people, and I really didn't want to [see that happen under the guise of RJC]." Name withheld.

48. Frank London, "Radical New Jewish Culture Festival," Knitting Factory, New York City, 7–11 April 1993. Spelling as in the original. The magazine *Tikkun* (est. 1986) brought into common use in Jewish liberal circles the notion of "healing the world" (from the Hebrew *tikkun olam*) through ethical action. *Tikkun* cites itself as having

originated "in part as a progressive Jewish alternative to *Commentary* magazine, pushing back against neo-conservatism in the Jewish world and U.S. politics." The magazine gained wider recognition for its controversial critiques of Israel's military policies in the West Bank and Gaza Strip after the first Palestinian uprising of 1987. It now describes itself as "rooted in Judaism and also interfaith" (http://www.tikkun.org/nextgen/about). The notion of *tikkun,* which I revisit in later chapters, served as an ethical touchstone for several downtown artists.

49. Pnina Werbner, "Introduction: The Materiality of Diaspora—Between Aesthetic and 'Real' Politics," *Diaspora* 9/1 (2000), 6–7. Werbner places James Clifford, Paul Gilroy, and Stuart Hall in the first camp and Jonathan and Daniel Boyarin, Amitabh Ghosh, and, again, Hall in the second. Related debates echo through the history of Jewish music. See, for example, James Loeffler, *A Most Musical Nation: Jews and Culture in the Late Russian Empire* (New Haven, Conn.: Yale University Press, 2007). For a recent discussion of the notion of diaspora in regard to contemporary Jewish music, see Jeff Janeczko, "A Tale of Four Diasporas: Case Studies on the Relevance of 'Diaspora' in Contemporary Jewish Music," in *Perspectives on Jewish Music: Secular and Sacred,* ed. Jonathan L. Friedmann (Lanham, Md.: Lexington Books, 2009), 9–40.

50. Not surprisingly, differences around Israeli politics and policies played a part in these conversations and occasionally rose to the surface; major conflicts that arose among artists involved in the 2003 Artists Against the Occupation benefit at the Knitting Factory are perhaps an indication of why these issues were otherwise not a major part of their discussions around RJC. Artists' sharp resistance to seemingly innocuous notions of cultural celebration and national solidarity were inflected by other contemporaneous events, particularly the rise of violent nationalism, the splintering of pluralistic communities, and the ethnic cleansing of the brutal Balkan wars of the early 1990s.

### 1. JEWISH MUSIC

1. Philip V. Bohlman, *Jewish Music and Modernity* (New York: Oxford University Press, 2008), 240.

2. Mark Slobin, *Fiddler on the Move: Exploring the Klezmer World* (New York: Oxford University Press, 2003), 26. Cf. Ruth Ellen Gruber, *Virtually Jewish: Reinventing Jewish Culture in Europe* (Berkeley: University of California Press, 2002), 200.

3. Benjamin Filene, *Romancing the Folk: Public Memory and American Roots Music* (Chapel Hill: University of North Carolina Press, 2000).

4. Henry Sapoznik, *Klezmer! Jewish Music from Old World to Our World* (New York: Schirmer Books, 1999).

5. Bohlman, *Jewish Music and Modernity,* 241. Emphasis added.

6. Bohlman also proposes a fourth story, whose "narratives concern themselves with the possibility that the present is substantively not radically different from the past." This story is based not on the notion of preserving an unchanging tradition, but on modernist ideas, in that it "seeks to represent the ways in which Jewish music has expressed complex and contradictory conditions for centuries." Ibid., 240–41.

7. Ibid., 241.

8. Clifford Geertz, "Art as a Cultural System," in *Local Knowledge: Further Essays in Interpretive Anthropology* (New York: Basic Books, 1983 [1976]), 99, 199–20.

9. *Geduldig und Thimann, A Haymish Groove* (Vienna: Extraplatte, 1992).

10. Roy Nathanson interview, 10 September 2003.

11. Anthony Coleman interview (roundtable), Paris Museum of Jewish Art and History, 18 April 2010; Roy Nathanson, "Dear Brother," on *Subway Moon* (Köln: Buddy's Knife Jazzedition, 2009).

12. Gary Lucas interview, 27 June 2003. Arnold Schoenberg, *Verklärte Nacht* (Transfigured Night), after a poem by Dehmel (1899, premiered 1902).

13. Shelley Hirsch, "I Am a Jew" (1980), on *States* (Tellus, 1997).

14. Hirsch, *States,* liner notes to the recording.

15. Shelley Hirsch interview, 24 February 2003.

16. Elliott Sharp, "Obvious" (1980), on *NOTS* (Berlin: Atonal, 1992). The image on the cover of this recording shows Sharp in profile—perhaps in reference to the notion of a Jewish "racial look," exemplified by an aquiline nose shown in profile. For an exploration of this notion, see Sander Gilman, *The Jew's Body* (New York: Routledge, 1991), 169–93. Elliott Sharp interview, 18 February 2003.

17. A recent multidisciplinary anthology addressing this idea is Susan A. Glenn and Naomi B. Sokoloff, *Boundaries of Jewish Identity* (Seattle: University of Washington Press, 2010).

18. Two examples of this kind of work are the novel by Harry Mulisch, *The Assault* (New York: Random House, 2011 [1982]), and the visual art project by Shimon Attie, *The Writing on the Wall: Projections in Berlin's Jewish Quarter* (1992–93), http://www.shimonattie.net/index.php?option=com_content&view=article&id=13.

19. For an illustration of how one may relate a subjective listening practice to more traditional kinds of musical analysis, see Charles Fisk, "Chopin's 'Duets'—and Mine," *19th-Century Music* 35/3 (Spring 2012), particularly the discussion of "musical intersubjectivity" on 185–86.

20. "Tikkun," on Jazz Passengers, *The Jazz Passengers Live at the Knitting Factory* (Knitting Factory Records, 1991).

21. This notion was a familiar one in avant-garde jazz circles; it is reflected, for example, in the titles of John Coltrane, *A Love Supreme* (Impulse! 1964), and Albert Ayler, *Music Is the Healing Force of the Universe* (Impulse! 1969).

22. Other musicians have posited similar conceptual and sonic links between Jewish prayer services and experimental music. Guitarist Alan Licht, for example, asserted that synagogue services prepared him for the repetition and long forms of the postwar classical avant-garde, which reflected what he framed as a Jewish aesthetic: "There are certain things about a Jewish [religious] background which uniquely suits musicians for the avant-garde. [On] Yom Kippur, you have this *extreme* repetition, you sing 'Kol Nidre' three times in a row, which is already like a ten-minute-long thing. And . . . depending on how Orthodox you are, services last all day. That kind of prepared me . . . for long-duration [compositions] . . . [Composer] Charlemagne Palestine, who . . . had these long piano concerts . . . was also a boy soprano in synagogue. He spent many hours singing in choir and has said a lot in interviews [that] it . . . prepared him for doing that kind of music. And it's also [part of] avant-garde film, where you have these very long films that involve a lot of repetition, like [filmmaker] Chantal Akerman or [artist] Andy Warhol. So to me there's kind of an inherent aesthetic in a lot of the Jewish ceremonies that also shows up in these avant-garde traditions, at least from the sixties and seventies." Alan Licht interview, 28 September 2000.

23. Howard Mandel, *Future Jazz* (New York: Oxford University Press, 1999), 189.

24. In regard to the notion of playing that offers a rough approximation of cantorial *nusach,* Nathanson's playing could be characterized as what William Sharlin calls "unsophisticated *davening.*" (*Nusach* refers to the codified intonation of the Jewish liturgy; *davening* is praying.) See Sharlin, "*Davening* and Congregational Song," in *Emotions in Jewish Music: Personal and Scholarly Reflections,* ed. Jonathan L. Friedman (Lanham, Md.: University Press of America, 2012), 47–48. On word repetitions, melodic intensifications, and embellishments in prayer sung by cantors in the Ashkenazic tradition, see Sholom Kalib, "Techniques of Embellishment: The Chenl, Dreydl, and *Coloratura,*" in *The Musical Tradition of the Eastern European Synagogue, vol. 2: The Weekday Services* (Syracuse: Syracuse University Press, 2005), 112–14. In the context of chazzanic technique, Kalin notes, "the Yiddish infinitive *zu dreen,* meaning to turn or twist . . . meant to embellish or extend a chant line. . . . [Such] techniques rendered more effectively the emotional impact of the text through intensified interpretation resulting from emphasis placed on words [and] syllables. Other liberties included more extensive *coloraturas* and word repetition. . . . A chazz'n would intone an entire sentence or two, or even more, then return to the beginning, all for the purposes of musical development and extension as well as devotional and emotional intensification."

25. One key recording is Roy Nathanson, *Camp Stories* (Knitting Factory Works, 1996).

26. C. K. Szego, "Praxial Foundations of Multicultural Music Education," in *Praxial Music Education Reflections and Dialogues,* ed. David J. Elliot (New York: Oxford University Press, 2009), 206–7. Szego is paraphrasing Feld here.

27. Steven Feld, "Communication, Music, and Speech about Music," *Yearbook for Traditional Music* 16 (1984), 1–18, and Judith Becker, *Deep Listeners: Music, Emotion, and Trancing* (Bloomington: Indiana University Press, 2004), 71. Cf. Charles Fisk, "Chopin's Duets" (2012), and Fisk, *Returning Cycles: Contexts for the Interpretation of Schubert's Impromptus and Last Sonatas* (Berkeley: University of California Press, 2001), particularly the discussion of personal versus cultural meaning on 283–84.

28. Judith Becker, *Deep Listeners: Music, Emotion, and Trancing* (Bloomington: Indiana University Press, 2004), 69. Cf. Louise Meintjes, "Paul Simon's *Graceland,* South Africa, and the Mediation of Musical Meaning," *Ethnomusicology* 34/1 (Winter 1990), 37–73.

29. Marc Ribot, "The Representation of Jewish Identity in Downtown Music" (1996), unpublished manuscript (courtesy of the author).

30. Elizabeth Hafkin Pleck, *Celebrating the Family: Ethnicity, Consumer Culture, and Family Rituals* (Cambridge, Mass.: Harvard University Press, 2000), 69.

31. Coleman, "Hanukkah Bush," on *Guide to the Perplexed* (1998); Coleman interview, August 2001.

32. By 1990 MMK was central enough to the Knitting Factory scene that Dorf included one of the band's pieces on his compilation series, *Live at the Knitting Factory,* and the band headlined the Knit's five-night "Klezmer Festival" in 1990, an unofficial milestone when the club stamped klezmer music with its hip imprimatur. This was the Knit's first Jewish music festival, and it would be repeated yearly under different rubrics until 2003, when the club came under new ownership. Other bands on the festival program spanned the klezmer spectrum, from the revivalist group Kapelye to the Klezmatics and post-bop New Klezmer Trio to the first iteration of Nathanson and Coleman's music-theater-comedy duo, for which Nathanson played an arrangement of one of the Yiddish songs he had learned from his uncle at the family's Passover table. Nathanson interview, 2003. MMK made one recording, *Don Byron Plays the Music of Mickey Katz* (Elektra Nonesuch,

1993), on which Byron notably draws on material from *Tuskegee Experiments* (Elektra, 1992), his tribute to the African American farmers whose syphilis was left untreated as part of a medical experiment in the 1930s. MMK also performs three tracks on *Live at the Knitting Factory, Volume 3* (A&M Records, 1990). Byron recently reconvened the band, with new personnel. Cf. Byron, "Voliner," on *Klezmania* (1997).

33. For a general overview, see Jeffrey Shandler, "Queer Yiddishkeit: Practice and Theory," in *Shofar: An Interdisciplinary Journal of Jewish Studies* 25/1 (Fall 2006), 90–113. For a focus on klezmer, see Dana Astman, "Freylekhe Felker: Queer Subculture in the Klezmer Revival," in *Discourses in Music* 4/3 (Summer 2003), http://www.discourses.ca /v4n3a2.html. Cf. David Kaminsky, "'And We Sing Gay Songs': The Klezmatics: Negotiating the Boundaries of Jewish identity," in *Studies in Jewish Musical Traditions*, ed. Kay K. Shelemay (Cambridge, Mass.: Harvard College Library, 2001), 51–87. Of note in this regard is the first Klezmatics album, *Shvaygn = Toyt* (Silence=Death) (Pirahna, 1988). As a Yiddish translation of SILENCE=DEATH, the slogan of ACT-UP, the era's most prominent AIDS activist organization, the album's title "outed" the band on multiple fronts, conflating the process of coming out as gay both with coming out as Jewish to the mainstream and with bringing Yiddish squarely back into the Jewish cultural purview. With the band's co-founders, violinist Alicia Svigals and trumpeter Frank London, clarinetist David Krakauer was present at the 1992 Munich festival, where London and Krakauer played in the premiere of Zorn's *Kristallnacht*. As Krakauer averred, "I thought about that too, in the [Munich] Radical Jewish Culture festival, of Lou Reed, in particular, *outing* himself as a Jew. You don't think of Lou Reed as Jewish. And then suddenly he appears in this Radical Jewish Culture festival." Krakauer interview, 11 April 2001.

34. For an example of Krakauer's formal innovations, hear "Congo Square Doina"; for a wide range of electronic effects and stylistic influences, hear, for example, "The Meeting," both on Krakauer/*Klezmer Madness! Klezmer, NY* (Tzadik, 1998).

35. Harpist Zeena Parkins was another artist who explored language, in this case Rottwelsch, a Jewish thieves argot, on *Mouth=maul=betrayer* (Tzadik, 1996).

36. NKT had a companion in Boston-based band Naftule's Dream, whose composer/ improviser members pushed klezmer toward contemporary rock and jazz.

37. By the time they were young adults, klezmer had become a familiar part of their musical landscape, with a strong identity as a genre that wore its "revived" aspect proudly. As students at the New England Conservatory, clarinetists Don Byron and Matt Darriau and trumpeter London and had all played in the Klezmer Conservatory Band. In San Diego in the 1980s, clarinetist Marty Ehrlich and bassist Mark Dresser played in klezmer ensembles led by violinist and revivalist Yale Strom, and West Coast– based clarinetist Ben Goldberg spent several years in the mid-1980s in the revival band Klezmorim before forming his experimentalist New Klezmer Trio. In addition to working with Strom, Dresser had also worked in cellist Ron Robboy's Big Jewish Band, an ensemble of Jewishly identified music with experimentalist leanings, which was a West Coast precursor to both neo-klezmer and RJC. Dresser interview, 2004; Ehrlich interview, 2004.

38. Reich published *Tehillim* in 1981 and *Different Trains* in 1988. Curran released the piece he performed at the Munich festival, "Why Is This Night Different from All Other Nights?" on *Animal Behavior* (Tzadik, 1995).

39. In some cases, downtown artists were not aware of composers who had preceded them in searching for a "usable Jewish aesthetic" suited to a particular Jewish context.

See, for example, Mark Kligman, "Reestablishing a 'Jewish Spirit' in American Synagogue Music: The Music of A. W. Binder," in *The Art of Being Jewish in Modern Times,* eds. Barbara Kirshenblatt-Gimblett and Jonathan Karp (Philadelphia: University of Pennsylvania Press, 2007), 270–87.

40. The question of race in the Jewish community has more dimensions, but I refer here to the majority of Ashkenazic Jews in the United States.

41. Marc Ribot interview, 6 June 2003.

42. Albin Zak, *The Poetics of Rock: Cutting Tracks, Making Records* (Berkeley: University of California Press, 2004), 77.

43. On gestures of pastness, see Ludwig Wittgenstein, "The Brown Book," 184, in *The Blue and Brown Books: Preliminary Studies for the "Philosophical Investigations"* (New York: Harper Collins, 1965). Cf. Malcolm Budd, "Wittgenstein on Aesthetics," in *Aesthetic Essays* (New York: Oxford University Press, 2008), 252–77.

44. *Tzitzit* are the fringes on a Jewish prayer garment. *Yechida* is the feminine form in Hebrew for "singular" or "unique."

45. Quoted (in translation) in Andreas B. Kilcher, "Philology as Kabbalah," in *Kabbalah and Modernity: Interpretations, Transformations, Adaptations,* eds. Boaz Huss, Marco Pasi, and Kocku von Stuckrad (Leiden: Brill, 2010), 27. From Scholem, "Zene unhistorische Sätze über Kabbala" (Ten unhistorical aphorisms on Kabbalah) (Zurich: Rhein-Verlag, 1958), 264.

46. Although the notion of complex Jewish identities is ubiquitous, I take this particular phrase from Matthew Baigell and Milly Heyd, *Complex Identities: Jewish Consciousness and Modern Art* (New Brunswick, N.J.: Rutgers University Press, 2001). Maria Damon, "Alan Sondheim's Internet Diaspora," in *Diasporic Avant-Gardes: Experimental Poetics and Cultural Displacement,* eds. Carrie Noland and Barrett Watten (New York: Palgrave Macmillan, 2009), 61.

47. For an exploration of the role a related notion has played in jazz, see Ajay Heble, *Landing on the Wrong Note: Jazz, Dissonance, and Critical Practice* (New York: Routledge, 2000).

## 2. BREAKING A THICK SILENCE

1. The 1992 Munich Art Projekt ran from 27 August to 9 September.

2. Howard Mandel, *Future Jazz* (New York: Oxford University Press, 1999), 189. "Commit a Crime" (words and music, Chester Burnett).

3. Elliott Sharp, liner notes to *Intifada,* on *Xenocodex* (Tzadik, 1996).

4. Composer Alvin Curran recalls having participated in 1990 in a precursor to the Munich festival, focusing on classical composers: the Musik der Zeit series (broadcast in Cologne, West German radio, WDR), which included a "Diaspora Meets Israel" festival with pieces by Curran, Feldman, Kagel, Ligeti, Tal, Teitelbaum, Schnittke, and Wolpe. http://www.alvincurran.com.

5. *Der Golem, wie er in die Welt kam,* 1920, directed by Paul Wegener.

6. Shelley Hirsch interview, 24 February 2003.

7. Books addressing the role of Jews in late twentieth-century popular music include Scott R. Benarde, *Stars of David: Rock 'N' Roll's Jewish Stories* (Lebanon, N.H.: University Press of New England, 2003); Steven Lee Beeber, *The Heebie-Jeebies at CBGB's: A Secret History of Jewish Punk* (Chicago: Chicago Review Press, 2008); Jon Stratton, *Jews, Race and Popular Music* (Surrey: Ashgate, 2009); and Bruce Zuckerman,

Josh Kun, and Lisa Ansel, eds., *The Song Is Not the Same: Jews and American Popular Music* (West Lafayette, Ind.: Purdue University Press, 2010). Cf. Michael Alexander, *Jazz Age Jews* (Princeton, N.J.: Princeton University Press, 2001), Ted Merwin, *In Their Own Image: New York Jews in Jazz Age Popular Culture* (New Brunswick, N.J.: Rutgers University Press, 2006), and Mike Gerber, *Jazz Jews* (Nottingham: Five Leaves, 2010). The literature is more substantial on Jews in television and popular media; a few examples include Neal Gabler, Frank Rich, and Joyce Antler, eds., *Television's Changing Image of American Jews* (Los Angeles: Norman Lear Center, 2000); Vincent Brook, *Something Ain't Kosher Here: The Rise of the "Jewish" Sitcom* (New Brunswick, N.J.: Rutgers University Press, 2003); David Zurawick, *The Jews of Prime Time* (Lebanon, N.H.: University Press of New England, 2003); Paul Buhle, *From the Lower East Side to Hollywood: Jews in American Popular Culture* (Brooklyn: Verso, 2004); and Brook, ed., *You Should See Yourself*, and Paul Buhle, ed., *Jews and American Popular Culture: Movies, Radio, and Television*, vols. 1–3 (Westport, Conn.: Praeger , 2007).

8. See Ruth R. Wisse, "Writing Beyond Alienation: Saul Bellow, Cynthia Ozick, and Philip Roth," in *The Modern Jewish Canon: A Journey through Language and Culture* (Chicago: University of Chicago Press, 2003), 295–322. For a first-person account, see Daniel R. Schwarz, "Eating Jewish Ivy: Jews as Literary Intellectuals," in *The New York Public Intellectuals and Beyond: Exploring Liberal Humanism, Jewish Identity, and the American Protest Tradition*, eds. Ethan Goffmann and Daniel Morris (West Lafayette, Ind.: Purdue University Press, 2009), 47–59. Jonathan D. Sarna, *American Judaism: A History* (New Haven, Conn.: Yale University Press, 2004), 273.

9. *Funny Girl* (1968, dir. William Wyler, original stage production and cast album 1964); *Fiddler on the Roof* (1971, dir. Norman Jewison, original stage production and cast album 1964).

10. Downtown artists had also grown up amidst a mounting popular awareness in the United States of two fundamental realities of contemporary Jewish life: the destruction wrought by the Holocaust and the founding of the State of Israel. As Jeffrey Shandler has illustrated, "By the mid-1970s the Holocaust had become a fixture of American Jewish consciousness, and greater numbers of non-Jewish Americans were aware of it both as a historical event and as a focus of Jewish memory, political activism, creativity, and scholarship." Shandler, *While America Watches: Televising the Holocaust* (New York: Oxford University Press, 1999), 155–56. For example, in the United States the 1950s and 1960s saw the publication of *Anne Frank: The Diary of a Young Girl* (New York: Doubleday, 1952 [1944]), Leon Uris, *Exodus* (New York: Bantam Books, 1958), and Elie Wiesel, *Night* (New York: Hill and Wang, 1960 [1952]), as well as the release of the films *The Diary of Anne Frank* (dir. George Stevens, 1959), *Exodus* (dir. Otto Preminger, 1960), *Judgment at Nuremberg* (dir. Stanley Kramer, 1961), and *The Pawnbroker* (dir. Sidney Lumet, 1964). *Anne Frank: The Diary of a Young Girl* was broadcast as a made-for-television movie in 1967 (dir. Alex Segal), and the American-made television miniseries *Holocaust* (dir. Marvin J. Chomsky) was broadcast in the United States in 1978 (and in Germany in 1979).

11. See Larry Wines, "Somewhere Out There: The Klezmatics," *Folkworks* (5 March 2009), http://www.folkworks.org/columns/somewhere-out-there-larry-wines/35862?task=view.

12. As historian Hasia Diner argues in *We Remember with Reverence and Love: American Jews and the Myth of Silence after the Holocaust, 1945–1962* (New York: New York

University Press, 2010), such silence was one response among many; indeed, it is striking that for some musicians, the mandate to stay quiet about Jewish identity prevailed even amidst well-established Jewish institutions in the United States, large Jewish communities in many cities, and a growing array of books, television programs, and films devoted to Jewish culture and history, including the Holocaust.

13. John Cohen, ed., *The Essential Lenny Bruce* (New York: Bell Publishing, 1970 [1967]), 31.

14. Elliott Sharp, in *Traces* (Paris: Museum of Jewish Art and History, 2010) (video).

15. The cover image is reproduced from Burt Levy, "How Passover Will Be Observed on the East Side," *New York Times*, 16 April 1905. The program included photocopies of this illustration and several others from David Geffen, ed., *American Heritage Haggadah: The Passover Experience* (Jerusalem: Gefen Publishing House and David Geffen, 1992).

16. The statement is dated "Purim 1993." (The festival took place a few weeks later, during the Passover holiday.) Dorf released a recording with a similar title but with a focus on neo-klezmer, *Klezmer 1993, New York City: The Tradition Continues on the Lower East Side* (Knitting Factory Works, 1993).

17. The Eldridge Street Project, which renovates the historic Eldridge Street Synagogue, was incorporated in 1986. The Lower East Side Tenement Museum, which addresses migrant and immigrant life in the neighborhood and sponsors related projects, was chartered in 1988. In using the phrase "heritage restoration," I am paraphrasing Barbara Kirshenblatt-Gimblett, who writes about the klezmer revival and Jewish American heritage tours to Eastern Europe in "Sounds of Sensibility," *Judaism* 47/1 (1999), 49–78.

18. The Downtown seders incorporated some local references, including a montage drawn not from the LES but from a neighboring borough, showing video clips of hasidic Jews in Brooklyn baking matzoh for Passover. Seth Rogovoy, "The Klezmatics Revitalize Their Roots," *Sing Out!* 43/3 (Winter 1999). http://www.berkshireweb.com/rogovoy /interviews/klezmatics.html. The deep cultural and religious differences between Downtown seder participants and hasidic communities of Williamsburg and Borough Park suggest that the videos functioned as a bit of selective tribal solidarity, and not a wholesale embrace.

19. Examples include quotas for Jewish students and faculty members at some universities, as well as the practice of excluding Jews from institutions such as resorts, golf courses, and country clubs, both of which continued through the 1950s. See Martha J. Synott, "Numerus Clausus (United States)," 514–15, and Amy Hill Shevita, "Restricted Public Accommodations, United States," 597, in *Antisemitism: A Historical Encyclopedia of Prejudice and Persecution*, vol. 1, ed. Richard S. Levy (Santa Barbara, Calif.: ABC-CLIO, 2005).

20. Coleman, in *Traces*.

21. I defer to Sarna in generally avoiding the vexed word "assimilation." However, in light of Coleman's comments here, the word seems appropriate. Sarna, *American Judaism*, xix.

22. Catherine Jauniaux, program notes for the Radical New Jewish Culture Festival, 7–11 April 1993.

23. I am referring to in particular to personal transmission of memories from one generation to the next, and not the issue of how the U.S. Jewish community confronted the Holocaust in the public sphere. For a discussion of what psychologist Yael Danieli

has termed the "conspiracy of silence," which encompasses both, see Danieli, ed., *International Handbook of Multigenerational Legacies of Trauma* (Philadelphia: Springer, 1998), particularly the chapter by Irit Felsen, "Transgenerational Transmission of Effects of the Holocaust," 43–68.

24. Joey Baron interview, 20 June 2001.

25. Sharon Topper and Craig Flanagin interview, 10 August 2004.

26. Debra Renee Kaufman, "Post-Memory and Post-Holocaust Jewish Identity Narratives," in *Sociology Confronts the Holocaust: Memories and Identities in Jewish Diasporas,* eds. Judith M. Gerson and Diane L. Wolf (Durham, N.C.: Duke University Press, 2007), 39–40. Cf. Marianne Hirsch, *The Generation of Postmemory: Writing and Visual Culture after the Holocaust* (New York: Columbia University Press, 2012).

27. On the issue of representations of Jews and gender, particularly in regard to masculinity, see, for example, Gilman, *The Jew's Body* (1991); Ann Pellegrini, "Whiteface Performances: 'Race,' Gender, and Jewish Bodies," 108–75, in *The New Jewish Cultural Studies,* eds. Jonathan Boyarin and Daniel Boyarin (Minneapolis: University of Minnesota Press, 1997); Daniel Boyarin, Daniel Itzkovitz, and Ann Pellegrini, eds., *Queer Theory and the Jewish Question* (New York: Columbia University Press, 2003); and Judah Cohen, "Hip-Hop Judaica: The Politics of Representin' Heebster Heritage," *Popular Music* 28/1 (January 2009), 1–18.

28. Marc Ribot, "Rad Jewish Music" (28 February 1996), unpublished manuscript (courtesy of the author).

29. Self-references to Jewish identity came up on rare occasions in underground rock. See, for example, Randall Rothenberg, "A Fix on the Founding Fug," *New York Magazine* (7 May 1979), 82–83.

30. With attention to issues of masculinity and gender, a useful overview of the depiction of Jews in popular media is Daniel Itzkovitz, "They All Are Jews," in *You Should See Yourself: Jewish Identity in Postmodern American Culture,* ed. Vincent Brook (New Brunswick, N.J.: Rutgers University Press, 2006), 230–52; cf. Maurice Berger, "The Mouse That Never Roared: Jewish Masculinity on American Television," in *Too Jewish? Challenging Traditional Identities,* ed. Norman L. Kleeblatt (New Brunswick, N.J.: Rutgers University Press, 1996), 93–107.

31. Although there is general agreement that since World War II Jews in the United States, who are predominantly of Ashkenazic origin, have increasingly identified and been identified as white, scholars have critiqued as overly simplistic the narrative of American "Jews becoming white folks," which is typified in Karen Brodkin, *How Jews Became White Folks and What That Says about Race in America* (New Brunswick, N.J.: Rutgers University Press, 1998). For an overview of these critiques, see Freedman, *Klezmer America,* 28–37. A collection that addresses the complexities accruing to the issue of race in the United States before World War II is Mitchell Bryan Hart, ed., *Jews and Race: Writings on Identity and Difference, 1880–1940* (Lebanon, N.H.: University Press of New England, 2011). For a nuanced historical overview of the topic, see Eric L. Goldstein, *The Price of Whiteness: Jews, Race, and American Identity* (Princeton, N.J.: Princeton University Press, 2007); for a contemporary assessment see Susan A. Glenn and Naomi B. Sokolof, eds., *Boundaries of Jewish Identity* (Seattle: University of Washington Press, 2010). For an overview of the evolution of conceptions of race and ethnicity in the United States, see Matthew Frye Jacobson, "Hyphen Nation," in *Roots Too: White Ethnic Revival in Post Civil-Rights America* (Cambridge, Mass.: Harvard University Press, 2006), 11–71.

32. Ingrid Monson, *Freedom Sounds: Civil Rights Call Out to Jazz and Africa* (New York: Oxford University Press, 2007), 7.

33. Baron interview, 2001. Baron started his professional drumming career at age eleven.

34. Gerber, *Jazz Jews*, contains many recollections by jazz musicians on this front. In another example of the chains of self-revelation such recollections can spark, reading that book led jazz critic Nat Hentoff to reveal, "I knew Artie Shaw (birth name: Arshawsky), but never asked him about his childhood. What I found out in *Jazz Jews* is that, as a kid, he was often sharply wounded by anti-Semitism. That resonates with my having grown up in Boston, which was then the most anti-Semitic city in the country. In my Jewish ghetto, a boy alone at night ran the risk of being punished by invaders as a 'Christ-killer.' I lost some teeth that way. That's when I became an outsider to the point back then that I didn't go into certain Boston stores, because I figured they didn't want to have anything to do with Jews. . . . What I didn't know when I used to talk to Artie Shaw is that he felt so marginalized growing up Jewish that, as Mike Gerber writes, 'Those anti-Semitic episodes haunted Shaw to such an extent that having Anglicized his name . . . for years he avoided disclosing his Jewish roots to fellow musicians.'" Nat Hentoff, "Jews in the Family of Jazz," *Jazz Times* (May 2010), http://jazztimes.com/articles/25939-jews-in-the-family-of-jazz.

35. Piekut, *Experimentalism Otherwise*, 119. Emphasis added.

36. Monson, *Freedom Sounds*, 12. Monson also complicates the notion of dual ideological camps and black-white racial binaries, addressing the range of attitudes about race held among black and white musicians alike.

37. The classic text on this topic is Amiri Baraka, *Blues People: Negro Music in White America* (New York: HarperCollins, 1999 [1963]).

38. See, for example, Ronald Radano, "Jazzin' the Classics: The A A C M's Challenge to Mainstream Aesthetics," *Black Music Research Journal* 12/1 (Spring 1992), 79–95.

39. Ehrlich interview, 2004.

40. Ibid.

41. From their earliest presence in the United States, Jews had grappled with their own perceptions of Jewishness vis-à-vis the pervasive paradigm of "race." As Eric Goldstein has illustrated, before the nineteenth century belonging to the Jewish "race"—in a now archaic version of the concept—was often a matter of pride. As phenotype and physical appearance began to dominate Americans' understanding of race, and as that concept became divided more clearly into two categories—white and black—Jews, like other non-Anglo groups later termed "white ethnics," occupied uncertain territory. Seen through the contemporaneous lens of race, Jews were not black, but also not quite white. Goldstein, *Price of Whiteness*.

42. Nathanson interview, 2003.

43. Ehrlich interview, 2004.

44. Baron interview, 2001. Indeed, the question of downtown's relationship to the creative legacy of African American music was ever present on the scene. The artists on whom I focus have often made this awareness central to their work, which pays tribute to creative progenitors in jazz through names and repertoire. Artists also use their work to signify on their relationship—as experimentalists, and as composer/improvisers drawing on a wide range of influences—to the organically unified concept that was once implied by the phrase "the jazz tradition." Thus, Nathanson and Curtis Fowlkes derived

the name of their band Jazz Passengers from Art Blakey's Jazz Messengers. In the 1980s, Zorn led Spy vs. Spy, a hardcore band devoted to the music of Ornette Coleman. Ribot's bands, Spiritual Unity and Sun Ship, are named for recordings by Albert Ayler and John Coltrane. Sharp's electric blues band is named Terraplane in reference to Robert Johnson's "Terraplane Blues" from 1936. Anthony Coleman's *Freakish* (Tzadik, 2009) is a solo piano recording interpreting the work of Jelly Roll Morton, and Hirsch has radically reconfigured many jazz classics from the American songbook, including the Rodgers and Hart song "Blue Moon."

45. All statements quoted from the manifesto refer to Marc Ribot and John Zorn, program notes to "Radical Jewish Culture at the Knitting Factory," 8–11 October 1992. The excerpts presented here have been edited for spelling and typographical errors.

46. Ribot, "Rad Jewish Music;" Marc Ribot interview, 6 June 2003.

47. The authors were not aware of contemporaneous literature about related topics, e.g., Alexander L. Ringer, *Schoenberg: The Composer as Jew* (New York: Oxford University Press, 1990). Indeed, at the time of the Munich festival, most of this literature was still to be published.

48. See Iain Anderson, "Jazz Outside the Marketplace: Free Improvisation and Nonprofit Sponsorship of the Arts, 1965–1980," in *American Music* 20/2 (Summer 2002), 131–67.

49. Sharp interview, 2003.

50. Mark Slobin, *Fiddler on the Move: Exploring the Klezmer World* (New York: Oxford University Press, 2003), 52. Cf. the musician interviews on 56–58.

51. Coleman interview, August 2001.

52. Gary Lucas, "Letter from Jedwabne," unpublished manuscript (courtesy of the author). See Jan T. Gross, *Neighbors: The Destruction of the Jewish Community in Jedwabne, Poland* (Princeton, N.J.: Princeton University Press, 2001), and Antony Polonsky and Joanna B. Michlic, eds., *The Neighbors Respond: The Controversy over the Jedwabne Massacre in Poland* (Princeton, N.J.: Princeton University Press, 2004). Like Lucas, Sharp had a closer connection than most downtown musicians to the destruction of European Jewry. Sharp described the genesis of his string piece *Intifada* as indirectly linked to that history. In regard to the piece's title and the geopolitics of Israel and the Palestinian territories, he asserted, "It's a very complex issue, although I must say that I'm absolutely against the occupation [Israel's military command of land won in the 1967 war] as a Jew and as the son of a Holocaust survivor. You know, Zionism in its original form was a very spiritual movement. It was transcendent, metaphorical." Patrick Ambrose, "Elliott Sharp's Instrumental Vision," *Morning News,* 4 October 2005, http://www.themorningnews.org/article/elliott-sharps-instrumental-vision.

53. Shelley Hirsch, in *Traces.*

54. Shelley Hirsch and Simon Ho, "Hitchhiking/Heinz," on *Where Were You Then?* (Tzadik, 2012); *Tohu Wa Bohu* (from the Biblical Hebrew phrase, "And the earth was without form and void") is an installation piece Hirsch designed with visual artist Ursula Scherrer, which premiered at the Donaufestival in Krems, Germany, in 2013.

55. Ribot, "Rad Jewish Music."

56. See Roger Sabin, "'I Won't Let That Dago Go By:' Rethinking Punk and Racism," in *White Riot: Punk Rock and the Politics of Race,* eds. Stephen Duncombe and Maxwell Tremblay (Brooklyn: Verso, 2011), 57–68, and Timothy S. Brown, "Subcultures, Pop Music and Politics: Skinheads and 'Nazi Rock' in England and Germany," *Journal of Social History* 38/1 (2004), 157–78.

57. Slan was named after an A. E. van Vogt science fiction novel of the same title (New York: Orb, 1998 [1940]). Slan, "Z.O.G.," on *Live at the Knitting Factory, vol. 3* (A&M Records, 1990). In 1993 Zorn recorded a piece entitled "Metaltov" with his hardcore band, Naked City. Zorn, "Metaltov," on Naked City, *Radio* (Avant, 1993).

58. Alicia Svigals, "Why We Do This Anyway: Klezmer as Jewish Youth Subculture," in *Klezmer: Its Roots and Offshoots*, ed. Mark Slobin (Berkeley: University of California Press, 2002), 216–17. Cf. Warren Hoffman, ed., *The Passing Game: Queering Jewish American Culture* (Syracuse: Syracuse University Press, 2009).

59. In their communal quality they resembled the public seders that had been conducted at hotels and restaurants in the United States since the early twentieth century. Depending on which organization was hosting the seder, these public affairs emphasized different themes—socialism at the Workmen's Circle seder, Zionism at the seder hosted by the Histadrut (an Israeli trade union organization). Historian Elizabeth Hafkin Pleck traces the rise of public seders in the United States, usually as catered events hosted by hotels, to the period after World War I. See Pleck, *Celebrating the Family: Ethnicity, Consumer Culture, and Family Rituals* (Cambridge, Mass.: Harvard University Press, 2000), 101–2; cf. Neil Levin, liner notes to "Third Seder of the Arbeter Ring," on *Legend of Toil and Celebration: Songs of Solidarity, Social Awareness, and Yiddish Americana* (Milken Archive Digital, 2012). Pleck also mentions a thematic, performance-oriented seder held by the Workmen's Circle in the Grand Ballroom of the Waldorf Astoria in New York City, which followed their original haggadah and used "Yiddish poetry, singing, and dancing as a means of planting their own version of socialism on American soil," 101. Another one of Manhattan's alternative seder traditions began in 1993 with Ma'yan (the Jewish Women's Project) hosting its first feminist seder. See Maida E. Solomon, "Claiming Our Questions: Feminism and Judaism in Women's Haggadot," in *Talking Back: Images of Jewish Women in American Popular Culture*, ed. Joyce Antler (Lebanon, N.H.: University Press of New England, 1998), 237.

60. Mandel, *Future Jazz*, 186–87.

61. Ehrlich interview, 2004.

### 3. FROM THE INEXORABLE TO THE INEFFABLE

Zorn did not share his imagery or music for this book, but the images and music I discuss here are readily available online.

1. Zorn established Tzadik with Kazunori Sugiyama, having worked in the 1980s as a curator, in partnership with Sugiyama, for Avant, a subsidiary label for the Japanese label DWI. The first Masada releases appeared on Avant. (Zorn spent much of the 1980s and 1990s living in Japan.)

2. Zorn has since commissioned a proliferation of new music for Tzadik, for the Aleph-Bet Project at the San Francisco Jewish Museum, and in conjunction with Masada *Book II: The Book of Angels*. In addition to *Kristallnacht* (Tzadik, 1995 [1992]) and around forty recordings from the Masada songbook, his catalog of Jewish-identified recordings includes "Metaltov" (1992, recorded by Naked City and Electric Masada), as well as *Angelus Novus* (a wind octet, 1993), *Zohar* (1995), *Kol Nidre* (a string quartet, 1996), *Shibboleth* (a piano quartet with strings and percussion, 1997), and *Shir ha Shirim* (a choral work for five female voices, 2007). After the Munich festival Zorn also continued writing new work without a Jewish focus. Indeed, in addition to compositional tributes to influential figures such as filmmaker Harry Smith (*Memento Mori*, 1999 [1992]), artist Joseph Cornell (*Untitled*, 1999), and composer Elliott Carter (*Passagen*, 2011),

his work comprises pieces that allude to satanism (*Necronomicon,* 2003), Christianity (*The Temptations of St. Anthony,* 2012), and goddess worship (*Jumalatteret,* 2012). Zorn's scores for topical Jewish films include *Port of Last Resort* on *Filmworks VIII 1997* (1998); *Filmworks IX: Trembling before G-d* (2000); *Filmworks XI: Secret Lives* (2002); *Filmworks XVI: Protocols of Zion* (2005); and *Filmworks XX: Sholem Aleichem* (2008). Zorn also wrote a score for alto saxophone, contrabass, and drums, which as of this writing had not been released on Tzadik, and which he performs live (with a trio) to artist Wallace Berman's experimental film, *Aleph.* Outside his obviously Jewish-identified work, Jewish signifiers also occasionally turn up elsewhere, for example, through using transliterated Hebrew words as the titles for "Mayim [water]," "Makkot [strikes, knocks]," and "Zeraim [seeds]" on his recording, *Taboo and Exile* (1999), which he released on Tzadik's Archival series. Another *Angelus Novus* example is "a kabbalistic piece for winds dedicated to Jewish cultural theorist Walter Benjamin. In five movements: Peshat [simplification], Tzomet [intersection], Aliya [ascent], Herut [freedom], Pardes [orchard]." Hips Road website, http://www.hipsroadedition.com.

3. Edward Strickland, *American Composers: Dialogues on Contemporary Music* (Bloomington: Indiana University Press, 1987), 133, and Ann McCutchan, *The Muse That Sings* (New York: Oxford University Press, 1999), 165.

4. Strickland, *American Composers,* 127.

5. John Zorn, *A Tribute to Mickey Spillane* (Elektra Nonesuch, 1987). McCutchan, *Muse,* 165.

6. McCutchan, *Muse,* 166. As Albin Zak has argued, in popular music, recordings are the "scores." *The Poetics of Rock: Cutting Tracks, Making Records* (Berkeley: University of California Press, 2004).

7. Naked City included Zorn on alto saxophone, Bill Frisell on guitar, Wayne Horvitz on keyboards, Fred Frith on bass, Joey Baron on drums, and Yamantaka Eye on vocals. The band's name is borrowed from the title of the book by Weegee (Arthur Felling), *Naked City* (1945), and the film of the same title (1948, dir. Jules Dassin).

8. Zorn also recorded long-form works with Naked City, including *Leng Tch'e* (1992), as well as an album that fell well outside the hardcore idiom, *Absinthe* (1992), but the band's signature style was particularly evident in Zorn's so-called "hardcore miniatures," the brief, explosive pieces featured on *Torture Garden* (1985). McCutchan, *Muse,* 167.

9. John Brackett, *John Zorn: Tradition and Transgression* (Bloomington: Indiana University Press, 2008), 22.

10. Ibid., 30.

11. "Improv 21: = Q + A: An Informance with John Zorn" (ROVA: Arts, 2007). Other Minds Video Archive. http://archive.org/details/IMP_2007_11_15.

12. This phenomenon was of particular importance among visual artists and experimental filmmakers on the downtown scene of the 1970s–1980s, including those interested in camp, such as Jack Smith, one of Zorn's main influences. The phenomenon of downtown's subversions of low/high culture in particular was addressed in an exhibit called "Salon de Refuse" at *The Downtown Show: The New York Art Scene 1974–1984* in 2006 at NYU's Gray Art Gallery. Cf. Bernard Gendron, *Between Montmartre and the Mudd Club: Popular Music and the Avant Garde* (Chicago: University of Chicago Press, 2002), 289.

13. Strickland, *American Composers,* 135–36.

14. Marc Ribot, written communication, 25 October 2012. Ribot has noted elsewhere Zorn's comprehensive understanding of the electric guitar and its full complement of ef-

fects, two of which he mentions here. "Reverb" refers to ambience, or the "sound of the room," the reflections from the walls or objects in a physical space as they interact with the original sound. Distortion, often described as fuzz or noise, results from an overdriven circuit, which creates an electronically corrupted waveform. Electric guitarists have a variety of reverb and distortion effects at their disposal.

15. Dave Douglas, "Music of Masada" seminar at The Stone, New York City (10 May 2010).

16. He has also sometimes used baldly literal programmatic elements that leave little room for multiplex interpretations. As he notes about his string quartet, *The Dead Man* (1990), "Screams, scrapes, scratches and howls in the night. These thirteen short movements, inspired by the book of the same name by French philosopher Georges Bataille, contain perhaps the most overt S/M subtexts in all of my work." Hips Road website, http://www.hipsroadedition.com.

17. "Informance" (2007). Zorn has championed the work of several avant-garde filmmakers and has written several film scores. He has also on occasion included projected slides or film in his own performances. Zorn develops his packaging in collaboration with his long-time designer, Chippy (Heung Heung Chin).

18. Clifford Geertz, drawing on sociologist Max Weber, in *Local Knowledge: Further Essays in Interpretive Anthropology* (New York: Basic Books, 1983), 5.

19. For a recent discussion of this controversy, see Kenneth Gloag, *Postmodernism in Music* (Cambridge: Cambridge University Press, 2012), 105–6. Cf. Ellie M. Hisama, "John Zorn and the Postmodern Condition," in *Locating East Asia in Western Art Music*, eds. Yayoi Uno Everett and Frederick Lau (Middletown, Conn.: Wesleyan University Press, 2004), 72–84.

20. The image and its exegesis are both borrowed from Bataille. Liner notes to *Naked City: Torture Garden and Leng Tch'e: 20th Anniversary Edition* (Tzadik, 2011 [1985 and 1992]).

21. *Naked City: The Complete Studio Recordings* (Tzadik, 2005 [1990]).

22. In response to the controversies (which extended to international decency laws in the United States and Japan), Zorn first repackaged *Torture Garden* and *Leng Tch'e* in a "Black Box," which moved the images to the inside of the packaging and included a third-person statement, and in 2011 he released a twentieth-anniversary edition with a new personal statement. Brackett also makes an important argument about the relationship between "reality" and "fantasy" in Zorn's work.

23. Jonathan Petropoulos, *The Faustian Bargain: The Art World in Nazi Germany* (New York: Oxford University Press, 2000), 262–71. "Hingebung" is German for submission or devotion. The Thorak sculpture is titled "Frauenakt." I am not aware of a connection between the two titles. The compact disc's cover image was a facsimile of the yellow Nazi badge in the shape of a Star of David, labeled "Jude" (German for "Jew"). The liner notes also contained an archival image of the burning of a synagogue, an original prose poem by downtown poet Lynne Tillman, and two text excerpts, one by poet Edmund Jabès and one by avant-garde playwright Richard Foreman.

24. Tzadik Records website, http://www.tzadik.com.

25. *Kristallnacht* is described in Michael Scott Cuthbert, "Free Improvisation and the Construction of Jewish Identity through Music," in *Studies in Jewish Musical Traditions*, ed. Kay K. Shelemay (Cambridge, Mass.: Harvard College Library, 2001), 1–31.

26. *Crystal Psalms*, a seventy-three-minute commemoration of the "Night of Broken Glass," is a two-movement piece for chorus, string quartet, accordion, percus-

sion, brass, and winds. In 1988, Curran had directed a live radio simulcast in several European countries of the piece. Live performances by six different ensembles were broadcast simultaneously over the radio in six European nations—Denmark, West Germany, Austria, France, Italy, and Holland. Perhaps not surprisingly, given that both pieces were written to commemorate the same event, *Kristallnacht* and *Crystal Psalms* use similar sonic devices. Such devices include snippets of taped cantorial singing and German/Nazi voices; archival snippets of cabaret singing; a sonic representation of glass breaking; an evocation of gunshots; an oom-pah dance played on accordion; structural disintegrations achieved through group improvisation; and, notably, an extended, high-pitched shriek. And like Reich's *Different Trains* (1988), *Kristallnacht* also uses recorded voices and is organized by means of programmatic titles with a historical sweep; in *Different Trains*, the titles are "America—Before the war," "Europe—During the war," and "After the war."

27. This body of Holocaust-commemorative work includes Arnold Schoenberg, *A Survivor from Warsaw*, Op. 46 (1946); Dmitri Shostakovich, *Symphony No. 13* in B-flat Minor, Op. 113 (1962), whose first movement commemorates the killings at Babi Yar; David Amram, *The Final Ingredient* (1965); Luigi Nono, *Ricorda cosa ti hanno fatto in Auschwitz* (Remember What They Did to You in Auschwitz) (1966); and Krzysztof Pederecki, *Dies Irae* (1967). Such programmatic works were part of a wider musical response that included resistance songs and non-programmatic concert music. In experimental jazz and rock, influential idioms on the downtown scene, there have been rare attempts to write music in response to this topic; Captain Beefheart (Don Van Vliet) of the rock underground recorded a brief instrumental piece titled "Dachau Blues" in 1969 on Captain Beefheart and the Magic Band, *Trout Mask Replica* (Reprise, 1969). Alternate version on *Grow Fins: Rarities 1965–82* (Revenant, 1999). Brett Werb, "Music," in *Oxford Handbook of Holocaust Studies,* eds. Peter Hayes and John K. Roth (New York: Oxford University Press, 2010), 484–85.

28. Ribot, "Representation."

29. Jon Pareles, "Evoking a Terrible Night in 1938," *New York Times* (19 December 1992). Eleven years later, journalist Phil Zampino recalled that "the premier of this piece at the Knitting Factory in 1992 was an experience this writer will not soon forget. The room was [darkened], all chairs and tables had been removed and the crowd stood sweating and shoved together as though they were in a cattle car on their way to a concentration camp." Phil Zampino, "Kristallnacht: Tonic," *Squid's Ear* (23 September 2003), http://www.squidsear.com/cgi-bin/news/newsView.cgi?newsID=296.

30. Susan Sontag, "Happenings: An Art of Radical Juxtaposition," in *Against Interpretation and Other Essays* (New York: Macmillan, 2001 [1966]), 265. Cf. Allan Kaprow, "Happenings in the New York Scene," in *Essays on the Blurring of Art and Life* (Berkeley: University of California Press, 1993), 15–26.

31. Zorn also had colleagues outside the hardcore rock scene who used extremely high volumes to explore overtone content, notably composer Rhys Chatham in his *Guitar Trio* (1977).

32. The performance was at Tonic. Dresser was the one to propose the yellow stars to Zorn. Dresser interview, 2004.

33. Painkiller, for example, was pithily described on one of Zorn's fan sites as "a guerrilla unit targeting the body and the soul on the most basic of all levels: physical punishment" (http://www.guypetersreviews.com/johnzorn.php).

34. Suzanne G. Cusick, "Music as Torture/Music as Weapon," *TRANS-Transcultural Music Review* 10, article no. 11 (2006), http://www.sibetrans.com/trans/a152/music-as -torture-music-as-weapon.

35. Liner notes to *Kristallnacht*.

36. "Informance" (2007).

37. The organization, founded by Meir Kahane, based its logo and founding principle on a Zionist determination that Jews defend themselves against antisemitic violence and oppression. See Ehud Sprinzak, "Kach and Meir Kahane: The Emergence of Jewish Quasi-Fascism II: Ideology and Politics," *Patterns of Prejudice, 19/4* (1985), n.p. Cf. Judith Tydor Baumel, *The "Bergson Boys" and the Origins of Contemporary Zionist Militancy* (Syracuse: Syracuse University Press, 2005 [1999]), 268–73. As Baumel notes, "Kahane . . . took the concepts of 'militarism' and 'barzel' to their greatest extreme," 272. By the late 2000s, Zorn was distancing himself pointedly from the implication that the title had any connection to Kahane's jingoistic agenda. As he pointed out immediately when asked about the meaning of "radical Jewish culture" in 2007, "Well, radical Judaism has a lot of interpretations right there. And just so that there's no misunderstanding, we're not talking about Meir Kahane here, because there've been too many misunderstandings when it comes to that kind of shit. I'm not, you know, a radical Zionist or anything like that." "Informance" (2007).

38. All spellings in English and Hebrew are as in the liner notes to the piece.

39. "Informance" (2007).

40. Indeed, Zorn asserted recently that he used the number 1948, the year of the founding of the State of Israel, as a compositional device in "The New Settlement." Exhibition notes to *Radical Jewish Culture at the Berlin Jewish Museum,* 9. Given Zorn's fluency in English and Japanese, in which his Japanese colleagues describe him as extremely proficient, his evident lack of attention to detail in Hebrew here is surprising.

41. "John Zorn at the Knitting Factory" (September 1993), program notes. Personal collection, courtesy Marc Ribot.

42. Locus Solus was the name of both the ensemble and a recording, made in 1983, which Zorn re-released on Tzadik in 1997.

43. Zorn and Coleman had worked intensively to choose samples for the piece, some of which (including the breaking glass of "Never Again") came installed on Coleman's sampler and others they borrowed from recent re-releases of archival recordings. Coleman also used the instrument's then-novel capability to loop and layer many of the samples in fragments, with loops starting at different points in the sample, and he manipulated many of the samples to make them more stylized, marking their presence as simulacra of a violently "disappeared" past. Interview with Anthony Coleman, 21 June 2012.

44. For a discussion of Schoenberg's interest in numerology, see Ethan Haimo, "Schoenberg, Numerology, and Moses und Aron," *Opera Quarterly* 23/4 (Autumn 2007), 385–94.

45. There are in fact several different gematria systems; I focus here on the two that seem most relevant to *Kristallnacht: Mispar Hekhrekhi,* "absolute or normative value, in which each letter is given a specific numerical equivalent," and *Mispar Katan Mispari,* "integral reduced value, [which] reduces the total value of the word to a single digit." David Derovan, "Gematria," in *Encyclopaedia Judaica,* eds. Michael Berenbaum and Fred Skolnik, 2nd ed. (Detroit: Macmillan Reference USA, 2007), 7:424–27.

46. McCutchan, *Muse,* 164.

47. "Informance" (2007). Brackett provides a detailed analysis of such numerological processes in *Necronomicon* (2007) and *IAO* (2002). Brackett, *Tradition and Transgression*, 40–78.

48. McCutchan, *Muse*, 169.

49. By naming a "Moses motif," Zorn suggests a connection not only to *Moses und Aron*, but also in particular a link to the character of Moses, who has a single sung utterance in Schoenberg's opera: "Purify your thinking. Free it from worthless things. Let it be righteous." Klára Móricz, *Jewish Identities: Nationalism, Racism, and Utopianism in Twentieth-Century Music* (Berkeley: University of California Press, 2008), 234. In making this injunction Schoenberg's Moses seems to be indexing Jewish theological ideas about separating the pure from impure and casting out that which is unworthy. Zorn's notion of using music to turn society's trash into treasure does not map neatly onto this concept. To the contrary, Zorn's aim is better described as to free oneself from notions of pure versus impure, and to champion the damaged, trivial, or "unmusical" sonic material that others have spurned.

50. Karl H. Wörner, *Schoenberg's "Moses and Aaron"* (New York: Faber and Faber, 1959), 94, is the source for the tone-row material in most of the musical examples that follow.

51. Móricz, *Jewish Identities*, 235.

52. *Berlin Jewish Museum*, 9. "Lili Marleen" was composed by Norbert Schulze, with words based on a poem by Hans Leip, "The Song of a Young Sentry" (1939).

53. This notion is drawn from Valentine Daniel, *Fluid Signs: Being a Person in the Tamil Way* (Berkeley: University of California Press, 1987), 267–68. Cf. Primo Levi, *Survival in Auschwitz / If This Is a Man* (BN Publishing, 2008 [1958]).

54. Marc Ribot, email communication, 15 June 2012.

55. *Berlin Jewish Museum*, 9.

56. One can hear analogous sounds, for example, on "S&M Sniper" and "Fuck the Facts" on Naked City, *Torture Garden*.

57. "John Zorn at the Knitting Factory" (September 1993).

58. "Garin" is Hebrew for seed, kernel, or nucleus.

59. *Berlin Jewish Museum*, 9.

60. "John Zorn at the Knitting Factory" (September 1993).

61. Ornette Coleman, "Lonely Woman," *The Shape of Jazz to Come* (Atlantic, 1959). *Spy vs. Spy: The Music of Ornette Coleman* (Nonesuch, 1988).

62. The number nine here may refer to the words *garin* or *geulah*, both of which have a gematria value of nine according to a gematria system that reduces words to a single integer.

63. Those invitations have resulted in such recordings as *Masada Guitars* (with Ribot, Bill Frisell, and Tim Sparks) and *Malphas: Book of Angels, Volume 3* (with violinist Mark Feldman and pianist Sylvie Courvoisier). Zorn premiered *Masada Book 3: The Book Beriah*, on March, 19, 2014, at Town Hall in New York City.

64. "Mibi" is one example. *Book of Angels 2: Azazel* (Tzadik, 2005).

65. http://www.tzadik.com.

66. Zorn, Chris Comer radio interview (24 August 1999), http://www.chriscomer radio.com/john_zorn/john_zorn8-24-1999.htm.

67. Liner notes to *Sanhedrin: Masada Unreleased Studio Recordings* (Tzadik, 2005).

68. The modes are named after liturgical settings; *Mi Shebberakh* is Hebrew for "May the One who Blesses," and *Ahavah Rabbah* is Hebrew for "Great Love." Zorn had

occasionally used similar scales in the past; for example, he uses a scale with lowered third degree and raised fourth degree in "Cairo Chop Shop," on Naked City, *Torture Garden*. Idelsohn discusses *Mi Shebberakh* as the name that Eastern European cantors, who used it only occasionally, gave to the mode he describes as Ukrainian-Dorian (Dorian mode with raised fourth degree). Abraham Z. Idelsohn, *Jewish Music: Its Historical Development* (New York: Dover Publications, 1992 [1929]), 184–85. Using the spelling associated with Ashkenazic pronounciation of the Hebrew, Idelsohn describes the *Ahavah Rabbah* mode on 84–89. The modal scales he discusses use microtones, which are not included here; Seroussi gives major and minor versions of the *Ahavah Rabbah* scale, in ascending and descending form, discusses its tendency to modulate, and gives melodic motifs typical of the mode. Edwin Seroussi et al., "Jewish music," *Grove Music Online. Oxford Music Online*, http://www.oxfordmusiconline.com.luna .wellesley.edu/subscriber/article/grove/music/41322, accessed May 6, 2014.

69. Sholem Aleichem, *Stempenyu: A Jewish Romance* (New York: Melville House Publishing, 2008 [1888]), 6.

70. He does occasionally imitate ululations, for example, in "Mibi."

71. More recently, Zorn has modified his concept, writing in 2005 that Masada was, indeed, conceived as a kind of neo-klezmer, and that "incorporating more contemporary influences into klezmer's 17th and 18th century amalgam of gypsy, Balkan, and Arabic music seemed organic and natural. Jazz, Rock, Classical, World Music, Blues . . . everything I loved and had learned from went into the new mix that I dubbed Masada/ Radical Jewish Culture." Liner notes to *Sanhedrin* (2005 [1994–97]).

72. Comer radio interview (1999).

73. *The Circle Maker: Issachar and Zevulun* (Tzadik, 1998).

74. "Idalah" (Joshua 19:15) is a place name of uncertain linguistic derivation in the Hebrew Bible, and "abal" is a primitive root for the Hebrew verb "to mourn" (for example, Lamentations 2:8). James Strong, *New Exhaustive Concordance of the Bible* (Nashville: T. Nelson Publishers, 1990).

75. Solos by drummer Joey Baron, not discussed here, are also a regular feature in Acoustic Masada's performances.

76. The heavy bass line and groove are reminiscent of Naked City, including "Facelifter," on *Torture Garden*.

77. This is a waveform of the uncompressed (wav) file, but the visual lack of dynamic shifts, though typical of the piece in performance, may also be due to audio compression applied during the mixing process.

78. Comer radio interview (1999).

79. Masada was a mountaintop fortress in the Judean desert, where in 73 CE a group of Jewish zealots committed suicide in the face of a Roman incursion. More recently, Zorn has used a plain, iridescent cardboard cover with a Star of David cutout, and he includes images only on the inside cover.

80. There is an irony in Zorn's choice of a quotation by Ahad Ha'am as a unifying device on his Masada releases. As historian Anita Shapira asserts, "Ahad Ha'am was by nature a rationalist. He was not given to romantic soul-searching or vague yearnings for something transcending reality." Anita Shapira, "The Origins of the Myth of the 'New Jew,'" in *The Fate of the European Jews, 1939–1945: Continuity or Contingency?*, ed. Jonathan Frankel, 256 (New York: Oxford University Press, 1997).

81. Obsessions Collective website, http://www.obsessionscollective.com. "Heal the world" functions here as an unmarked signifier for the Jewish spiritual notion of *tikkun*. As discussed earlier, because of its association with the Jewish magazine *Tikkun*, as well as its place in Gershom Scholem's introductory writings on Kabbalah, with which Zorn was familiar, it is likely that in using this phrase "heal the world" Zorn intended a specifically Jewish referent. See Gershom Scholem, *On the Mystical Shape of the Godhead: Basic Concepts in the Kabbalah* (New York: Schocken, 1991).

82. Bill Milkowski, "One Future, Two Views: Conversation with [Wynton Marsalis and] John Zorn," in *Jazz Times* (March 2000), 34.

83. Anthropologist Matti Bunzl expands upon the notion of "abject others" in *Symptoms of Modernity: Jews and Queers in Late Twentieth-Century Vienna* (Berkeley: University of California Press, 2004).

84. Program notes, "The Tradition Continues on the Lower East Side" (1993).

85. Arthur Hertzberg (1921–2006), quoted in the liner notes to *The Unknown Masada* (Tzadik, 2003).

86. Jonathan Boyarin, *Storm from Paradise: The Politics of Jewish Memory* (Minneapolis: University of Minnesota Press, 1992), 2.

87. The Stone is named as a memorial to an important figure—Irving Stone. Cf. 264n44.

88. For example, in New York City Zorn recently performed at the benefit concert "Save the Village" to raise funds toward countering the further expansion of New York University into Greenwich Village (October 2012); he performed at the 7th Film-Makers' Cooperative Benefit Concert (March 2013); and he organized three concerts to raise money for victims of Japan's earthquake and tsunami (March and April 2011).

89. See Hannah Arendt, "The Jew as Pariah: A Hidden Tradition," in *Hannah Arendt: The Jewish Writings*, eds. Jerome Kohn and Ron H. Feldman (New York: Schocken Books, 2007) [1944]), 275–97.

90. Liner notes to *Mount Analogue* (2012). References to mysticism are also common in heavy metal discourse, and are thus familiar and legible to fans in one of Zorn's main audiences.

91. At its most intense, Zorn's work is designed to confront an inassimilable sphere, where the "music, the accompanying artwork, and the interaction between the two create an unstable space where we are confronted with the seemingly impossible, unthinkable, or unimaginable." Brackett, *Tradition and Transgression*, 30.

92. Liner notes to *Masada First Live: 1993* (Tzadik, 2002). Suspension points in original; bracketed ellipses added.

93. "Informance" (2007).

94. See Mel Gordon, "Gurdjieff's Movement Demonstrations: The Theatre of the Miraculous," in *The Drama Review: TDR* 22/2, Occult and Bizarre Issue (June 1978), 32–44, and John Mangan, "Thomas de Hartmann: A Composer's Life," in *Notes*, Second Series 53/1 (September 1996), 18–29. Cf. Michael S. Pittman, *Classical Spirituality in Contemporary America: The Confluence and Contribution of G. I. Gurdjieff and Sufism* (New York: Continuum International Publishing Group, 2012).

95. Laurence Rosenthal, "Gurdjieff and Music," in *Gurdjieff: Essays and Reflections on the Man and His Teaching*, eds. Jacob Needleman and George Baker (New York: Continuum, 1996), 301–10.

96. Liner notes to *Mount Analogue* (Tzadik, 2012).

97. Gordon, "Gurdjieff," 41.

98. Ibid., 39.

#### 4. RETHINKING IDENTITY

1. Roee Rosen, "Sounds of 'Shtetl Metal': Radical Jewish Music Hits Downtown Clubs," *Forward* (15 July 1994).

2. *Nuggets,* a double-LP compilation produced by guitarist Lenny Kaye, had served as a kind of Rosetta Stone for many punk rockers, who used it to locate a usable past in 1960s garage rock—a genre peopled mostly by white suburban teens. *Nuggets: Original Artyfacts from the First Psychedelic Era, 1965–1968* (Elektra, 1972). Punk was preceded by so-called "proto punk" bands of the 1960s, many of which had a political edge, including Iggy Pop, the Velvet Underground, and the MC5.

3. Composer Brian Eno helped reify No Wave's canon on a compilation he produced, titled *No New York* (Antilles, 1978).

4. Bernice Martin, "The Sacralization of Disorder: Symbolism in Rock Music," in *Sociological Analysis* 40/2 (Summer 1979), 95.

5. In the mid-1990s, the band had its own label, The Making of Americans, and several of its members ran another band as a side project, the Hattifatteners, which played a genre they called "Moomincore," after *Moomins,* a children's book series by Finnish author Tove Jansson.

6. The classic text on the semiotics of punk style, with a focus on the United Kingdom, is Dick Hebdige, *Subculture: The Meaning of Style* (New York: Methuen, 1979). Cf. David A. Ensminger, "Coloring Between the Lines of Punk and Hardcore," in *Visual Vitriol: The Street Art and Subcultures of the Punk and Hardcore Generation* (Jackson: University Press of Mississippi, 2011), 242–89. A recent film, *A Band Called Death* (Drafthouse Films, 2013), has also added a new dimension to punk historiography by focusing on an African American band from punk's earliest years.

7. Efren del Valle, "Marc Ribot" (24 December 2002), http://www.tomajazz.com.

8. Eric Lott, *Love and Theft: Blackface Minstrelsy and the American Working Class* (New York: Oxford University Press, 2013 [1993]).

9. "We Signify" (Craig Flanagin, Fly and Gilles Reider), on God Is My Co-Pilot, *Straight Not* (Outpunk Records, 1993). The title was likely in reference to Henry Louis Gates's influential book *Signifying Monkey,* which was released around the same time. Gates, *The Signifying Monkey: A Theory of African-American Literary Criticism* (New York: Oxford University Press, 1989).

10. Queercore developed in parallel to the Queer Yiddishkeit scene, to which the downtown band the Klezmatics were important contributors. In "Ale Brider" (All are brothers)—based on the poem by Morris Winchevsky, "Akhdes" (Brotherhood)—the band added extra layers to the metaphor of "coming out of the closet," allying their embrace of Yiddish with the act of coming out as gay. Of course, the message was lost on audience members who did not know Yiddish. In a humorous side note, when GodCo learned the song, one of the band members thought the title meant "all are breeders" —"breeder" being slang for heterosexual. GodCo concert program, 1993.

11. Flanagin, liner notes to *Straight Not* (1993).

12. Janne Maki-Turja, "G-d Is My Co-Pilot," *Mutiny!* (Finland, [1993]).

13. Ibid.

14. Ibid.

15. See, for example, Frank Alvarez-Pereyre and Simha Aron, "Ethnomusicology and the Emic/Etic Issue," *World of Music* 35/1 (1993), 7–31.

16. Homi K. Bhabha, *The Location of Culture* (New York: Routledge, 1994), 2. For a brief but important critique of Bhabha's formulation in regard to notions of musical hybridity, see Denis Constant-Martin, *Sounding the Cape: Music, Identity and Politics in South Africa* (Somerset West: African Minds, 2013), 58–59; for a consideration of this notion in regard to RJC, see Jeff Janeczko, "Negotiating Boundaries: Musical Hybridity in Tzadik's Radical Jewish Culture Series," in *The Song Is Not the Same: Jews and American Popular Music*, eds. Bruce Zuckerman, Josh Kun, and Lisa Ansell (West Lafayette, Ind.: Purdue University Press, 2010), 143–48. An illuminating discussion of the relationship between nationalism, music, and the notion of the in-between space is Philip V. Bohlman, *Music, Nationalism, and the Making of the New Europe* (New York: Routledge, 2010 [2004]), 211–14.

17. Ribot, "Rad Jewish Music" (1996).

18. Jill Hamburg, "Out on the Edge," *Jerusalem Report*, 20 May 1993, 42–43. The event was a Radical New Jewish Culture Festival at the Knitting Factory, 7–11 April 1993.

19. Marc Ribot, *Yo! I Killed Your God* (Tzadik, 1999 [1992]).

20. Laurence J. Silberstein, "Others Within and Others Without," in *The Other in Jewish Thought and History: Constructions of Jewish Culture and Identity*, eds. Laurence Silberstein and Robert L. Cohn (New York: New York University Press, 1994), 11.

21. Flanagin and Topper interview, 2004.

22. Ibid.

23. Ibid.

24. Ibid.

25. G-d Is My Co-Pilot, *Mir Shlufn Nisht* [We Don't Sleep] (Disk Union/Avant, 1994). The phrase "We don't sleep" is drawn from "The Thunder, Perfect Mind," the Nag Hammadi codex. Cf. n. 52.

26. Sharon Topper, "Haggadah shel G-d Is My Co-Pilot" [G-d Is My Co-Pilot's Haggadah], Radical Jewish Culture Festival at the Knitting Factory, 8–11 October 1992. Personal collection, courtesy Sharon Topper and Craig Flanagin.

27. Strikethrough in the original. Sharon Topper, "G-d Is My Co-Pilot, What Kann You Mach? Es Ist Amerikeh!" [What can you do? It's America!] Radical New Jewish Culture festival at the Knitting Factory, 7–11 April 1993. Personal collection, courtesy Sharon Topper and Craig Flanagin.

28. Flanagin and Topper interview, 2004.

29. Topper, "Haggadah," 1992.

30. Topper, "What Kann You Mach?," 1993.

31. Flanagin and Topper interview, 2004. Women's prayers usher in the Sabbath and Jewish holidays.

32. The title is taken from the chorus of a song by Aaron Lebedeff, recorded by klezmer clarinetist Dave Tarras, on *Yiddish-American Klezmer Music, 1925–1956* (Yazoo, 1995 [1925]).

33. Flanagin and Topper interview, 2004.

34. Bhabha, *Location of Culture*, 56. Bhabha makes these comments in the context of a larger argument about cultural displacement, cultural translation, and the negotiation of knowledge, identities, and power in the post-colonialist era.

35. French feminist Hélène Cixous developed the classic formulation of this idea, known as *écriture feminine,* in *Le Rire de la Méduse* (The Medusa's Laugh) (1975). For a recent overview and illustration, see Rebecca Walker, "Experiments in *Critique de Performance:* An Experimental Review of *Experiments in Écriture Féminine,"* *Text and Performance Quarterly* 33/4 (October 2013), 407–13.

36. Topper, "Haggadah," 1992.

37. As Bohlman reminds us, "The history of a national music begins with a folk-melos, that is, folk melodies that reflect the cultural and historical unity of a people," and the notion of a Jewish folk-melos emerged in nineteenth-century Russia, given new attention in the context of establishing a Jewish national state. Philip V. Bohlman, *Central European Folk Music: An Annotated Bibliography of Sources in German* (New York: Psychology Press, 1997), 297, and Bohlman, "Afterword: Shirei 'Am, Shirei Medina (Folk Song, National Song)," in *Israeli Folk Music: Songs of the Early Pioneers,* eds. Hans Nathan and Philip V. Bohlman (Madison, Wisc.: A-R Editions, 1994), 40. "Ha-Tikvah" (The Hope) (words by Naphtali Herz Imber; music by Samuel Cohen), based on a Moldavian-Romanian folk song, "Carul cu Boi" (Cart and oxen).

38. Bohlman, *Israeli Folk Music,* 39–55.

39. Joel Engel (Yuli Dimitriyevich, 1868–1927) and Avigdor Hameiri (Feuerstein) (1890–1970). "Halutz, Beneh!" was first published in 1929 in a collection of newly composed pioneer songs, *Mizimrat ha-Aretz* (Tunes of the Land), sponsored by the Jewish National Fund (*Keren Kayemet le-Yisrael*). See Natan Shahar, "The Eretz Israeli Song and the Jewish National Fund," in *Modern Jews and Their Musical Agendas,* ed. Ezra Mendelsohn (New York: Oxford University Press, 1993), 78–91.

40. Bohlman, *Israeli Folk Music,* 42–43.

41. Meyer W. Weisgal, liner notes to *Once upon a Time: Israeli Hit Tunes of Yesteryear* (Hed-Arzi, 1960).

42. "Hay, Hay, Naalayim," *Israeli Hit Tunes of Yesteryear;* Joel Engel and Avigdor Hameiri, "Halutz, Build On: Chalutz, Beʿnëh / Hay, Hay Naalayim," arranged for mixed voices (s.a.t.b.) by Avraham Soltes, English version by Babette Deutsch (New York: Transcontinental Music Corp., 1942), TCL 219.

43. The recording is similar to GodCo's in only one respect: It creates unresolved tension by ending on a half-cadence that occurs at a midway point in the published score.

44. The friend was the late Stephanie Stone, a jazz pianist and the wife of the late Irving Stone; the couple were downtown scene stalwarts and inspired the name of Zorn's club, The Stone. The source may have been Harry Coopersmith, *Songs of Zion* (New York: Behrman House, 1942), where the song is included under "Zionist Songs: Songs of Toil."

45. The original words (in translation) are, "Without shoe soles; the stone burns the feet; Burns burns burns / It doesn't matter, it's nothing; It's nothing, it's nothing, it's nothing; Pioneer, build, build Jerusalem / Build! Pioneer! Build! Build, emigrate, and build—hey!" Instead of "Beneh Yerushalayim" (Build Jerusalem), Topper sings something nonsensical that sounds like "Beneh chalushulaim," probably an accidental blending of "chalutz" (pioneer) with "Yerushalayim" (Jerusalem), and another result of imperfect transmission. The text recalls the Zionist hymn "Birkat Am" (The people's blessing), a poem written by Jewish national poet Hayyim Nahman Bialik (1873–1934): "We came to the land, to build and be built in it."

46. Tom Segev, *One Palestine, Complete: Jews and Arabs under the Palestinian Mandate* (New York: Macmillan, 2001), 255–60.

47. Topper, "What Kann You Mach?," 1993.

48. Flanagin and Topper interview, 2004.

49. Ibid.

50. Topper, "What Kann You Mach?," 1993. The main ethnographic source on music and hasidic worship is Ellen Koskoff, *Music in Lubavitcher Life* (Urbana: University of Illinois Press, 2001). Cf. Koskoff, "The Sound of a Woman's Voice: Gender and Music in a New York Hasidic Community," in *Women and Music in Cross-Cultural Perspective,* ed. Ellen Koskoff (Westport, Conn.: Greenwood Press, 1987), 213–23.

51. Flanagin and Topper interview, 2004 The Second Temple period was 20 BCE– 70 CE.

52. The text "The Thunder, Perfect Mind" is a "revelation discourse" (not necessarily Jewish) discovered in Nag Hammadi, Egypt, in the mid-twentieth century, whose protagonist is a female divine figure who declaims in "I am" style, e.g., "I am the honored one and the scorned one / I am the whore and holy one." George W. MacRay, "'The Thunder Perfect Mind (VI, 2)," ed. Douglas M. Parrott, in *The Nag Hammadi Library in English,* eds. James McConkey Robinson and Richard Smith (Leiden: Brill, 1996), 295.

53. Topper, "What Kann You Mach?," 1993. Apocryphal or pseudepigraphical works are those works that are omitted from some canons of the Bible and included in others.

54. Ibid.

55. Valle, "Marc Ribot."

56. Melissa Raphael, "Feminist Theology and the Jewish Tradition," in *Oxford Handbook of Feminist Theology,* eds. Mary McClintock Fulkerson and Sheila Briggs (New York: Oxford University Press, 2011), 52.

### 5. SHELLEY HIRSCH AND ANTHONY COLEMAN

1. The more familiar notion of a memory place, or *lieu de memoire,* is drawn from Pierre Nora, "Between Memory and History: Les Lieux de Mémoire," trans. Marc Roudebush, *Representations* 26 (1989), 7–24. Nora developed the concept to describe monuments, but because music and ideas are conceptual spaces and not geographic places, instead of the phrase "memory place" I use "memory space."

2. This was a view klezmer revivalist Henry Sapoznik expressed in a book about the history of the genre, asserting that "downtown musicians, proud of being Jews, express that pride through the creation of 'identity art' that pays scant allegiance to the klezmer style on which it is based. . . . As [another musician] has observed, *'Fusion* is short for *confusion.*' Henry Sapoznik, *Klezmer! From Old World to Our World* (New York: Schirmer Books, 1999), 252–54. A few years earlier, Sapoznik had produced a klezmer compilation, *Klezmania: Klezmer for the New Millennium* (Shanachie, 1997), which included some ambitiously "out" pieces, including Don Byron, "Voliner"; New Klezmer Trio, "Washing Machine"; and "Sadegurer Khosid'l" by Anthony Coleman and Roy Nathanson. Performance studies scholar Barbara Kirshenblatt-Gimblett, whose nuanced study of the klezmer revival is an essential piece of klezmer scholarship, also charged downtown musicians with inhabiting a "nowhere place." Barbara Kirshenblatt-Gimblett, "Sounds of Sensibility," in *American Klezmer: Its Roots and Offshoots,* ed. Mark Slobin (Berkeley: University of California Press, 2002), 129–73. This article is a revised version of the original, which appeared in *Judaism* 47/1 (Winter 1998), 49–78.

3. Anthony Coleman interview, August 2001.

4. See Barbara Kirshenblatt-Gimblett, "Folklore's Crisis," *Journal of American Folklore* 111/441 (Summer 1998), 281–327. R. Murray Schafer discussed this notion in *The New Soundscape: A Handbook for the Modern Music Teacher* (New York: Associated Music Publishers, 1969). As he noted presciently, "The big sound sewer of the future will be the sky" (58). There is a far-reaching and ever-expanding literature in ethnomusicology, anthropology, and folklore that builds on and critiques his formulation of schizophonia. A key text is Steven Feld, "From Schizophonia to Schismogenesis: On the Discourses and Commodification Practices of 'World Music' and 'World Beat,'" in *The Traffic in Culture: Refiguring Art and Anthropology,* eds. George E. Marcus and Fred R. Myers (Berkeley: University of California Press, 1995), 96–126.

5. As performance studies scholar Marcus Cheng Chye Tan has recently observed, there is a close correspondence between schizophonia and theories of postmodernism: "Cultures, and cultural sounds, are displaced from historicity and exist as articles of schizophonic mimicry, in many ways echoing the postmodern schizophrenic condition articulated by Fredric Jameson." Marcus Cheng Chye Tan, *Acoustic Interculturalism: Listening to Performance* (New York: Palgrave Macmillan, 2012), 210; cf. 209–13.

6. Kirshenblatt-Gimblett, "Sounds of Sensibility," 143. Kirshenblatt-Gimblett, who has elsewhere delved in depth into the complexities of this notion, here glosses the schizophonic condition. The notion of the nowhere place has an ironic resonance with the antisemitic slur after which Ribot named one of his earliest bands, before the advent of RJC, Rootless Cosmopolitans.

7. Irene Heskes offers an overview of this topic in *Passport to Jewish Music* (New York: Tara Publications), 69–86, and Mark L. Kligman provides us with an ethnographic study in *Maqām and Liturgy: Ritual, Music, and Aesthetics of Syrian Jews in Brooklyn* (Detroit: Wayne State University Press, 2008). For a case study, see Boaz Tarsi, "How Music Articulates Liturgical Structure, Meaning, and Perception: The Kaddish," in *The Experience of Jewish Liturgy: Studies Dedicated to Menahem Schmelzer,* ed. Debra Reed Blank, 309–40 (Leiden: Brill, 2011).

8. Jacob Neusner, *The Enchantments of Judaism: Rites of Transformation from Birth through Death* (New York: Basic Books, 1987).

9. Marc Ribot, "The Representation of Jewish Identity in Downtown Music" (1996). Unpublished manuscript, courtesy of the author.

10. Ribot, in *Munich* (Paris: Museum of Jewish Art and History, 2010) (video).

11. Two examples (published after Ribot wrote his essay) are Mark Godfrey, *Abstraction and the Holocaust* (New Haven, Conn.: Yale University Press, 2007), and Stephen Paul Miller and Daniel Morris, eds., *Radical Poetics and Secular Jewish Culture* (Tuscaloosa: University of Alabama Press, 2010).

12. Marc Ribot, "Rad Jewish Music" (28 February 1996). Unpublished manuscript, courtesy of the author. He is referring here to Anthony Coleman's Selfhaters.

13. Walter Benn Michaels, "Race into Culture: A Critical Genealogy of Cultural Identity," *Critical Inquiry* 18/4 (Summer 1992), 683. See Daniel Boyarin and Jonathan Boyarin, "Diaspora: Generation and the Ground of Jewish Identity," *Critical Inquiry* 19/4 (Summer 1993), 702–706, for a stringent critique.

14. Marc Ribot, "Klezmer authenticity draft" (2002). Unpublished manuscript, courtesy of the author.

15. Ribot, "Klezmer authenticity draft." The concert was held in December 1995 at Merkin Concert Hall in Manhattan.

16. Kay Kaufman Shelemay, *Let Jasmine Rain Down: Song and Remembrance among Syrian Jews* (Chicago: University of Chicago Press, 1998), and Ellen Koskoff, *Music in Lubavitcher Life* (Urbana: University of Illinois Press, 2001).

17. Marc Ribot interview, 6 June 2003.

18. The title of the piece is a wink at the Christmas carol "O Little Town of Bethlehem" (words by Rev. Phillips Brooks, music by Lewis H. Redner, 1865–66). Hirsch developed this piece, commissioned by New American Radio in 1991–92, into a recording for Tzadik in 1995. She also mined this material for other narrative pieces, including *The Vidzer Family* (1992–1993), a radio play based on one of the characters depicted in *O Little Town;* a different version of "The Vidzer Family" appears on *The Far In, Far Out Worlds of Shelley Hirsch* (Tzadik, 2002).

19. A recent collection that engages the place of personal and Jewish narrative in the work of some of these writers is Derek Parker Royal, ed., *Unfinalized Moments: Essays in the Development of Contemporary Jewish Narrative* (West Lafayette, Ind.: Purdue University Press, 2011). Also useful here is Janet Burstein's exploration of work by Jewish female memoirists who explore the relationship with home, family, and the past, in "Recalling Home from Beneath the Shadow of the Holocaust: American Jewish Women Writers of the New Wave," in Vincent Brook, ed. *You Should See Yourself: Jewish Identity in Postmodern American Culture* (New Brunswick, N.J.: Rutgers University Press, 2006), 37–54. For an exploration of the role of women's personal narratives during an earlier era of Jewish social history, see Melissa R. Klapper, *Jewish Girls Coming of Age in America, 1860–1920* (New York: New York University Press, 2005).

20. Hirsch, *States;* Shelley Hirsch interview, 29 December 2010.

21. Hasia R. Diner, *Lower East Side Memories: A Jewish Place in America* (Princeton, N.J.: Princeton University Press, 2002).

22. Hirsch interview, 24 February 2003.

23. Ibid. The recording to which she is referring is Arnold Schoenberg, *Pierrot Lunaire, Op. 21* (Nonesuch Records, 1971).

24. Hirsch interview, 2003.

25. Hirsch interview, 2010.

26. Ibid.

27. Hirsch interview, 2003.

28. Hirsch interview, 2010.

29. Johnny Mathis with Ray Ellis and his Orchestra, "Come to Me" (P. H. Hayes and Robert Allen) (Columbia, 1957).

30. Anthony Coleman Trio, *Sephardic Tinge* (Tzadik, 1995), *Morenica* (1998), and *Our Beautiful Garden Is Open* (2002); Selfhaters' Orchestra, *Selfhaters* (1996) and *The Abysmal Richness of the Infinite Proximity of the Same* (1998); and Coleman, *Schmutzige Magnaten: Coleman Plays Gebirtig* (2006). Cf. Coleman, "Hanukkah Bush," on *Jewish Alternative Movement* (1998); Anthony Coleman, *With Every Breath: The Music of Shabbat at BJ* (Knitting Factory, 1999); and *The Coming Great Millennium* (Knitting Factory Works, 1992), *Lobster and Friend* (Knitting Factory Records, 1993), and *I Could've Been a Drum* (Tzadik, 1997), all with saxophonist Roy Nathanson.

31. Coleman interview, August 2001.

32. Anthony Coleman, in *Klezmer* (Paris: Museum of Jewish Art and History, 2010) (video).

33. Coleman, *Klezmer.*

34. Coleman, liner notes to *Sephardic Tinge* (1995).

35. Coleman interview, August 2001.

36. Anthony Coleman, *disco by night* (Tokyo: Disk Union, 1992).

37. Coleman interview, April 2010.

38. Anthony Coleman, interview with John Ronsen, *monk mink pink punk* 4 (June 1994). Online at http://ronsen.org/monkminkpinkpunk/4/anthonycoleman.html.

39. Ibid.

40. Coleman interview, August 2001.

41. Coleman interview, 2010.

42. Coleman interview, August 2001.

43. Both Coleman and Nathanson, who attended this concert together, described it as revelatory. The concert was organized by two klezmer revivalists, clarinetist and mandolinist Andy Statman and cimbalom player Zev Feldman. It took place at the Educational Alliance, which was originally part of the Balkan Folk Arts Center (now the Center for Traditional Music and Dance).

44. Coleman interview, August 2001.

45. Coleman interview, April 2010.

46. Coleman interview, August 2001.

47. Coleman, *monk mink pink punk* 4.

48. Coleman interview, April 2010.

49. Howard Mandel, "Vibes from the Tribe: Jewish Identity, Music, and Jazz," *Jazz Times* (September 2001), http://jazztimes.com/articles/20131-vibes-from-the-tribe-jewish-identity-music-and-jazz.

50. Ben Goldberg, "'New Klezmer Trio' and the Origins of 'Radical Jewish Culture'" (8 February 2012), http://www.bengoldberg.net/media.

51. Mark Slobin, *Fiddler on the Move: Exploring the Klezmer World* (New York: Oxford University Press, 2003), 98–107, 118.

52. Coleman, *Klezmer.*

53. "The Mooche" (Duke Ellington / Irving Mills [/ James Wesley "Bubber" Miley]).

54. Anthony Coleman, in Claudia Heurmann, *Sabbath in Paradise* (Tzadik, 2007 [1997]), (video).

55. "His Masquerade" is a reference to the Herman Melville book *The Confidence-Man: His Masquerade* (1857); "Fifty-Seven Something" is a reference to the "57 Varieties" slogan of Heinz ketchup.

56. See, for example, Slobin, *Fiddler on the Move,* 54–55.

### EPILOGUE

1. Issue Project room (founded 2003) moved to Brooklyn in 2005, the Knit (1987) in 2009, and Roulette (1978) in 2011.

2. John Rockwell, "Reverberations," *New York Times,* 23 April 2004.

3. The conference proceedings are included in Ajay Heble and Rob Wallace, eds., *"People Get Ready!" The Future of Jazz is Now* (Durham, N.C.: Duke University Press, 2013).

4. Walter Benjamin, *Illuminations: Essays and Reflections,* ed. Hannah Arendt (New York: Harcourt Brace Jovanovich, 1968).

5. Howard Eiland, "Superimposition in Walter Benjamin's *Arcades Projects,*" *Telos* 138 (Spring 2007), 121–38.

6. Lurie performs with the Billy Tipton Memorial Quartet, "Frailoch," on the Knitting Factory compilation *Klezmer 1993.*

7. Roger Bennett and Josh Kun, eds., *And You Shall Know Us by the Trail of Our Vinyl: The Jewish Past as Told by the Records We Have Loved and Lost* (New York: Crown Publishers, 2008), http://idelsohnsociety.com.

# SOURCES

**PRINT**

Abu-Lughod, Janet L. *From Urban Village to East Village: The Battle for New York's Lower East Side.* Cambridge, Mass.: Blackwell, 1994.

Alexander, Michael. *Jazz Age Jews.* Princeton, N.J.: Princeton University Press, 2001.

Alpert, Lukas I. "Knitting Factory Settles with Musicians." *Associated Press,* 16 December 2004.

Alvarez-Pereyre, Frank, and Simha Aron. "Ethnomusicology and the Emic/Etic Issue." *World of Music* 35/1 (1993), 7–31.

Anderson, Benedict. *Imagined Communities: Reflections on the Origin and Spread of Nationalism.* London: Verso: 1983.

Anderson, Iain. "Jazz Outside the Marketplace: Free Improvisation and Nonprofit Sponsorship of the Arts, 1965–1980." *American Music* 20/2 (Summer 2002), 131–67.

Astman, Dana. "Freylekhe Felker: Queer Subculture in the Klezmer Revival." *Discourses in Music* 4/3 (Summer 2003), [n.p.]. http://www.discourses.ca/v4n3a2.html

Baigell, Matthew, and Milly Heyd. *Complex Identities: Jewish Consciousness and Modern Art.* New Brunswick, N.J.: Rutgers University Press, 2001.

Baraka, Amiri. *Blues People: Negro Music in White America.* New York: HarperCollins, 1999 [1963].

Barzel, Tamar. "The Praxis of Composition/Improvisation and the Poetics of Creative Kinship." In *Jazz/Not Jazz: The Music and Its Boundaries,* eds. David Ake, Charles Hiroshi Garrett, and Daniel Goldmark, 171–89. Berkeley: University of California Press, 2012.

Baumel, Judith Tydor. *The "Bergson Boys" and the Origins of Contemporary Zionist Militancy.* Syracuse: Syracuse University Press, 2005 [1999].

Becker, Judith. *Deep Listeners: Music, Emotion, and Trancing.* Bloomington: Indiana University Press, 2004.

Beeber, Steven Lee. *The Heebie-Jeebies at CBGB's: A Secret History of Jewish Punk.* Chicago: Chicago Review Press, 2008.

Benarde, Scott R. *Stars of David: Rock 'n' Roll's Jewish Stories.* Lebanon, N.H.: University Press of New England, 2003.

Benjamin, Walter. *Illuminations: Essays and Reflections.* Ed. Hannah Arendt. New York: Harcourt Brace Jovanovich, 1968.

Benn Michaels, Walter. "Race into Culture: A Critical Genealogy of Cultural Identity." *Critical Inquiry* 18/4 (Summer 1992), 655–85.

Bennett, Roger, and Josh Kun, eds., *And You Shall Know Us by the Trail of Our Vinyl: The Jewish Past as Told by the Records We Have Loved and Lost.* New York: Crown Publishers, 2008.

Berger, Maurice. "The Mouse That Never Roared: Jewish Masculinity on American Television." In *Too Jewish? Challenging Traditional Identities,* ed. Norman L. Kleeblatt, 93–107. New Brunswick, N.J.: Rutgers University Press, 1996.

Berliner, Paul. *Thinking in Jazz: The Infinite Art of Improvisation.* Chicago: University of Chicago Press, 1994.

Bhabha, Homi K. *The Location of Culture.* New York: Routledge, 1994.

Biale, Henry. *Acting Jewish: Negotiating Ethnicity on the American Stage & Screen.* Ann Arbor: University of Michigan Press, 2005.

Bohlman, Philip V. *Central European Folk Music: An Annotated Bibliography of Sources in German.* New York: Psychology Press, 1997.

———. *Jewish Music and Modernity.* New York: Oxford University Press, 2008.

———. *The Study of Folk Music in the Modern World.* Bloomington: Indiana University Press, 1988.

Bohlman, Philip V., and Hans Nathan, eds. *Israeli Folk Music: Songs of the Early Pioneers.* Madison, Wisc.: A-R Editions, 1994.

Boyarin, Daniel. *A Radical Jew: Paul and the Politics of Identity.* Berkeley: University of California Press, 1997.

Boyarin, Daniel, and Jonathan Boyarin. "Diaspora: Generation and the Ground of Jewish Identity." *Critical Inquiry* 19/4 (Summer 1993), 693–725.

Boyarin, Daniel, Daniel Itzkovitz, and Ann Pellegrini, eds. *Queer Theory and the Jewish Question.* New York: Columbia University Press, 2003.

Boyarin, Jonathan. *Storm from Paradise: The Politics of Jewish Memory.* Minneapolis: University of Minnesota Press, 1992.

Brackett, John. *John Zorn: Tradition and Transgression.* Bloomington: Indiana University Press, 2008.

Brodkin, Karen. *How Jews Became White Folks and What That Says about Race in America.* New Brunswick, N.J.: Rutgers University Press, 1998.

Brook, Vincent. *Something Ain't Kosher Here: The Rise of the "Jewish" Sitcom.* New Brunswick, N.J.: Rutgers University Press, 2003.

———, ed. *You Should See Yourself: Jewish Identity in Postmodern American Culture.* New Brunswick, N.J.: Rutgers University Press, 2006.

Brown, Timothy S. "Subcultures, Pop Music and Politics: Skinheads and 'Nazi Rock' in England and Germany." *Journal of Social History* 38/1 (2004): 157–78.

Budd, Malcolm. *Aesthetic Essays.* New York: Oxford University Press, 2008.

Buhle, Paul. *From the Lower East Side to Hollywood: Jews in American Popular Culture.* Brooklyn: Verso, 2004.

———, ed. *Jews and American Popular Culture: Movies, Radio, and Television,* vols. 1–3. Westport, Conn.: Praeger Publishers, 2007.

Bunzl, Matti. *Symptoms of Modernity: Jews and Queers in Late-Twentieth-Century Vienna.* Berkeley: University of California Press, 2004.

Burstein, Janet. "Recalling Home from Beneath the Shadow of the Holocaust: American Jewish Women Writers of the New Wave." In *You Should See Yourself: Jewish Identity in Postmodern American Culture,* ed. Vincent Brook, 37–54. New Brunswick, N.J.: Rutgers University Press, 2006.

———. *Telling the Little Secrets: American Jewish Writing since the 1980s.* Madison: University of Wisconsin Press, 2006.

Cateforis, Theo, and Elena Humphreys. "Constructing Communities and Identities: Riot Grrrl New York City." In *Musics of Multicultural America: A Study of Twelve Musical Communities,* eds. Kip Lornell and Anne Rasmussen, 317–42. New York: Schirmer, 1997.

Cixous, Hélène. *The Laugh of the Medusa* [*Le Rire de la Méduse,* 1975]. Trans. Keith Cohen and Paula Cohen. In *New French Feminisms,* eds. Elaine Marks and Isabel Courtivron, 245–64. New York: Schocken Books, 1981.

Cohen, John ed. *The Essential Lenny Bruce.* New York: Bell Publishing, 1970 [1967].

Cohen, Judah. "Hip-Hop Judaica: The Politics of Representin' Heebster Heritage." *Popular Music* 28/1 (January 2009), 1–18.

Coleman, Anthony. "Reflections in J" [in Flemish]. *Etcetera* 20/81 (April 2002).

Coleman, Anthony, Catherine Jauniaux, Frank London, Michael Dorf, John Zorn. "The Tradition Continues on the Lower East Side: Radical New Jewish Culture Festival." Knitting Factory, New York City. 7–11 April 1993. Program notes.

Constant-Martin, Denis. *Sounding the Cape: Music, Identity and Politics in South Africa.* Somerset West, South Africa: African Minds, 2013.

Coopersmith, Harry, ed. *Songs of Zion.* New York: Behrman House, 1942.

Cuthbert, Michael Scott. "Free Improvisation and the Construction of Jewish Identity through Music." In *Studies in Jewish Musical Traditions,* ed. Kay K. Shelemay, 1–31. Cambridge, Mass.: Harvard College Library, 2001.

Damon, Maria. "Alan Sondheim's Internet Diaspora." In *Diasporic Avant-Gardes: Experimental Poetics and Cultural Displacement,* eds. Carrie Noland and Barrett Watten, 51–76. New York: Palgrave Macmillan, 2009.

Daniel, Valentine. *Fluid Signs: Being a Person in the Tamil Way.* Berkeley: University of California Press, 1987.

Danieli, Yael, ed. *International Handbook of Multigenerational Legacies of Trauma.* Philadelphia: Springer, 1998.

Derovan, David. "Gematria." *Encyclopaedia Judaica.* Eds. Michael Berenbaum and Fred Skolnik. 2nd ed. 7:424–27. Detroit: Macmillan Reference USA.

Diner, Hasia R., ed. *How the Other Half Lives: Authoritative Text, Contexts, Criticism.* New York: W. W. Norton, 2010.

———. *Lower East Side Memories: A Jewish Place in America.* Princeton, N.J.: Princeton University Press, 2002.

———. *We Remember with Reverence and Love: American Jews and the Myth of Silence after the Holocaust, 1945–1962.* New York: New York University Press, 2010.

Dorf, Michael. *Knitting Music: A Five-Year History of the Knitting Factory.* New York: Knitting Factory Works, 1992.

Eiland, Howard. "Superimposition in Walter Benjamin's *Arcades Projects.*" *Telos* 138 (Spring 2007), 121–38.

Ensminger, David A. *Visual Vitriol: The Street Art and Subcultures of the Punk and Hardcore Generation.* Jackson: University Press of Mississippi, 2011.

Feld, Steven. "Aesthetics as Iconicity of Style, or 'Lift-up-over Sounding': Getting into the Kaluli Groove." *Yearbook for Traditional Music* 20 (1988), 74–113.

———. "Communication, Music, and Speech about Music." *Yearbook for Traditional Music* 16 (1984), 1–18.

———. "From Schizophonia to Schismogenesis: On the Discourses and Commodification Practices of 'World Music' and 'World Beat.'" In *The Traffic in Culture: Refiguring Art and Anthropology,* eds. George E. Marcus and Fred R. Myers, 96–126. Berkeley: University of California Press, 1995.

Filene, Benjamin. *Romancing the Folk: Public Memory and American Roots Music.* Chapel Hill: University of North Carolina Press, 2000.

Fisk, Charles. "Chopin's 'Duets'—and Mine." *19th-Century Music* 35/3 (Spring 2012), 182–203.

———. *Returning Cycles: Contexts for the Interpretation of Schubert's Impromptus and Last Sonatas.* Berkeley: University of California Press, 2001.

Finkelstein, Norman. *Not One of Them in Place: Modern Poetry and Jewish American Identity.* Albany: State University of New York Press, 2001.

Frank, Anne. *Anne Frank: The Diary of a Young Girl.* New York: Doubleday, 1952 [1944].

Freedman, Jonathan. *Klezmer America: Jewishness, Ethnicity, Modernity.* New York: Columbia University Press, 2008.

Fulkerson, Mary McClintock, and Sheila Briggs, eds. *Oxford Handbook of Feminist Theology.* New York: Oxford University Press, 2011.

Gabler, Neal, Frank Rich, and Joyce Antler, eds. *Television's Changing Image of American Jews.* Los Angeles: Norman Lear Center, 2000.

Gates, Henry Louis. *The Signifying Monkey: A Theory of African-American Literary Criticism.* New York: Oxford University Press, 1989.

Geertz, Clifford. "Art as a Cultural System." In *Local Knowledge: Further Essays in Interpretive Anthropology,* 94–120. New York: Basic Books, 1983 [1976].

Geffen, David, ed. *American Heritage Haggadah: The Passover Experience.* Jerusalem: Gefen Publishing House and David Geffen, 1992.

Gendron, Bernard. *Between Montmartre and the Mudd Club: Popular Music and the Avant Garde.* Chicago: University of Chicago Press, 2002.

———. "The Downtown Music Scene." In *The Downtown Book: The New York Art Scene 1974–1984,* ed. Marvin J. Taylor, 41–65. Princeton, N.J.: Princeton University Press, 2005.

"General Introduction." *Encyclopaedia Judaica.* Eds. Michael Berenbaum and Fred Skolnik. 2nd ed. 1:15–32. Detroit: Macmillan Reference USA.

Gerber, Mike. *Jazz Jews.* Nottingham: Five Leaves, 2010.

Gilman, Sander. *The Jew's Body.* New York: Routledge, 1991.

Glenn, Susan A., and Naomi B. Sokolof, eds. *Boundaries of Jewish Identity.* Seattle: University of Washington Press, 2010.

Gloag, Kenneth. *Postmodernism in Music.* Cambridge: Cambridge University Press, 2012.

Godfrey, Mark. *Abstraction and the Holocaust.* New Haven, Conn.: Yale University Press, 2007.

Goldstein, Eric L. *The Price of Whiteness: Jews, Race, and American Identity.* Princeton, N.J.: Princeton University Press, 2007.

Gordon, Mel. "Gurdjieff's Movement Demonstrations: The Theatre of the Miraculous." In *Drama Review: TDR* 22/2 (Occult and Bizarre Issue) (June 1978), 32–44.

Gross, Jan T. *Neighbors: The Destruction of the Jewish Community in Jedwabne, Poland* Princeton, N.J.: Princeton University Press, 2001.

Gruber, Ruth Ellen. *Virtually Jewish: Reinventing Jewish Culture in Europe.* Berkeley: University of California Press, 2002.

Haimo, Ethan. "Schoenberg, Numerology, and *Moses und Aron.*" *Opera Quarterly* 23/4 (Autumn 2007), 385–94.

Hamburg, Jill. "Out on the Edge." *Jerusalem Report,* 20 May 1993, 42–43.

Hart, Mitchell Bryan, ed. *Jews and Race: Writings on Identity and Difference, 1880–1940.* Lebanon, N.H.: University Press of New England, 2011.

Hebdige, Dick. *Subculture: The Meaning of Style.* New York: Methuen, 1979.

Heble, Ajay. *Landing on the Wrong Note: Jazz, Dissonance, and Critical Practice.* New York: Routledge, 2000.

Heble, Ajay, and Rob Wallace, eds. *"People Get Ready!" The Future of Jazz Is Now.* Durham, N.C.: Duke University Press, 2013.

Hentoff, Nat. "Jews in the Family of Jazz." *JazzTimes.* May 2010, [n.p.]. http://jazztimes .com/articles/25939-jews-in-the-family-of-jazz.

Heskes, Irene. *Passport to Jewish Music.* New York: Tara Publications.

Hisama, Ellie M. "John Zorn and the Postmodern Condition." In *Locating East Asia in Western Art Music,* eds. Yayoi Uno Everett and Frederick Lau, 72–84. Middletown, Conn.: Wesleyan University Press, 2004.

Hoffman, Warren. *The Passing Game: Queering Jewish American Culture.* Syracuse: Syracuse University Press, 2009.

Idelsohn, Abraham Z. *Jewish Music: Its Historical Development.* New York: Dover Publications, 1992 [1929].

Itzkovitz, Daniel. "They All Are Jews." In *You Should See Yourself: Jewish Identity in Postmodern American Culture,* ed. Vincent Brook, 230–52. New Brunswick, N.J.: Rutgers University Press, 2006.

Jacobson, Matthew Frye. *Roots Too: White Ethnic Revival in Post-Civil Rights America.* Cambridge, Mass.: Harvard University Press, 2006.

Jameson, Fredric. *Postmodernism, or the Cultural Logic of Late Capitalism.* Durham, N.C.: Duke University Press, 1991.

Janeczko, Jeff. "Negotiating Boundaries: Musical Hybridity in Tzadik's Radical Jewish Culture Series." In *The Song Is Not the Same: Jews and American Popular Music,* eds. Bruce Zuckerman, Josh Kun, and Lisa Ansell, 137–68. West Lafayette, Ind.: Purdue University Press, 2010.

———. "A Tale of Four Diasporas: Case Studies on the Relevance of 'Diaspora' in Contemporary Jewish Music." In *Perspectives on Jewish Music: Secular and Sacred,* ed. Jonathan L. Friedmann, 9–40. Lanham, Md.: Lexington Books, 2009.

Kajikawa, Loren. "The Sound of Struggle: Black Revolutionary Nationalism and Asian American Jazz." In *Jazz/Not Jazz: The Music and Its Boundaries,* eds. David Ake, Charles Hiroshi Garret, and Daniel Goldmark, 190–216. Berkeley: University of California Press, 2012.

Kalib, Sholom. *The Musical Tradition of the Eastern European Synagogue, Vol. 2: The Weekday Services.* Syracuse: Syracuse University Press, 2005.

Kaminsky, David. "'And We Sing Gay Songs': The Klezmatics: Negotiating the Boundaries of Jewish Identity." In *Studies in Jewish Musical Traditions,* ed. Kay K. Shelemay, 51–87. Cambridge, Mass.: Harvard College Library, 2001.

Kaprow, Allan. *Essays on the Blurring of Art and Life.* Berkeley: University of California Press, 1993.

Kaufman, Debra Renee. "Post-Memory and Post-Holocaust Jewish Identity Narratives." In *Sociology Confronts the Holocaust: Memories and Identities in Jewish Diasporas,* eds. Judith M. Gerson and Diane L. Wolf, 39–54. Durham, N.C.: Duke University Press, 2007.

Kilcher, Andreas B. "Philology as Kabbalah." In *Kabbalah and Modernity: Interpretations, Transformations, Adaptations,* eds. Boaz Huss, Marco Pasi, and Kocku von Stuckrad, 13–28. Leiden: Brill, 2010.

Kirshenblatt-Gimblett, Barbara. "Sounds of Sensibility." In *American Klezmer: Its Roots and Offshoots,* ed. Mark Slobin, 129–73. Berkeley: University of California Press, 2002 [1998].

———. "Sounds of Sensibility." *Judaism* (Winter 1998), 49–78.

Klapper, Melissa R. *Jewish Girls Coming of Age in America,* 1860–1920. New York: New York University Press, 2005.

Kligman, Mark. "Reestablishing a 'Jewish Spirit' in American Synagogue Music: The Music of A. W. Binder." In *The Art of Being Jewish in Modern Times,* eds. Barbara Kirshenblatt-Gimblett and Jonathan Karp, 270–87. Philadelphia: University of Pennsylvania Press, 2007.

Kligman, Mark L. *Maqām and Liturgy: Ritual, Music, and Aesthetics of Syrian Jews in Brooklyn.* Detroit: Wayne State University Press, 2008.

Kohn, Jerome, and Ron H. Feldman, eds. *Hannah Arendt: The Jewish Writings.* New York: Schocken Books, 2007.

Koskoff, Ellen. *Music in Lubavitcher Life.* Urbana: University of Illinois Press, 2001.

———. "The Sound of a Woman's Voice: Gender and Music in a New York Hasidic Community." In *Women and Music in Cross-Cultural Perspective,* ed. Ellen Koskoff, 213–23. Westport, Conn.: Greenwood Press, 1987.

Kun, Josh. "The Yiddish Are Coming: Mickey Katz, Antic-Semitism, and the Sound of Jewish Difference." *American Jewish History* 87/4 (1999), 343–74.

Levi, Primo. *Survival in Auschwitz.* New York: Touchstone, 2011 [1958].

Levy, Burt. "How Passover Will Be Observed on the East Side." *New York Times,* 16 April 1905.

Levy, Richard S., ed. *Antisemitism: A Historical Encyclopedia of Prejudice and Persecution,* vol. 1. Santa Barbara, Calif.: ABC-CLIO, 2005.

Lewis, George E. "Experimental Music in Black and White: The AACM in New York, 1970–1985." *Current Musicology* (Spring 2001–2002), 100–157.

———. *A Power Stronger Than Itself: The AACM and American Experimental Music.* Chicago: University of Chicago Press, 2008.

Loeffler, James Benjamin. *The Most Musical Nation: Jews and Culture in the Late Russian Empire.* New Haven, Conn.: Yale University Press, 2010.

Lott, Eric. *Love and Theft: Blackface Minstrelsy and the American Working Class.* New York: Oxford University Press, 2013 [1993].

Lucas, Gary. "Letter from Jedwabne." 2001. Unpublished manuscript.

———. "Me and the Golem." 10 June 2001. Unpublished manuscript.

Mandel, Howard. *Future Jazz.* New York: Oxford University Press, 1999.

———. "Vibes from the Tribe: Jewish Identity, Music, and Jazz." *JazzTimes* (September 2001), 60–65, 136–38, 145. http://jazztimes.com/articles/20131-vibes-from-the-tribe-jewish-identity-music-and-jazz.

Mangan, John. "Thomas de Hartmann: A Composer's Life." *Notes,* 2nd ser., 53/1 (September 1996), 18–29.

Martin, Bernice. "The Sacralization of Disorder: Symbolism in Rock Music." *Sociological Analysis* 40/2 (Summer 1979), 87–124.

McAllester, David P. *Enemy Way Music: A Study of Social and Esthetic Values as Seen in Navaho Music.* Cambridge, Mass.: Peabody Museum, 1954.

McCutchan, Ann. *The Muse That Sings.* New York: Oxford University Press, 1999.

Meintjes, Louise. "Paul Simon's *Graceland,* South Africa, and the Mediation of Musical Meaning." *Ethnomusicology* 34/1 (Winter 1990), 37–73.

Mele, Christopher. *Selling the Lower East Side: Culture, Real Estate, and Resistance in New York City.* Minneapolis: University of Minnesota Press, 2000.

Merwin, Ted. *In Their Own Image: New York Jews in Jazz Age Popular Culture.* New Brunswick, N.J.: Rutgers University Press, 2006.

Michels, Tony. *A Fire in Their Hearts: Yiddish Socialists in New York.* Cambridge, Mass.: Harvard University Press, 2009 [2005].

Milkowski, Bill. "One Future, Two Views: Conversation with [Wynton Marsalis and] John Zorn." *JazzTimes* (March 2000), 28–38, 118–21.

Miller, Stephen Paul, and Daniel Morris, eds. *Radical Poetics and Secular Jewish Culture.* Tuscaloosa, Ala.: University of Alabama Press, 2010.

Miron, Dan. *From Continuity to Contiguity: Toward a New Jewish Literary Thinking.* Stanford, Calif.: Stanford University Press, 2010.

Monson, Ingrid. *Freedom Sounds: Civil Rights Call Out to Jazz and Africa.* New York: Oxford University Press, 2007.

———. *Saying Something: Jazz Improvisation and Interaction.* Chicago: University of Chicago Press, 1996.

Moore, Rebecca. "The Sweet Sound of Success: Knitting Factory Recording Artists Win Historic Settlement." *Allegro* 55/2 (February 2005), [n.p.]. http://www.loca1802afm.org/2005/02/the-sweet-sound-of-success.

Móricz, Klára. *Jewish Identities: Nationalism, Racism, and Utopianism in Twentieth-Century Music.* Berkeley: University of California Press, 2008.

Mulisch, Harry. *The Assault.* New York: Random House, 2011 [1982].

Needleman, Jacob, and George Baker, eds. *Gurdjieff: Essays and Reflections on the Man and His Teaching.* New York: Continuum, 1996.

Neusner, Jacob. *The Enchantments of Judaism: Rites of Transformation from Birth through Death.* New York: Basic Books, 1987.

———. *The Presence of the Past, the Pastness of the Present: History, Time, and Paradigm in Rabbinic Judaism.* Bethesda, Md.: CDL Press, 1996.

Nora, Pierre. "Between Memory and History: Les Lieux de Mémoire." Trans. Marc Roudebush. *Representations* 26 (1989), 7–24.

Pareles, Jon. "Evoking a Terrible Night in 1938." *New York Times,* 19 December 1992.

Pellegrini, Ann. "Whiteface Performances: 'Race,' Gender, and Jewish Bodies." In *The New Jewish Cultural Studies,* eds. Jonathan and Daniel Boyarin, 108–75. Minneapolis: University of Minnesota Press, 1997.

Petropoulos, Jonathan. *The Faustian Bargain: The Art World in Nazi Germany.* New York: Oxford University Press, 2000.

Piekut, Benjamin. *Experimentalism Otherwise: The New York Avant-Garde and Its Limits.* Berkeley: University of California Press, 2011.

Pittman, Michael S. *Classical Spirituality in Contemporary America: The Confluence and Contribution of G. I. Gurdjieff and Sufism.* New York: Continuum International Publishing Group, 2012.

Pleck, Elizabeth Hafkin. *Celebrating the Family: Ethnicity, Consumer Culture, and Family Rituals.* Cambridge, Mass.: Harvard University Press, 2000.

Polonsky, Antony, and Joanna B. Michlic, eds. *The Neighbors Respond: The Controversy over the Jedwabne Massacre in Poland.* Princeton, N.J.: Princeton University Press, 2004.

Radano, Ronald. "Jazzin' the Classics: The AACM's Challenge to Mainstream Aesthetics." *Black Music Research Journal* 12/1 (Spring 1992), 79–95.

Ribot, Marc. "Klezmer Authenticity draft" and "Authenticity Klez edit." 2002. Unpublished manuscript.

———. "Rad Jewish Music." 28 February 1996. Unpublished manuscript.

———. "The Representation of Jewish Identity in Downtown Music." 1996. Unpublished manuscript.

Ribot, Marc, and John Zorn. "Radical Jewish Culture at the Knitting Factory." 8–11 October 1992. Program notes.

Ringer, Alexander L. *Schoenberg: The Composer as Jew.* New York: Oxford University Press, 1990.

Robinson, James McConkey, and Richard Smith, eds. *The Nag Hammadi Library in English.* Leiden: Brill, 1996.

Rockwell, John. "Reverberations." *New York Times,* 23 April 2004.

Rogovoy, Seth. *The Essential Klezmer: A Music Lover's Guide to Jewish Roots and Soul Music, from the Old World to the Jazz Age to the Downtown Avant-Garde.* Chapel Hill, N.C.: Algonquin Books, 2000.

———. "The Klezmatics Revitalizing Their Roots." *Sing Out!* 43/3 (Winter 1999), 48–55.

Rothenberg, Randall. "A Fix on the Founding Fug." *New York Magazine,* 7 May 1979, 82–83.

Rosen, Roee. "Sounds of 'Shtetl Metal': Radical Jewish Music Hits Downtown Clubs." *Forward,* 15 July 1994.

Roskies, David G. *The Jewish Search for a Usable Past.* Bloomington: Indiana University Press, 2008.

Royal, Derek Parker, ed. *Unfinalized Moments: Essays in the Development of Contemporary Jewish Narrative.* West Lafayette, Ind.: Purdue University Press, 2011.

Rubin, Ruth. *Voices of a People: The Story of Yiddish Folksong.* Urbana: University of Illinois Press, 2000 [1974].

Sabin, Roger. "'I Won't Let That Dago Go By:' Rethinking Punk and Racism." In *White Riot: Punk Rock and the Politics of Race,* eds. Stephen Duncombe and Maxwell Tremblay, 57–68. Brooklyn: Verso, 2011.

Sapoznik, Henry. *Klezmer! From Old World to Our World.* New York: Schirmer Books, 1999.

Sarna, Jonathan D. *American Judaism: A History.* New Haven, Conn.: Yale University Press, 2004.

Scholem, Gershom. *On the Mystical Shape of the Godhead: Basic Concepts in the Kabbalah.* New York: Schocken, 1991.

———. "Zene unhistorische Sätze über Kabbala" [Ten unhistorical aphorisms on Kabbalah]. Zurich: Rhein-Verlag, 1958.

Schwarz, Daniel R. "Eating Jewish Ivy: Jews as Literary Intellectuals." In *The New York Public Intellectuals and Beyond: Exploring Liberal Humanism, Jewish Identity, and the American Protest Tradition,* eds. Ethan Goffmann and Daniel Morris, 47–59. West Lafayette, Ind.: Purdue University Press, 2009.

Segev, Tom. *One Palestine, Complete: Jews and Arabs under the Palestinian Mandate.* New York: Macmillan, 2001.

Shafer, R. Murray. *The New Soundscape: A Handbook for the Modern Music Teacher.* New York: Associated Music Publishers, 1969.

Shahar, Natan. "The Eretz Israeli Song and the Jewish National Fund." In *Modern Jews and Their Musical Agendas,* ed. Ezra Mendelsohn, 78–91. New York: Oxford University Press, 1993.

Shandler, Jeffrey. "Queer Yiddishkeit: Practice and Theory." *Shofar: An Interdisciplinary Journal of Jewish Studies* 25/1 (Fall 2006): 90–113.

———. *While America Watches: Televising the Holocaust.* New York: Oxford University Press, 1999.

Shapira, Anita. "The Origins of the Myth of the 'New Jew.'" In *The Fate of the European Jews, 1939–1945: Continuity or Contingency?,* ed. Jonathan Frankel, 253–70. New York: Oxford University Press, 1997.

Sharlin, William. "*Davening* and Congregational Song." In *Emotions in Jewish Music: Personal and Scholarly Reflections,* ed. Jonathan L. Friedman, 45–53. Lanham, Md.: University Press of America, 2012.

Shelemay, Kay Kaufman. *Let Jasmine Rain Down: Song and Remembrance among Syrian Jews.* Chicago: University of Chicago Press, 1998.

Shohat, Ella, and Robert Stam. "Narrativizing Visual Culture: Toward a Polycentric Aesthetics." In *The Visual Culture Reader,* ed. Nicholas Mirzoeff, 37–59. New York: Psychology Press, 2002.

Silberstein, Laurence J., and Robert L. Cohn, eds. *The Other in Jewish Thought and History: Constructions of Jewish Culture and Identity.* New York: New York University Press, 1994.

Silver, Mitchell. *Respecting the Wicked Child: A Philosophy of Secular Jewish Identity and Education.* Amherst: University of Massachusetts Press, 1998.

Slobin, Mark, ed. *American Klezmer: Its Roots and Offshoots.* Berkeley: University of California Press, 2002.

———. *Fiddler on the Move: Exploring the Klezmer World.* New York: Oxford University Press, 2003.

Sollors, Werner. *Neither Black nor White yet Both: Thematic Explorations of Interracial Literature.* Cambridge, Mass.: Harvard University Press, 1999.

Solomon, Maida E. "Claiming Our Questions: Feminism and Judaism in Women's Haggadot." In *Talking Back: Images of Jewish Women in American Popular Culture,* ed. Joyce Antler, 220–41. Lebanon, N.H.: University Press of New England, 1998.

Sontag, Susan. *Against Interpretation and Other Essays.* New York: Macmillan, 2001 [1966].

Sprinzak, Ehud. "Kach and Meir Kahane: The Emergence of Jewish Quasi-Fascism II: Ideology and Politics." *Patterns of Prejudice* 19/4 (1985), [n.p.].

Stansell, Christine. *American Moderns: Bohemian New York and the Creation of a New Century.* Princeton, N.J.: Princeton University Press, 2009 [2000].

Stone, Ruth. *Let the Inside Be Sweet: The Interpretation of Music Event among the Kpelle of Liberia.* Bloomington: Indiana University Press, 1982.

Stratton, Jon. *Jews, Race and Popular Music.* Surrey: Ashgate, 2009.

Strickland, Edward. *American Composers: Dialogues on Contemporary Music.* Bloomington: Indiana University Press, 1987.

Strong, James. *New Exhaustive Concordance of the Bible.* Nashville: T. Nelson Publishers, 1990.

Sutcliffe, Adam, and Ross Braun, eds. *Renewing the Past, Reconfiguring Jewish Culture: From Al-Andalus to the Haskalah.* Philadelphia: University of Pennsylvania Press, 2004.

Svigals, Alicia. "Why We Do This Anyway: Klezmer as Jewish Youth Subculture." In *Klezmer: Its Roots and Offshoots,* ed. Mark Slobin, 211–19. Berkeley: University of California Press, 2002.

Szego, C. K. "Praxial Foundations of Multicultural Music Education." In *Praxial Music Education: Reflections and Dialogues,* ed. David J. Elliot, 196–218. New York: Oxford University Press, 2009.

Tan, Marcus Cheng Chye. *Acoustic Interculturalism: Listening to Performance.* New York: Palgrave Macmillan, 2012.

Tarsi, Boaz. "How Music Articulates Liturgical Structure, Meaning, and Perception: The Kaddish." In *The Experience of Jewish Liturgy: Studies Dedicated to Menahem Schmelzer,* ed. Debra Reed Blank, 309–40. Leiden: Brill, 2011.

Taruskin, Richard. "The Pastness of the Present and the Presence of the Past." In *Authenticity and Early Music,* ed. Nicholas Kenyon, 137–210. New York: Oxford University Press, 1988.

Topper, Sharon, and Craig Flanagin. "G-d Is My Co-Pilot, What Kann You Mach? Es Ist Amerikeh!" [What can you do? It's America!]. Radical New Jewish Culture Festival at the Knitting Factory, 7–11 April 1993. Program notes.

———. "Haggadah shel G-d Is My Co-Pilot" [G-d Is My Co-Pilot's Haggadah]. Radical Jewish Culture Festival at the Knitting Factory, 8–11 October 1992. Program notes.

Uris, Leon. *Exodus.* New York: Bantam Books, 1958.

Walker, Rebecca. "Experiments in *Critique de Performance:* An Experimental Review of *Experiments in Écriture Féminine.*" *Text and Performance Quarterly* 33/4 (October 2013), 407–13.

Weegee (Arthur Felling). *Naked City.* New York: Da Capo Press, 1978 [1945].

Werb, Brett. "Music." In *Oxford Handbook of Holocaust Studies,* eds. Peter Hayes and John K. Roth, 484–85. New York: Oxford University Press, 2010.

Werbner, Pnina. "Introduction: The Materiality of Diaspora—Between Aesthetic and 'Real' Politics." *Diaspora* 9/1 (2000), 6–7.

Wilson, Eric. "A Necessary Stop." *New York Times,* 29 May 2013.

Wiesel, Elie. *Night.* New York: Macmillan, 2012 [1952].

Wisse, Ruth R. *The Modern Jewish Canon: A Journey through Language and Culture.* Chicago: University of Chicago Press, 2003.

Wittgenstein, Ludwig. *The Blue and Brown Books: Preliminary Studies for the "Philosophical Investigations."* New York: HarperCollins, 1965.

Wundmüller, Sonja. "Trash Museums: Exhibiting In-Between." In *Trash Culture: Objects and Obsolescence in Cultural Perspective,* ed. Gillian Pye, 39–58. New York: Oxford University Press, 2010.

Zak, Albin. *The Poetics of Rock: Cutting Tracks, Making Records.* Berkeley: University of California Press, 2004.

Zorn, John. "John Zorn at the Knitting Factory." September 1993. Program notes.

———. "Radical Jewish Culture at the Berlin Jewish Museum." Exhibition notes. April 2011.

Zuckerman, Bruce, Josh Kun, and Lisa Ansel, eds. *The Song Is Not the Same: Jews and American Popular Music.* West Lafayette, Ind.: Purdue University Press, 2010.

Zurawick, David. *The Jews of Prime Time.* Hanover, N.H.: University Press of New England, 2003.

### ONLINE SOURCES

Ambrose, Patrick. "Elliott Sharp's Instrumental Vision." *Morning News,* 4 October 2005. http://www.themorningnews.org/article/elliott-sharps-instrumental-vision.

Attie, Shimon. *The Writing on the Wall: Projections in Berlin's Jewish Quarter.* 1992–93. http://www.shimonattie.net/index.php?option=com_content&view=article &id=13.

Comer, Chris. Radio interview with John Zorn. 24 August 1999. http://www.chris comerradio.com/john_zorn/john_zorn8-24-1999.htm.

Curran, Alvin. Personal website. http://www.alvincurran.com.

Cusick, Suzanne G. "Music as Torture/Music as Weapon." *TRANS-Transcultural Music Review* 10/11 (2006). http://www.sibetrans.com/trans/a152/music-as-torture-music -as-weapon.

Dessen, Michael. "Asian Americans and Creative Music Legacies." *Critical Studies in Improvisation / Études critiques en improvisation* 1/3 (May 2006). http://www .criticalimprov.com/article/view/56/89.

Feld, Steven. "From Ethnomusicology to Echo-Muse-Ecology: Reading R. Murray Schafer in the Papua New Guinea Rainforest." *Soundscape Newsletter* 8 (June 1994). http://www.acousticecology.org/writings/echomuseecology.html.

Goldberg, Ben. "'New Klezmer Trio' and the Origins of Radical Jewish Culture." 8 February 2012. http://www.bengoldberg.net/media. Idelsohn Society for Musical Preservation. http://idelsohnsociety.com.

"Improv 21: = Q + A: An Informance with John Zorn." ROVA: Arts, 2007. Other Minds Video Archive. http://archive.org/details/IMP_2007_11_15.

Maki-Turja, Janne. "Me Emme Nuku [We Don't Sleep]." *Mutiny!* Finland, 1993, [n.p.]. http://allan.hise.org/godco/articles/mutiny.html.

Peterson, Guy. Personal website. http://www.guypetersreviews.com/johnzorn.php.

Ronsen, Josh. "Interview with Anthony Coleman." *Monk Mink Pink Punk* 4. June 1994. http://ronsen.org/monkminkpinkpunk/4/anthonycoleman.html.

———. "Interview: Anthony Coleman [September] 2004." *Monk Mink Pink Punk* 11/1. July 2005. http://ronsen.org/monkminkpinkpunk/11/anthonycoleman2004.html.

———. "Interview with God Is My Co-Pilot." *Monk Mink Pink Punk* 3. Fall 1995. http:// allan.hise.org/godco/articles/mmpp.html.

Seroussi, Edwin et al. "Jewish music." *Grove Music Online. Oxford Music Online.* Oxford: Oxford University Press. http://0-www.oxfordmusiconline.com.luna.wellesley.edu /subscriber/article/grove/music/41322.

*Tikkun* magazine. http://www.tikkun.org.

Valle, Efren del. "Marc Ribot." 24 December 2004. http://www.tomajazz.com/perfiles /ribot_marc_eng.htm.

Wines, Larry. "Somewhere Out There: The Klezmatics." *Folkworks.* 5 March 2009. http://www.folkworks.org/columns/somewhere-out-there-larry-wines/35862?task =view.

Wong, Deborah. "Asian American Improvisation in Chicago: Tatsu Aoki and the 'New' Japanese American Taiko." *Critical Studies in Improvisation / Études critiques en improvisation* 1/3 (May 2006). http://www.criticalimprov.com/article/view/50.

Zampino, Phil. "Kristallnacht: Tonic." *Squid's Ear,* 23 September 2003. http://www .squidsear.com/cgi-bin/news/newsView.cgi?newsID=296.

[Zorn, John.] Hips Road Edition website. http://www.hipsroadedition.com.

[———.] Obsessions Collective. http://www.obsessionscollective.com.

[———.] Tzadik Records. http://www.tzadik.com.

## SELECTED INTERVIEWS AND OTHER COMMUNICATIONS

Baron, Joey. 20 June 2001. New York City. Interview.

Byron, Don. 12 February 2004. New York City. Interview.

Cohen, Greg, Marty Ehrlich, Jessica Lurie, Roy Nathanson, and Marc Ribot. 15 May 2010. Kolot Chayeinu, Brooklyn, New York. Roundtable interview.

Coleman, Anthony. 13 August 2001. New York City. Interview.

———. 28 December 2001. New York City. Interview.

———. 13 October 2002. E-mail exchange.

———. 18 April 2010. Paris Museum of Jewish Art and History. Roundtable interview.

———. 21 June 2012. Phone interview.

Douglas, Dave. "Music of Masada." The Stone, New York City. 10 May 2010.

Dresser, Mark. 24 January 2004. New York City. Interview.

Ehrlich, Marty. 1 February 2004. New York City. Interview.

———. 29 May 2004. Written statement.

———. 20 April 2010. E-mail exchange.

———. 24 July 2010. E-mail exchange.

Hirsch, Shelley. 24 February 2003. New York City. Interview.

———. 26 December 2009. New York City. Interview.

———. 29 December 2010. New York City. Interview.

———. 26 December 2013. New York City. Interview.

Krakauer, David. 11 April 2001. New York City. Interview.

Licht, Alan. 28 September 2000. New York City. Interview.

Lucas, Gary. 27 June 2003. New York City. Interview.

———. 28 June 2013. E-mail exchange.

Lurie, Jessica. 12 May 2010. Phone conversation.

Nathanson, Roy. 10 September 2003. New York City. Interview.

Ribot, Marc. 6 June 2003. New York City. Interview.

———. 20 April 2010. E-mail exchange.

———. 23 April 2010. E-mail exchange.

———. 15 June 2012. E-mail exchange.

———. 25 October 2012. Written communication.

———. 28 October 2012. Phone conversation.

Sharp, Elliott. 18 February 2003. New York City. Interview.

Topper, Sharon. 10 June 2010. E-mail exchange.

Topper, Sharon, and Craig Flanagin. 10 August 2004. New York City. Interview.

———. 9 October 2009. E-mail exchange.

Zorn, John. 14 December 2000. Phone conversation.
———. 5 May 2011. E-mail exchange.
———. 23 May 2011. E-mail exchange.

### ELECTRONIC MEDIA

#### Recordings (Compilations)

Geduldig und Thimann. *A Haymish Groove*. Extraplatte, 1992.
*The Jewish Alternative Movement—A Guide For The Perplexed*. Knitting Factory Records, 1998.
*Klezmania: Klezmer for the New Millennium*. Shanachie, 1997.
*Klezmer 1993, New York City: The Tradition Continues on the Lower East Side*. Knitting Factory Works, 1993.
*Klezmer Festival 1998: Live at the Knitting Factory* Knitting Factory Works, 1998.
*Knitting on the Roof*. Knitting Factory Works, 1998.
*Legend of Toil and Celebration: Songs of Solidarity, Social Awareness, and Yiddish Americana*. Milken Archive Digital, 2012.
*Live at the Knitting Factory, Volume 3*. A&M Records, 1990.
*New York Noise: Dance Music from the New York Underground, 1978–1982*. Soul Jazz, 2003.
*Nuggets: Original Artyfacts from the First Psychedelic Era, 1965–1968*. Elektra, 1972.
*Once upon a Time—Israeli Hit Tunes of Yesteryear 1*. Hed-Arzi, 1960.

#### Selected Recordings and Scores (Artists and Ensembles)

Amram, David, Arnold Weinstein, and Reginald Rose. *The Final Ingredient of the Holocaust: An Opera in One Act*. Premier Recordings, 1996. Score published New York: C.F. Peters, 1965.
Ayler, Albert. *Music Is the Healing Force of the Universe*. Impulse! 1969.
Byron, Don. *Don Byron Plays the Music of Mickey Katz*. Elektra Nonesuch, 1993.
———. *Tuskegee Experiments*. Elektra, 1992.
Captain Beefheart (Don Van Vliet) and the Magic Band. *Grow Fins: Rarities 1965–82*. Revenant, 1999.
———. *Trout Mask Replica*. Reprise, 1969.
Chatham, Rhys. "Guitar Trio" (1977). On *An Angel Moves Too Fast to See: Selected Works, 1971–1989*. Table of the Elements, 2002.
Coleman, Anthony. *disco by night*. Disk Union, 1992.
———. *Freakish*. Tzadik, 2009.
———. *Schmutzige Magnaten: Coleman Plays Gebirtig*. Tzadik, 2006.
Coleman, Anthony / Anthony Coleman Trio. *Morenica*. Tzadik, 1998.
———. *Our Beautiful Garden Is Open*. Tzadik, 2002.
———. *Sephardic Tinge*. Tzadik, 1995.
Coleman, Anthony / Selfhaters. *The Abysmal Richness of the Infinite Proximity of the Same*. Tzadik, 1998.
———. *Selfhaters*. Tzadik, 1996.
Coleman, Anthony, and Roy Nathanson. *The Coming Great Millennium*. Knitting Factory Works, 1992.

―――. *I Could've Been a Drum*. Tzadik, 1997.

―――. *Lobster and Friend*. Knitting Factory Works, 1993.

Coleman, Ornette. *The Shape of Jazz to Come*. Atlantic, 1959.

Coltrane, John. *A Love Supreme*. Impulse! 1964.

Curran, Alvin. *Animal Behavior*. Tzadik, 1995.

―――. *Crystal Psalms*. New Albion Records, 1994 [1988].

Eno, Brian. *No New York*. Antilles, 1978.

Engel, Joel, and Avigdor Hameiri. "Halutz, Build On: Chalutz, Bᵉnëh / Hay, Hay Naa-layim." Arranged for mixed voices (s.a.t.b.) by Avraham Soltes. English version by Babette Deutsch. New York: Transcontinental Music Corp., 1942.

Ginsberg, Allen. *The Lion for Real*. Island Records, 1997 [1990].

God Is My Co-Pilot. *Straight Not*. Outpunk Records, 1993.

G-d Is My Co-Pilot. *Mir Shlufn Nisht* [We Don't Sleep]. Disk Union/Avant, 1994.

Goldberg, Ben. *Speech Communication*. Tzadik, 2009.

Goldberg, Ben / New Klezmer Trio. *Masks and Faces*. Tzadik, 1991.

―――. *Melt/Zonk/Rewire*. Tzadik, 1995.

―――. *Short for Something*. Tzadik, 2000.

Hirsch, Shelley. *The Far In, Far Out Worlds of Shelley Hirsch*. Tzadik, 2002.

―――. *O Little Town of East New York*. New American Radio and Performing Arts, 1992.

―――. *O Little Town of East New York*. Tzadik, 1995.

―――. *States*. Tellus, 1997.

Hirsch, Shelley, and Simon Ho. *Where Were You Then?* Tzadik, 2012.

Jazz Passengers. *The Jazz Passengers Live at the Knitting Factory*. Knitting Factory Records, 1991.

Klezmatics. *Rhythm + Jews*. Pirahna/Rounder, 1990.

―――. *Shvaygn=Toyt*. Piranha, 1988.

Krakauer, David / Klezmer Madness! *Klezmer, NY*. Tzadik, 1998.

Mathis, Johnny, with Ray Ellis and His Orchestra. "Come to Me" (P. H. Hayes and Robert Allen). Columbia, 1957.

Nathanson, Roy. *Camp Stories*. Knitting Factory Works, 1996.

―――. *Subway Moon*. Buddy's Knife Jazzedition, 2009.

Nono, Luigi. *Ricorda cosa ti hanno fatto in Auschwitz* (Remember what they did to you in Auschwitz). On *Complete Works for Solo Tape*. Milan: Ricordi Oggi, 2006. Score published Munich: G. Ricordi Bühnen- und Musikverlag, 1966.

Parkins, Zeena. *Mouth=maul=betrayer*. Tzadik, 1996.

Penderecki, Krzysztof. *Dies Irae: oratorium ob memoriam in perniciei castris in Oswiecim necatorum inexstinguibilem reddendam* (Oratorio dedicated to the memory of those murdered at Auschwitz). On *A Polish Requiem*. Naxos, 2004. Score published Celle: Moeck, 1967.

Reich, Steve. *Different Trains*. On *Works 1965–1995*. Nonesuch, 1997. Score published New York: Hendon Music, 1988.

―――. *Tehillim*. On *Works 1965–1995*. Nonesuch, 1997. Score published New York: Hendon Music, 1981.

Ribot, Marc. *Yo! I Killed Your God*. Tzadik, 1999 [1992].

Schoenberg, Arnold. *Pierrot Lunaire, Op. 21*. Nonesuch Records, 1971. Score published Vienna: Universal Edition, 1914.

————. *A Survivor from Warsaw*, Op. 46. Vienna: Vienna Modern Masters, 1992. Score published, Long Island City, N.Y.: Bomart Music Publications, 1949.

Sharp, Elliott. *NOTS*. Berlin: Atonal, 1992.

————. "Intifada." *Xenocodex*. Tzadik, 1996 [1992].

Shostakovich, Dmitri. Symphony No. 13 in B-flat Minor, Op. 113 ("Babi Yar"). EMI Classics, 2005. Score published London: Anglo-Soviet Music Press, 1971.

Smith, Patti. *Horses*. Arista, 1975.

Tarras, Dave. *Yiddish-American Klezmer Music 1925–1956*. Yazoo, 1992.

Teitelbaum, Richard. *Golem I*. Tzadik, 1995 [1988].

Zorn, John. *Angelus Novus*. Tzadik, 1998 [1993].

————. *The Circle Maker: Issachar and Zevulun*. Tzadik, 1998.

————. *Filmworks IX: Trembling before G-d*. Tzadik, 2000.

————. *Filmworks XI: Secret Lives*. Tzadik, 2002.

————. *Filmworks XVI: Protocols of Zion*. Tzadik, 2005.

————. *Filmworks XX: Sholom Aleichem*. Tzadik, 2008.

————. *Jumalatteret*. Tzadik, 2012.

————. *Kol Nidre*. Tzadik, 1996.

————. *Kristallnacht*. Tzadik, 1995 [1992].

————. *Masada String Trio: Book of Angels 2: Azazel*. Tzadik, 2005.

————. *Memento Mori*. Tzadik, 1998 [1992].

————. *Mount Analogue*. Tzadik, 2012.

————. *Naked City: The Complete Studio Recordings*. Tzadik, 2005.

————. *Naked City: Torture Garden and Leng Tch'e: 20th Anniversary Edition*. Tzadik, 2011 [1985, 1992].

————. *Necronomicon*. Tzadik, 2003.

————. *Passagen*. Tzadik, 2011.

————. *Port of Last Resort* on *Filmworks VIII 1997*. Tzadik, 1998.

————. *Sanhedrin: Masada Unreleased Studio Recordings*. Tzadik, 2005 [1994–97].

————. *Shibboleth*. Tzadik, 1997.

————. *Shir Hashirim*. Tzadik, 2007.

————. *Spy vs. Spy: The Music of Ornette Coleman*. Nonesuch, 1988.

————. *Taboo and Exile*. Tzadik, 1999.

————. *The Temptations of St. Anthony*. Tzadik, 2012.

————. *A Tribute to Mickey Spillane*. Elektra Nonesuch, 1987.

————. *The Unknown Masada*. Tzadik, 2003.

————. *Untitled*. Tzadik, 1999.

————. *Zohar*. Tzadik, 1995.

## Interviews and Performances on Film and Video

Ben Goldberg Trio. "Speech Communication: Anglais." Paris Museum of Jewish Art and History. Akadem, 2010.

*Descent into Baldness*. Dir. Cassis Birgit Staudt and Joerg Soechting. http://www-marcribot-descentintobaldness.com.

Hirsch, Shelley. *States*. Roulette TV, 2001.

————. *O Little Town of East New York*. Dance Theater Workshop, 1990.

*Klezmer*. Paris Museum of Jewish Art and History. 2010.

*Munich*. Paris Museum of Jewish Art and History. 2010.

"La Radical Jewish Culture" and Anthony Coleman, "Ecouter le flâneur flâner," Paris Museum of Jewish Art and History. Akadem, 2010.

*Sabbath in Paradise*. Dir. Claudia Heurmann. Tzadik, 2007 [1997].

*Shibboleth*. Paris Museum of Jewish Art and History. 2010.

*Traces*. Paris Museum of Jewish Art and History. 2010.

## Other Film and Video

*Anne Frank: The Diary of a Young Girl*. Dir. Alex Segal. 1967.

*A Band Called Death*. Drafthouse Films. 2013.

*The Diary of Anne Frank*. Dir. George Stevens. 1959.

*Exodus*. Dir. Otto Preminger. 1960.

*Fiddler on the Roof*. Dir. Norman Jewison. 1971.

*Funny Girl*. Dir. William Wyler. 1968.

*Der Golem, wie er in die Welt kam*. Dir. Paul Wegener and Carl Boese. 1920. Music by Gary Lucas and Walter Horn, 1990.

*Holocaust* (television miniseries). Dir. Marvin J. Chomsky. NBC, 1978.

*Judgment at Nuremberg*. Dir. Stanley Kramer. 1961.

*Naked City*. Dir. Jules Dassin. 1948.

*The Pawnbroker*. Dir. Sidney Lumet. 1967.

# INDEX

Page numbers in *italics* indicate illustrations, photographs, or musical examples.

TAMAR BARZEL is an ethnomusicologist whose research focuses on experimental music, with an emphasis on late twentieth-century jazz and the Jewish avant-garde. Drawing on both ethnographic and archival research, her work explores the convergence of cultural studies, creative identity, and musical sound. She has presented papers at scholarly meetings world-wide and has published articles in the *Journal of the Society for American Music* (2010), *Jazz/Not Jazz: The Music and Its Boundaries* (2012), and *"People Get Ready": The Future of Jazz Is Now* (2013).